The
Literatu
the
celts

The Literature of the Celts

Magnus Maclean

SENATE

The Literature of the Celts

First published in 1902 by Blackie & Son Ltd, London

This edition published in 1998 by Senate,
an imprint of Tiger Books International PLC,
26A York Street, Twickenham,
Middlesex TW1 3LJ, United Kingdom

Cover design © Tiger Books International 1998

1 3 5 7 9 10 8 6 4 2

ISBN 1 85958 524 8

Printed and bound in the UK by
Cox & Wyman, Reading, England

PREFACE

CELTIC studies have grown apace within recent years. The old scorn, the old apathy and neglect are visibly giving way to a lively wonder and interest as the public gradually realise that scholars have lighted upon a literary treasure hid for ages. This new enthusiasm, generated in great part on the Continent—in Germany, France, and Italy, as well as in Britain and Ireland, has already spread to the northern nations—to Denmark, Sweden, and Norway, and is now beginning to take root in America.

A remarkable change it certainly presents from the days when Dr. Johnson affirmed that there was not in all the world a Gaelic MS. one hundred years old; and the documents were so derelict and forgotten, so little known and studied, that though this prince of letters travelled in the Highlands expressly to satisfy himself, Celtic knowledge of the existing materials and Celtic studies were so deficient that they proved wholly inadequate to the task of disproving his bold statement.

It was left to the scholarship of the nineteenth century to unearth the ancient treasures and to show that Gaelic was a literary language long before English literature came into existence, and that there are still extant Celtic-Latin MSS. almost as old as the very oldest codexes of the Bible.

There is undoubtedly a charm in the thought that all over the Continent of Europe, in the libraries of many of its romantic cities and towns, there are scores of MSS., some of them upwards of a thousand years old, fugitives in the early times from these much harassed islands ; and that European scholars of the highest erudition, such as Zeuss, Ebel, Nigra, Ascoli, Windisch, Zimmer, and Whitley Stokes have been profoundly interested in these literary relics, and have devoted much of their time to the work of studying, translating, elucidating, and editing the Gaelic texts or glosses found in them.

To-day the number of those engaged in similar research at home and abroad is vastly on the increase, and augurs well for the future of this department of knowledge.

Professor Kuno Meyer, Ph.D., himself a distinguished German Celticist, in reviewing the present state of Celtic studies last year at Dublin, made the following significant statement :—

" I cannot conclude without casting a glance into the future. I am convinced that the present is but the beginning of an era of still greater activity in all departments of Celtic studies. Everything points to that.

" The more reliable text-books and hand-books will be published, the greater will be the numbers of those taking up Celtic studies. As the fields of other more ancient and more recognised studies become exhausted, there will come a rush of students on to the fresh, and often, almost virgin soil of Celtic research, to study the great Celtic civilisation at its source, to collect the last lingering remnants of a mighty tradition.

" Again and again it has happened during recent years that workers in other subjects have in their researches finally been led on to the Celtic soil, where lie the roots of much medieval lore, of many institutions, of important phases of thought.

"And another thing, too, I will foretell. The re-discovery, as it were, of ancient Celtic literature will not only arouse abroad a greater interest in the Celtic nations, but it will lead to beneficial results among those nations themselves."

Mr. W. B. Yeats, in the *Treasury of Irish Poetry*, 1900, gives pen to similar reflections and anticipations :—

"Modern poetry," he writes, "grows weary of using over and over again the personages and stories and metaphors that have come to us through Greece and Rome, or from Wales and Brittany through the Middle Ages, and has found new life in the Norse and German legends. The Irish legends in popular tradition and in old Gaelic literature are more numerous and as beautiful, and alone among great European legends have the beauty and wonder of altogether new things. May one not say then, without saying anything improbable, that they will have a predominant influence in the coming century, and that their influence will pass through many countries."

The interest thus lately evolved in the literature of the Celts, who were among the earliest inhabitants of the country, and whose blood still courses in our British veins, has naturally awakened a desire in many minds to know the nature and extent of the literary legacy they have bequeathed—its substance and quality, and also to gain some acquaintance with the opinions and results of recent scholarship on the subject.

But, strange to say, notwithstanding the activity of Celticists, no book has yet appeared which professes to give in short compass a general survey of the whole field. There is thus, I venture to think, room for such a volume as the present, which is intended to serve as a popular introduction to the study of the literature. Containing, as it does, the gist of two series of lectures which I delivered under the Maccallum Bequest in the University of Glasgow during the sessions 1900-1 and 1901-2, it is now prepared and issued with a view to meeting the demands not only of the general reader, but also of the private student in quest of a guide to the original sources, the authorities, and books on the subject.

In its preparation, in addition to the numerous published works mentioned in the text, I have received valuable help from Professor Mackinnon, Edinburgh University, and Dr. Alexander Macbain, Inverness, both of whom supplied me not only with many of their printed papers embodying the fruits of their own personal research, but also with other useful information. To the former I am still further indebted for interesting details regarding the life and work of several of the scholars, and to Professor Rhys of Jesus College, Oxford, for kindly reviewing in MS. form the chapter on Welsh Literature.

And, finally, I have to record my special indebtedness to the kind assistance of my friend, Mr. David Mackeggie, M.A., whose knowledge of Celtic history and literature is both extensive and accurate, and who, besides giving me much suggestive aid in the preparation of the lectures, read the proofs of this volume.

MAGNUS MACLEAN

The Technical College,
Glasgow, *May* 1902.

CONTENTS

CHAPTER I

THE ARRIVAL OF THE CELT IN HISTORY AND LITERATURE

PAGE

The Celts in primitive Europe—Advent in British Isles—Two branches —Observations of Cæsar and Tacitus—Main facts of Celtic progress on the Continent—A vast empire—Interview with Alexander the Great—Colony in Galatia—Cup of conquest full—Disintegration— The scattered remnants—Recent statistics—The ancient Celts as seen through Greek and Roman eyes—Literary awakening—Ogam writings—First men of letters—Earliest written Gaelic now extant— Modern linguistic discovery—The place of Celtic in the Aryan group I

CHAPTER II

ST. PATRICK, THE PIONEER OF CELTIC WRITERS

The historical Patrick—Authentic records—Earliest known Gaelic litterateur—Dates elusive—Birthplace—Autobiographical details of his youth—Taken captive—Escape—Obscure wanderings—Return home—The rôle of missionary in Ireland—Epoch-making career— Remarkable Patrician Dialogues—His own literary work—The "Confession"—"Epistle to Coroticus"—"Deer's Cry"—Ireland's oldest book—Three other antique compositions from the Book of Hymns—A curious prophecy—Personal character—Death . . 22

CHAPTER III

ST. COLUMBA AND THE DAWN OF LETTERS IN SCOTLAND

The fugitive MSS.—Gaelic a literary language for ages—Scotland's first writer—St. Columba one of the rarer master-spirits—His peculiar

ix

PAGE

qualities—Intellectual standpoint—Birth—Early life—A fateful
incident—Sets sail for Pictland—Motive—Arrival in pagan Scotland
—His missionary enterprise—Lights the lamp of literature—An
ardent scholar, penman, and poet—The famous " Cathrach "—
His Gaelic poems—Latin hymns—The Columban renaissance—
Encouragement of bards and scholars—The *Amra Choluimcille*—Iona
as an educational centre—European fame and influence   .   .   40

CHAPTER IV

ADAMNAN'S " VITA COLUMBÆ "

Oldest Scottish book in existence—A sturdy survival—Criteria of age—
Dorbene the copyist—Romantic history of the MS.—Now in
Schaffhausen—Adamnan, a rare personality—Abbot and scholar—
Influential career—Attitude to the two great questions that divided
the Celtic churches—Pathetic estrangement—" Lex Adamnani "—A
mighty social revolution—Death—His writings—" The Vision of
Adamnan "—His *Life of Columba* in three parts—Remarkable con-
tents—Most valuable monument of the early Celtic Church—List of
MSS. in which preserved—Latin *versus* Gaelic   .   .   .   58

CHAPTER V

THE BOOK OF DEER

An ancient curio—Second oldest book of Scotland—Where did it come
from ?—Its contents threefold—Gaelic colophon from the ninth
century—The work of a native scribe of Alba—Peculiarities—The
ecclesiastical art of the period—The Gaelic entries—" Legend of
Deer "—Drostan's tears—Some very quaint history—The earliest
source for Scottish Gaelic—Authentic glimpses into the Celtic condition of Scotland—Origin of shires, parishes, burghs, individual
freedom, and the use of the English language—Three editions of the
Gaelic of the Book of Deer—Now one of the very oldest MSS. of
native origin that Cambridge can boast of   79

CHAPTER VI

THE MS. LEGACY OF THE PAST

A fresh start in the study of Celtic literature—Advent of foremost scholars
—The new basis found by Zeuss—Resurrection of ancient texts—

Unexpected light—H. d'Arbois de Jubainville and his mission to this
country—The numbers, dates, and localities of Gaelic MSS. : (1) on
the Continent ; (2) in the British Isles—Subject matter—Examples
of the oldest written Gaelic poetry in Europe—The great books of
saga—Leabhar Na h'Uidhre—Books of Leinster, Ballymote, and
Lismore—Quotations—Account of the Ancient Annals—Tighernach
—The *Chronicon Scotorum*—The *Four Masters*—Romance of the
fugitive documents   96

CHAPTER VII

THE SCOTTISH COLLECTION OF CELTIC MSS.

Cabinet in Advocates' Library—Curious assortment of vernacular literature
—Number and character—Origin of the collection—Highland Society
and Kilbride MSS.—Subsidiary additions—Work for the expert—
Fate of some luckless documents—Value of MSS. XL., LIII., and
LVI.—Three literary monuments of the Western Highlands : (1) The
Book of the Dean of Lismore—History, description, value, contents,
extracts, names of contributors; (2) The Fernaig MS.—Characteristics
—Interesting details of supposed author ; (3) The Book of Clanranald
—Quaint relic—Two MSS., the Red and the Black—History and
contents, with specimen prose-poem and elegy .   .   .   115

CHAPTER VIII

THE MYTHOLOGICAL CYCLE

A rich and abundant saga literature—Three leading periods or cycles—The
myths and folk-tales—Problems to men of science—The philologists
and anthropologists take opposite sides—Their theories—Attitude of
the annalists and romancists of Ireland—Their craze for genealogy—
Early settlers in Erin—Advent of the Milesians or Gaels—The Three
Sorrows of Gaelic Storydom : (1) "The Tragedy of the Children of
Tuireann" ; (2) The fascinating "Aided of the Children of Lir" ;
(3) Story of "Deirdre and the Sons of Uisneach"—Extraordinary
interest evinced in this saga—Marvellous output of texts and translations   134

CHAPTER IX

THE HEROIC CYCLE

The golden age of Gaelic romance—Number of the tales—Cuchulinn—
His early adventures—The Wooing of Eimer—Training in Skye—The

PAGE

Bridge of the Cliffs—Tragedy of Conlaoch—Elopement—The "Táin Bó Chuailgné," and exploits of Cuchulinn—Ferdia at the ford—The two champions of Western Europe—Cuchulinn in the Deaf Valley—Death—The Red Rout of Conall Cearnach—Instruction of Cuchulinn to a prince—His "Phantom Chariot"—Modern translations of these rare sagas 153

CHAPTER X

THE OSSIANIC CYCLE

The old order changes—Who were the Feinn?—Ossian, his name and relation to the bardic literature—The Ossianic tales and poems very numerous — Earliest references — First remarkable development — Original home of the Ossianic romance—The leading heroes—A famous tract—Legends regarding Fionn, and curious details of his warrior-band—The literature divided into four classes—Most ancient poems of Ossian, and the Feinn—Quotations—"The Dialogue of the Ancients"—Ossian and Patrick—Story of Crede—Miscellaneous poems—Prose tales—"Pursuit of Diarmad and Grainne"—"Lay of Diarmad"—Norse Ballads—Dream figures, a remarkable Gaelic tradition 174

CHAPTER XI

THE INFLUENCE OF THE NORSE INVASIONS ON GAELIC LITERATURE

The dreaded Vikings—In English waters—Descents on Iona—Monasteries favourite objects of attack—Destruction of books—Their own eddas and sagas—Modern discovery of the wonderful Icelandic literature—The Northmen in a new light—Literary effects of their invasions—Arrested development—Lamentable dispersion of the literary classes—Pilgrim Scots—The rise of Scottish Gaelic—Present-day differences between it and Irish—Introduction of Norse words—Decay of inflection—Gaelic examples of Viking beliefs and superstitions—The Norseman still with us 198

CHAPTER XII

THE FOUR ANCIENT BOOKS OF WALES

The *Myvyrian Archaiology*—Oldest texts—The Black Book or Caermarthen—The Book of Aneurin—The Book of Taliessin—The Red

Book of Hergest — Gildas and Nennius — The ancient Laws and Institutes — A great dialectic battle — The princes of song — " I Yscolan " — A Welsh Ossianic poem — Characteristics of the early poetry — The medieval romances — Their history — Modern translations of the Mabinogion — Two classes of tales — The legend of Taliessin — His curious odes — Kilhwch and Olwen — The Lady of the Fountain — Three striking features of the Arthurian romances — Their influence on Western Europe 217

CHAPTER XIII

CELTIC LITERARY REVIVALS

Sixth century awakening throughout Celtdom — Illustrious names — Brittany's wonderful cycle of song — Charming examples — Dearth of tenth century — A strange trait of Celtic life — The brilliant medieval renaissance — Output of Ireland, Wales, and Brittany — The Cornish dramas — Last speaker of that dialect — Period of inactivity and decline — Recrudescence — 1745-1800 the highwater mark of Highland production — A galaxy of poets — Splendid lyrical outburst — New Ossianic cycle — Seana Dana — Caledonian Bards — The Welsh Eisteddfod — Latest Celtic renaissance — Some characteristic features, results, manifestations — Antiquity, thou wondrous charm ! . . 239

CHAPTER XIV

HIGHLAND BARDS BEFORE THE FORTY-FIVE

"The Owlet "—Three Macgregor songs—The old bardic system superseded—Era of modern Gaelic poetry—Mary Macleod—Details of her life—Famous songs—Iain Lom—Ardent poet and politician—His " Vow "—Eventful career—Poems—Created Gaelic Poet-Laureate— Influence on Highland history—Other minor bards and bardesses— Imitations by Sir Walter Scott—The blind harper, and the blind piper — A comic poet — Two major bards — Maccodrum's Muse— Characteristics of the group before the Forty-five . . . 262

CHAPTER XV

THE INFLUENCE OF THE CHURCH ON GAELIC LITERATURE

The origins of Celtic literature—Two streams—The Pagan—The Christian —Influence of the early Celtic Church as patron of letters—Originates a written literature—Attitude towards the ancient sagas—Medieval obscurantism—The Dialogues between Ossian and Patrick quoted and discussed—Their significance—Bishop Carsewell and the Reformation—The rival influences of Naturalism and the Church—Decline of Gaelic oral literature—The Nineteenth, a century of gleaning rather than of creative work — Reasons — Present - day return to nature— Splendid services of individual Churchmen . . . 286

CHAPTER XVI

THE INFLUENCE OF CELTIC, ON ENGLISH LITERATURE

Earliest contact—Loan-words—Three periods of marked literary influence —Layamon's " Brut "—A fascinating study for critics—The development of the Arthurian Romance—Sir Thomas Malory—Question as to origin of rhyme—A Celtic claim—Elements in Scottish poetry —in English literature—Gray's " Bard "—Macpherson's " Ossian " —Influence on Wordsworth and his contemporaries—Moore's " Irish Melodies "—Sir Walter Scott—Tennyson—Interesting comparison —Arnold, Shairp, Blackie—Novelists after Scott—Living writers . 304

CHAPTER XVII

THE PRINTED LITERATURE OF THE SCOTTISH GAEL

Two interesting bibliographies—Surprising revelations—First Gaelic printed book—Meagre output prior to the Forty-five—Earliest original works issued—No complete Bible in type before 1801— Nineteenth century activity—The Highlander's favourite books—A revelation of character—His printed literature mainly religious— Translations—The two books in greatest demand—Dearth of the masterpieces of other languages—The most popular of English religious writers—of native bards—Gaelic poetry—The printed succession—Notable books—Account of the Gaelic grammars— Dictionaries—Periodicals—Value of the literature . . . 325

CHAPTER XVIII

THE MASTER GLEANERS OF GAELIC POETRY

The work of the gleaner—Authors of the three most precious relics of Celtic literature, Leabhar Na h'Uidhre, Book of Hymns, and Book of Leinster—of the three Highland treasures, Book of the Dean of Lismore, Fernaig MS., and Book of Clanranald—Advent of Mac-

pherson—Collections and collectors between 1750 and 1820—First
printed gleaning—Four nineteenth-century monuments, Campbell's .
Leabhar na Feinne, Mackenzie's Beauties of Gaelic Poetry, Sinclair's
Songster, and Carmichael's Carmina Gadelica—Other recent gleaners
and their books   347

CHAPTER XIX

THE MASTER SCHOLARS OF CELTIC LITERATURE

The bards and seanachies—Six men of outstanding literary eminence—
The earliest pioneer of the modern philological movement—Representatives of the older scholarship—Those of the new—The brilliant
Zeuss—Foreign periodicals dealing with Celtic—Foremost scholars
of the various nations—Italian—German—French—Danish—Scandinavian—American—British, including English, Irish, Welsh, Manx,
and Scottish—Many literary problems solved—The promise of future
harvests   367

INDEX OF NAMES   387

INDEX OF SUBJECTS   397

CHAPTER I

THE ARRIVAL OF THE CELT IN HISTORY AND LITERATURE

The Celts in primitive Europe—Advent in British Isles—Two branches—
Observations of Cæsar and Tacitus—Main facts of Celtic progress on the
Continent—A vast empire—Interview with Alexander the Great—Colony in
Galatia—Cup of conquest full—Disintegration—The scattered remnants—
Recent statistics—The ancient Celts as seen through Greek and Roman eyes
—Literary awakening—Ogam writings—First men of letters—Earliest
written Gaelic now extant—Modern linguistic discovery—The place of Celtic
in the Aryan group.

EMERSON, looking forth from the new time on the nations
of Europe, gave pen to the reflection, "The Celts are of the
oldest blood in the world. Some peoples are deciduous or
transitory. Where are the Greeks? Where the Etrurians?
Where the Romans? But the Celts are an old family
of whose beginning there is no memory, and their end is
likely to be still more remote in the future, for they have
endurance and productiveness—a hidden and precarious
genius."

A sweeping statement withal, yet the thoughtful finding
of an eminently studious and dispassionate mind.

When the curtain lifts over primitive Europe, and
authentic history first begins, the Celts are already there,
and loom formidable in the heart of the Continent. Not
the earliest inhabitants by any means; archæology points
to anterior races. These the ethnologists designate according to the shape of their heads and supposed colour of their

hair. Their remains have been found in caves, and in what are known to science as the Neolithic or Stone Age barrows. And they present types of humanity widely differing from the succeeding so-called Aryans.[1] But beyond their material survivals, and the people who were supposed to have been descended from them, there is absolutely no record of these vanished races. They belong to pre-historic times.

So do the Celts in great part, but unlike their predecessors they have emerged in history, and projected themselves on its pages to this day. They have stepped out of the impenetrable haze, and appear at the opening of the written drama of Europe.

History finds them for the first time located about the upper reaches of the Danube, in the lands corresponding to modern Bavaria, Wurtemburg, Baden, and the country drained by the Maine to the east of the Rhine. The idea of an ingress from Asia has lately been abandoned. Research seems to have effectively exploded it.[2]

They were barbarians from our point of view, not savages ; not civilised, but apparently a good stage onward from earlier types. It was they who gave names to many of the rivers and mountains of Europe—"names which are poems," says Matthew Arnold, "and which imitate the pure voices of nature."

Hyperboreans they seemed to have been called by the original Greeks, but since the time of Hecatæus and Herodotus, that is, from about 500 B.C., they came to be known to the classic writers as κελται or κελτοι—a name which at that early period the Greeks applied indiscriminately to all the people of north and west Europe who were not Iberians.

[1] "In Europe the ancient races were all, according to Schaafhausen, 'lower in the scale than the rudest living savages,' they must therefore have differed to a certain extent from any existing race."—Darwin's *Descent of Man*, chap. vii. p. 281.

[2] "There is no proof of any migration of Asiatics into Europe west of the basin of the Dnieper down to the time of Attila."—Huxley.

To them, as well as to the Romans, all that stretch of the Continent appeared to be occupied mainly by κελτοι. And though the Germans lived from time immemorial beyond them in the north, not till the first century B.C. did the Romans discover that they were a different people. Cæsar himself was one of the earliest to observe and chronicle the fact.

But there were reasons for this apparent ubiquity of the Celts. Apart from their chronic unrest and frequent migrations, we can well understand why the Germans appeared merged in them. The Germans were early deprived of their independence, and held in slavish subordination till they recovered their freedom about 300 B.C. For centuries before that date, conqueror and conquered apparently lived under a common regime, obeying the same chiefs, and fighting in the same armies, though generally in the relation of dominant masters and subject slaves. In this way they even came to have many words in common, as their respective languages show.

At what time the Celts entered Gaul, Britain, and Ireland is a question unhappily beyond the knowledge of man. The seventh century B.C., or even the tenth as the Irish tradition maintains, is given as an approximate date. But of this there is no authentic record. Nor yet of a second immigration assumed to have followed in the third century B.C.

That there were two such invasions of Britain with a considerable interval between them is one of the pet theories of philology. For two branches of an originally parent stock may be traced, known as the Gadelic and the Brittonic, or more recently as the Q and P groups. The one includes the Irish, Manx, and Gaelic-speaking peoples, and was the earlier to arrive ; the other embraces the Welsh, Cornish, and Breton, who came later.

This linguistic fact might be represented tabularly, thus :—

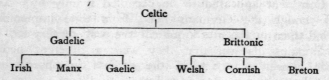

The main difference between those two branches is, that in Gadelic the original guttural of the Aryan tongue came gradually to be *c* with the sound *k*, ogam *qu*, and that in Brittonic it became *p*. So we say :—

English	Gaelic	Welsh	Latin
Four	*c*eithir	*p*edwar	quatuor
Five	*c*oig	*p*imp	quinque

Such a distinction points to a great change from the common speech of earlier Celtic times. It existed prior to the Christian era, and is still strikingly in evidence. Edward Lhuyd, the illustrious Welsh antiquary, writing in the early part of the eighteenth century, noted that there were scarcely any words in the Irish that began with *p*, beyond what were borrowed from Latin or some other language. So much was this the case, that in an ancient alphabetical vocabulary which he had beside him, the letter *p* was entirely omitted. Other instances might be given. For example, in O'Reilly's Irish Dictionary, out of upwards of 700 pages, only twelve are occupied with that letter ; and when we come to examine the most recent Gaelic collection of words—the etymological dictionary of Dr. Macbain—we find about 270 beginning with *p* out of a total of well over 7000 ; and even of these, the majority are derived or borrowed from Norse or English. There is a MS. of the eighteenth century in the Laing collection of Edinburgh University, which puts the case succinctly, when in the sections of what promised to be a good Gaelic grammar, it observes that of old no word, except *exotic* words, began in Gaelic with a *p*. Fastening on so characteristic a distinction Professor Rhys, some years ago, decided to call the Brittonic the P, and the Gadelic the Q group, as the more simple and fundamental classification.

Thus far philology helps to differentiate between the two branches, and points to a remote advent of the Gael in Britain.

But when we turn to history we find there is nothing definite on this most attractive subject till Cæsar arrives and makes personal observation. Speaking of the south—for he had not penetrated the northern parts—he tells us that he found two races in possession: one in the interior, which considered itself indigenous ; the other on the sea-coast, roving adventurers from the Continent who arrived later. Tacitus, writing nearly a century and a half after Cæsar, namely, about 82 A.D., practically confirms Cæsar's report of a double occupation, and adds the further interesting details, that the one race was dark complexioned and had curly hair, while the other, resembling the Gauls, had red hair and were tall of stature. In the eighth century A.D. we know, on the authority of Bede, that there were in these islands five written languages, viz. those of the Angles, the Brythons, the Scottis, the Picts, and the Latins, the first four[1] of which were spoken. It is the ever-puzzling yet fascinating work of philology and ethnology to trace the origin and exact racial connection of these—a work which hitherto has proved as elusive as the finding of the North Pole. Who are the dark complexioned race of the South? and who the Picts of the North? are questions of perennial interest to the experts.

But though early British and German history is so elusive, we are on sure ground with the main facts of Celtic progress on the Continent from the fifth century B.C. Authentic history then opens with the advent of the classical writers just at the time when the Celts were entering upon a series of conquests which for the next 200 years made them the dominant race in Europe.[2] It is needless to

---

[1] Adamnan refers to the same four peoples.

[2] " The first great movements of the European population of which there is

follow their various migrations, even if it were possible.   As
their territories became congested on the Danube, they sent
forth horde after horde of conquering tribes who surged
every way.   Now westward for the most part, till, in the
graphic language of Galgacus, uttered centuries after, " there
was now no nation beyond—nothing save the waves and
the rocks " (Nulla jam gens ultra ; nihil nisi fluctus et
saxa), then, like the back-rushing tides, they receded
eastwards.

" Tumults," the Romans called these irrepressible out-
bursts, and most felicitously too, for they were the terror of
Europe.

A cursory glance at some of the more famous of their
invasions suffices to show the restless energy of the Celts
and their far-reaching conquests.

From Gaul, where they appear to have established themselves north of the Garonne and about the Seine and Loire,
the hungry tribes made a dash for Spain, shortly before 500
B.C., and wrested the peninsula from the hands of the
Phœnicians.   One hundred and twenty years later North Italy
shared the same fate.   Surging through the passes of the
Alps they overthrew the Etruscans on their own ground in the
great battle of Allia, 390 B.C., and annexed their territory.
Flushed with the victory they pressed forward, and within
three days stormed and sacked the town of Rome itself.
Indeed, it is with this momentous incursion that authentic
Roman history begins.

One more mighty invasion of the East, and the Illyrians
along the Danube are vanquished, thus rendering the
conquerors masters of a vast territory extending from that
river and the Adriatic to the Atlantic, and bounded on the
north by the Rhine and Mid-Germany, and on the south by
Mid-Italy and Mid-Spain, and including the British Isles—
a magnificent empire rivalling that of Alexander or of Cæsar

any conclusive evidence are that series of Gaulish invasions of the east and
south which ultimately extended from North Italy to Galatia in Asia Minor."—
Huxley.

in their palmy days. Goldsmith's lines might well apply to them—

> One only master grasps the whole domain,
> And half a tillage stints the smiling plain.

So formidable, indeed, were the Celts during the period of their ascendency that it served the purpose of the classic nations — Greeks and Romans — to keep the peace with them as best they could, and even to play them off against their own hereditary foes. And so the expansive tribes were for the most part on friendly terms with both, especially with the Greeks. We have an account in Strabo of an interview which Alexander the Great had with their ambassadors. It is given on the authority of Ptolemy, his general. The young potentate knew well the advantage of cultivating good fellowship with his powerful neighbours, and when the tribes of the Adriatic sent delegates he received them with all due courtesy and respect.

While they were drinking, says the general, Alexander asked them what was the object of their greatest fear, thinking they would say himself. But the imaginative Celts had quite other views. They feared no man. One thing only alarmed them, they replied, and that was lest the heavens should one day fall and crush them. Still, they added, that they valued the friendship of such a man as he was above everything.

" How vainglorious these Celts are ! " muttered the young autocrat to his courtiers, a little piqued, perhaps, at their rejoinder. Yet, if such were really the object of their superstitious dread, the promise they made was not without its own grim cogency. " If we fulfil not our engagement," they said, " may the sky falling upon us crush us, may the earth opening swallow us, may the sea overflowing its borders drown us."

With Alexander they kept their pledge, but in 280 B.C., when another king ruled Macedonia, they over-ran his territories, slew him in battle, and pillaged the temple of

Delphi itself—an act of vandalism so shocking to the Greeks that it roused their patriotism to such a pitch that they were able to repulse the enemy in the neighbouring gorges.

Thus compelled to evacuate Greece, the Celts invaded Asia Minor in 278 B.C., and established there the well-known colony of Galatia. It was to their descendants that St. Paul addressed his trenchant epistle, and the words, " O foolish Galatians, who hath druided you ? "

For six centuries after they continued to speak their language there, so that St. Paul must have heard one dialect at least of the ancient tongue.

It may surprise students of the classics to learn that the Celts claim Hercules as one of their own potentates. In an old Gaelic MS. in the Advocates' Library, Edinburgh, we find the renowned hero figuring thus : " Ercoill mac Amphitrionis, mhic Antestis, mhic Andlis, mhic Mitonis, mhic Festime, mhic Athol, mhic Gregais, mhic Gomer, mhic Jafed, mhic Noe "—a truly wonderful genealogy, tracing him up to Noah through the Cymric Gomer.

The Greek version of the myth is interesting. It tells how Hercules, on his expedition against Geryon, turned aside into Gaul and married there a handsome Gaulish lady, by whom he had a son, Galates. This Galates, surpassing all his countrymen in strength and prowess, led the way to conquest, and exercising a wide sway, his territory and subjects eventually came to be named after him—the one Galatia, the other Galatæ.

In whatever way the classic story originated, it is matter of history that after the Celtic invasion of Greece, Galatæ became the popular Greek name for the people hitherto known as κελτοι, even as Galli was the favourite Roman one.

But already, before the Greek repulse, the Celtic cup of conquest was full, and their vast empire began to crumble and disintegrate. The first great shock was given by the revolt of their born thralls, the Germans, about 300 B.C. In the struggle for independence these recovered their liberty and big stretches of territory. Besides falling out with the Greeks, the flurried tribes in that wild consternation of defeat came to blows with the Romans also, who in two different battles got the victory over them. Forced to ally themselves with former foes, now with the Etruscans, again with the Carthaginians, the Celts still fought desperately, but all in vain. Their dominion was doomed. And as if to hasten the swift debacle, the various sections of the same great people attacked and dispossessed each other. It was probably in the pressure of those times that the Brittonic invaders surged into Britain and elbowed their Gaelic kinsmen into more straitened circumstances ; for all the continental Celts were simultaneously in the throes of a lamentable dispersion. Reverse followed reverse with singular fatality. Every attempt to redeem their desperate fortunes seemed to fail. " They went to the war, but they always fell," said their own sad bard afterwards, summing up in one terse antithesis the history of their collapse.

The failure was crushing and irretrievable. They lost Spain, they lost the north of Italy, they lost Gaul, and subsequently Britain.

The story of Cæsar's conquests needs no rehearsal. By 80 A.D. all Britain south of the Firth of Forth figured as a Roman province.

Meantime the Celtic dialects of Gaul and Spain were gradually being superseded by the Latin, and even the laws, habits, and civil administration of the people were becoming Roman, until in the third century of our era scarcely a vestige of the ancient régime remained outside of the British Isles and Brittany, except to the south of the latter, where the influence of the discarded dialect on the adopted Latin might be traced.[1]

In Britain the Romanising process was suddenly arrested by the hasty departure of the conqueror ; and in the helpless

---

[1] " Two centuries after Cæsar's conquest the Celtic tongue had all but disappeared from Gaul, still that language did not perish without leaving behind it slight but yet distinct traces."—A. Brachet.

abandonment that ensued the Saxons found an open door.
The same fate that they had themselves formerly inflicted
on their kinsmen now overtook the Britons, who were
hustled in great numbers into the wilds of Cornwall, of
Wales, and Strathclyde. And the last stage of the driving
west remained to be accomplished in the case of the Irish,
when the Anglo-Celts arrived in the twelfth century.

Since the great debacle of their race the Celtic remnants
have continued to speak one or other of the dialects bequeathed from their ancestors. Five of these are living
tongues. Apart from the number that speak them abroad,
it is estimated there are upwards of 3,000,000 people in
Brittany and the British Isles whose mother tongue is
Celtic. The distribution and proportion, according to the
latest available statistics,[1] are full of interest, in view of the
long struggle for existence of the language and people, and
the extraordinary vitality they have evinced in defying the
tooth of time. These facts may be crisply tabulated thus :—

Gaelic.[2]	254,415.	Chiefly in the Highlands of Scotland.
Irish.	679,145.	West of a line in Ireland from Dun-garvon Bay to Loch Swilly.
Manx.	3,000.	West Coast, Isle of Man.
Welsh.	900,000.	Over Wales.
Cornish.	Extinct.	Formerly Cornwall.
Breton.	1,300,000.	In Brittany, N.W. corner of France.

A sadly dwindling minority are these fag-ends of once
so mighty a race. There can be no doubt that we see the
isolated parts gradually expiring on the horizon, and with
more accelerated speed within the last few decades than for
centuries before. Modern industrialism now woos them
away from the strongholds of their own characteristic life,
and the separate units get absorbed in the common national
life and the common civilisation. Numbers of them—of the
Irish especially—are still seeking a home, following the

[1] Census, 1891.

[2] The number in Scotland who could speak Gaelic in 1901 was 230,806, and
who could speak Gaelic only, 28,106. The census of 1891 gave 43,738 speaking
Gaelic only, and 38,192 speaking Irish only.

hereditary instincts of their ancestors, and hiving westwards to America, only to lose their distinctive Celtic existence and to be merged in the larger life of that great nation.

The facts are sufficiently patent, but to show the rapidity with which the disintegration is going on it may be mentioned that since 1851, 3,925,133 persons have emigrated from Ireland alone—a number larger than that of all the remaining Celtic-speaking population in Europe. In 1899 the number was 43,760; in 1900, 47,107; in 1901, 39,870, the vast majority of whom were from the western Irish-speaking provinces; and, as in the depopulation of the Highlands, it is largely a drain of the best blood, the land being left in the hands of the old and the feeble.

There are those who still write and dream of laying the foundations of a new Celtic civilisation, but in view of the present subtle and swift dissolution it is hard to know what they mean, unless indeed it be a leavening of the existing civilisation by a recrudescence of the Celtic spirit and Celtic aspirations.

In the main the race has already become fused with the population of Europe, disappearing as Gallo-Grecians in the east, as Celt-Iberians in Spain, as Gallo-Franks and Anglo-Celts in the north-west—all but the Celtic fringes that are shedding their past.

Thus far the history, and from what we have said it will appear that the Celts first emerge in literature in the fifth century B.C., from which time the classical writers make frequent, though generally short and meagre allusions to them. Dr. W. Z. Ripley,[1] one of the latest authorities on ethnology, would discount their evidence as of little value for the purposes of modern scientific research into race origins and affinities, yet, nevertheless, so far as it goes, it is highly interesting and important.

The earliest of all the Greek authors to mention the Celts, if we except the geographer Hecatæus (520 B.C.), is Herodotus (484-425 ?), who twice refers to them in his history as

[1] *Races of Europe.*

dwelling at the sources of the Danube and bordering on the Kunesii, the westermost inhabitants of Europe. Xenophon, at a later period (390), speaking of them as mercenaries with Dionysius of Syracuse in 368 B.C., remarks that "the ships brought Keltoi and Iberes." Plato, Ephorus, Pytheas, and Scylax all furnish hints in the same century. Aristotle also knew about this extraordinary people, who, he was told, feared "neither earthquake nor floods," living in a country so cold that even the ass did not thrive there, yet putting little clothing on their children. It appears he had also heard that they had sacked Rome. Timæus popularised the new name Galatæ in bringing into notice Galatia, which, he avers, is named after "Galates, son of Cyclops and Galatia."

From this time onward we get fuller details of the Celtic character, manners, and customs. And to show the number and variety of authorities from which information may be gleaned, the following may be selected : Polybius, a Greek writer of the second century B.C., and Posidonius of the first. Julius Cæsar and his contemporary Diodorus Siculus, Strabo, a geographer of the early part of the first century A.D., Virgil, Cicero, Livy, Tacitus, Dion Cassius, Pliny, Ptolemy, and Ammianus Marcellinus, the latter bringing the list down towards the end of the fourth century, when the Roman Empire in its own turn began to break up, and the Gaels were at length prepared to enter the arena of literature and speak for themselves.

It is outwith the scope of this chapter to go into many of the interesting details which these various authors furnish, but a few of those which astonished the writers may be noted in passing, such as, the Celts' intellectual cleverness ; their numbers and great size ; the magnificence of their funerals, and their belief in the immortality of the soul. Their cities were forests, and though otherwise cleanly in their eating, lion-like, they were wont to take up huge joints and gnaw at them. Other features of striking peculiarity were their figurative, exaggerated language ; the functions of bards and druids ; their chariots and excellent horsemanship ;

the fierceness and noise of their first onset in battle; their readiness to be disheartened by reverse; their astounding clothes,—dyed tunics, flowered with various colours, flaming and fantastic, striped cloaks buckled on their shoulders, and breeches. Their chiefs generally appeared with a retinue of followers. Of old, the Celts devoted themselves to plundering other people's countries. The heads of their fallen enemies they cut off and hung to their horses' manes; they were warlike, passionate, and always ready for fighting; otherwise simple, frank, hospitable to strangers, but vain, quarrelsome, fickle, and ever prone to waste their strength on personal feuds and factions. Such were some of the curious traits and customs of our Celtic progenitors as seen through Greek and Roman eyes.

Scarcely had the Romans finally abandoned Britain than the Celts enter upon a new rôle. They annex the Roman script, the Roman language for literary work, and the Roman art of writing. And thus equipped, they proceed to produce a literature of their own in Latin and Gaelic. The wonder is that with their natural quickness and thirst for knowledge they did not achieve a record in this direction before.

When we reflect on the other great nations of antiquity, we find that they generally had a literature of some kind, written down, if not in books, then on skins or slabs and in temples. The Egyptians had their "Book of the Dead," the Indians their "Rig-veda," the Persians their "Zend-avesta," the Chinese and Hebrews their "Sacred Books," the Greeks and Romans their classics, and we naturally ask, "What had the Celts in the zenith of their power?" say between 500 and 300 B.C. No writing at all that we know of. At this day only a few inscriptions remain in the Gaulish language of Cæsar's time and later, but nothing earlier. These nomadic warrior populations may have had their bardic compositions and tales floating by oral tradition, but we have no evidence that they developed a literature, though some of them may have known Greek letters.

It is to the insular Gaels, to those of Ireland and Scotland in the fifth and sixth centuries of our era, that we have to look for the early beginnings of Celtic literature. The Irish first showed signs of a rude awakening to activity in this direction. They invented a system of writing peculiar to themselves, simple and ingenious, and good enough for rough inscriptions on stones, but too cumbrous for the needs of literature.

Their earliest records are to be found in this Ogam script, which consists of a number of short lines drawn straight or slanting, either above, below, or through a long stem-line. Thus—

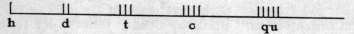

represents the letters h, d, t, c, qu, being the first letters of the first five numerals in Gaelic, h'aon, dha, tri, ceithir, coig ; the last in Manx is queig ; in Irish cuig ; and in Latin quinque.

The vowels are similarly represented, broad vowels, a, o, u ; small vowels, e, i—   .

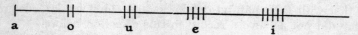

Over two hundred stones have been found inscribed with Ogam writing, most of them in the south-west of Ireland, from twenty to thirty in Wales and Devonshire, and ten in Scotland. The Book of Ballymote, a MS. of the fourteenth century, fortunately contains a key to some of these inscriptions, so that many of them have been read, though not all.

Who introduced this peculiar mode of writing? and when? are questions that have never yet been determined. Brash, who made personal inspection of most of the stones, was of opinion that they are of pre-Christian origin, whereas Dr. Graves has attempted to prove that they belong to a period between the fifth and seventh centuries A.D.

References to Ogam inscriptions are frequently met with in the earliest Celtic literature, and some examined contain grammatical forms alleged to be older than those of the most ancient MSS., and corresponding even with the archaic forms of the antique Gaulish monuments.

The Ogam used to be written on wood and stone, and it is not improbable that many of the genealogies and bits of legendary lore may have been handed down from generation to generation in this way, as well as by oral tradition.

It is with the great wave of Christian evangelisation that passed over Ireland and Scotland successively, through the labours of St. Patrick and St. Columba, that the use of the Roman script became widely general, and we trace the dawn of letters. Round the names of these two men there shines a lustre which the lapse of ages has failed to dim. They not only kindled the torch of a higher faith and purer life among their Celtic brethren, but they lighted also the lamp of literature, which has continued to burn with more or less radiance for 1500 years.

St. Patrick, as the earlier of the two, is really the Cæd-mon of Gaelic literature. Born in Scotland, probably, as the later critics think, at Old Kilpatrick, near Dumbarton, he was, while yet a youth of sixteen, carried captive to Hiberio, and though he escaped after six years from his hard fate as his master's thrall and feeder of cattle, his missionary zeal, new kindled, urged him to return as evangelist to the land of his former oppression. The visions of his early captivity, as he lay down to rest of nights near the cattle, remind us of Cædmon's vision in the stable at Whitby, upwards of two hundred years after—a vision which issued in the birth of English literature, as did those of St. Patrick in that of Gaelic.

And so the unassuming herd emerges as the first known writer of the ancient Celtic people, the first of whom we have any definite authentic knowledge.

Three literary compositions stand in his name, namely, his "Confession," written in rugged Latin, his "Epistle to Coroticus," in similar language and style, and the "Deer's Cry," a lorica or prayer in Gaelic. This hymn has always been regarded, and rightly too, as a gem of sacred song.

The religious and literary dawn that lit up Ireland in the fifth century reached Scotland in the sixth through the advent of the heroic Columba. He too, by unhappy circumstances driven over sea, lived an exile in "the land of his adoption tried," and with even more brilliance and learning did for Scotland what St. Patrick did for Ireland. So that the school of Iona became for centuries after his death a centre of light and leading in religion and letters, not only for Scotland and Ireland, but also for many parts of Europe.

His own special contributions to literature include several beautiful poems in Gaelic and Latin, and many transcripts in Latin of parts of books of Scripture, such as the Cathrach, a copy of the Psalter believed to have been made while he was yet a student, and perhaps also the Book of Durrow and the Book of Kells—two wonderful specimens of penmanship and early Celtic art. If these latter are not exactly the work of his own hands they belong at least to the Columban period, an era of great literary activity, which produced, among other well-known works, the *Amra Choluimcille* of Dallan Forgaill, Adamnan's *Life of Columba*, and the Book of Deer.

It will thus be seen that the earliest written MSS. of the Celtic people are essentially a Christian literature, which ignored almost entirely the pagan traditions of the race in its effort to supersede them. But the atmosphere was heavy with these, and apparently from pre-Christian times there had come floating down by oral transmission a great mass of heroic saga which at length found written expression in the seventh or eighth century A.D. So that now to the purely Christian literature there was added the purely pagan, which much more faithfully reflected the characteristic flavour of the race, its strength, and its weakness, its facts, its fancies, and its foibles. Professing to go back to a remote antiquity, it is significant that the setting of this ancient saga is confined exclusively to these islands. None of the stories belong to Europe or the doings of the parent stock in its palmy days. As compared with the Christian, this pagan contribution is by far the more important from a literary point of view. Yet it must be borne in mind that though there are still extant in Ireland Celtic Latin MSS. which reach up to the time of St. Patrick and St. Columba, there is none existing which contains actual Gaelic writing prior to the eighth century.

Almost the only specimen of continuous prose written by the end of the eighth century now known to exist is a portion of a Gaelic sermon on temperance and self-denial from the text, " If any man will come after me, let him deny himself, and take up his cross, and follow me." This curious relic is in the town library of Cambray, in a MS. containing the canons of an Irish council held in 684. The MS., however, bears direct evidence that it was not written until about a century afterwards.

The earliest written Gaelic is contained in MSS. on the Continent, such as those at Milan, Cambray, Vienna, St. Gall, and other places. And even these are not books of saga, but generally Latin books with some Gaelic poems jotted on the leaf margins, or glosses, and other explanatory writing. There are a few such literary monuments also in the British Isles, containing ancient Gaelic. The Book of Armagh, for example, dates from 807, and in addition to vernacular notes, preserves the Latin " Confessions " of St. Patrick, copied, it is believed, from the apostle's own autograph MS. The Book of Deer, almost equally venerable, with a Gaelic colophon, belongs to the same century. To its original contents were added in the eleventh and twelfth centuries Gaelic entries which are of uncommon philological and historical interest and value.

But setting aside these Latin books in which the Gaelic jottings are purely incidental and secondary, we need to come down as far as the eleventh century to reach the existing sources of the earliest written compositions in the native tongue. It is in such MSS. as the Leabhar Na h'Uidhre, the Book of Hymns, and the other great Middle-

Age gleanings of after days that we find the Patrician and Columban literature as well as the ancient sagas.

Till within very recent times the Celt had no idea that he was heir to such a vast literary inheritance as really exists. As in the olden times men sometimes buried their wealth to save it from the hands of ruthless foes, and, dying themselves or falling in the fray, lived not to indicate to others the site of their hid treasures, so it has happened in the case of Gaelic literature. Much of it perished at the hands of the enemy and the avenger. What was saved from the wreck of the more stormy and turbulent periods of our history owes its existence to-day very largely to concealment and neglect. And as the plough or the spade occasionally turns up an old stone cist, or a casket of ancient coins, or a canoe of primitive man, so the casual researches of antiquarians and scholars have brought to light a hidden mass of ancient writings which appear to have been scattered broadcast over Europe and the British Isles. These Gaelic relics are now jealously preserved in various countries, and within the last century have been made the subject of the most interested scrutiny by leading Continental and British philologists, with the result that they have thrown a welcome light on some of the darker problems of history, philology, and ethnology. For example, as late as the first quarter of last century few people had any idea that the Celtic populations were allied with the southern nations of Europe, or that their language had any connection whatever with the Romance and Teutonic tongues. One solitary scholar,[1] indeed, threw out the hint as early as 1786, but offered no proof; and it remained a visionary hypothesis until the long list of documents reappearing one by one enabled scholars to establish the point beyond question, that linguistically the Celtic people are a branch of the great Aryan family, and thus closely allied with the Teutonic, and still more nearly with the Greek and the Latin peoples. Roughly, this relationship may be represented as under. The table is not meant to

[1] Sir William Jones.

indicate race affinities, which it is very far indeed from doing, but simply to exhibit the affinities of language which modern philological studies have traced :——

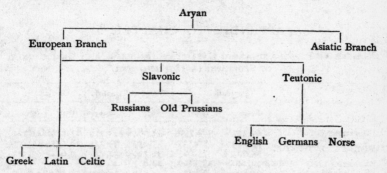

It is this important and surprising discovery, that we are a part of a vast Indo-European family spread to the east over a great part of Asia, and to the west over the most of Europe including Russia, that has given such impetus to Celtic studies within recent years. The Gaelic has been found to have roots which go far down towards the parent stock. And its literature, therefore, is of the utmost value to all who seek to read the riddle of the past and to push back the horizons of knowledge beyond the age even of Herodotus, " the father of history."

There is a fascination and refining influence in the study of the Greek and Roman classics, but for the man of large outlook and broad human sympathies there is much also to interest and attract in the literature of the Gael—so old, so weird, so fanciful.

Wordsworth, as he listened to the song of the Highland maid in the harvest field, felt the pathos of the past in that moving Gaelic product, and would fain learn its story. Hence his reverie—

> Will no one tell me what she sings?
> Perhaps the plaintive numbers flow
> For old unhappy far-off things,
> And battles long ago.

That is just what they do; dealing with much brighter
things too. For the spirit of the race is enshrined in these
old writings, and the fortunes of the race in their history.

APPENDIX TO CHAPTER I

NUMBER OF PERSONS SPEAKING GAELIC AND ENGLISH, AND GAELIC ONLY,
IN SCOTLAND IN 1891 AND 1901.

County.	Population.		Gaelic and English.		Gaelic only.	
	1891.	1901.	1891.	1901.	1891.	1901.
Inverness . .	89,317	89,796	44,084	43,179	17,276	11,721
Ross and Cromarty	77,810	76,135	37,437	39,235	18,577	12,171
Argyll . . .	75,003	73,083	36,720	34,224	6,042	3,313
Lanark . .	1,046,040	1,337,886	22,887	26,695	84	101
Sutherland . .	21,896	21,239	14,786	14,076	1,115	469
Perth . . .	126,199	123,276	13,847	11,446	304	78
Renfrew . .	290,798	268,459	8,435	5,585	63	40
Edinburgh . .	434,159	487,702	6,308	5,745	19	75
Caithness . .	37,177	33,623	4,068	2,865	76	20
Dumbarton . .	94,495	113,627	3,556	3,040	36	14
Bute . . .	18,404	18,641	3,482	2,713	29	20
Nairn . . .	10,019	9,291	2,487	1,325	53	10
Elgin . . .	43,453	44,749	2,263	1,860	12	2
Stirling . .	125,608	141,847	1,840	2,021	2	10
Ayr . . .	226,283	254,165	1,827	1,654	14	16
Aberdeen . .	281,332	303,908	1,534	1,331	8	8
Forfar . . .	277,773	283,736	1,461	1,303	8	13
Fife . . .	187,346	218,347	726	840	6	3
Banff . . .	64,190	61,440	639	499	3	...
Haddington . .	37,485	38,656	575	459	7	7
Linlithgow . .	52,808	64,796	486	575	2	5
Clackmannan .	28,432	31,994	215	170	1	1
Dumfries . .	74,221	72,564	201	176	...	1
Roxburgh . .	53,741	48,804	177	132	...	...
Kincardine . .	35,647	40,896	116	103	1	...
Berwick . .	32,406	30,793	89	74	...	1
Orkney . .	30,453	27,727	88	70	...	...
Selkirk . .	27,353	23,356	73	57	...	...
Peebles . .	14,761	15,066	70	72	...	1
Kirkcudbright .	39,985	39,335	69	98	...	...
Wigton . .	36,062	32,593	68	84	...	...
Shetland . .	28,711	27,736	67	52	...	...
Kinross . .	6,280	6,981	56	55	...	...
Persons on Board Ship in Scottish Waters . .	...	9,856	...	887	...	6
Total . .	4,025,647	4,472,103	210,677	202,700	43,738	28,106

In the census of 1901 the schedule restricts the entries in the Gaelic column to persons over three years of age. According to the previous census the number of persons under three years of age amounted to $7\frac{1}{2}$ per cent of the whole population. This must be taken into account in order to institute a fair comparison between the returns of the Gaelic-speaking population in 1891 and 1901.

CHAPTER II

ST. PATRICK, THE PIONEER OF CELTIC WRITERS

The historical Patrick—Authentic records—Earliest known Gaelic litterateur—Dates elusive—Birthplace—Autobiographical details of his youth—Taken captive—Escape—Obscure wanderings—Return home—The rôle of missionary in Ireland—Epoch-making career—Remarkable Patrician Dialogues—His own literary work—The "Confession"—"Epistle to Coroticus"—"Deer's Cry"—Ireland's oldest book—Three other antique compositions from the Book of Hymns—A curious prophecy—Personal character—Death.

IT is a characteristic of our age to doubt, if not to deny, the historical reality of many of the heroic figures that hover in the background of history. And such a doubt has extended even to St. Patrick, due largely to the fact that he is not mentioned by the early historians Prosper of Aquitaine (402-463) and Bede (673-735), both of whom attribute the conversion of Ireland to Palladius.

But this seeming omission has been explained on the highly probable assumption that Patrick [1] was the Palladius of these writers; and against the merely negative inference there is the positive and almost overwhelming voice of history and tradition, which puts the essential features of Ireland's apostle beyond all doubt.

The authentic records of his career are numerous and very old, dating back, we may say, to his own handwriting. For in the Book of Armagh we have what professes to be a copy of the autobiographical "Confession" which he wrote

[1] Professor Zimmer, among others, believes that they were one and the same person.

himself late in life.   This Book of Armagh, one of the most
ancient and exquisite of the Irish MSS., is itself nearly
1100 years old, having been written in 807 by a scribe
Ferdomnach, and, in addition to the " Confession " and other
interesting contents, it has preserved to us various Patrician
documents.   That the writer had before him the actual
autograph MS. of the saint when copying the " Confession "
is inferred from his own words, " Thus far the volume which
Patrick wrote with his own hand.   On the seventeenth day
of March was Patrick translated to the heavens."   And also
from his frequent marks of interrogation and casual hints,
such as, " The Book is uncertain here," showing that during
the intervening centuries since Patrick wrote the writing
must have become faded and even illegible in some places.

Besides his own personal account, there is no lack of
early lives by other authors.   Among those that may still
be consulted are : (1) the biographical Hymn by Fiacc of
Sletty, one of the saint's own contemporaries ; (2) two
seventh-century Lives known as Tirechan's and Muirchu
Mac Cumachteni's, found in the Book of Armagh ; (3) the
Tripartite Life, largest of all, from three very ancient
Gaelic MSS., believed by Colgan, though not by later critics,
to belong to the early part of the sixth century, and translated by him in his *Trias Thaumaturga*, 1645 ; (4) the
Monk Jocelin's memoir, twelfth century ; and (5) other
MSS. of the eleventh and fifteenth centuries.   Subsequent
authors, of course, are mainly dependent on these.

A great historic character was this St. Patrick, who
could not be buried in documents.   His own words have
far-reaching significance, beyond even what he himself meant
to convey when he wrote, " He who is mighty came and in
his mercy supported me, and raised me up and placed me
on the top of a wall."   On this eminence St. Patrick is
great, not merely as apostle of Ireland, but also as occupy-
ing a niche in the origins of Celtic literature.   Essentially
a man of religious initiative, and making no claim to distinction as a writer, he is nevertheless the earliest known

pioneer of letters in Ireland—the first of whose work we
have definite records to attest the authenticity.

What share he had in making the latter a literary
country it is difficult to say; but from his missionary
advent in Ireland a knowledge of letters seems to have
spread rapidly over the land. His monasteries and
churches were centres and nurseries of learning. "He
used," as Tirechan tells us, "to baptize men daily and to
read letters and abgatoriae with them."

There is a high probability that the Ogam writing
peculiar to Ireland originated before his time, and even the
beautiful modification of the Roman alphabet found in Irish
books. These are still matters for research. But one
thing, at least, is claimed for the saint and his Christian
followers, that they made the use of the Roman script for
the first time widely general. And this had far-reaching
results for the future, since only by its adaptation, as apart
from the rude and cumbrous though ingeniously simple
Ogam, was any real literature possible.

In view of the mass of biographical material that has
collected round the venerated name of St. Patrick, it might
be supposed that every event of his life would stand out
clear and luminous. Yet such is the perversity of historic
authorship, that names and dates and even oft-told incidents
are hard to get at in their true setting. The career of the
apostle is inextricably jumbled up and confused with that of
two others—the traditional Palladius and another Patrick,
both of which semi-mythical characters appear and dis-
appear again and again, crossing his path like his double;
insomuch that it has been conjectured that the incidents of
one life are often transferred to another, and the saint is
credited with experiences which really belonged to the
history of the other two, such, for example, as his alleged
mandate from the Pope and the superior continental training
under Germanus.

Dates especially are wonderfully elusive. The usual
chronology for St. Patrick's career is given as follows:

Birth, 387; missionary advent in Ireland, 432; death, 492 or 493. Yet each of these dates is still under discussion. Dr. Whitley Stokes puts the advent as early as 397; Dr. Todd as late as 439 or 440. And so, after all that has been said and searched, we are dependent for the essential features and outstanding facts of his life upon the apostle's own writings.

Such historical details as are generally accepted may be briefly given. But in this case there is an advantage in quoting the *ipsissima verba* of the saint, and thus allow him to tell his own tale at critical points of his career, for his style and matter are themselves a revelation of character.

He first projects himself on the canvas of literary history by relating early circumstances and the pregnant event which changed the whole aspect of his life, and gave it the direction it afterwards took. Thus he begins :—

I, Patrick, a sinner, the rudest and least of all the faithful and the most despicable among most men, had for my father Calpornius a deacon, son of the late Potitus a presbyter, who was of the town of Bonaven Taberniæ; for he had a farm in the neighbourhood where I was taken captive. I was then sixteen years old. I knew not the true God, and I was carried in captivity to Hiberio with many thousands of men according to our deserts, because we had gone back from God and had not kept His commandments, and were not obedient to our priests who used to warn us for our salvation.

Bonaven Taberniæ has been the subject of much eager inquiry to this day. Where is it? or Nemthur, the alternative name furnished by Fiacc of Sletty? Many places claim the honour of being the birthplace of the saint. Boulogne, Bristol, Glastonbury, Carlisle, Tours, Caerleon, and Ireland have all contended at one time or another for the prestige. But the best authorities in recent times seem to favour Old Kilpatrick, near Dumbarton, as the most likely locality from which sprung the saint, and as fulfilling better than any of the others the actual suggestions of the records. In the river opposite the town there is a rock visible at low water, called St. Patrick's stone, tradition alleging that the ship in which he sailed away to Ireland struck against it, but continued its voyage unharmed.

In captivity in Antrim he remained for six years, his daily employment being to feed cattle. Then the love of God entered his heart, he tells us, and a spirit of prayer grew upon him. Often he would say a hundred prayers in a day, and rise of nights to resort to the woods and mountains in snow, and frost, and rain, for the same purpose.

While thus exercised, one night, in a dream, a voice came to him saying, " Thy fasting is well ; thou shalt soon return to thy country." Later on, the dream was repeated, the same voice assuring him that the ship was now ready, 200 miles away.

Waiting no longer, the poor enthused slave fled from his master, and, after long wandering, reached the port, where he found indeed a ship, but the captain of it proved rough and hostile, and refused to have anything to do with him. On the way back to his hut he was recalled by a sailor, the upshot of the parley being that he accompanied the crew on the voyage. Afterwards he seems to have been detained by them on shore, perhaps in Gaul, as they wandered in a desert and suffered great hardships. " How is it, Christian ? ", said the captain one day when no food could be had. Patrick gave a characteristic reply, and he tells us that they were saved from starvation on that occasion by a herd of swine soon after appearing, some of which they killed and ate.

There is no mention in his account of any Continental sojourn,[1] though almost all the Lives make reference to such. Fiacc of Sletty waxes poetical over it :—

He went across all the Alps—great God, it was a marvel of a
    journey—
Until he staid with German in the south, in the south part of
    Latium ;

---

[1] Dr. Whitley Stokes thinks this sojourn took place between his first missionary advent to Ireland in 397 and his second in 432.

In the isles of the Tyrrhene Sea he remained, therein he
    meditated,
He read the Canon with German ; it is this that writings declare
To Ireland God's angels were bringing him in his course,
Often was it seen in vision that he would come thither again.

If such wandering took place, it was probably after he
escaped from the mariners. For, over twenty-two years of
his life at this period seem to be a blank, unless accounted
for by some such sojourn in this country or abroad. At
length, after great privations and lonely struggle, he made
his way back to his parents, who received him " as a son,
and earnestly besought him not to expose himself to fresh
dangers, but to remain with them henceforth."

For a while he did stay, and then the apostolic spirit
came upon him. " In the dead of night," he says, " I saw
a man coming to me as if from Hiberio, whose name was
Victoricus, having innumerable epistles. And he gave me
one of them, and I read the beginning of it, which contained
the words, ' The voice of the Irish.' And whilst I was
repeating the beginning of the epistle, I imagined that I
heard in my mind the voice of those who were near the
wood of Foclut, which is near the Western Sea, and then
they cried, ' We pray thee, holy youth, to come and henceforth walk amongst us.' "

He is supposed to have been forty-five years of age then.
His mission, we see, he attributed solely to an inward call
or divine command. There is no mention of any authority
from the Pope, of any visit to Rome or Gaul, or even of
the superior education he is credited with having received
on the Continent under Germanus. On the contrary, he
speaks of himself in his early condition as " a rustic, a fugitive,
unlearned, and not knowing how to provide for the coming
day ; " spiritually, " like a stone lying in the deep mud."
And in later life, in reference to the " Confession," " Wherefore I thought of writing long ago, but hesitated till now,
for I feared I should not fall into the language of men ;
because I have not read like others who have been taught

sacred letters in the best manner, and have never changed their language from infancy, but were always adding to its perfection ; for my language and speech is translated into a foreign tongue. Indeed, it can be easily perceived from the childishness of my writing after what manner I have been instructed and taught."

He had used Latin, no doubt, as his mother tongue in boyhood, but, not having received much instruction in it, he had never cultivated it as a literary language, and consequently it had, during his captivity, fallen very much into abeyance, so that it was difficult for him in later days to write this language of the learned as fluently as he would wish.

His father was of Roman descent. His mother is said to have been British—a merely conjectural statement.

Like St. Columba in after years, St. Patrick addressed the tribesmen through their chiefs and kings, and was tolerant of contemporary superstitions, seeking rather to graft the new faith upon the old. He adopted the pagan festivals and associated them with Christian events. At Tara, however, he attacked paganism in its stronghold and burnt the druidical books, extorting from King Laoghaire a reluctant acquiescence in his work. From the chief, Daire, he obtained the site for his famous monastery at Armagh, which became his headquarters. He threw down, in what is the present county of Cavan, the great idol Crom Cruach —object of immemorial veneration and savage rites. From the huge stone, which bowed westward on that day of doom, the demon is reported to have fled to hell, leaving his fallen image leaning over, so that what was once called " The Chief of the Mound " was henceforth known as " The Crooked one [Crom Cruach] of the Mound."

As his work advanced, a vast following of missionaries, bishops, and even chiefs and sub-kings, with their subjects, came under his influence. He had a share also in reforming the ancient druidical laws of Ireland, and bringing them more into harmony with Christian principles. According to the "Four Masters," it was in 438 the part of the Brehon Law known as the Seanchus Mor, and still preserved in venerable documents, was redacted. Much of the work may be of later dates, but tradition credits St. Patrick with having undertaken the task along with others, and with having effected a drastic purification in his own lifetime.

Many legends have gathered round his name during the ages, and superstitious beliefs, as one might expect. Yet, so great is his prestige in the land of his adoption to this day, that not only are thousands called by his name, but the peasantry of Ireland actually believe that St. Patrick banished snakes from the island.

The historical records know nothing of any meeting between Ossian and the saint; yet in some of the older MSS. there are Dialogues [1] in the heroic style reported as having been carried on between them, the bard representing the pagan ideal of his ancestors, the saint the Christian ideal of the Church. They are evidently the work of later times, some centuries, no doubt, after the saint's time. But, both from a literary and religious point of view, they are profoundly interesting.

Besides these characteristic Dialogues reported in the Book of Lismore and other ancient MSS., and assumed to have taken place between St. Patrick and Ossian, there is a romantic and beautiful one recorded by Tirechan, and repeated with more or less variations in the Lives of St. Patrick, and consequently of great antiquity. It is taken from the Book of Armagh.

The saint had come to the well called Clebach, and before sunrise sat down beside it with his followers.

And lo! the two daughters of King Laoghaire, Ethne the fair and Fedelm the ruddy, came early to the well to wash after the manner of women, and they found near the well a synod of holy Bishops with Patrick. And they knew not whence they were or in what form or from what people, or from what country; but they

---

[1] For examples, see Chap. XV.

supposed them to be divine sidhe, or gods of the earth, or a phantasm, and the virgins said unto them, "Who are ye! and whence come ye?" And Patrick said unto them, "It were better for you to confess to our true God, than to inquire concerning our race."

The first virgin said,
"Who is God?
And where is God?
And of what (nature) is God?
And where is His dwelling-place?
Has your God sons and daughters, gold and silver?
Is He ever living?
Is He beautiful?
Did Mary foster His Son?
Are His daughters dear and beautiful to men of the world?
Is He in heaven or in earth?
In the sea?
In rivers?
In mountainous places?
In valleys?
Declare unto us a knowledge of Him,
How shall He be seen?
How is He to be loved?
How is He to be found?
Is it in youth?
Is it in old age that He is to be found?"

With swift strides the narrative goes on to tell how the saint enlightened the two maidens, how they believed and were baptized, how they received the eucharist of God and slept in death. Thereafter they were laid on the same bed, covered with garments, while their friends raised great lamentation for them.

Such is a summary of the chief events in St. Patrick's long and epoch-making career in Ireland, taken generally to have lasted sixty years, so that he must have lived to a ripe old age, if the records report with any exactness.

Leaving now the biographical and coming to the purely literary aspect of his life, we find that there are three pieces of literature assigned to him, namely, the "Confession" and the "Epistle to Coroticus," both in Latin, and the

" Deer's Cry " in Gaelic.   The two former are sometimes
styled his epistles, numbered I. and II., the history of
whose preservation to our own time is not without its
peculiar interest.

Besides the copy of the " Confession " in the Book of
Armagh, there are four other MSS. in existence : (1)
the Cottonian, in the British Museum ; (2) two MSS. in
the Bodleian Library, Oxford, formerly preserved in the
Salisbury Cathedral ; (3) one MS. in the Public Library of
Arras.   The text of the Bollandist Fathers was taken from
the Arras MS. and published at Antwerp in 1668 in their
Acta Sanctorum.   A copy of the " Epistle to Coroticus " ac-
companies each of the above except that in the Book of
Armagh.

Of the " Confession," the style and gist may be gathered
from the extracts given as we recounted his life.   It is
perhaps the earliest piece of authentic Celtic literature we
have, inasmuch as it is the first of which the authorship
can be definitely and historically asserted.   Its Latin is rude
and archaic, answering to the description St. Patrick gives of
his own writing.   It quotes from the pre-Vulgate version of
the Scriptures, and contains nothing inconsistent with the
period in which it professes to have been written.

The saint appears to have penned this document as a
kind of defence of his apostolic work against the attacks of
men who regarded the whole undertaking as arrogant and
presumptuous in view of his own rusticity.   " The rustic
condition was created by the Most High," he gently reminds
them, and adds some plain truths which show that, like
Jesus, and St. Paul, and St. Francis of Assisi, and other
great master-spirits of the Christian Evangel, he did not
disdain poverty, but voluntarily assumed it for the promotion
of the Gospel.   It would be tedious, he says, to relate even
a portion of the many toils and dangers he had gone
through.   Twelve times his life was in imminent peril.
Never one farthing did he receive for all his preaching and
teaching.   He challenges his detractors to say if he did

and it will be returned. The people, indeed, were generous and offered innumerable gifts, which, out of principle, he refused, lest it might furnish an opportunity for cavil against the disinterestedness of his mission. On one occasion, on being told that his own nephew declared that his preaching would be perfect if he insisted a little more on the necessity of giving, he gave the noble reply, that " for the sake of charity he forebore to preach charity."

The " Epistle to Coroticus " is evidently from the same pen. The Latin and the literary style are similar. It also quotes from the pre-Vulgate version, and there is no internal evidence against the assumption that it was written by the saint. Though not found in the Book of Armagh, it is preserved in the other MSS. cited, some of which may be as old as the eleventh and twelfth centuries.

Certain authorities identify Coroticus with the Welsh prince Caredig. Other more recent scholars, such as Drs. Skene, Whitley Stokes, and Douglas Hyde, contend that he was a prince of Strathclyde, Ceretic by name, who had his capital at Alclwyd, the modern Dumbarton, and thus that he hailed from St. Patrick's own district.

At any rate, the soldiers and allies of this nominally Christian king suddenly made a descent on the eastern shores of Ireland, which they harried, carrying away many of St. Patrick's converts to be sold as slaves, and ruthlessly killing numbers of them on the very day after their baptism, while the symbol of their faith, as he says, was still wet upon their foreheads, and these neophytes were yet clad in their white vestments. The letter was sent as a remonstrance against such barbarous conduct, and to urge the lawless prince to restore the captives. But to little effect, for the invader treated messengers and letters alike with ridicule and contempt, delivering the converts abducted into the hands of the Picts and Scots.

In this letter, as in the " Confession," St. Patrick gives interesting personal details. A few extracts are worth quoting. For example :—

I, Patrick, an unlearned sinner do truly acknowledge that I have been constituted a bishop in Ireland.   I accept it of God that I am.   I dwell among barbarians a proselyte and an exile for the love of God.

I have written these words to be given and delivered to the soldiers and by them to Coroticus. . . . I do not say to my fellow-citizens nor to fellow-citizens of pious Romans, but to fellow-citizens of demons, through their evil deeds. . . . I was of noble birth according to the flesh, my father being a Decurio.   For I bartered my nobility—I do not blush nor regret it—for the benefit of others. No thanks to me.   But God hath put in my heart the anxious desire that I should be one of the hunters or fishers who as God formerly announced should appear in the last days. . . . What shall I do, Lord?   I am greatly despised.   Lo thy sheep are torn to pieces around me and plundered by these aforesaid marauders under the command of Coroticus.

In this letter he mentions also that he is constrained by the Spirit not to see any of his kindred.

For St. Patrick's beautiful hymn, the "Deer's Cry," we are indebted to the Book of Hymns of the eleventh century, which, like the Book of Armagh, contains several Patrician pieces.   It is a Gaelic composition alleged to have been made by the saint while on his way to the great Court of Tara. It was celebrated for generations before the English conquest as a *lorica* or prayer for protection.   Dr. Todd says, "That this hymn is a composition of great antiquity cannot be questioned.   It is written in a very ancient dialect of the Irish Celtic.   It was evidently composed during the existence of pagan usages in the country.   It makes no allusion to Arianism or any of the heresies prevalent in the Continental Church.   It notices no doctrine or practice of the Church that is not known to have existed before the fifth century. In its style and diction, although written in a different language, there is nothing very dissimilar to the Confession and the letter about Coroticus, and nothing absolutely inconsistent with the opinion that it may be by the same author."   Beyond this no positive proof can be given.

In the *Liber Hymnorum* it is prefaced by the following distinctive account in Gaelic :—

Patrick made this hymn. In the time of Laoghaire son of Nial it was made. The cause of making it however was to protect himself with his monks against the deadly enemies who were in ambush against the clerics. And this is a corselet of faith for the protection of body and soul against demons and human beings and vices. Every one who shall say it every day with pious meditation on God, demons shall not stay before him. It will be a safeguard to him against every poison and envy; it will be a comna to him against sudden death; it will be a corselet to his soul after dying. Patrick sung this when the ambuscades were sent against him by Laoghaire that he might not go to Tara to sow the faith, so that there seemed before the ambuscaders to be wild deer and a fawn after them, to wit, Benen;[1] and faed fiada (guard's cry) is its name.

Apparently the assassins mistook the chanting of the lorica for the cry of the deer. This saved the party, and furnished a name for the hymn.

A very remarkable and striking piece of literature it is, and one that does credit to the language in which it is clothed. " For its glow of imagination and fervour of devotion," says Dr. Dowden, the author of the *Early Celtic Church in Scotland,* " it will always challenge a high place in the history of Christian hymnology."

It it well worth transcribing also as exhibiting the saint's creed, his belief in contemporary superstitions and attitude towards them, his piety and poetic gift. In all probability we have here a very fair representation of the gist of his teaching. Like the authors of the Vedic hymns, and the votaries of all primitive religions, he invokes the powers of nature, a phase of the religious spirit which seems to have fallen devotionally in abeyance in modern times. What strikes our age perhaps as more curious and superstitious, he prays for protection against the spells of women, smiths, and Druids, like any good heathen.

I[2] bind myself to-day to a strong virtue, an invocation of (the) Trinity. I believe in a Threeness with confession of an Oneness in (the) Creator of (the) Universe.

---

[1] Benen, name of Saint's follower, St. Benignus.
[2] Version by Whitley Stokes in his Goidelica.

I bind myself to-day to the virtue of Christ's birth with his
    baptism,
  To the virtue of his crucifixion with his burial,
  To the virtue of his resurrection with his ascension,
  To the virtue of his coming to the Judgment of Doom.
I bind myself to-day to the virtue of ranks of Cherubim,
  In obedience of angels,
  (In service of archangels),
  In hope of resurrection for reward,
  In prayers of patriarchs,
  In predictions of prophets,
  In preachings of apostles,
  In faiths of confessors,
  In innocence of holy virgins,
  In deeds of righteous men.
I bind myself to-day to the virtue of Heaven,
  In light of sun,
  In brightness of snow,
  In splendour of fire,
  In speed of lightning,
  In swiftness of wind,
  In depth of sea,
  In stability of earth,
  In compactness of rock.
I bind myself to-day to God's virtue to pilot me,
  God's might to uphold me,
  God's wisdom to guide me,
  God's eye to look before me,
  God's ear to hear me,
  God's word to speak for me,
  God's hand to guard me,
  God's way to lie before me,
  God's shield to protect me,
  God's host to secure me,
    Against snares of demons,
    Against seductions of vices,
    Against lusts (?) of nature,
    Against every one who wishes ill to me,
    Afar and anear,
    Alone and in a multitude,
So have I invoked all these virtues between me (and these)
  Against every cruel, merciless power which may come, against
    my body and my soul,

Against incantations of false prophets.
Against black laws of heathenry,
Against false laws of heretics,
Against craft of idolatry,
Against spells of women, and smiths, and Druids,
Against every knowledge that defiles men's souls,
   Christ to protect me to-day.
Against poison, against burning, against drowning, against
      death wound,
   Until a multitude of rewards come to me !
Christ with me, Christ before me, Christ behind me, Christ in
   me !
Christ below me, Christ above me, Christ at my right, Christ
   at my left,
Christ in breadth, Christ in length, Christ in height !
Christ in the heart of every one who thinks of me,
Christ in the mouth of every one who speaks to me,
Christ in every eye who sees me,
Christ in every ear who hears me.
I bind myself to-day to a strong virtue, an invocation of (the)
   Trinity,
I believe in a Threeness with confession of an Oneness in (the)
   Creator of (the) Universe
Domini est salus, Domini est salus, Christi est salus,
Salus tua Domine, sit semper nobiscum:

The oldest book in Ireland is now believed to be the
Domhnach Airgid, a copy of the four Gospels in Latin
presented, according to the " Tripartite Life," by St. Patrick
to St. Aedh Maccarthenn of Clogher.   For protection it
has a triple shrine of yew, silver-plated copper, and gold-
plated silver.   Shrine and MS. are to-day among the most
prized treasures of the Royal Irish Academy.   It is highly
probable, says Professor G. T. Stokes and Dr. Wright, that
it was the veritable copy used by St. Patrick himself.

The Book of Hymns has also three other very interesting
compositions, which profess to date back to his time.

First there is Sechnall's Hymn in praise of St. Patrick,
supposed to have been written during his lifetime, and
generally regarded as genuine.   St. Sechnall, or Secundius

as he is sometimes called, was the nephew and disciple of
Patrick, and associated with him in the See of Armagh,
either as contemporaneous bishop or as his successor. It
was he who annoyed the saint by his sordid remark about
preaching on the necessity of giving. To condone for the
pain he gave his uncle, the penitent Sechnall composed this
poem of twenty-two stanzas in his praise, thus constitut-
ing himself, if written before the " Deer's Cry," the first
known poet of Christian Ireland. In view of its alleged
acceptance by St. Patrick, the hymn has been held in great
veneration, and sung as one of his honours on the days of
his Festival.

A second Patrician piece in the Book of Hymns is Fiacc
of Sletty's metrical life—also called a Hymn. It is purely
biographical, and written after St. Patrick's death, according
to the introduction in the above ancient MS. Here we are
told in Gaelic, with Latin words curiously interpolated, that
Patrick said to Dubthach, chief bard of Ireland, " ' Seek for
me a man of rank, of good race, well-moralled, one wife
and one child with him only.' ' Why dost thou seek that,
to wit a man of that kind ? ' said Dubthach. ' For him
to go into orders,' said Patrick. ' Fiacc is that,' said
Dubthach, ' and he has gone on a circuit in Connaught.'
Now while they were talking, it is then came Fiacc from his
circuit. ' There,' said Dubthach, ' is he of whom we spake.'
' Though he be,' said Patrick, ' yet what we say may not
be pleasing to him.' ' Let a trial be made to tonsure me,'
said Dubthach, ' so that Fiacc may see.' So when Fiacc
saw he asked, ' Wherefore is the trial made ? ' ' To tonsure
Dubthach,' say they. ' That is idle,' said he, ' for there is
not in Ireland a poet his equal.' ' Thou wouldst be taken
in his place,' said Patrick. ' My loss to Ireland,' says
Fiacc, ' is less than Dubthach's (would be).' So Patrick
shore his beard from Fiacc then, and great glee came upon
him thereafter, so that he read all the ecclesiastical ordo in
one night—or fifteen days, as some say—and so that a
bishop's rank was conferred on him, and so that it is he

who is Archbishop of Leinster thenceforward and his successor after him."

Dr. Todd thinks it impossible to attribute so high an antiquity to the Hymn as Fiacc's own time, since it contains an allusion to the desolation of Tara. Colgan 250 years previously met the difficulty by regarding the latter reference as prophetic.

We must not omit a very curious prophecy regarding St. Patrick which the Scholiast on Fiacc's Hymn has preserved. It is in the copy of the Book of Hymns now in the convent of St. Isidore at Rome, a MS. of the eleventh or twelfth century. From internal evidence it may be recognised that the stanza cannot be older than the beginning of the seventh century, but it is written in a very ancient dialect of the Gaelic, and purported to be an old-time prediction by a pagan Druid.

> Ticfa tailcend
> Tar muir murcend,
> A brat tollcend,
> A crand chromcend,
> A mias in iarthur a thigi,
> Frisgerad a muinter uili
> Amen, Amen.

He comes, he comes, with shaven crown, from off the storm-toss'd sea,
His garment pierced at the neck, with crook-like staff comes he,
Far in his house, at its east end, his cups and patens lie,
His people answer to his voice. Amen, Amen, they cry.
> Amen, Amen.

A third Patrician fragment in the Book of Hymns, eleventh century, is entitled Ninine's Prayer, with the explanatory head-line, " Ninine the poet made this prayer, or Fiacc of Sletty." It runs :—

We put trust in St. Patrick, chief apostle of Ireland,
Conspicuous his name, wonderful ; a flame that baptized Gentiles,
He fought against hard-hearted Druids ; he thrust down proud men
with the aid of Our Lord of fair heavens.

He purified the great offspring of meadow-landed Erin,
We pray to Patrick, chief apostle, who will save us at the Judgment
    from doom to the malevolences of dark demons.
God be with me with the prayer of Patrick, chief apostle !

In all this varied literature, reaching from his own time till ours, the Apostle of Ireland stands forth a commanding personality, as different from St. Columba as St. Francis was from St. Bernard. Genial, earnest, humble, sensitively sympathetic, with commanding force of character and irresistible determination as the agent of a Divine Mission, his enthusiasm made way for him. Less impulsive, less warlike, and less learned than Columcille, he carried on his spiritual campaign in a spirit of self-denying devotion and love of men. "Patrick, without loftiness or arrogance," as Fiacc describes him, "it was much of good he thought." At the end of the day we find him in poverty and misery writing his Confession, not sure but the morrow of his life may bring a violent death, or slavery, or some other dread evil.

Yet true to the last in his unquenchable zeal, his own words seem to sum up the high aim of his life : " Therefore it is very fitting that we should spread our nets that a copious multitude and crowd may be taken for God, and that everywhere there may be clergy who shall baptize a needy and desiring people."

He died at Saul, while on a visit there from Armagh, and his grave is believed to be at Downpatrick, to which place tradition says the remains of St. Columba were transported from Iona in the more troublous times, and reinterred beside those of his great forerunner.

CHAPTER III

ST. COLUMBA AND THE DAWN OF LETTERS IN SCOTLAND

The fugitive MSS.—Gaelic a literary language for ages—Scotland's first writer—
St. Columba one of the rarer master-spirits—His peculiar qualities—Intellec-
tual standpoint—Birth—Early life—A fateful incident—Sets sail for Pictland
—Motive—Arrival in pagan Scotland—His missionary enterprise—Lights
the lamp of literature—An ardent scholar, penman, and poet—The famous
" Cathrach "—His Gaelic poems—Latin hymns—The Columban renais-
sance—Encouragement of bards and scholars—The *Amra Choluimcille*—
Iona as an educational centre—European fame and influence.

MODERN research and historical criticism have done much
for Celtic literature. Not long ago the subject might be
regarded as a tangled web of fact and fiction. Inquirers
found it hard to thread their way through the unsifted mass
of materials, to know the true from the fabulous, authentic
history from myth and legend.

All the more because the original documents, like the
graves of a household, were " severed far and wide by mount
and stream and sea," and for the most part inaccessible. It
must be matter of astonishment to many to learn that very
few of our older Celtic MSS.——MSS. written in these islands
—have found a home in Scotland. They have long ago
been transferred to the Continent, to France, Italy, Holland,
Switzerland, Austria, and Germany. So that to-day scores
of these venerable relics are preserved in places as distant
and far apart as Milan, St. Gall, Würzburg, Carlsruhe,
Brussels, Turin, Vienna, Berne, Leyden, Nancy, Paris. Even
the oldest MS. now existing that can be proved to have

been written in Scotland, is kept not in Edinburgh or Glasgow, but in the public library of Schaffhausen in Switzerland.

One reason for this seems to have been that the Irish or Scots gave so many evangelists and professors in those early days to the Continent, men like Columbanus and St. Gall, and their followers ; and another, when the books were in danger in the British Isles from the depredations of the Norsemen, they were removed for security to the monasteries and seats of learning presided over by these Celtic scholars.

The records thus available, here and there, carry us back over a period of well nigh 1500 years to the days of St. Patrick and St. Columba. As Cædmon was the pioneer of English literature, so is St. Patrick the first known litterateur of Ireland, and St. Columba the first of Scotland. From the time of the introduction of Christianity by these men, Celtic literature has a history, continuous and verifiable. Beyond their day all is uncertain and cloudy. Pagan Scotland lies in the dim background enveloped in haze. Sagas and myths and poems and romances it undoubtedly had in abundance, floating by oral tradition, but no written record. In almost every instance of its old-time lore, authorship is unknown. That by-past is the region of conjecture, and we can be as little certain of the origins as Greek scholars are of the genesis of the *Iliad* or of the *Odyssey*.

In this study, then, we go back to the march between Pagan and Christian times, and leaving behind at present the doubtful and uncertain, we shall endeavour to trace the dawn of letters in Scotland.

On that far horizon the first man we encounter with a pen and a passion for writing is the wonderful St. Columba. Across the ages his impressive figure still stands out massive and strong in the background of history. Among the men of fame—the rarer master-spirits who have helped to make Scotland what she is—Columcille stands earliest. Vividly and terribly in earnest himself, he stamped his religious convictions not only upon many districts of Ireland, but also upon heathen Alba.

He possessed just the qualities that were best fitted to give him an ascendancy over men in that rude age. Unlike most of the great evangelists of Christianity, he was of princely origin, descended both on his father's and his mother's side from illustrious Irish kings. This noble lineage, combined with the patronage of his own kinsman Conall, King of Dalriada—our modern Argyllshire—gave him an immense influence in an age when the tribes, even in matters of religion, followed their king or chief.

But Columcille was personally a born leader of men. Physically and intellectually he towered above his fellows. Of a tall and commanding appearance, powerful frame, broad face, close and curly hair, his grey eyes large and luminous, he looked the saint he was, joyful and radiant, with a love for everything beautiful in nature, animate and inanimate. Withal he had a loud and resonant voice, well adapted for impassioned speech. When preaching, tradition says that he could be easily understood across the Sound of Mull. And Adamnan assures us that when singing with his brethren in the church, the venerable man raised his voice so wonderfully that it was sometimes heard at the distance of 1000 paces, while from the "Old Irish Life" we learn that his reading carried even farther. A voice to soothe the savage breast with its plaintive sweetness, and yet of power and range sufficient to awe the pagan mind.

For this apostle of Scotland, despite his name, was no mere cooing dove. He could be very terrifying when roused. Of a hot and passionate temper, he was in reality a perfervid Celt; stern and even vindictive at times, he would fight his battles with the carnal weapons, if need be, just as readily as he would with the spiritual. Three battles at least, fierce and sanguinary, stand to his account in history, he their instigator, two of these even after he became Abbot of Iona.

Altogether a strange character to contemplate was this father and founder of monasteries, especially when viewed from our scientific age—the intellectual standpoint of his time was so wholly different from ours. He continually moved in a halo of miracles, prophecies, and angels, as real to him as physical laws and nerves and germs are to us. So credulous was he that he never seemed even to question the magical impostures of his opponents, the Druids. He is not represented as trying to expose their marvels, but rather as endeavouring to outrival them by greater miracles of his own. The one set he believed to be from the evil one, the other of God. For him the seen always merged in the unseen ; the natural is construed in terms of the supernatural. Science, of course, had not then formulated laws or facts as we know them, and St. Columba was a child of his age, imbued with the same credulity as the contemporary heathen around him, and very much the same superstitions. He believed he could bless men or blight them by his inter-cessions, and sometimes in the exercise of this power he did not even hesitate to curse irreconcilables and consign them to future destruction.

On one occasion, exasperated with a thief of noble birth who had twice plundered the house of a man of humble condition, and mocked and laughed at the rebukes of the saint himself, the irate Columba—and this is a picture for an artist—followed him to the water's edge, and wading up to the knees in the clear green sea-water, raised both his hands to heaven and solemnly invoked a curse on the man. Returning to the dry ground he sat down, and forthwith told his companions what the fate of the scamp would be. No maudlin saint was the imperious Columcille. Gentle, affectionate, and kind, yet a man to impress the wild Pictish tribes with awe and reverence.

Born at Gartan, Donegal, in the north of Ireland in 521, and brought up from youth in Christian principles, he was trained under the best masters, and apparently caught up in the wave of evangelisation that swept over Ireland from St. Patrick's time. At any rate, when twenty-five years of age he founded the Church of Derry, and seven years later the

Monastery of Durrow. Other establishments soon followed, springing up here and there under his initiative and fostering care, until when full forty years old an event occurred which in a manner changed the whole aspect of his career, and gave a new direction to his energies. This was the battle of Cooldrevna, of far-reaching import.

Two causes are usually assigned for the fight. St. Finnian of Moville, under whom the future abbot first studied, brought back with him from Rome a copy of the Psalms, supposed to be the first copy of St. Jerome's Vulgate that appeared in Ireland. This the master treasured, and wished to keep private and reserved. But Columcille, then an ardent student and rapid writer, sat up for nights together and surreptitiously transcribed the book for his own use. Hearing of this, Finnian claimed the copy, but in vain. His disciple refused to part with it, and the matter was referred to King Diarmad at Tara. This monarch, to whom no doubt a legal quarrel over a book was new, could find nothing in the Brehon Law to adjudicate the case by, except the practical adage, *le gach boin a boinin* (with every cow her calf), and being perhaps more disposed to favour Finnian, as of his own kin and jurisdiction, he, not unnaturally, adapted this precedent to the case in point, giving the judgment, " As with every cow her calf, so with every book its son."

This decision is the first we know in the law of copyright. It gave dire offence to Columba, which was greatly heightened some time after by another regal affront. It happened at the Great Convention of Tara that a young prince, in utter violation of the law of sanctuary, slew the son of the king's steward, and knowing the penalty to be certain death, fled for refuge to the northern princes, who placed him under the sheltering wing of their kinsman, the sacred Columba. Ignoring the saint's authority, the king had the refugee promptly seized and put to death. This, it appears, exasperated the imperious Columcille to the last degree, and he immediately made his way north, and roused to arms the race of Hy-Neill, the northern branch against the southern.

And with the King of Connaught, whose son had been slain, they marched their forces southward. A furious battle ensued at Cooldrevna, in the red ruin and carnage of which King Diarmad was defeated with the loss of 3000 men.

Two years after, the Hegira took place, when the saint fled or migrated on his great mission to Scotland—henceforth an exile from Erin.

Speculation has been rife as to the real motive that drove this intensely patriotic Irishman over the wave. Many would fain believe, in view of its epoch-making significance, that this momentous step was purely voluntary " for the love of Christ," as the " Old Irish Life " puts it. Adamnan, while connecting it with the battle, also puts this construction upon it. " In the second year after the battle of Culdreimhne," he says, " and in the 42nd year of his age, St. Columba resolving to emigrate for Christ sailed from Scotia (that is Ireland) to Britain." Many other saints had wandered elsewhere on similar missions. But there is a persistent tradition that this unique missionary was banished by the Synod of the Saints in Ireland for the bloodshed he had caused ; and that this sentence was confirmed by St. Molaise, whom the unhappy Columba consulted, and who advised him to seek as many souls in conversion among the heathen as there fell of men in battle. Some, on the other hand, construe his action as a voluntary penance, self-inflicted. Others find mainly a political motive in his removal to Dalriada, where he might be of immense service to his kinsmen in helping to avert the ever increasing and harassing incursions of the Picts. Certainly he became a bulwark to them.

Imbued with a high missionary zeal, there is no doubt that ultimately he went forth to the new spiritual campaign voluntarily, but, as in the case of most fateful careers, it is evident that circumstances wound him up to the task, the most conspicuous and compelling of which was Cooldrevna. That the parting from Erin was bitter, a very tearing of the heart, is matter of history. The verses, the records attributed to himself on this occasion, reveal the depths of his feelings.

" How rapid the speed of my coracle and its stern turned toward Derry. I grieve at the errand over the proud seas, travelling to Alba of the Ravens. There is a grey eye that looks back upon Erin, it shall not see during life the men of Erin nor their wives. My vision over the brine I stretch from the ample oaken planks ; large is the tear from my soft grey eye when I look back upon Erin. Upon Erin is my attention fixed, upon Loch Leven, upon Linè, upon the land the Ultonians own ; upon smooth Munster, upon Meath."

As Dr. Douglas Hyde has sympathetically observed, " Columcille is the first example in the saddened page of Irish history of the exiled Gael grieving for his native land and refusing to be comforted, and as such he has become the very type and embodiment of Irish fate and Irish character."

A pity it is that history has not photographed the dramatic scene when the great monk, forty-two years old, tall and powerful, lands from his curach the " Liath Bhalaidh," with twelve followers on the island of Hy, now the famous Iona. It was in 563 that he took possession of this future home, of which he had received a grant from the King of Dalriada, which was afterwards confirmed by King Brude. Modern Scotland had not yet emerged, being in early fragments. And it is important to note, for it has been very confusing to historians, that in Columba's day Ireland was Scotia, from whence in earlier days the Scots had come, who then occupied Dalriada, or, as it is known to-day, Argyllshire. North and east were the Picts, possessing the body of Alba, as modern Scotland was then called ; and in Strathclyde the Britons. Not till centuries after was the name of Scotia or Scotland finally transferred from Erin to Alba.

The Dalriadic Scots, though not destitute of a primitive civilisation, were rude and barbarous. Slavery and polygamy were common, blood feuds incessant. Women fought side by side with the men in battle, until first Columba and afterwards Adamnan obtained exemption for them. The heathen Picts were even more degraded, under the tyranny of a Druid regime, full of sorcery and superstition. No ray of Christianity seemed as yet to have penetrated their darkness.

Such were the wild and waste lands into which the devoted Columba threw himself as a deliverer. For two years he remained in Hy, organising his base, and, it is thought, learning the Pictish language, before setting out on his visit to " the powerful king of the Pictish nation."

His missionary labours for the next thirty-two years, in collaboration with the devoted band of men who imbibed his spirit and adopted his methods, have caught the eye of the world.

But there is another aspect of his enterprise, far-reaching and magnificent, which has been largely overlooked and overshadowed by our one-sided veneration for his religious genius. And that is the significance of his literary work. It is not so generally known that the Apostle of Scotland was a patron of letters, intensely interested in literature, an ardent writer and disseminator of knowledge—one in fact who has left his literary mark on the ages, and who was the first to help to raise Scotland to the proud eminence in education which she occupies to-day.

As in the great awakening in Europe in the sixteenth century there were two movements, independent of each other and yet going on side by side—a revival of religion and a revival of learning, known as the Reformation and the Renaissance ; so, in St. Columba's enterprise two similar movements were fostered, not as separate and hostile to each other, but as mutually helpful and conjoined.

The abbot was from youth a great lover of books and an unwearied scribe. His standard biographer, Adamnan, says that he never could spend the space even of one hour without study, or prayer, or writing, or some other holy occupation, watching or fasting. This love of books continued in his case to the very end. Not till the day of his demise was the pen finally laid aside. On that day, after blessing the Monastery, he descended from the hill and sat in his hut transcribing the Psalter. But the vitality of that once deft hand and brain was now well-nigh spent, and answered feebly, like the diminishing flow of water from a spout. "Here," cried the saint, at length, conscious of the impending change, "at the end of the page I must stop, and what follows let Baithene write."

It was his love of literature that got him into trouble with St. Finnian, and in the "Calendar of Aengus" the story goes that he once visited a man, Longarad, noted for his collection of books. In anticipation of the visit, and mindful perhaps of Cooldrevna, the *sai* or saoidh (wise man) hid his treasures, whereupon Columba left "a word," that is, a curse, on the books, so that when in after ages they had become unintelligible from various causes, this was deemed the full and sufficient reason. "May your books be of no use after you, since you have exercised inhospitality in withholding them."

He composed a book of hymns for the office of every day in the week, and in the "Old Irish Life" he is credited with having written "three hundred gifted, lasting, illuminated noble books." It is highly probable that those thus referred to were simply transcribed by him, for we have no evidence that he wrote any prose literature.

The three books still existing in Ireland which tradition and some high authorities regard as the work of his own hand are simply transcripts. They are certainly very ancient, even if they do not quite reach up to his day. Two of them are in Trinity College, Dublin, and the third in the Royal Irish Academy. The former, known as the Book of Durrow and the Book of Kells,[1] are copies of the Gospels in Latin, the one finished, the other not, but the Book of Kells, which is the unfinished one, contains on its blank pages copies of charters of the eleventh and twelfth centuries, connected with the endowment of the Institution. The other book referred to as in the Royal Irish Academy is the famous

[1] The Book of Kells is held by the more competent authorities to belong to the end of the seventh century.

"Cathrach," believed to be the identical copy of the Psalter that Columba made when he was a student. The skill displayed in the penmanship and decoration of these ancient MSS. is astonishing, and they have covers which are brilliant specimens of early Celtic art. The Book of Kells, in particular, is spoken of as "the unapproachable glory of Irish illumination." In fact, the codex known as the "Four Masters" alleges that "it was the principal relic of the western world on account of its remarkable cover."

Great interest attaches to the celebrated "Cathrach" or "Battler," so called from the circumstance that a battle was fought on account of it. It continued an heirloom in the successive generations of the saint's family, the O'Donnells, until a comparatively recent representative, exiled as a supporter of James II. carried it with him to the Continent in the beautiful shrine prepared for it at the end of the eleventh century. In early days it used to be carried three times round the army when Cinal Conaill went to battle, in the belief that if thus carried on the breast of a cleric free from mortal sin it would get them the victory.

In 1802 the precious relic was recovered from the Continent and opened. Within was found a decayed wooden box covering a mass of vellum stuck together and hardened into a single lump. By careful moistening treatment, the various leaves at length came asunder, and proved a real Psalter, written in Latin in a "neat but hurried hand." Fifty-eight leaves remained, containing from the 31st to the 106th Psalm, and an examination of this text has shown that it is precisely a copy of the second revision of the Psalter from the Vulgate of St. Jerome, which strengthens the belief so long and tenaciously held, that this may have been the very book for which 3000 warriors fell.

From very early times Columba was spoken of as a poet. That he wrote verse and befriended the bards is attested by the oldest tradition and some of the most ancient records. Many Gaelic poems are attributed to him. "Thrice fifty noble lays," says one poet—

Some in Latin which were beguiling,
Some in Gaelic, fair the tale.

Among his reputed Gaelic poems may be mentioned three that Colgan considered genuine, 250 years ago, and were printed by Dr. Reeves in his first edition of Adamnan's *Life of St. Columba :* his "Farewell to Ara," published in the *Gaelic Miscellany* of 1808 ; and another on his escape from King Diarmad, reproduced in the *Miscellany of the Irish Archæological Society.* There are three verses composed as a prayer at the battle of Cooldrevna, ascribed to him in the *Chronicon Scotorum ;* and there is a collection of fifteen poems in the O'Clery MSS. at Brussels. But by far the largest collection is contained in an oblong MS. of the Bodleian Library at Oxford. This document embraces everything in the shape of poem or fragment anywhere believed as his, and that could be collected about the middle of the sixteenth century.

None of these are found in the oldest MSS., though not a few are apparently very ancient and beautiful, breathing the intensity of feeling and passion so characteristic of the Gael. Dr. Hyde is perhaps not far off the mark when he says that of the great number of Irish poems attributed to him, only a few — half a dozen at the most — are likely to be even partly genuine. It is very hard to say how much or how little is his. But this authority is inclined to agree with Dr. Healy, author of *Ireland's Schools and Scholars*, that at least the three considered genuine by Colgan represent substantially poems that were really written by the saint. " They breathe his pious spirit," says Healy, " his ardent love for nature, and his undying affection for his native land. Although retouched, perhaps, by a later hand, they savour so strongly of the true Columban spirit that we are disposed to reckon them amongst the genuine compositions of the saint."

A few specimens are worth quoting, by way of illustrating Columba's poetic genius :—

Were the tribute of all Alba mine, from its centre to its border, I would prefer the sight of one house in the middle of Derry. The reason I love Derry is for its quietness, for its purity and for the crowds of white angels from the one end to the other. . . . My Derry, my little oak-grove, my dwelling and my little cell, O eternal God in heaven above, woe be to him who violates it.

Ara was a little isle, like Iona, in the west of Ireland, where St. Enda lived, and was visited by the saints.

Farewell from me to Ara. It anguishes my heart not to be in the west among her waves, amid groups of the saints of heaven. It is far, alas! it is far, alas! I have been sent from Ara West out towards the population of Mona to visit the Albanachs. Ara Sun, oh Ara Sun, my affection lies buried in her in the west, it is the same to be beneath her pure soil as to be beneath the soil of Paul and Peter. Ara blessed, O Ara blessed, woe to him who is hostile to her, may he be given shortness of life and hell.

The next, so characteristic of the saint's love of nature, is taken from the poem on Cormac's visit—one of the three considered genuine :—

It were delightful, O Son of my God, with a moving train,
To glide o'er the waves of the deluge fountain to the land of Erin,
O'er Moy-n Eolarg, past Ben-Eigny. O'er Loch Feval,
Where we should hear pleasing music from the swans,
The host of gulls would make joyful, with eager singing,
Should it reach the port of stern rejoicers, the *Dewy Red*,
I am filled with wealth without Erin, did I think it sufficient.

In the unknown land of my sojourn of sadness and distress,
Alas, the voyage that was enjoined me, O King of secrets,
For having gone myself to the battle of Cuil.
How happy the son of Dima of the devout church
When he hears in Durrow the desire of his mind
The sound of the wind against the elms when 'tis played,
The blackbird's joyous note when he claps his wings,
To listen at early dawn in Ros-grencha to the cattle,
The cooing of the cuckoo from the tree on the brink of summer,
Three objects I have left, the dearest to me on this peopled world,
Durrow, Derry, the noble angelic land, and Tir-Luighdech,
I have loved Erin's land of cascades, all but its government.
My visit to Comgall and feast with Cainnech was indeed delightful.

Of his Latin hymns only three remain. They are preserved in the *Liber Hymnorum*, a MS. probably of the end of the eleventh century, and are known as the " Altus," " In te Christo," and " Noli Pater." No doubt exists as to the genuineness of the " Altus." It is the most famous of the three, and is supposed to have been written after the battle of Cooldrevna. The poem takes its name from the first word, and each of its twenty-two stanzas begins in order with a letter of the alphabet, probably as a help to the memory. The stanzas are rudely constructed, with a kind of rhyme between every two lines. The poem has enjoyed a great reputation, and has been variously rendered into English. Perhaps the best translation is that of the Rev. Anthony Mitchell :—

> Ancient of Days ; enthroned on high ;
> The Father unbegotten He,
> Whom space containeth not nor time,
> Who was and is and aye shall be ;
> And one-born Son and Holy Ghost,
> Who co-eternal glory share.
> One only God of Persons Three
> We praise, acknowledge and declare.

Attention has been directed by Dr. Dowden, Bishop of Edinburgh, to the saint's curious conceptions of the physical causes of clouds, and rain, and tides, in the stanza beginning with I :—

> In the three quarters of the sea,
> Three mighty fountains hidden lie,
> Whence rise through whirling water-spouts,
> Rich-laden clouds that clothe the sky :
> On winds from out his treasure house,
> They speed to swell bud, vine, and grain ;
> While the sea-shallows emptied wait
> Until the tides return again.

In the R stanza we have a picture of the judgment not unlike the " Dies Iræ " :—

Riseth the dawn :—the day is near
Day of the Lord, the King of Kings ;
A day of wrath and vengeance just,
Of darkness, clouds, and thunderings :
A day of anguish, cries, and tears,
When glow of women's love shall pale ;
When man shall cease to strive with man,
And all the world's desires shall fail.

What now are we to think of this new literature and the other productions, Latin and Gaelic, to which the monasteries of the period gave rise ? Is the Columban renaissance really a decadence in comparison with what went before, the old unwritten inheritance ? " Yes," says Darmesteter, and if we accept the antiquity of the oral tradition, I think we must admit the truth of it. The sagas and historic tales, and the poetry that is mingled with them, are of far greater importance from a purely literary point of view. With a wild freedom of imagination and an old-time conception of life untouched by Christian thought, they breathe the spirit of pre-Christian ages, very much in the primitive manner of Homeric poetry ; and being intensely human and heroic, they have a charm even for minds set to later ideals.

For example, in the *Colloquy or Dialogue of the Ancients*, it is recorded that St. Patrick himself felt a little uneasy at the delight with which he listened to the stories of the ancient Feinn, and in his over-scrupulous sanctity he feared it might be wrong to appreciate and enjoy so much, these worldly narratives. But when he consulted his two guardian angels they not only assured him that there was no harm in listening to the tales, but even desired him to get them written down in the words of ollamhs, " for," said these wise counsellors, " it will be a rejoicing to numbers and to the good people to the end of time to listen to these stories."

Yet for all this the Columban period *was* a renaissance. You cannot spring a new creed and new ideas upon a nation without a re - awakening of thought and corresponding progress.

Over and above his own personal contributions to literature, Columba helped forward the cause of letters in two other ways, namely, by encouraging the bards and the scholars.

In his day the bards in Ireland had become an intolerable nuisance—idle, numerous, and insolent; in fact they had developed into a loafing class, who quartered themselves on the working-classes, on the chiefs and farmers. They went about the country in bands, carrying a silver pot, nicknamed by the people " the pot of Avarice." Their tyranny was such that he who refused to contribute was mercilessly satirised and disgraced. Three attempts had been made to suppress them, but hitherto to no purpose. At length Aedh, the High King of Ireland, considering them to be too heavy a burden on the land, resolved to banish the whole profession. Summoning a great Convention of all Ireland to Drumceat in 590 to settle important national affairs, he made this one of the chief items. And the fate of the bardic institution would most certainly have been sealed had not Columcille averted it. With 140 followers he had crossed over to attend the Conference, and besides obtaining exemption from military service for the women, and independence and freedom from taxation for Dalriada, which was henceforth simply to help the parent kingdom in affairs of war, he also succeeded in moderating the fury of the chieftains against the bards. Their numbers were reduced and their prestige abated, but the profession was amply compensated for this by acquiring a new and recognised position in the State. No bards except those specially sanctioned were to pursue the poetic calling. But for the maintenance of these latter distinct public estates in land were set apart for the first time, in return for which they were obliged to give public instruction to all comers in the learning of the day, after the manner of university professors. The rate of reward for their poems was also legally fixed, so that from this time down to the seventeenth century the bardic colleges, as distinct from the ecclesiastical ones, taught poetry, law, and history, educating the lawyers, judges, and poets of the Irish nation.

In recognition of the service rendered them on this occasion the bards appeared before Columba in a body, with Dallan Forgaill, their chief, at their head, bringing the famous " Amra " or elegy which the latter had composed in his praise. This poem is in the Fenian dialect, so ancient and obscure as to be very baffling and almost unintelligible to scholars. It has come down to us heavily annotated with gloss and commentary in the eleventh century MS. (Leabhar Na h'Uidhre). So far as can be made out, it speaks of the saint in relation to the people as " their soul's light, their learned one, their chief from right, who was God's messenger, who dispelled fears from them, who used to explain the truth of words, a harp without a base chord, a perfect sage who believed in Christ ; he was learned, he was chaste, he was charitable, he was an abounding benefit of guests, he was eager, he was noble, he was gentle, he was the physician of the heart of every age ; he was to persons inscrutable, he was a shelter to the naked, he was a consolation to the poor, there went not from the world one who was more continual for a remembrance of the cross."

But a recent writer, Dr. Strachan of Manchester, casts doubts upon the antiquity of its present form, thinking it belongs, as transcribed, to a later date.

The other way in which St. Columba helped forward the cause of letters was by encouraging the scholars. The monasteries became great schools of learning as well as missionary centres. In all the institutions he founded, ample provision was made for the multiplication of books. The knowledge of Hebrew and Greek was fostered among the monks as well as of Latin and Gaelic. To the monastic houses founded throughout Pictland by the Columban clergy the tribes sent their youth to be trained. And for several centuries, as Skene has observed, there was not a Pictish boy taught his letters but received his education from a Columban monk. In later times students from the Continent flocked to the more famous of the Celtic seats of learning in Ireland

and Scotland, and we even hear of Iona sending professors to Cologne, Louvain, and Paris.

There is no evidence that the northern Picts had a knowledge of letters before Columba taught them. There is even doubt as to what language these tribes spoke. Yet in 710 A.D., a little more than a hundred years after his death, a knowledge of letters was common in Pictland. With reference to subsequent ecclesiastical changes, it is known that King Naitan sent a proclamation " by public command throughout all the provinces of the Picts to be transcribed, learned, and observed." This we have on the authority of Bede, a statement which shows that learning must have made considerable progress among the people even at that early date. So that in this respect we may very well endorse the opinion of Professor Mackinnon, when he says that " we have not yet perhaps fully realised the part which the School of Iona had in shaping the destinies of the Scottish nation." When in Scotland we discuss the past history of our national education, the figure of John Knox invariably rises before us as prime inaugurator of the first real system, but the great Abbot of Iona was at it 1000 years before him.

Shaping the destinies of the Scottish nation ; ay, and might we not add of literature ? For a further striking claim has been repeatedly put forward on behalf of the Celtic poets in the Columban period, namely this, that they taught Europe to rhyme. And this claim has been made not so much by partisans as by some of the foremost European scholars, including Zeuss and Nigra, who have remarked and pointed out that the Latin verses of Columcille and other early saints, either rhyme or have a strong tendency to rhyme. Referring to the advance towards final assonance in later times made by the English in their Latin poems, Zeuss says, " We must believe that this form was introduced among them by the Irish, as were the arts of writing and of painting and of ornamenting manuscripts, since they themselves, in common with the other Germanic nations, made use in their poetry of nothing but alliteration." It is only some 500 years after Columba that we find rhyme beginning to appear in English literature.

The other foreign writer of note, C. Nigra, with equal emphasis asserts that "final assonance or rhyme can have been derived only from the laws of Celtic phonology." Meanwhile this must be regarded as a moot point. For other eminent scholars, Thurneysen and Windisch, have professed their opinion that it may be traced to the Latin. But "this at least is clear," observes Dr. Hyde, who has gone very carefully into the matter, "that already in the seventh century the Irish not only rhymed, but made intricate Deibhidh and other rhyming metres, when for centuries after this period the Germanic nations could only alliterate."

It is our proud boast as an English-speaking people that we can go back as far as Cædmon to the beginnings of our literature ; yet how few British subjects realise that Gaelic was a literary language long before then in the hands of men like St. Patrick, St. Columba, and Dallan Forgaill, and that there are Latin MSS. still extant associated with Columba and the School of Iona which are almost as old as the very oldest existing codex of the Bible.

It is worth our while to think of this, and of the remarkable man who, in the obscurity of his island home, recognised the value and permanence of his own work, giving utterance to a sentiment which the ages have amply verified : " Small and mean though this place is, yet it shall be held in great and unusual honour, not only by Scotic kings and people, but also by the rulers of foreign and barbarous nations, and by their subjects ; the saints also even of other churches shall regard it with no common reverence." And it is so. Systems and dynasties have since fallen, yet the fame of Iona still stands secure, and continues to attract the saint and the foreigner.

CHAPTER IV

ADAMNAN'S "VITA COLUMBÆ"

Oldest Scottish book in existence—A sturdy survival—Criteria of age—Dorbene the copyist—Romantic history of the MS.—Now in Schaffhausen—Adamnan, a rare personality—Abbot and scholar—Influential career—Attitude to the two great questions that divided the Celtic churches—Pathetic estrangement—"Lex Adamnani".—A mighty social revolution—Death—His writings—"The Vision of Adamnan"—His *Life of Columba* in three parts—Remarkable contents—Most valuable monument of the early Celtic Church—List of MSS. in which preserved—Latin *versus* Gaelic.

MANY Scottish visitors visit Schaffhausen, on the Rhine in Switzerland, and perhaps few of them are aware that in the public library there, is deposited one of the rarest and most interesting relics of Scotland.

It is a parchment MS. of sixty-eight leaves, each about eleven inches by nine. The volume looks as if in the original binding. Its sides are of beechwood, greatly worm-eaten and covered with calfskin, the sewing of the back very rude and curious, and the front would seem to have been formerly secured by clasps.

This is not a Gaelic work, though Gaelic names appear in it. It is written in Latin in double columns. Capital letters abound, some of them of great size and adorned with red and yellow paint. The summaries at the beginning, the headings of chapters, and the colophon of the scribe are all in rubric which on the whole is wonderfully fresh and beautiful.

Three handwritings may be traced : the first, that peculiar

58

to the greater part of the book ; the second, in evidence towards the end, in all probability the work of the same writer, but with different pen and ink and in smaller, rounder letters ; the third, corrections in spelling by a later and much inferior penman.

The ink is dark, almost jet-black, except in some places where it has turned brown.

Such is the general appearance of the relic.   And marvel not if a vague, far-away look steals into the eye when one reflects that this book which he sees and handles is well nigh, if not quite, 1200 years old ; that it is, in fact, the oldest now existing, known to have been written in Scotland, and separated by the lapse of 100 years from the next most ancient.

A copy of Adamnan's *Life of St. Columba*, made by one of his contemporaries in Iona—this, the sturdy survival is taken to be.   And if the criteria of its age are not misleading, it dates from before 713 A.D.   These criteria are in themselves profoundly interesting.

1. It is recognised that the handwriting is that peculiar heavy kind found in the oldest Gaelic MSS.—not quite so round as that in the Books of Kells and Durrow, but possessing many features in common, and certainly anterior to that of the Book of Armagh, fixed at 807.

2. Similarly the Latin spelling corresponds with that of the more ancient Celtic MSS. at home and abroad.

3. The Greek characters which appear in the text are in the semi-uncials of the period, without accents or breathings.

4. The later corrections, supposed to have been made on the Continent, are reckoned by Dr. Ferdinand Keller, an expert in the handwriting of Charlemagne's time, to belong to the period between 800 and 820.

5. The parchment is in goat-skin, in colour and condition extremely ancient.

6. But more conclusive still is the remarkable colophon of the scribe at the end of the volume, where he says, " I

beseech those who wish to transcribe these books, yea, rather, I adjure them by Christ, the judge of the world, after they have diligently transcribed, carefully to compare and correct their copies with that from which they have copied them, and also to subjoin here this adjuration : ' Whoever readeth these books on the virtues of St. Columba let him pray to the Lord for me Dorbene that after death I may possess eternal life.' "

Here we have actually the name of the scribe—a splendid clue to the age of the MS. which critics have not been backward in availing themselves of.   The name is so rare in the records that they had only a choice between two, one anterior to Adamnan's day, the other his contemporary, and Abbot-elect of Iona in 7 1 3.   But this latter Dorbene died that same year before assuming office, and only nine years after Adamnan himself.   He in all probability it was who copied the *Life*.

To the objection, Why not by another of the same name ? Dr. Reeves replies in effect, " Not likely, as the name is almost unique and pointedly connected with the Columban society."   And to the further objection that it might possibly be by a later hand from the autograph of this Dorbene, he answers, " Even less likely, as the colophon in Irish MSS. is always peculiar to the actual scribe, and usually omitted by other transcribers.   And this is the only MS. of Adamnan's *Life* that has the name and the colophon."

The interest attaching to it on account of its extraordinary age and subject-matter is greatly enhanced when we consider its history.   For the old document had hairbreadth escapes and adventures, and if it could speak for itself doubtless could unfold a tale infinitely more surprising, because more real and tragic, than many of the miraculous incidents it does record.   All the long agony of the early, the middle, and the modern ages has transpired since first it went a-wandering.   Invasions, crusades, and revolutions, the rise and fall of systems and nations—whole populations passing swiftly and stormfully across the bosom of Europe

into oblivion, and the book in the heart of the troubled area
survives them all and emerges at length, as if from the debris,
to reassert that " there lived a man."

Adamnan, ninth Abbot of Iona, wrote the original in the
years 691 to 693—that is, ten or twelve years before his
death, which occurred in 704. In the second preface—for
there are two—he tells us that it is the substance of the
narratives learned from his predecessors, and is founded
either on written authorities anterior to his own time or on
what he heard himself from ancient men then living. And
we know that he was sufficiently near the fountainhead, both
in time and place, to be able to draw from authentic sources ;
for he wrote just a century after St. Columba's death, and
at the urgent request of his brethren. In his boyhood he
had frequent opportunities of conversing with those who had
seen and known the saint, and he was surrounded in the
monastery and in the island with all the halo of association
and piety in which the memory of his hero was enshrined.

The written material he could rely on was not meagre
even at so early a date. There was the narrative of
Cummene the Fair, seventh abbot of Iona, and thus
one of his own immediate predecessors. His account
Adamnan transferred entire and almost verbatim into the
third book of his own work. It was really a tract entitled
De virtutibus sancti Columbæ. In addition to this he had
at least one other Latin memoir and various Gaelic poems
in praise of the saint, such as the "Amra" of Dallan
Forgaill, and those of Baithene Mòr, and perhaps of St. Mura.

In another of his books (*De Locis Sanctis*) the author
informs us how he generally set about composing his literary
efforts. He wrote the first draft on waxen tablets, revised
and corrected it, and then from the text so prepared, a clean
copy was neatly written out on parchment.

Dorbene the Scribhnidh may have copied the *Life* in
Adamnan's own time ; if not quite so early, then shortly
after his death. And whatever became of Adamnan's
original, Dorbene's copy appears to have remained in the

monastery till the beginning of the ninth century, when it
was probably taken to Germany.   At that time a strong
tide of Scotic pilgrims set in towards Central Europe, owing
no doubt to the Norse invasions, which rendered life and
property insecure in Iona and elsewhere.

In 825 Blathmac was murdered in the monastery, along
with several of the brethren, because he refused to tell where
the Columban relics were hid.   The likelihood is that after
that narrow escape one of the fleeing monks carried the
book to St. Gall or Reichenau on the Rhine.   At any rate
it is significant that Walafridus Strabus, formerly Dean of
the Irish monastery of St. Gall in Switzerland, and then
Abbot of Reichenau from 842-849, knew of the tragic event
and wrote a poem in Latin on the death of Blathmac.   And
it was in this very house of Reichenau, that used to be
frequented so much by Scotic missionaries, that the MS.
was ultimately found.   And quite casually too.

Ages had elapsed when, in the beginning of the seven-
teenth century, Stephen White, a learned Irish Jesuit in search
of Gaelic documents on the Continent, luckily discovered it.
He immediately transcribed the venerable codex, and gave
Ussher, Colgan, and the Bollandists the benefit of his copy.
Both the latter published the text—Colgan in 1647, the
Bollandists in 1698.

Thereafter, a second time the original vanished.   When
or how it was removed from Reichenau is not known, but it
must have been before that monastery was suppressed in
1799.   Once more it emerged, this time at Schaffhausen,
rediscovered by Dr. Ferdinand Keller of Zurich, the distinguished archæologist.

Writing of the interesting find in January 1851, Dr.
Keller tells the story of its reappearance, showing into what
sorry neglect it had fallen before it reached its ultimate
coign of vantage.   " The present *proprietor* of the MS. of
St. Columba," he says, " is the town-library of Schaffhausen.
Here I found this codex in 1845 at the bottom of a high
book-chest, where it lay pell-mell with some other MSS.

and old books totally neglected, bearing neither title nor number." It was twice borrowed by Keller, and on the last occasion in 1851 he made a valuable collection of facsimiles from it.

Finally the aged record, after well-nigh 1200 years' vicissitudes, was published by Dr. Reeves, Bishop of Down, in 1856, and his work republished in 1874 by the publishers of the Series of Scottish Historians, this time with English translation and re-arrangement of the Notes, which Dr. Reeves permitted in order to adapt the book to a wider circle of readers.

A truly romantic history, taking it all in all, is this story of the ancient wanderer which has come to honour in a foreign land, but has not yet found a way home to its native soil. What would Schaffhausen take and part with it? Scotland has never asked. Some day she may, when she awakens to the fact that the very oldest and, at the same time, one of the most intensely interesting monuments of her literary history is an alien in a strange country.

Apart from the book itself, the hero of the book, and its faithful copyist, there is a fascination and much insight to be drawn from a study of the personality of its author. Adamnan, like Boswell, has achieved immortality through an enthusiastic and almost self-effacing hero-worship. His great object, as he tells us again and again, is to show up the wonderful character of the saintly Columba, and any deed or tale that he thinks will enhance the prestige of this " great father and founder of monasteries " goes down with unfailing devotion.

Born about the year 624 in Donegal, Adamnan, like Cummene, was a kinsman of St. Columba. Indeed, the three men were descended from three brothers, all of royal lineage. His peculiar name is understood to be a diminutive of Adam, and is frequently followed by the patronymic Ua Tinne, meaning grandson of Tinne. Of his father Ronan, or his mother Ronnat, we know absolutely nothing beyond their descent, which was of high degree. And of his own childhood and youth there remains only a single legend, supposed to be the creation of a later age, reporting his first meeting with Finnachta, afterwards monarch of Ireland, with whom Adamnan was on the most friendly terms. This Finnachta, as his biographer relates, was riding along one day to his sister's house with a numerous cavalcade, when he met a schoolboy with a jar of milk on his back. In his haste to get out of the way the stripling knocked his foot against a stone, and tripping, down went the jar with its contents upon the ground. Whereupon the great prince spoke kindly to the boy and assured him of protection, bidding him not to sorrow over it. To whom the latter replied, "O good man, I have cause for grief, for there are three goodly students in one house and three more of us are attendants upon them. And how we act is this : one attendant from among us goes out in turn to collect sustenance for the other five, and it was my turn to-day ; but what I had gathered for them has been spilled upon the ground, and what grieves me more, the borrowed jar is broken and I have not wherewith to pay for it."

These are the boyish and dramatic circumstances in which Adamnan emerges on the canvas of tradition. From his youth it would thus appear that he was inured to hardship, and consequently qualified for the rigorous discipline of the monastic life. Plain living went with high thinking, and the quiet, thoughtful student soon acquired a reputation for scholarship. He was just the kind of man to obtain entrance into the distinguished circle of Iona, and though we cannot trace his career as subordinate there, with certainty, we know that in 679, when fifty-five years of age, he became head of the institution. At that period the monastery was already known far and near for its learning. And there seems little doubt that the new abbot was, taking him all in all, the ablest and most accomplished of St. Columba's successors. A great linguist, he knew not only Latin, but, it may be inferred from his writings, Hebrew and Greek also.

Four years prior to his own promotion, Finnachta had become king in his native country.   That monarch, it would appear, never lost sight of the boy with the jar, whose whole bearing indicated a youth of rare promise.   The latter was afterwards invited to his court, and ultimately constituted the king's spiritual adviser (anamchara).   This we have on the authority of an ancient bardic composition in a vellum MS., formerly in the possession of W. Monck Mason, Esq.

Besides his interesting relations with Finnachta, Adamnan was fortunate in possessing the friendship of King Aldfrid of Northumbria.   This intimacy probably dates from the time when the latter as prince had occasion to seek refuge in Ireland from his intriguing foes.   At that time he may have even been, as Duald Mac Firbis's annals affirm, a pupil of Adamnan.

At any rate, with two such royal friends, the influence of the Ionan abbot was very great.   And on important occasions he served as ambassador or "go-between" in matters of State betwixt the two kings.   For example, after a raiding expedition by the North Saxons on Meath, Finnachta got him to undertake a mission to his friend Aldfrid to negotiate for the return of the captives, and the abbot had the satisfaction of personally conducting sixty of them back to Erin in 686.

Two years later he paid another visit to the Court in Northumbria.   On both occasions a dreadful plague was raging in that country, and throughout a great part of Europe.   In his usual ultra-rational manner Adamnan attributes his own immunity from the pestilence, and that of the Picts and Scots in general, to the intercession of his holy patron St. Columba.

On these tours he made the acquaintance of the leading clergy in the north of England.   It is supposed he met Bede, then a young man, at the Court also.   This distinguished historian gives various facts regarding the abbot and his movements.   He appears to have read Adamnan's book on the "Holy Places," though it may be that he never saw the biography, which was a much later production. At least he makes no mention of it anywhere.

There were two great questions that then divided the Celtic churches—the celebration of Easter and the tonsure. Through his intercourse with the English clergy in Northumbria, and more especially, it is affirmed, through a lively discussion he had with the learned Ceolfrid, Abbot of Jarrow, Adamnan was persuaded to adopt the Catholic in preference to the Celtic usage in these matters. On his return to Hy the brethren strenuously opposed the innovation, and there was a lasting difference of opinion thus originated by his change of views. For years the abbot, who was pre-eminently a man of peace and unity—and, like the great and pious scholar he was, always open to conviction,—earnestly strove to win them over to what he deemed to be the better method, but did not succeed in his own lifetime, though in after years the change was ultimately adopted. In 692 he visited Ireland, and again in 697, between which years he wrote the book that has made his name and memory immortal. A man of great energy and incessant diligence, he was much on the move convening synods and negotiating affairs. Like his extraordinary patron, he interested himself in politics as well as in religion and literature, of which he was a shining light.

Unhappily the law which St. Columba had got enacted, exempting women from fighting in actual warfare, had soon fallen into abeyance, and Adamnan resolved to have it re-enacted. According to a legend in the Leabhar Breac and Book of Lecain, his attention was called to the inhuman custom in the following accidental way. One day he happened to be travelling through the plain of Bregia, says the legend, with his mother on his back, when they saw two armies in deadly conflict. During the heat of the combat his mother's eye caught sight of a woman dragging another woman by means of an iron reaping-hook from the opposing battalion. The hook was fastened in the unfortunate victim's breast. Sitting down overcome by the sight, the distressed

Ronnat said to her son, " Thou shalt not take me from this spot until thou exemptest women for ever from being in this condition and from excursions and hostings." Adamnan promised it. And at the important Synod of Tara, convened in 697, with the approval of King Finnachta, the point was carried, involving a mighty social revolution from henceforth in the life and customs of the Gael. For under the old regime, men and women went equally to battle.

The enactments of this synod were afterwards known in Latin as " Lex Adamnani," and in Gaelic " Cain Adhamhnain." In addition to a certain privilege conceded to him and to his successors of levying contributions for sacred purposes, Dr. Reeves thinks it was on this occasion that the questions of Easter and the tonsure were publicly discussed, and Adamnan's views and usage adopted in Ireland.

Afterwards he seems to have been some years in that country promoting his reforms. He certainly was there in 701 ; and Bede mentions that he crossed from Erin to Hy the summer of the year that he died, and indicates that he had been there a considerable time previously. His death occurred on September 23rd, 704. It is thus touchingly commemorated by the great historian. " For it came to pass that before the next year came round he departed this life ; the Divine goodness so ordering it that, as he was a man most earnest for peace and unity, he should be taken away to everlasting life before the return of the season of Easter he should be obliged to differ still more seriously from those who were unwilling to follow him in the way of truth." He had apparently celebrated his last Easter in Ireland, and died at the mature age of seventy-seven.

His fame rests on his writings, chiefly the *Life of St. Columba*, and his book on the " Holy Places "—*De Locis Sanctis*. Adamnan himself saw not these Holy Land localities, but a French bishop on his return from the east was driven by a storm to spend the winter with Adamnan, who took down on waxen tablets his interesting accounts of the chief places visited, and afterwards wrote out, *brevi textu*, on parchment. It is better written and more fluent even than the biography, and when found many years after, it was published as "the earliest account coming from modern Christian Europe of the condition of Eastern lands and the cradle of Christianity."

Adamnan presented the book to King Aldfrid of Northumbria. There are extant MSS. of it as old as the eighth, ninth, and tenth centuries still on the Continent—at Rome, Corbey, Saltzburg, and other places.

Besides these chief Latin works he is credited with a *Life of St. Patrick ;* poems, quoted by Tighernach, the " Four Masters," and the Book of Lecain ; a *History of Ireland* to his own times, and *An Epitome of Irish Laws in Metre.* These two latter are only mentioned by Ward [1] (on what authority is not known), and may be probably only compilations of more modern times.

In the *Liber Hymnorum,* however, there is a short hymn in Gaelic entitled Adamnan's Prayer. It may be read in Dr. Stokes' *Goidelica.* And in the Leabhar Na h'Uidhre there is a more lengthy production known as " Fis Adhamhnain." It is in the form of a sermon, and may have been written down some two hundred years after the abbot's time. In this remarkable vision Adamnan figures as "the high sage of the western world," and like Aeneas or Dante, he is privileged on the festival of St. John the Baptist to visit heaven and hell. The scenes he beheld are depicted in the original Gaelic with a realism and power of vivid imaginary detail that puts even Thomas Boston in the shade. As Dante found his Florentine enemies in not too comfortable circumstances in the Inferno, so Adamnan is here represented as seeing the Aircinnich—the lay administrators of the church lands, who too often abused their trust, in similar dool. But this sentiment alone is sufficient to show that the composition is of later date than Adamnan's day, for such Aircinnich had yet to arise, and the broad acres they mismanaged.

[1] Ward or Vardaus, author of *Acta Sancti Rumoldi.*

It is said that at the time of the great Synod in 697 the public mind had for long been kept in such a state of suspense and alarm by the prevailing pestilences and portents, that the report of the abbot having some such vision made it so susceptible to his influence that he had far less difficulty in carrying into effect his revolutionary measures than he would have had in ordinary circumstances.

But all these things—writings and traditions alike— tend to show how this quiet, intellectual, studious, pious, and —from our point of view—amazingly credulous, yet influential scholar, impressed his own and succeeding ages.

Adamnan's best known book is essentially a Life of St. Columba, written not in any chronological order, but on a characteristic plan of his own.   There are two prefaces, and what would really be the gist and subject-matter of a modern biography is condensed by him into one short paragraph at the end of the second of these.   The work is then divided into three parts or books.   The first deals with prophetical revelations, the second with miracles, the third with visions of angels ; and under these titles he groups all the most striking stories of the saint's life.   All the collateral information—and it is not much—regarding the history of the time, the social life, the manners, customs, language, topography, etc., we get merely by the way in the telling of the tale.   Adamnan apparently had no thought that his readers would wish to know something of these, or if he had he did not deem it any part of his task to enlighten them.   He was writing for his own times, and he could not conceive that the eye of any monk or other reader could wander off from the central luminary to mere details of the environment.   It is at once the limitation and strength of the enthusiast and the specialist.   How could he know that he was writing for the far-distant future ?—this unassuming monk in his cell, unconsciously addressing a people who have emerged from his theory of the universe, and who listen and wonder at his stories, which to them have all the charm and interest of fairy tales.

Tempora mutantur, eheu ! The little facts that incidentally dropped from his pen are those most sought and valued
now, while the miracles, visions, and prophecies which he
took to be the soul and substance of the book, wear a
different aspect to modern eyes. It is these trifling details,
sometimes mere names, that give us glimpses into the state
of society in Ireland and Pictland, and into the civil and
ecclesiastical history of the time.

Adamnan's consuming desire at all times is to present
"the evidences which the venerable man gave of his power."
And when we reflect that he believed that "by some divine
intuition" St. Columba, "through a wonderful experience
of his inner soul, beheld the whole universe drawn together
and laid open to his sight, as in one ray of the sun," we
need not be surprised at the wonders unfolded. In the
first chapter of Book I., and before entering upon illustrative
examples, he gives a summary of his hero's supernatural
qualities. For example, he healed diseases ; expelled from
the island "innumerable hosts of malignant spirits, whom
he saw with his bodily eyes assailing himself and beginning
to bring deadly distemper on his monastic brotherhood."
The surging waves quickly became quiet at his prayer, and
contrary winds changed into fair. He took a white stone
from the river Ness and blessed it for healing purposes. This
famous pebble floated like an apple when placed in water.
In the country of the Picts he raised a dead child to life,
and while yet a young man in Hibernia turned water into
wine. An immense blaze of heavenly light was occasionally
seen to surround him in the light of day, and he was
frequently favoured with the society of bright hosts of
celestial beings. He often saw just men carried by angels
to the highest heavens, and reprobates hurried by demons
to hell. The blessed man even foretold the destinies of
individual men, pleasing or painful, according to their deserts.
And "in the dreadful crash of wars he obtained from God
by the virtue of prayer, that some kings should be conquered
and others come off victorious."

And now, coming to the substance of the separate books in order, we need not dwell on the prophetical revelations, numerous and curious though they are, beyond giving one or two as typical examples. The credulity of the author and his capacity for belief are passing strange, and even foreign to an age like our own. A peasant, he tells us, once asked the saint by what death he would die. "Not in the battle-field nor at sea," came the ready response, "but the travelling companion of whom thou hast no suspicion shall cause thy death." And the man died through the effects of a wound accidentally caused by his own knife.

One wonderful experience may be quoted, as quite in line with Professor James' argument in his Gifford Lectures at Edinburgh University (May, 1901). In discussing "The reality of the Unseen," this brilliant exponent of the new Psychology instanced a number of curious cases of the occurrence of a "presence" to individuals, and he maintained that the sentiment of reality could indeed attach itself to things of which the representative faculty could frame only the dimmest sort of an idea. And abstractions other than the ideas of pure reason had the power of making us feel presences that we were impotent articulately to describe. No more striking example of his contention could be desired than the following. It is entitled, "Of the consolation which the monks when they were weary on their journey, received from the saint visiting them in spirit."

Baithene and the brethren were returning in the evening to the monastery from the harvest work when something strange and unusual was felt by them all. It is thus described by an elder brother. "I perceive," he said to the others, "the fragrance of such a wonderful odour, just as if all the flowers on earth were gathered together into one place. I feel also a glow of heat within me, not at all painful, but most pleasing, and a certain unusual and inexpressible joy poured into my heart, which on a sudden so refreshes and gladdens me that I forget grief and weariness of every kind. Even the load, however heavy, which I carry on my back, is in some mysterious way so lightened from this place all the way to the monastery that I do not seem to have any weight to bear."

King Brude and his Druids had rather a different sensation when, outside their fortifications near Inverness, some of the latter tried to prevent the saint from chanting the evening hymns. Very much in the flesh this time, St. Columba began to sing the 44th Psalm so wonderfully loud, like the rattle of thunder, that king and people were terror-struck with the awful noise, and forthwith relented. Columba seems to have been more than a match for these pagan opponents. For in the second book, where the miracles are recorded, among other confusions to which he drove the resisting Picts, the following is recorded. When first he visited Brude, it happened that the king, elated by the pride of royalty, acted haughtily and would not open his gates to his distinguished visitors. But the man of God, observing this, approached the folding doors with his companions and, having first formed upon them the sign of the cross, he knocked and then laid his hand upon the gate, which instantly flew open of its own accord, the bolts sliding back with great force. The saint and his followers then passed through, and ever after, as long as he lived, king Brude knew how to respect and reverence his imperious visitor. It was to him that the latter gave the remarkable white pebble which effected cures. "And what is very wonderful," says our author, "when this same stone was sought for by those sick persons whose term of life had arrived, it could not be found." Even King Brude himself was abandoned *in articulo mortis* by the fateful pebble.

After giving examples of miraculous punishments inflicted on those who were opposed to St. Columba, Adamnan instances a few encounters with wild beasts, and as they relate to our own Scotland they are of ancient and exceptional interest.

"On one occasion," to quote our author, "when the blessed man was staying some days in the Scian island

(Skye), he left the brethren and went alone a little farther
than usual to pray; and having entered a dense forest he
met a huge wild boar that happened to be pursued by
hounds. As soon as the saint saw him at some distance he
stood looking intently at him. Then raising his holy hand
and invoking the name of God in fervent prayer, he said to
the beast, ' Thou shalt proceed no farther in this direction ;
perish on the spot where thou hast now reached.' And no
sooner were these fateful words uttered than it appears his
formidable opponent collapsed, expiring on the spot."

But an experience on the mainland of the Picts seems to
have been even more exciting. One day he had to cross the
river Ness. And when he reached the bank of the river he
saw some of the inhabitants burying an unfortunate man,
who, according to the accounts of those who were burying
him, was a short time before seized as he was swimming, and
bitten most severely by a monster that lived in the water ;
his wretched body was, though too late, taken out with a
hook by those who came to his assistance in a boat. The
blessed man, on hearing this, was so far from being dis-
mayed that he directed one of his companions to swim over
and row across the coble that was moored at the farther
bank. And Lugne Mocumin, hearing the command of the
excellent man, obeyed without the least delay, taking off all
his clothes except his tunic and leaping into the water. But
the monster, which, so far from being satiated, was only
roused for more prey, was lying at the bottom of the stream,
and when it felt the water disturbed by the man swimming,
suddenly rushed out, and giving an awful roar darted after
him with its mouth wide open, as the man swam in the
middle of the stream. Then the blessed man, observing
this, raised his holy hand, while all the rest, brethren as well
as strangers, were stupefied with terror, and invoking the
name of God, formed the saving sign of the cross in the air,
and commanded the ferocious monster, saying, " Thou shalt
go no farther, nor touch the man ; go back with all speed."
Then at the voice of the saint the monster was terrified, and

fled more quickly than if it had been pulled back with ropes, though it had just got so near Lugne as he swam that there was not more than the length of a spear staff between the man and the beast. Then the brethren, seeing that the monster had gone back, and that their comrade Lugne had returned to them in the boat safe and sound, were struck with admiration and gave glory to God in the blessed man. And even the barbarous heathens who were present were forced, by the greatness of this miracle which they themselves had seen, to magnify the God of the Christians.

The raising of the hand and forming the sign of the cross in the air seems to have been a frequent and effective expedient. In the case of a youth who was returning from the milking of the cows with his pail on his back, and who stopped at the door of the cell where the blessed man was writing, it was the means of driving out a demon that lurked in the milk pail. No sooner had he left than the saint made the sign. Instantly the air was greatly agitated. The bar which fastened the lid of the pail being pulled back through the two openings which received it, was shot away to a great distance, while the lid fell to the earth and the greater part of the milk was spilled upon the ground. The demon that lurked in the bottom of the pail could not endure the power of the sign, and fled thus violently in terror.

Such is the unvarying style of Adamnan. That he himself credited those versions of stories reported is beyond question. "Our belief in the miracles which we have recorded," he says, "but which we did not ourselves see, is confirmed beyond doubt by the miracles of which we were eye-witnesses." Three times in his own experience he saw unfavourable gales changed into propitious breezes.

As Book III., dealing with visions and angels, embodies Cummene's contribution, it is of the highest interest to consider some of its choice memories. "On a certain night," proceeds chap. ii., "between the conception and birth of the venerable man, an angel of the Lord appeared to his mother in dreams, bringing to her as he stood by her a

certain robe of extraordinary beauty, in which the most
beautiful colours, as it were, of all the flowers seemed to be
portrayed.   After a short time he asked it back and took
it out of her hands, and having raised it and spread it out
he let it fly through the air.   But she, being sad at the loss
of it, said to that man of venerable aspect, 'Why dost
thou take this lovely cloak away from me so soon?'   He
immediately replied, 'Because this mantle is so exceedingly
honourable that thou canst not retain it longer with thee.'
When this was said, the woman saw that the forementioned
robe was gradually receding from her in its flight, and that
then it expanded until its width exceeded the plains, and in
all its measurements was larger than the mountains and
forests.   Then she heard the following words, 'Woman, do
not grieve for the man to whom thou hast been bound by
the marriage bond; thou shalt bring forth a son of so
beautiful a character that he shall be reckoned among his
own people as one of the prophets of God, and he hath been
predestined by God to be the leader of innumerable souls to
the heavenly country.'   At these words the woman awoke
from her sleep."

A priest, to whose care the sacred youth had been con-
fided, upon returning home from the church after mass found
his house illuminated with a bright light, and saw in fact a
ball of fire standing over the face of the little boy as he lay
asleep.   And in after years a higher personage, St. Brendan,
reported that he observed a most brilliant pillar wreathed
with fiery tresses preceding the same wonderful individual.

It was not to be supposed that such a distinguished
ornament of the church militant could escape the attention
and intrigues of its arch-enemy.   And so, on another day,
while the holy man went to seek in the woods of Iona for a
place more remote from men and fitting for prayer, he
suddenly beheld, as he afterwards told a few of the brethren,
a very black host of demons fighting against him with iron
darts.   These wicked demons, as the Holy Spirit revealed
to the saint, wished to attack his monastery and kill with the

same spears many of the brethren. But he, single-handed, against innumerable foes of such a nature, fought with the utmost bravery, having received the armour of the apostle Paul. And thus the contest was maintained on both sides during the greater part of the day, nor could the demons, countless though they were, vanquish him ; nor was he able by himself to drive them from his island until the angels of God—as the saint afterwards told certain persons—and they few in number came to his aid, when the demons in terror gave way.

The chapter, which is far and away the most thrilling and humanly interesting, is the last of the volume, entitled, " How our patron Saint Columba passed to the Lord." It lingers with loving memory over the closing scene of this remarkable life, giving a minute account of the saint's last words and acts, his preparations for the impending change, and the manner and circumstances of his death. But as this is an oft-repeated and well-known passage, it need not be quoted here.

Adamnan's *Vita Columbæ* is not the only ancient *Life of St. Columba* after Cummene's, but it is undoubtedly the standard classic one, from which most of the subsequent biographies draw their facts and inspirations, with the exception, perhaps, of the " Old Irish Life," which furnishes particulars not mentioned in this one.

Neither is the Schaffhausen document the sole existing MS. copy of the great biography. Dr. Reeves consulted as many as seven distinct MSS., three of which contained a longer and four a shorter text. Besides these he had heard of five other extant copies, more or less complete.

The seven from which he obtained his own various readings are the following :—

I. Codex A.—The famous Schaffhausen one, the oldest of all, dating from the early years of the eighth century.

II. Codex B.—A vellum of the middle of the fifteenth century, preserved in the British Museum.

III. Codex C.—The Canisian text, which was published in 1604 from a MS. in the monastery of Windberg, Bavaria.

IV. Codex D.—The second tract in a large vellum of the thirteenth century, in Primate Marsh's library, Dublin.

V. Codex F.—A vellum consisting of fifty leaves, now in the Royal Library of Munich.

VI. Codex G.—A small quarto MS. on vellum of the early part of the ninth century, in the Library of St. Gall.

VII. Codex Cottonianus in the British Museum, also a vellum of the latter part of the twelfth century.

The others, which he had not seen, are variously distributed in Austria, Bavaria, Switzerland, and Belgium.

With all its defects, Adamnan's masterpiece is the most valuable monument of the early Celtic Church which has escaped the ravages of time ; imaginative, superstitious, magical, and steeped in hero-worship, it is characteristically Celtic and of surpassing interest to the archæologist and philologist.

Its value as such would have been vastly enhanced in these times had it been written in Gaelic, and doubtless, too, had the author condescended more on social and historical details. But Adamnan apparently had no high opinion of his native language as a literary medium. In his first preface he almost apologises for using Gaelic names of men and tribes and obscure places in the " base Scotic tongue," which he thinks rude in comparison with the languages of foreign nations, and begs his readers not to despise a record of useful deeds on account of these native words inserted.

Dr. Reeves seems to regret that Adamnan did not follow the method of Bede and give us an ecclesiastical history instead of a biography. We cannot all share his sentiment. Had it been other than it is—had it even been in Gaelic—the probability is that it might not have survived. In Gaelic it certainly never could have attained the celebrity it enjoyed on the continent of Europe during the Middle Ages, and which helped to perpetuate it. On the other hand, without the memoir as thus preserved, the life of St. Columba, the greatest pioneer of Scottish history, religion, and literature, would now be as vague and jumbled as that of any mythical hero, even as that of the historical St. Patrick outside his own " Confession " unfortunately is; and we should be ignorant of many points concerning which we have now first-hand information.

As it stands, the *Vita Columbæ* is still the most authentic voucher we have for various important particulars in the civil and religious history of the Picts and Scots, and the severe Pinkerton himself was perhaps never nearer the truth on Celtic subjects than when he pronounced it " the most complete piece of such biography that all Europe can boast of, not only at so early a period, but even through the whole Middle Ages."

CHAPTER V

THE BOOK OF DEER

An ancient curio—Second oldest book of Scotland—Where did it come from ?—
Its contents threefold—Gaelic colophon from the ninth century—The work
of a native scribe of Alba—Peculiarities—The ecclesiastical art of the period
—The Gaelic entries—"Legend of Deer"—Drostan's tears—Some very
quaint history—The earliest source for Scottish Gaelic—Authentic glimpses
into the Celtic condition of Scotland—Origin of shires, parishes, burghs,
individual freedom, and the use of the English language—Three editions of
the Gaelic of the Book of Deer—Now one of the very oldest MSS. of native
origin that Cambridge can boast of.

IN the year 1860, Mr. Henry Bradshaw, Librarian of
Cambridge University, while rummaging among old books,
came upon a curious production which at once usurped his
attention. Here, thought he, is surely a survival from some
remote time. And examining the MS., he found it to
consist of eighty-six parchment leaves, six inches long, four
and a half wide, and closely written on both sides.

The language was Latin, written in the Irish character,
"not very unlike the Bodleian Cædmon." Each page
showed marks of ruling with a sharp instrument, and the
letters hung from the ruled lines instead of resting on them.
The pages were surrounded by ornamented borders, most of
them filled in with interlaced work in panels, and with fret-
work of a peculiar kind.

On a casual inspection of the subject-matter, the accomplished librarian had no difficulty in ascertaining that it
consisted of the first six chapters of St. Matthew's Gospel,
and part (verses 1-22) of the seventh ; the first four chapters

of St. Mark, and part of the fifth (to middle of verse 35);
the first three chapters of St. Luke, with the first verse of
the fourth ; the whole of the Gospel of St. John ; a fragment
of an Office for the Visitation of the Sick, in a later hand ;
and the Apostles' Creed.   The writing of the Gospels was all
in one uniform hand, the ink dark-brown with age, and the
initial letters of paragraphs designed in fanciful dragonesque
forms and variously coloured.   At the end of the book, just
after the Apostles' Creed, the writer had added a colophon in
another language, which looked like Gaelic, and on the margins
and vacant spaces of the volume there was a number of entries
in the same vernacular, but evidently inserted much later.

What greatly enhanced the rarity and interest of this
remarkable codex, in the finder's eyes, was that it also contained a collection of coloured pictures and ornamental designs
contemporary with the writing, executed in the same style,
and apparently by the same hand that penned the Gospels.

Where did this ancient curio come from ?   It was easy
for him to trace its entrance into the Library, for he found
it among the remainder of the books of John Moore, at one
time Bishop of Norwich, and later of Ely.   These books
had come into the possession of the University in a very
interesting way.   After the prelate's death, which took
place in 1714, it appears that King George the First,
acting on the suggestion of Lord Townshend, bought the
extensive library of the deceased for the sum of 6000
guineas, and gifted it to the College Library.

The small octavo MS. of which we are speaking, and
now known as the Book of Deer, had formed part of
Bishop Moore's collection in 1697, and strange to say, after
its removal to Cambridge, it lay apparently neglected for a
century and a half on the shelves of that University Library,
until the discriminating eye of Mr. Bradshaw singled it out as
of exceptional antiquity and value—as, in fact, one of the very
oldest MSS. of native origin that Cambridge can boast of.

Thus far the history of the quaint foundling.   For the
rest, it must tell its own tale.

Obviously one of the few relics of the Celtic Church now extant, it required an expert in the Gaelic language and antiquities to elicit the desired information regarding its origin and long past. And when Whitley Stokes sought a perusal, we can almost fancy the eager Bradshaw addressing his fellow-linguist in the language of Marcellus to Horatio when the ghost of Hamlet's father suddenly appeared, " Thou art a scholar ; speak to it." Here was the worn and faded form of a book resurrected from the dust of oblivion, and, like the shade of the dead king, once more catching the eye of men, and making their hearts quiver with eerie curiosity.

A rising .Celticist, Mr. Whitley Stokes soon applied himself to the interesting inquisition, following the venerable scroll back for a thousand years to the ancient time when it first took shape. And in the *Saturday Review* of December 1860 appeared an anonymous article from his pen, in the form of an appreciative notice, giving translations of the Gaelic, and otherwise making known to the public the importance of this latest literary discovery.

In the contents of the volume he found sufficient internal evidence to be able to trace its past, so far as many details of its early origin and environment are concerned.

These contents, as already hinted, are threefold. First, the original substance of the book ; second, its ornamentations ; and third, the notes and memoranda inserted at a later time on the margins and blank pages.

And into what age and environment, we naturally ask, do these lead us ?

As on receipt of an unknown letter, the receiver turns with eager eyes to scan the signature at the end, so here the expert first directs his attention to the colophon or postscript of the scribe.

In this particular instance it happens to be in Gaelic, and may be rendered thus : " Be it on the conscience of every one in whom shall be for grace the booklet with splendour, that he give a blessing on the soul of the poor wretch (truagain) who wrote it " (" Forchubus caichduini imbia arrath inlebran colli aratardda bendacht forainmain in truagain rodscribai ").

This Gaelic, says Whitley Stokes, is identical with the oldest Irish glosses given by Zeuss in his *Grammatica Celtica*, and "certainly as old as the ninth century." Professor Westwood, from a study of the written characters, which are those at that time common to the Irish and Anglo-Saxon schools, came to the same conclusion as to the age of the book.

The version of the Gospels which it contains is one of a class which has been called "Irish," because, while mainly corresponding with Jerome's Vulgate, it preserves occasional readings from versions of earlier dates. The text, in other words, agrees with the text of the various Books of Gospel used in the Scoto-Irish monasteries of the period, such as the Books of Durrow, Kells, Dimna, Moling, Armagh, etc.

It would appear that Jerome's recension made its way early among Gaelic scholars, and during the isolation of the Celtic Church, there had been a sort of revision which produced a native version exhibiting characteristics peculiar to itself and common to all the above-mentioned texts. Hence the wonderful uniformity alike in the text and in the peculiarities of spelling found in all the surviving Gaelic MSS. of that early period.

It is not known whether the book was produced in the place whose name it bears or in Iona, or whether it was written by a Pict or a Scot. Scholars are content to affirm their opinion that it is the work of a native scribe of Alba, without particularising too confidently.

Dr. Stuart, who edited it for the Spalding Club in 1869, observed that though the handwriting is good and uniform, casual examination of the MS. will show that it is a careless transcript of a corrupt text. The spelling is frequently barbarous and capricious. There are many violations of grammar, with omissions, transpositions, repetitions and interpolations of various kinds, while the prepositions are almost always joined to the word which they govern.

Generally speaking, this Book of Deer exhibits many of

the peculiarities of spelling which Tischendorf noted in the Vulgate, for example :—

Magdalen*æ* for Magdalen*e*.
Ba*b*tismum for ba*p*tismum.
Oc*c*ulus for o*c*ulus.
Abra*c*ham for Abra*h*am.
*Ch*anna for *C*ana.
Pro*f*eta for pro*ph*eta.
Dic*i*ens for dic*e*ns.
*Z*abulus for *d*iabolus.
*H*oriens for *o*riens, etc.

But the copying is otherwise of such a kind that it appears very doubtful if the scribe really knew Latin well. It certainly indicates a great falling away from the high scholarship of Adamnan and the verbal accuracy of Baithene. And this itself might confirm us in the idea that it may have been written in Deer or somewhere in Buchan rather than in Iona.   Very curious blunders might be quoted ; but perhaps none more grotesque than that in the genealogy in St. Luke, where Seth is set down as the first man and father of Adam, or again in John xviii. 22, " Sic respondis Pontifici " (Answerest thou the high priest so ?) is written " Sicrespem dispontifici."   In other cases words are introduced which entirely destroy the sense.

The second feature of this remarkable codex to arrest the attention, is the decoration, which also is found to exhibit the character of the ecclesiastical art of the period at which it is presumed to have been written.   The style of ornament of the illuminations is in fact entirely similar to that used in the well known Irish Books of Gospel prior to the ninth century, and on its own account is exceedingly interesting. The first folio has its page divided into four panels by a plain Latin cross, with a rosette in the centre.   In these are four figures representing, most likely, the four evangelists, though they might very well stand for clerics.   Fronting the beginning of the first Gospel is a figure, full-page size, taken to represent St. Matthew, the author of that Evangel. He appears with a beard, and clothed in ecclesiastical vestments, all but the feet, which are bare. In his right hand he holds a sword of unusual form, turned downwards with the point of the scabbard resting between his feet ; the handle is guarded before and behind, the guards being curved and reversed.

On either side of the evangelist there looks forth a smaller figure, which seems to be intended for an angel.

At the beginning of St. Mark's Gospel is another figure in the same style, with an object in front of his breast like a book in ornamental binding. In his own place, St. Luke appears in the attitude of prayer, his arms outspread. St. John is surrounded by six smaller figures, similar to those accompanying St. Matthew. The two last pages of the MS. have also designs of which one repeats with variations that at the beginning of the book ; while the other is a combination of similar figures with geometric ornament. Throughout the volume are found here and there small drawings—quaint little flourishes representing fern leaves, birds, and animals, curiously wrought, and words as if in trial of the pen, some of which show very delicate and correct lines. The initial letter of each Gospel is enlarged and ornamented with patches of different colours, about two inches high, and the ends of the principal strokes of the letters terminate in dogs' heads.

Yet it must be added that with all its similarity of style and attractive colouring, the art is poor in comparison with that of contemporary Irish MSS.

Such are the original contents of the codex. There remain the later notes and memoranda on the margins and blank spaces. And these are of two kinds—those written in Latin and those in Gaelic. The Latin ones consist of (1) the fragment of an Office for the Visitation of the Sick inserted between Mark and Luke, and with a single line of Gaelic rubric in the body of it, namely, " Hisund dubeir sacorfaic dau " (" Here give the sacrifice to him "); (2) a Charter by King David confirming to the monks of Deer their lands and their privileges. As the Office for the Sick may have been the first insertion, perhaps 200 or 250 years after the original book was written, so the King's Charter, granted some time before his death in 1154, was with a single exception apparently the last, for in declaring that the clerics of Deer were free from all lay interference and undue exaction, "as it is written in their book," it is implied that the rest of the entries had already been made.

These latter are the six Gaelic ones, and they contribute the chief value to the Book of Deer. They all relate to grants of land and other privileges given from time to time to the Monastery of that name. At Banff and Aberdeen, in the early part of the twelfth century, the book was produced in the King's Courts in evidence of the rights of the clerics to the land in question, and their claim was thereby substantiated. The entries were made at different times, from the end of the tenth or the beginning of the eleventh century down to the middle of the twelfth. They occur in the earlier part of the book, and though inferior in point of penmanship and even of ink to the original contents of the MS., they are well written and perfectly legible throughout. Inscribed as they were in the Gaelic of the place and of the period, these entries introduce us direct and at once into the community of monks who owned the codex.

The first is of exceeding great interest. It is known as the "Legend of Deer." Based upon a tradition of some 500 years, it cannot be regarded as strictly historical, which all the others are. The tradition was that the monastery of Deer was founded by St. Columba. According to the legend, the great Abbot came with his pupil Drostan from Hy (Iona) to Abbordoboir, the modern Aberdour in Aberdeenshire, but whether by land or sea is not stated. The record simply says, "As God had directed them." Bede the Pict was, at the time, Mormaer or Grand Steward of Buchan, and gave them the town in freedom for ever from mormaer and toisech (chieftain). They came after that to the other town of the district, now known as Deer, and "it was pleasing to Columcille because it was full of God's grace," and he asked Bede to give him that one too, but the Pict refused.

Then a son of this ruler took ill and was at the point of death, when his father sent to the clerics—Columba and his pupil—to pray for the lad that he might recover, and he gave them in offering the land from " Cloch in tiprat to Cloch pette meic Garnait " (" From the stone of the well to the stone that marks the bounds of the son of Garnat's place "). They offered a prayer and health came to the dying youth. After that, Columcille departed from the district, gifting the town to Drostan. But before he set out he blessed it, and left as his " word," " Whosoever shall come against it, let him not be many-yeared or victorious."

Drostan's tears (deara), we are told, flowed freely on parting with his famous Chief, whereupon the immortal Columba said, " Let Dear be its name henceforward." And thus the town and monastery derived their name, since variously spelt as Dear, Der, Deir, Dere, and Deer.

The facts underlying the legend are not at all improbable. On the contrary, they are quite in keeping with the character of St. Columba and the range of his mission. Arguing from the circumstance that no Drostan is mentioned in history in connection with the saint, an attempt has been made by Dr. Macbain to show that the founder of the monastery may have been another individual of that name who lived about 700 A.D., but there is no sufficient data. The word is a diminutive of the British name Drust. And whoever Drostan was, as a saint he has been held in honour in the Buchan district from very early times. The church of Aberdour was dedicated to him, and Drustie's fair used to be held annually at Deer on the 14th of December.

In connection with the " word " said to have been left by Columcille, there is some very quaint history in after years. The Celtic Earls of Buchan, partly influenced by it, no doubt, showed a munificent spirit towards the Church of Deer till the fall of their House with the Comyns, when Robert the Bruce came to the throne.

The Comyns had opposed the latter and were so utterly overthrown that, according to a chronicle of the period, of a name which numbered at one time the three Earls of Buchan, Mar, and Menteith, and more than thirty belted knights, there remained no memorial in the land "save the orisons of the monks of Deer."

Sir Robert de Keith, the influential Marischal of Scotland and staunch supporter of the Bruce, got a grant of some pleasant lands in the neighbourhood of the monastery from the King as a reward for his services. Thereafter, partly through intermarriage, the Marischals in succession became the leading family in the district, and at the time of the Reformation were tenants of the abbey lands. By authority of a member of the family who had become "Abbot and Commendator of Deer," the property was by a certain process rather mendaciously made over to the Earl of the day. But the Earl's wife, "a woman both of a high spirit and of tender conscience, forbade her husband to leave such a consuming moth in his house as was the sacrilegious meddling with the Abisie of Deir." Unfortunately, however, "fourteen chalders of meill and beir was a sore tentatione, and he could not weel indure the randering back of such a morsell." Her demand was met with "absolut refusall." So she had a vision of the impending ruin of the house. It is thus curiously recorded by Patrick Gordon, a writer of the eighteenth century, in his book entitled, *A Short Abridgement of Britanes Distemper from the year of God 1739 to 1749.*

The night following, "in her sleepe, she saw a great number of religious men in their habit, cum forth of that Abbey to the stronge Craige of Dunnoture which is the principall residence of that familie. She saw them also sett themselves round about the rock, to gett it down and demolishe it, having no instruments nor toilles wherewith to perform this work, but only penknyves; wherewith they foolishly (as it seemed to her), began to pyk at the Craige. She smyled to sie them intend so frutles ane interpryse; and went to call her husband to scuffe and geyre them out of it. When she had fund him and brought him to sie these sillie religious monckes at their foolishe work, behold! the wholl Craige, with all his strong and statly buildings, was by their penknyves undermynded and fallen in the sea, so as ther remained nothing but the wrack of ther rich furniture and stufe flotting on the waves of a raging and tempestuous sea. Som of the wiser sort, divining upon this vission, attrebute to the penknyves the lenth of time befor this should com to pass; and it hath bein observed, by sundrie, that the Earles of that house before wer the richest in the kingdom, having treasure in store besyd them; but ever since the addition of this so great revenue, they have losed their stock by heavie burdeines of debt and ingagment."

The writer who relates this wonderful vision did not live to see the downfall of the House in the following century, or, it is surmised, he would have regarded it in the light of a literal fulfilment.

But a much more distinguished author in recent times, the French Comte de Montalembert, has not hesitated to connect the ruin of the family fortunes with the sinister "word" of the famous Columcille: "Whosoever shall come against it, let him not be many-yeared or victorious." The scribes who inserted the later entries had kept up the ominous prediction by concluding the fourth with the sentence, "And the Lord's blessing on every mormaer and on every toisech who shall fulfil this, and to their seed after them;" and the fifth, with the alternative, "And his blessing on every one who shall fulfil this after him, and his curse on every one who shall go against it."

In Gaelic entry No. 2 we suddenly emerge from the traditionary elements of the first into the region of historical fact. We need not detail the various grants referred to in the entries 2 to 6 or the names of the donors. Our chief interest in these vernacular addenda lies in the circumstance that they throw an ancient and fresh light on the language and history of the period. Philologically, they are of great value as the earliest specimens of Scottish Gaelic extant. In Adamnan's *Life of St. Columba* there are, of course, some Celtic words, but these are merely names of persons or places and the book is the work of a scholar born and educated in Ireland.

Hitherto, therefore, so far as the Gaelic literary monuments of Scotland have survived, they may all be regarded as more or less of Irish origin, character, and inspiration. But here at length and for the first time we have one that is distinctly Scottish, both in language and the manner of writing. As Windisch has expressed it in his *Celtic Speeches*, "the oldest source for Scottish Gaelic is the Book of Deer." After it there is no other for 400 years, till the Dean of Lismore's book is produced between 1512 and 1526.

Before the sixteenth century you will look in vain for a scrap of any literature or even record in Scottish Gaelic outside the Book of Deer. The arguments that may be adduced to show that in the latter we have the genuine native vernacular, as distinct from the Irish Gaelic in vogue in contemporary MSS., are these.

First, the book was evolved in a corner of Scotland as remote as could be from Ireland. The district formed part of the country of the Picts, who had asserted a kind of independence in ecclesiastical affairs.

Second, the Norsemen by their frequent incursions had inserted a wedge as it were between the two countries that hitherto had so much in common. They destroyed Iona and forced the Church to adopt Dunkeld as its chief abbatial centre. Since Malcolm Canmore's time, Scotland was thus becoming a separate kingdom, independent of English and Irish influences, and the establishment of bishoprics by the Kings Alexander and David freed even the Church from both England and Ireland. The twelfth century was therefore a likely time for the birth of a native literature.

Third, the writing in the Book of Deer is of a thoroughly practical kind, relating to business transactions, and the Gaelic of the district must have been used. The very purpose of the memoranda was to substantiate claims against future mormaers and toisechs who might be disposed to dispute their legality.

Fourth, it is believed that even in the Western Highlands, not to speak of Buchan, the difference between Irish and Scottish Gaelic was then wider than the literature would lead us to infer. For this reason, that the Gaelic MSS. of the period were produced by men who derived their culture from Ireland and naturally followed the Irish standard in their written compositions. The contents of the Book of Deer fully justify that conclusion.

The Gaelic text is of the same age with that in the Leabhar Na h'Uidhre and Book of Hymns. Yet a comparison with these typical Irish monuments shows that the monks of Deer had developed peculiarities in writing Gaelic which differed considerably from the standard of the Irish scholars. Windisch, commenting upon this circumstance, says, " The manner of expression, words, and forms are as in the Irish, but the manner of writing shows already a stronger phonetic decay ; whether it be that the Scotch Gaelic has lived faster, or that only the manner of writing has remained less ancient, and has fitted itself more exactly to the pronunciation of the time."

It is in this respect more like the Middle than the Ancient Irish.

Those who are interested in the study of archaic words and grammatical forms will find the Book of Deer not a bad quarry ; in fact our very oldest bed-rock for Scottish idioms. There are few declensional specimens, it is true, but these suffice to show, as Dr. Whitley Stokes observed, that the Highlanders declined their nouns in the eleventh century as fully as the Irish, which is very far from being the case to-day. Some of the peculiarities of the newly-fledged Scottish Gaelic may here be noticed. For example, that distinction of vowels so noticeable in the Authorised Version of the Scriptures, where we have the Irish *o* in *focal* instead of the Scottish *a* as in *facal*, may be observed in the colophon of the Book of Deer, where we have *truagain*, " the poor wretch," and not *trogan* as in the Irish Priscian of St. Gall. Another feature is the confusion of vowels if ending words, as *i* for *e*, the sinking of *c* and *t* to *g* and *d*, and the assimilation of *ld* and *ln* to *ll*. The spelling has further local characteristics, perhaps due to Pictish influence, as, for example, *cc* for *ch* ; thus *imacc* is for *imach*, modern *a mach*, "out of," "henceforth ;" *buadacc* is for *buad(h)ach*, "victorious."

The aspirated *d* or *g* is dropped, as in *blienee*, just as from Jocelyn of Furness (1180) we learn that the pronunciation of *tighearn* was at that time *tyern*, though in Irish *tigerna*. Another Gaelic Scotticism is the manner of treating *n* in the preposition *in*. In early Irish the *n* disappears before *s* and *p*; here it is retained, as *insaere, inpett*. We also find *ibbidbin* for *im-bidbin* and *ig-ginn* for *in-cinn*. Thus the two peculiar features of Celtic grammar known as aspiration and eclipsis, or vocalic infection and nasal infection of tenues, are observed.

The great rule for spelling known as " Leathan ri leathan is caol ri caol," that is, " broad (vowel) to broad, and small (vowel) to small," forced on Scottish Gaelic from Ireland, is, with very rare exceptions, ignored in the Book of Deer. The orthography of the latter has many contractions, and is more phonetic than that of the Irish MSS. All of which peculiarities and circumstances point to the conclusion arrived at by Celtic scholars in general, that the Scottish Gaelic dialect of the eleventh and the twelfth centuries, and especially the accent, differed much from the language of educated Irishmen.

The next two literary monuments of this vernacular, namely, those of the Dean of Lismore and of Duncan Macrae of Inverinate, both of whom wrote phonetically, bring out this difference between the two dialects still more clearly. It is an interesting fact, apparent from the Book of Deer, that the present Aberdeenshire, now so Teutonic, was, when the entries were made, a Gaelic-speaking district. The names of the kings, mormaers, and toisechs mentioned are all Celtic, indeed most of them are common enough names to-day in the Highlands,——Cathal, Domnall, Muridach, Maelcolum, Cainnech, Donnchad, Gartnait, Aedh, Comgall, Maledoun, Matadin ; Nectan was Bishop of Aberdeen, Leot Abbot of Brechin, Domangart, a ferlegin or " man of learning," and Cormac Abbot of Turiff. A few are non-Celtic, such as Andrew, Samson, and David. Unhappily, in these records the names of women do not figure much. Two very euphonious and beautiful ones, however, are given,—Eua, the "wedded wife" of Colban, and Ete, daughter of Gillemichel. It is a wonder that these delightful names, especially Ete or Eite, have gone out of use in the Highlands.

The Celts seem to have had a genius for coining melodious appellations, sweet and endearing, as well as strong, rough, and uncouth.

Unlike Adamnan's *Vita Columbæ* and Bede's *History*, there is no hint in this MS. of any language other than Latin and Gaelic. The latter was in evidence in the Courts of Banff and Aberdeen, and we would gather from the line of vernacular inserted in the Latin fragment of an Office for the Visitation of the Sick that the monks of Deer were more familiar with their Gaelic than their Latin ; for in the Irish Book of Dimna the direction is not the Gaelic "Hisund dubeir sacorfaic dau," but it is the Latin "Das ei Eucharistan."

But apart from their philological value, the memoranda in the Book of Deer throw a welcome light on an early and obscure period of our national history. Where the student of the social, political, and ecclesiastical machinery of the time would otherwise have to grope his way among dim and doubtful hints and analogies, he has here authentic glimpses into the Celtic condition of Scotland.

And these notices are all the more valuable because they were made at the time when a great social and ecclesiastical revolution was impending. There was, on one side, the change from the primitive patriarchal polity to the feudal regime, and on the other, from the monastic to the parochial system. The period covered by the entries is towards the close of the Celtic epoch, before this momentous transition had taken place. We see the old order ready to depart, and we get some light on the origin of the new institutions which were about to supersede it.

Queen Margaret, wife of Malcolm Canmore, had much to do with the remoulding of the ancient structure of society in Scotland. This old system of inherited peculiarity was first confronted with one founded on different principles, when the Celtic clergy of Scotland met in council, to listen during three days to the addresses of the Saxon princess, whose speeches were translated into the language of the Gael by her husband the King. Just as in the other great social movements of later times in the Highlands, the influences that undermined the old order were not the result of natural progress in the Celtic polity, but of foreign ideas and principles introduced from without. It was these that led to the destruction of the civil and ecclesiastical institutions on which the old regime rested. In the train of Queen Margaret had come into Scotland a race of Saxon, and afterwards of Norman settlers, whose presence in the country led to a quickening of the national life, and the awakening of a feeling of unity such as could find no place among the divided clans of a Celtic people.

In the Book of Deer we still have the old patriarchal system in full swing. There is the Ardrigh or High King. Under him and over the provinces are the mormaers, and under the mormaers the tribal or district chieftains known as toisechs. All these had their exactions out of the land, besides having their own fat manor lands. They had rights of personal service, civil and military; of entertainment when travelling; and of exacting rent in kind or in money. There were neither dioceses nor parishes as yet. The patriarchal idea was carried out even in the monastic system. Each tribe or tuath had a monastery. Its abbot belonged to a leading family of the tuath or of the founder, in which family the office was hereditary. The system gave rise to great abuses; for as the monastery grew rich in lands the abbot took to do more with the temporal than with the spiritual management, and often the lands passed out of the possession of the monastery altogether into the hands of the laymen.

" It was not so in the case of Deer, the clerics of which down to the middle of the twelfth century were still receiving from the bounty of the Gaelic chiefs of this district additions to their monastic inheritance, in the whole of which they were secured by King David I., with full immunity from all secular exactions." It is plain, however, from the terms of the royal charter, that attempts had been made to fleece them, and that they were able to maintain their rights in virtue of the grants recorded in their book.

The abuses of the lay abbacies, though not wholly removed, were fairly checked by Queen Margaret and her sons, through the creation of bishoprics and the gradual supersession of the monastic by the parochial system. Soon, dioceses and parishes, which cannot be traced farther back than the time of Alexander I., began to appear in the records. They had been established in England much earlier.

Other new civil divisions and distinctions emerge. The old "countries" and "provinces" become shires. Towns spring up, and the number of individuals and corporations holding personal property and corporate rights increased. A large part of the best land was given by charter from King David to men who held of the crown in feudal tenure.

The mormaer became merged in the Earl, and the toisech in the Thane. In short, with the growth of feudal law, and the change to the parochial system, the old Celtic regime was fast becoming a thing of the past, though many of the customs and traditions associated therewith lingered on till the great overthrow of the Forty-five, and even in some localities almost to our own times.

We are thus able, through the medium of this venerable Book of Deer, to reach a hand over time to Columcille and his faithful Drostan, to Bede the Pict, to the monks of Buchan, and that succession of the Ardrighs, mormaers, and toisechs who lived in the old and primitive conditions, before the new institutions and the regime under which we ourselves exist were evolved. We can hardly think of Scotland to-day apart from the categories of parishes, burghs, individual freedom, English language, and many others, and yet in these far-off times the monks of Deer and their contemporaries had to be doing without them. For all this, these men were not lacking in culture or pious devotion.

Their book shows us that they revered the spiritual Columba as their Chief, and founder of their monastery, and besides being expert caligraphists, having some skill in painting and illumination, they were educated with a sufficient knowledge of Latin to transcribe it intelligently and use it in the services of the church. "This is not much to say of them," says Dr. Anderson in his Rhind Lectures, "but," he adds, "it is a great deal more than we have it in our power to say of any other community or institution from similar evidence, if we except the parent community of Iona itself."

Of the Gaelic of the Book of Deer there are three editions. The first was prepared, Latin and Gaelic together, with valuable preface and facsimile plates, by Dr. Stuart, and published by the Spalding Club in 1869. It is one of the many excellent and beautifully printed volumes we owe to that distinguished Association. Mr. Stokes was responsible for the English translation. The second publication he has given himself, in his own *Goidelica*. There we find all the later entries of the codex with translation, notes, and glossary. A similar service has since been rendered by Dr. Macbain of Inverness, who provides the text with translation, notes, and glossary of his own, founded on the work of the previous editors, but throwing additional light on the vocabulary. This contribution appears in the eleventh volume of the *Transactions of the Gaelic Society of Inverness* (1884-85), and is a welcome aid to the study of the text.

As in the case of the oldest book of Scotland, so in the case of this second oldest, it is to be regretted that the Book of Deer has strayed outwith our own land, yet no doubt, it is to this fact that we owe the existence of both to-day; for no other book of so ancient a calibre has been able to survive the many stormy convulsions and turbulent ferments known as Scottish history. Cast up like flotsam and jetsam in a late age, and treasured in the high places of learning, they both add a lustre and a glory now to our ancient language and literature which we would otherwise in vain desiderate.

CHAPTER VI

THE MS. LEGACY OF THE PAST

A fresh start in the study of Celtic literature—Advent of foremost scholars—The new basis found by Zeuss — Resurrection of ancient texts — Unexpected light—H. d'Arbois de Jubainville and his mission to this country—The numbers, dates, and localities of Gaelic MSS. : (1) on the Continent ; (2) in the British Isles—Subject matter—Examples of the oldest written Gaelic poetry in Europe—The great books of saga—Leabhar Na h'Uidhre—Books of Leinster, Ballymote, and Lismore—Quotations—Account of the Ancient Annals—Tighernach—The *Chronicon Scotorum*—The "Four Masters" —Romance of the fugitive documents.

IT is practically within the last fifty years that the great revival in the study of Celtic literature has taken place. About the middle of last century the foremost scholars began to arrive, and since then there has been quite a galaxy of experts, both on the Continent and in the British Isles, who have approached the subject on scientific lines, and by careful literary research have not only opened to us the treasures of the past, but have also thrown a flood of light on them.

Prior to their advent, Celtic studies had no solid basis, for the sufficient reason that the materials were not available. Old-time convulsions had dispersed the documents to the four winds, and they remained where they lay, buried for ages from the public eye.

Such learned men as occupied themselves with these studies before the middle of last century confined their attention in great part to the languages and literatures of the Neo-Celtic races—the Welsh and the Bretons. They sought in these light to dissipate the obscurity that hung over the early history of the Celtic race—the period anterior to the conquest of Gaul by the Romans. They consulted grammars and dictionaries published in Brittany, Wales, Scotland, and Ireland, during the last three centuries. Of the texts themselves, the oldest they knew were Welsh, dating from about the thirteenth century; and some poems of Welsh bards preserved in MSS., of which the most ancient went no farther back than the end of the twelfth century. These were literary treasures indeed, with the characteristic Celtic flavour, as may be seen from the beautiful critiques of Renan and Matthew Arnold, both of whom were charmed by the spirit and sentiment they breathe.

But in general it may be said that the early scholars had only mastered the more modern forms of the language, and it was from texts comparatively recent that they sought illumination of a past removed from them by more than nineteen centuries.

Such was the stage Celtic study had reached—a kind of arrested development—when suddenly a unique resuscitation took place.

The first of the new scholars to arrive were O'Donovan and O'Curry. Eugene O'Curry, Professor of the Catholic University of Ireland, went straight to the necessities of the case by publishing in 1849 a catalogue of the Gaelic MSS. in the British Museum, and then, of those in the Royal Academy of his native land. Afterwards, besides other valuable contributions, he gave to the world his *Lectures on the MS. Materials of Irish History*, enhancing the interest of the work by putting a very large and varied selection of facsimiles of the ancient writings in the appendix. A very Tischendorf was this indefatigable MS. hunter and interpreter. Very aptly indeed did he speak of himself as an underground worker. Much had been done by other labourers, but the foundation was still to seek and still to lay. And it is significant of former methods, that he knew not one man previous to his own time who had qualified himself for the work in hand, either by mastering the ancient Gaelic, or by making himself acquainted with the MSS. And yet these are the genuine sources of historical and antiquarian knowledge in this department.

Close after O'Curry came the great Continental savant Zeuss, who may be regarded as the real founder of the new and solid basis on which Celtic studies now rest. His monumental work, the erudite *Grammatica Celtica*, appeared in Leipzig in 1853, giving a new impetus all over Europe to a study which hitherto had attracted but a languid, or at the best, a restricted attention. And when, following up this great work, the German grammarian published the glosses found in some of the oldest Gaelic MSS. on the Continent, it was recognised that he had opened up a new and most fertile field for future explorers. These latter were immediately forthcoming — learned authorities, like Nigra, Ascoli, Ebel, Stokes, Windisch, and Zimmer, who brought to light other important documents and explained their significance. Thus was the new movement in Celtic study duly inaugurated, with what results we shall see.

The glosses published by Zeuss, though they furnish no fresh ideas, offer to the learned world a grammatical interest of the highest kind. They belong, some to the eighth century, others to the ninth, and the venerable Gaelic in which they are couched presents certain antique and curious characteristics which are entirely lacking to the Welsh of the same period, and still more to that of the twelfth and following centuries—the only forms known to the scholars before Zeuss.

Since his time the new basis which he found for Celtic studies has been wonderfully enlarged, chiefly through the discovery of other Gaelic texts contemporary with some of those that served for his own beautiful work. And then the remarkable publications of erudite men in Dublin, and the excellent work of Windisch, Professor of Sanskrit at

Leipzig, have called the attention of experts on the continent to a great mass of documentary material in the British Isles. Under the transcription and retouching of many of these MSS. by later copyists, there are found original compositions, primarily in the ancient Gaelic of which Zeuss was the first interpreter.

Unlike the glosses, they furnish us with a vast storehouse of new ideas and traditions of every sort, comprising especially the mythological and legendary, the legal also, and even the grammatical under various forms. Their originality is unquestionable. These texts, in carrying us back to pagan times, throw quite unexpected light on the incomplete though precious accounts which ancient writers like Cæsar, Diodorus of Sicily, and Strabo have given of the primitive civilisation of the Gauls. We should expect to find in this mass of curious heroic literature some expression of the traditions common to all the Celtic race before the settlement of the different branches in the countries which now bear their name, and we are not disappointed. The MSS. preserved do give us a crowd of fresh thoughts on the beliefs and customs of the Celts in the most ancient epochs of their history.

In this respect they help to gratify the longing desire of living men to know something of the actions, the range of thought, the character of mind, the habits, the tastes, the arts, the religion, and, in short, the everyday life of so old and venerable a race as our own, which has played such a wonderful part in the drama of history.

The French authorities have been fully alive to the value of these studies, and on one occasion, at least, the Minister of Public Instruction showed his interest in a very practical and laudable way. In February of 1881 Jules Ferry, who was in office at the time, appointed H. d'Arbois de Jubainville, Professor of Celtic in the College of France, as a special commissioner to visit the British Isles, and investigate and make a list of all the Gaelic MSS. he could find. This literary mission De Jubainville carried out the same year, subsequently embodying his report in a book which gives not only his catalogue of MSS. inspected in England and Ireland, but also a list of those on the Continent.   For some reason or other he omitted to include Scotland in the area of his research, and so the large collection of valuable documents in the Advocates' Library, Edinburgh, is not chronicled in his interesting résumé.   Yet still, we have now for the first time a pretty general estimate of all the more important material available.

We need not follow this enthusiastic MS. hunter in his peregrinations through the British Isles and on the Continent, entering, as he frequently did, the precincts of ancient universities, cloisters, and museums, sitting in odd corners in libraries, poring over musty leaves, deciphering antique characters, looking at some documents through glass cases which he would fain see opened, handling others with eager, hurried scrutiny, while a verger or a monk mounts sentry over the inquisitive foreigner, watching the precious relics with jealous care, and limiting the time for observation.

What concerns us most are the tabulated results ; and we might look in the passing at some of the more striking facts which they exhibit.

And first of all it is not a little surprising to learn that, while the libraries of the Continent possess twenty MSS., or more correctly twenty portions of MSS., written in the Gaelic language before the eleventh century, in the libraries of England and Ireland there are only seven of that remote age.   But after that date the British libraries take the lead, since the number of their Gaelic MSS. before the seventeenth century amount to 133, whereas the total on the Continent down to the seventeenth century is only thirty-five.   Of course this excludes the Celtic Latin MSS., of which there are upwards of 200 in European libraries.

Altogether there are just fifty-six Gaelic documents that are known to be on the Continent of dates ranging from the eighth to the nineteenth century, and these are distributed as follows :—

8th century . . .	2	Milan, Cambray.
8th to 9th century .	2	St. Paul in Carinthia, Vienna.
9th century . .	13	Berne, Carlsruhe (2), Dresden, Laon, Leyden, Nancy, Paris (2), Rome, St. Gall (2), Turin.
9th to 10th century .	1	Würzburg.
10th century . .	2	Paris.
11th century . .	6	Carlsruhe, Rome (2), St. Gall, Vienna (2).
11th to 12th century .	1	Klosterneuburg.
12th century . .	1	Engelberg.
13th to 15th century .	1	Rennes.
14th to 16th century .	1	Paris.
16th century . .	1	Stockholm.
17th century . .	12	Brussels (11), Paris.
18th century . .	5	Paris (4), Rouen.
19th century . .	4	Paris (2), Rouen (2).
Dates uncertain . .	4	Berne, Florence, Milan (2).

Besides the number, antiquity, and wide distribution of these MSS., we are struck with two things. First, the fact that Milan and Cambray, two Continental cities, have the honour of possessing the two most ancient Gaelic MSS. now extant. One of these relics is a Latin commentary on the Psalms, the other a Latin sermon, but in both there are glosses in Irish or Gaelic written in the eighth century. Earlier than that we cannot go for actual writing still extant in the native tongue.

The other striking thing about the list is the entire absence of Gaelic MSS. in the northern countries of Europe, such as Norway, Sweden, and Denmark, where we should most expect to find them. There is one indeed at Stockholm, but it is merely a copy written in the sixteenth century. Surely this goes far to confirm the sinister reputation of the marauding Danes and Norsemen with regard to learning. Keating, writing 250 years ago, asserts their destructiveness. " It was not allowed to give instruction in letters. . . . No scholars, no clerics, no books, no holy relics, were left in church or monastery through dread of them. Neither bard nor philosopher nor musician pursued his wonted profession in the land."

Apparently these northern pillagers, who laid waste so many monasteries, instead of removing the rare and precious books to their own lands, were no better than the Vandals in their mad business of burning and destroying on the spot what they evidently themselves could not value or appreciate.

But coming now to the British Isles, we might briefly consider the literary legacy which the learned Frenchman found in those libraries of England and Ireland that he visited. In all, he mentions 953 as the number of MSS. to which he had access, and these were located as follows :—

At Cambridge	3
„ British Museum	166
„ Oxford	15
„ Royal Irish Academy	560
„ Trinity College, Dublin	63
„ Franciscans, Dublin	22
„ Lord Ashburnham	63
„ Some special libraries	61
Total . .	953

So far from being exhaustive, our literary commissioner thinks these figures very far below the actual number of Gaelic MSS. in the British Isles. Though he makes no reference in this respect to Wales or Scotland, he is aware that there must be many in private libraries that he has not indicated. And he admits that, according to O'Curry, Trinity College has 140 instead of the 63 he mentions. And besides its 559 catalogued MSS., the Royal Academy of Ireland possesses about as many more not catalogued, of which only one, the Book of Fermoy, was described to him as worthy of his special attention.

Though in point of antiquity there is none of all these British MSS. to compare with the oldest glosses on the Continent, there are two which come near it. They date from the ninth century, and are both located in Trinity College. These are the Book of Armagh and the Book of Dimna. Next in order, between the ninth and tenth centuries, come (1) the Irish Canons at Cambridge; (2) the Gospel of Maeielbrid Mac Durnâin, tenth century, at Lambeth Palace; (3) the Psalter of Southampton, end of the tenth century or beginning of the eleventh, at St. John's College, Cambridge; (4) The Book of Deer, with its Latin, ninth to tenth, and Gaelic entries tenth to twelfth, also at Cambridge in the University Library; and (5) the Gaelic portion of the Missal of Stowe, bought by the British Government with the rest of Lord Ashburnham's collection for their Museum.

These seven MSS. are the most ancient, the only ones, in fact, in which you find Gaelic written before the eleventh century within the British Isles. Yet they are not Gaelic MSS., strictly speaking, but Latin ones in which are found some words or phrases or paragraphs written in the native tongue. The Gospel of Maeielbrid, for example, contains only a line and a half of Gaelic, the Book of Armagh four pages.

To find what we would strictly call Gaelic documents, we must come down as far as the closing years of the eleventh century, which yields us four. Henceforth there is no lack of abundant and rich material. The twelfth century is credited with seven, the thirteenth with eight, the fourteenth with eleven, the fifteenth and sixteenth with ninety-six, the seventeenth with sixty-six, the first half of the eighteenth with seventy-seven. Total down to the year 1750, 276 MSS. in the British Isles of the whole number 953 catalogued by De Jubainville. So that the remainder, the vast majority of the British MSS., are of comparatively recent date, subsequent in fact even to the days of Macpherson of Ossianic fame.

More important than the number, dates, and distribution is the subject-matter of our literary legacy, and this now falls to be considered. It is very difficult to classify the MSS. according to their contents, as so many of them are miscellaneous. Yet they do admit of being brought under certain categories. Leaving aside for the present all the later ones written after 1600, we have in all 168 Continental and British documents to deal with.

Of these we must place in a section apart all the Latin ones that only contain glosses or poems or notes in Gaelic which are additional or secondary to the original text. This is the case with all the Continental MSS. concerned, except three, one at Rennes, one at Paris, and one at Stockholm. It is also the case with ten Britishers, viz. (1) the Book of Deer, (2) the Irish Canons, (3) the Psalter at Cambridge, (4) the Gospel of Maelbrigte hua Maelûanaig, (5) the Book of Dimna, (6) the Book of Armagh, (7) the Book of Kells, (8) the fragment of Psalter attributed to St. Camin, (9) the Missal of Stowe, and (10) the Gospel of Maeielbrid Mac Durnâin at Lambeth Palace.

That makes a total of forty-two in which the Gaelic is only added in notes to a Latin original. Yet they comprise the most ancient of all we have, and though their grammatical value is very considerable, their literary interest is but meagre —almost nil in fact—with the exception of the few poems at Milan, St. Gall, Dresden, St. Paul in Carinthia, and Klosterneuburg.

As these poems seem to lie like wayside flowers in our path, it is worth our while, before passing on, to turn aside for a little to cull some of the verses.

Of the two poems in the Milan codex, Dr. Stokes declares they are difficult to decipher and more difficult to translate. But of the four quatrains on the margin of the Priscian of St. Gall, here are two charming examples, very characteristic of the Gael's love of nature and learning, as well as reminiscent of his wild environment. The first is not unlike the lyric of Columcille himself, when he describes the peace of Durrow :—

> A grove surrounds me :
> The swift lay of the blackbird makes music to me—

> I will not hide it;
> Over my much-lined little book,
> The song of the birds makes music to me.

The author of the second, as Professor Mackinnon has fancied, must often have seen the storm burst upon a wild spot on the west of Ireland, or, more likely still, on Iona, Tiree, Oronsay, or Skye.

> Is acher in gaith innocht:
> Tufuasna fairggae findfholt;
> Ni ágor reimm mora minn
> Dond laechraid lainn oa Lochlind.

> Wild blows the wind to-night:
> The white-haired billows rage;
> The bold warriors from Norway
> Fear not the path of a clear sea.

In the Codex Boernerianus of Dresden we have the following lines. Translated literally, they run thus :—

> To go to Rome is much of trouble, little of profit. The King whom thou seekest here, unless thou bring him with thee thou findest not.
> Great folly, great madness, great loss of sense, great folly since thou hast proposed (?) to go to death, to be under the unwill of Mary's Son.

It was the late Herr Mone, Archivdirektor at Carlsruhe, who discovered the Gaelic poems in the MS. belonging to St. Paul in Carinthia, and sent the first verse of the first of these poems to Dr. Reeves. Thereafter Dr. Whitley Stokes wrote him requesting to be favoured with the remainder, with which request he not only complied, but also sent two other extracts from the same codex, and a letter dated Carlsruhe, January 24th, 1859. There are in all five short Gaelic poems or fragments in the MS.

The first, of eight stanzas, is in praise of Aedh, son of Diarmad, and has been translated by Eugene O'Curry. We give here simply the first and last verses :—

> Aedh great to institute hilarity,
> Aedh anxious (desirous) to dispense festivity,
> The Straight Rod, the most beautiful,
> Of the hills of cleared Ro-er-enn.
>
> At ale-drinking, poems are sung
> By companies among people's houses
> Sweet-singing bards announce
> In pools of ale the name of Aedh.

The next to be quoted is part of a longer poem found in the Books of Leinster, Ballymote, Glendaloch, Lismore, and a Bodleian MS. The copy from the Book of Leinster is given in full by Dr. Whitley Stokes in his *Goidelica*, but here are the two quatrains of it in the Carinthian codex :—

> He is a bird round which a trap shuts,
> He is a leaky bark in dangerous peril,
> He is an empty vessel, he is a withered tree,
> Who so doth not the will of the King above.
>
> He is pure gold, he is a heaven round the sun,
> He is a vessel of silver full of wine,
> He is an angel, he is wisdom of saints,
> Every one who doth the will of the King.

The third poem, Dr. Stokes says, is exceedingly obscure. It seems to mean—

There remains a fort in Tuain Inbir . . . . with its stars last night, with its sun, with its moon.

Gobhan made that : let its story be perceived by you : my heartlet, God of heaven, he is the thatcher that thatched it.

A house wherein thou gettest not moisture ; a place wherein thou fearest not spear-points. More radiant it is than a garden, and it without an *udnacht* around it.

Another of the pieces in this Carinthian MS. is of a very different order. A monk in a humorous and facetious strain, according to Professor Zimmer, contrasts his own serious studies with the very different pursuits of another person whom he calls Pan Gurban (or Panqur ban, Windisch), a

Slavonic name, meaning, as Zimmer thinks, " Mr. Hunch-back."

Omitting the forty-two Gaelic documents from the 168, we have 126 remaining which have been written before the year 1600, and these deal with a great variety of subjects : religion, law, medicine, astronomy, grammar, history, and legendary history.

The texts that treat of theology, mysticism, lives of saints, and martyrologies, are very numerous ; those of law few. Medicine figures in a class apart. Astronomy gets even a smaller place than medicine. Its most ancient monument dates from the fourteenth century.

One of the most curious and least known of all the Gaelic relics is a treatise on Gaelic grammar, written in Gaelic. It is divided into four books, and is preserved to us in ten MSS. of the fourteenth, fifteenth, and sixteenth centuries. The four books of which it is composed are attributed, the first to Cennfaelad, an historic personage who died in 678 ; the other three to mythical, prehistoric authors, such as Fercertné, Amergin Glûngel, and Fenius Farsaid. The antiquity and ability of the latter grammarian for the work, may be inferred from the somewhat startling statement that he is said to have composed the Gaelic tongue out of seventy-two languages, and afterwards his son Nial visited Egypt to teach the languages after the confusion of Babel. Verily the Celts were an enterprising race to have a grammarian first in the field, and the nebulous Fenius Farsaid deserves a grave as high as Browning's hero, for even before Moses " ground he at grammar." It is a pity that this rare old treatise which Ireland possessed in the Middle Ages has not been published. The MSS. are in the British Museum, Royal Academy of Ireland, Trinity College, and with the Franciscans of Dublin.

But not in any of the above-named categories do we find the body and soul of Celtic literature. The real breathing spirit of the past speaks to us rather in the great MSS. of the Middle Ages, those which deal with romance and history—the earlier sagas and the later annals ; and these deserve more than a passing reference. The saga or heroic literature is far and away the most curious and abundant. De Jubainville himself chronicles no less than 540 pieces of this class. But its greatest monuments are the miscellaneous MSS. known as the Leabhar Na h'Uidhre, the Book of Leinster, Book of Ballymote, Book of Lecain, and Book of Lismore.

No more precious and important document in the whole range of ancient Gaelic literature has reached us than the Leabhar Na h'Uidhre, or Book of the Dun Cow, said to be so called after an original text of that name now lost, but of which it contains a copy. St. Ciaran, it appears, wrote down from the dictation of the risen Fergus, the tale of the " Táin Bó Chuailgné," in a book which he had made from the hide of his pet cow. This favourite from its colour was called the Odhar (or Dun), of which Na h'Uidhre is the genitive. The existing Leabhar Na h'Uidhre is a MS. of the end of the eleventh century, and, even more than the Book of Hymns, its contemporary, it merits the distinction of being the earliest exclusively Gaelic document that we have. Besides preserving St. Ciaran's version of the Táin, it contains a copy of Dallan Forgaill's famous " Amra " in praise of Columcille, and quite a number of ancient sacred and secular pieces, some of which are of great interest. The compiler of this venerable codex was Maelmuiri, son of the son of Conn nam-Bocht, a writer who met his death in 1106 in the middle of the great stone church of Clonmacnois, at the hands of a band of robbers. There is a quaint inscription at the top of folio 45 in his own original handwriting. The words run, " This is a trial of his pen here by Maelmuiri, son of the son of Conn."

Next in importance to Leabhar Na h'Uidhre comes the Book of Leinster, written fifty years later. Rich in saga, it contains the fullest account of the "Táin Bó Chuailgné." O'Curry sets so high a value upon this codex that he writes : " I think I may say with sorrow that there is not in all

Europe any nation but this of ours that would not long since have made a national literary fortune out of such a volume, had any other country in Europe been fortunate enough to possess such an heirloom of history."

The Book of Ballymote belongs to the end of the fourteenth century—that of Lismore to the fifteenth. The latter is the property of the Duke of Devonshire, having been discovered in his Castle of Lismore, county of Waterford, Ireland, so late as the year 1814. Besides containing Lives of saints, etc., it is considered specially important in point of view of the Ossianic cycle.

Of all the heroic sagas the greatest and the longest is that for which we are indebted to the Book of Leinster and Leabhar Na h'Uidhre—the "Táin Bó Chuailgné." This is not the place to deal with such a lengthy story ; but by way of illustrating the quality and literary interest of these old world MSS., preserving as they do the most characteristic traits of Celtic genius in the age before writing, we give two quotations from this wonderful saga.

And the first will show the keen perception, the wealth of pictorial detail, and descriptive power of language so characteristic of the Gaelic ursguels and poems. It is the personal account of the Ulster chiefs as given in the Táin.

"There came another company there," said Mac Roth; "no champion could be found more comely than he who leads them. His hair is of a deep-red yellow, and bushy ; his forehead broad and his face tapering ; thin red lips ; pearly shining teeth ; a white smooth body. A red and white cloak flutters about him ; a golden brooch in that cloak at his breast ; a shirt of white kingly linen with gold embroidery at his skin ; a white shield with gold fastenings at his shoulder ; a gold-hilted long sword at his left side ; a long, sharp, dark-green spear with a rich band and carved silver rivets in his hand." "Who is he, O Fergus ?" said Ailill. "The man who has come there is in himself half a battle ; the fury of the slaughter hound," etc.

Truly a wonderful accoutred warrior was this, and gorgeous in his apparel for his age. Like our Oriental Nabobs and savage chiefs he believed in colour and luxurious display.

But I fancy it would be hard to beat the second quotation as an illustration of the riotous luxuriance of the Celtic imagination in the days when it was at its best, unsobered by science, unrestricted by reason. The quotation is from the description of the fight between the two rival bulls in Queen Meve's country. In the poetic language of the tale, " the province rang with the echoes of their roaring, the sky was darkened by the sods of earth they threw up with their feet, and the foam that flew from their mouths ; faint-hearted men, women, and children hid themselves in caves, caverns, and clefts of the rocks, whilst even the most veteran warriors but dared to view the combat from the neighbouring hills and eminences. The Finnbheannach or White-horned at length gave way, and retreated towards a certain pass which opened into the plain in which the battle raged, and where sixteen warriors bolder than the rest had planted themselves ; but so rapid was the retreat and the pursuit that not only were all these trampled to the ground, but they were buried several feet in it. The Donn Chuailgne at last coming up with his opponent, raised him on his horns, ran off with him, passed the gates of Meve's palace, tossing and shaking him as he went, until at last he shattered him to pieces, dropping his disjointed members as he went along. And wherever a part fell, that place retained the name of that joint ever after." And thus it was that " Ath Luain, now Athlone, which was before called Ath Mor or the Great Ford, received its present name from the Finnbheannach's luan or loin having been dropped there."

This "Táin Bó Chuailgné" opens a window upon the past, and were it only for the rich and abundant historical details it so lavishly furnishes, must be held a treasure. " Notwithstanding the extreme wildness of the legend," says O'Curry, " I am not acquainted with any tale in the whole range of our literature in which the student will find more of valuable details concerning general and local history ; more of description of the manners and customs of the people ; of the druidical and fairy influence supposed to be exercised in the affairs of men ; of the laws of Irish chivalry and honour ; of the standards of beauty, morality, valour, truth, and fidelity exercised by the people of old ; of the regal power and dignity of the monarch and the provincial kings, as well as much concerning the division of the country into its local dependencies ; lists of its chieftains and chieftaincies ; many valuable topographical names ; the names and kinds of articles of dress and ornament ; of military weapons ; of horses, chariots, and trappings ; of leechcraft as well as instances of perhaps every occurrence that could be supposed to happen in ancient Irish life. All of these details are of the utmost value to the student of history, even though mixed up with any amount of the marvellous or incredible in poetical traditions."

So much for the sagas and monuments of heroic literature. There remain the other great class of MSS. to which we have referred—the Annals. They serve as a basis for Irish history, and only the more quaint and important need be mentioned here, such as the Annals of Tighernach, the *Chronicon Scotorum*, the Annals of Innisfallen, the Annals of Boyle, the Annals of Ulster, the Annals of Loch Cé, the Annals of Clonmacnois, and most important of all, the book called the " Four Masters."

Of all these the Annals of Tighernach is the most ancient and most reliable, having for author the abbot of that name who died in 1088. It is supposed that in compiling this work he had as basis a chronicle kept by the monks from the founding of the abbey in 544. The MS. of this history belongs to the twelfth and thirteenth centuries. A considerable part of it is in Gaelic, interspersed with numerous quotations from Latin and Greek authors. Dr. O'Conor, commenting on this, remarks that Tighernach's balancing of these authorities against each other manifests a degree of criticism uncommon in the early age in which he lived.

The precious historical composition known as the *Chronicon Scotorum* exists in a copy written towards 1650 by Duald Mac Firbis. The original belonged to the twelfth century, the chronicle itself ending in 1135. It begins with the following title and short preface by the compiler :—

The chronicle of the Scots (or Irish) begins here—

Understand, O Reader, that it is for a certain reason, and particularly to avoid tediousness that our intention is to make only a short abstract and compendium of the history of the Scots in this book, omitting the lengthened details of the historical books ; wherefore it is that we beg of you not to criticise us on that account as we know that it is an exceedingly great deficiency.

He then passes rapidly over the first three ages of the world,—the earlier colonisation of Ireland, the death of the colonists at Tallaght in the county of Dublin, and the visit of Nial, the son of Fenius Farsaid, to Egypt to teach the languages. With winged speed the compiler reaches the year 375, when St. Patrick was born, and then the red letter date 432 which witnessed his arrival in Ireland. Columcille's prayer at the battle of Cooldrevna is given under the year 561, and numerous scraps of poems here and there quoted as authorities. A large deficiency occurs between 722 and 805 A.D., where the compiler has written, " The breasts (or fronts) of two leaves of the old book out of which I write this, are wanting here, and I leave what is before me of this page for them, I am, Dubhaltach Firbisigh." A similar defect, it may be noted, occurs in the Annals of Tighernach from 756 to 973.

The other Annals above-mentioned carry the history down towards the end of the sixteenth century.

Almost contemporary with the *Chronicon Scotorum* arose the greatest of all, *The Annals of the Kingdom of Ireland by the Four Masters*, commonly cited as the " Four Masters," a name given to its authors by Colgan. It was the work of Michael O'Clery and other three great scholars, begun in 1632 and finished in 1636. All the best and most copious Annals he could find throughout Ireland were collected by him for this *magnum opus*. Like so many others of these historical compilations, it begins far back, in the year of the world 2242, and finishes in 1616 A.D. "There is no event of Irish history," says Dr. Hyde, "from the birth of Christ to the beginning of the seventeenth century, that the first inquiry of the student will not be, 'What do the "Four Masters" say about it?' for the great value of the work consists in this, that we have here in condensed form the pith and substance of the old books of Ireland which were then in existence, but which, as the Four Masters anticipated, have long since perished."

The work has been published by O'Donovan in 1851. His is regarded as the best and most complete edition in translation and notes. It forms six volumes, without counting the supplementary index. The autograph MS. still exists, composed of two volumes, of which the first, stopping at the year 1169, forms No. XXI. of the Stowe Collection. Of the second volume there are two autograph copies: the one complete, in the library of the Royal Academy of Ireland; the other, comprising only the years 1335 to 1605, is preserved at Trinity College, Dublin.

And now looking back over this long legacy of vellum, is there not something eerie in the thought of these old-world musty MSS. creeping out once more into the light, after ages of gravelike oblivion?

If we could follow their actual history, from their slow genesis under the pen of ancient amanuenses through their subsequent fortunes, when perhaps some of them under the cloak of a fleeing monk, or in a shaky coracle at sea, barely escaped the fury of illiterate warriors or the waves; some of them other perils on land in their wanderings through the British Isles and the Continent,—what a revelation of life and destiny that would be! They have slept a long sleep through turbulent ages since then, apparently unappreciated, buried, neglected, and forgotten, but now in this new age, as we have seen, there is a mighty hunt and scramble for the resurrected relics. Many of them have been already published, and there is a movement afoot by the Irish Text Society to print the more important of the rest. Libraries and individuals compete with each other for possession of the originals. So that now, in the eyes of the wise and the wealthy, the hitherto obsolete MSS., often cast aside in odd chests and closets as mere brown rubbish, are more prized and coveted as rare treasure than even their rivals of to-day. And what a legacy of vellum all-told we owe to the old scribes of cell and cloister ; from the legended Fenius Farsaid all the way down to the " Four Masters."

CHAPTER VII

THE SCOTTISH COLLECTION OF CELTIC MSS.

Cabinet in Advocates' Library—Curious assortment of vernacular literature—
Number and character—Origin of the collection—Highland Society and
Kilbride MSS.—Subsidiary additions—Work for the expert—Fate of some
luckless documents—Value of MSS. XL., LIII., and LVI.—Three literary
monuments of the Western Highlands: (1) The Book of the Dean of Lismore
—History, description, value, contents, extracts, names of contributors; (2)
The Fernaig MS.—Characteristics—Interesting details of supposed author;
(3) The Book of Clanranald—Quaint relic—Two MSS., the Red and the
Black—History and contents, with specimen prose-poem and elegy.

IN a cabinet in the Advocates' Library, Edinburgh, may be
seen what looks like the decayed and mouldering remains of
some obsolete literature. Very rarely is the case opened,
and only once in a while does the casual observer show any
more than a passing interest in these faded and tattered
remnants. Why should he? In comparison with the vast
variety of neatly printed and handsomely bound volumes
around, their appearance is uninviting. Handwritten, many
of them with frayed edges, leaves missing, ink faded, words
illegible, it is only too apparent they have not escaped the
marks of age, damp, soot, and moths.

Here is No. IX., for example, a portion of a single leaf
of dirty paper—no more. And No. LII., loose leaves and
scraps gathered together under one cover; XXXVII., one of
the best known of all, with several of its leaves torn, and in
many places quite illegible. No. XL., five layers of different
origin stitched together in a vellum cover. And what shall we

say of the curious little volume only two inches long and one and a half in breadth and thickness, bound together with thongs in quite primitive fashion? On a page in the middle is written: "Is e so leabhar Neil Oig" ("This is Neil the Younger's book"). And here and there on some other musty records we find such entries as these: "Is mise Eoin o Albain" ("I am John from Scotland"), or "Is mise Domhnall a foghlumach Maigbeathadh" ("I am Donald Bethune the Scholar").

All are not equally tattered and faded. The handwriting in several is fresh and clear as on the day of production. It varies from the coarse and careless to the highly finished and artistic, from the merest daubs to the richly coloured and ornamental.

Yet to the superficial observer with no antiquarian tastes, there is little here to attract, the more because most of these torn and dirty fragments exhibit a language and orthography hard to decipher, and much harder to read and understand. It took the late Dr. Maclauchlan of Edinburgh five years to decipher and copy a single MS.—No. XXXVII., and he tells us pathetically that it was the hardest piece of work he was ever engaged in.

The interested spectator, on the other hand, if his eye happens to be directed to the obscure and tattered miscellany, naturally inquires, and learns to his surprise that this is the Scottish collection of Gaelic MSS., all that could be gathered into one place in this country of the vernacular MS. literature of the past. A swift inspection shows upwards of threescore documents, of which thirty-six at least are parchments, the rest paper or paper and parchment combined. Alongside lie later volumes—transcripts of tales, ballads, and other lore. A few of the parchments hail from the fourteenth century, but the majority were written in the fifteenth and sixteenth. The paper MSS. were all produced within the last 350 years, mainly in the end of the seventeenth and the first half of the eighteenth centuries, while the adjacent accretions of transcripts and books belonged to men who lived within the last 100 years.

It is easy to tell the tale of this assortment. Ireland, England, and the Continent had their rich collections long ago. With Scotland such a thing seems to have been an afterthought. Only in 1861 were these literary monuments of the past brought together and deposited as a kind of national treasury in the Advocates' Library, and this laudable result is due mainly to the energy and interest of Dr. Skene, author of *Celtic Scotland*, and formerly Historiographer-Royal in Edinburgh.

He knew of two collections fairly large and representative that had been made earlier, and exerted himself to have them united and housed where they might be reasonably accessible. These belonged, one to the Highland Society, the other to the Kilbride family.

The former was made in the opening years of the nineteenth century, while the battle still raged over the authenticity of Macpherson's Ossian. With Mr. Henry Mackenzie, author of the *Man of Feeling*, as their chairman, the Society instituted an inquiry into the whole question, and scoured the country far and near for Ossianic MS. literature. In this way they secured a good many documents, the greater number of which came from London through Macpherson's literary executor. It was well known that in his lifetime Macpherson had carried away from the North-West Highlands and Islands some very old literary MSS., which he afterwards deposited with his London publishers for public inspection. But so few cared to see them that the originals thus exhibited cannot now be identified.

It is highly probable that some of those which the Highland Society received from the Metropolis were among the number. The rest came to them from other quarters. Some were purchased, and the whole reported on in the Proceedings of 1805.

The history of the Kilbride [1] collection is even more fortuitous. A letter from Lord Bannatyne to the Chairman

---

[1] There are various Kilbrides in Scotland, several even in Lorn, but this one is in the island of Seil, near Easdale.

of the Society and Committee tells how it was first discovered. Acting on the suggestion of Lord Hailes, Bannatyne
when Sheriff of Bute, and accustomed to attend the Circuit
at Inverary, made inquiries among the Highland gentlemen
he met there regarding any fugitive Gaelic MSS. they might
happen to be cognisant of, and in this way there came into
his hands one of the Kilbride collection, belonging to Major
Maclachlan. It appears that from the time of the
Reformation, the Kilbride family had cultivated a taste for
Celtic antiquities, as a result of which they possessed a very
large number of Celtic documents, gleaned partly in the
Highlands and partly in Ireland. Following up the clue thus
incidentally found, the enthusiastic Sheriff obtained permis-
sion for a delegate " to take inspection and bring an account
of the MSS. in Major Maclachlan's possession." These
were found to number twenty-two, exclusive of five that were
lent. They are catalogued V. to XXXI. in the Edinburgh
Cabinet.

We need not dwell upon the subsidiary additions to this
original and double nucleus in the Advocates' Library. But
it may be noted, there are besides in the University Library
of Edinburgh, a Gaelic medical MS. ; one collection of poetry
made in the middle of the eighteenth century, by Jerome
Stone; another in the beginning of the nineteenth, by Irvine,
and a fragment of a Gaelic grammar. The Library of Scottish
Antiquaries also exhibits a Gaelic curio in the form of a
translation of the " Lilium Medicinæ " of Bernardus Gordonus,
a foreign physician. And counting the few extra productions
in private hands, these comprehend all the MS. literature of
the Gael now extant in Scotland, so far as known.

Not a satisfying sum-total by any means. The harvest
truly was plentiful but the gleaners were few, and this forlorn
remnant hardly does credit to our national prestige and
veneration for the past. It cannot compare either in number,
variety, antiquity, or content, with the rich assortments elsewhere, such as those in Ireland, England, and the Continent.
Yet this collection, such as it is, has a value of its own, and

in some important respects supplements the material of other more ancient and valued documents.

The wonder is that so many of these manuscripts have survived to tell their tale of dool, considering the haphazard way in which they have been preserved. There is something to be said for the apparent apathy and neglect, when we remember the stormy past, the national vicissitudes and convulsions that continued down almost to last century.

And how should our Scottish ancestors know that there was any purpose to be served in preserving books which nobody could read? The peculiar idiom and orthography had long since become obsolete. Until fifty years ago no scholar could interpret the scrolls, and the wiseacres of the past, no less than the multitude of illiterate clansmen, might well be pardoned if it never occurred to them that the brain of a modern critic would some day forge a key for these old-world hieroglyphics, and through the study of the derelict parchments, make a dead language speak.

Instances are on record of the fate of some luckless MSS., which serve to illustrate the doom of many more.

Before the Forty-five, for example, a valuable collection of old Gaelic poetry was made in Strathglass, which afterwards found its way to the Catholic College of Douay. The last heard of this vagrant volume was that the Principal, while yet a student there, saw the leaves of the mutilated document torn out to kindle the fire in their stove.

A similar vandalism overtook the library of the Macvurichs, seanachies of Clanranald, who had been accumulating material for seventeen generations, from the time of Muireach Albanach, about 1200. There were many parchments, according to the testimony of a recent illiterate descendant, and among them the Red Book made of paper, but none of these are now to be found, because, when deprived of their lands, his family lost their literary taste and zeal. He knew not what became of the parchments. Two or three he saw cut down by tailors to make measuring tapes, and although he himself fell heir to some after his father's death, being without education, he set no value upon them and they disappeared.

Dr. Skene has prepared a general catalogue of the Scottish collection.　But half of the documents have never been read or described.　No Zeuss or Zimmer has yet arisen in Scotland with leisure or patience enough to decipher them.

Strange that the cry " Made in Germany " should apply even to the key to the ancient Gaelic, that the Continent had to come to our aid to interpret our own literature, and that now, the key having been handed over, these remaining relics should continue, hieroglyphically locked in the land of their nativity.　Yet it is so.　With the exception of a few specimens culled here and there, we have no English rendering of some of the finest pieces of this MS. literature.

Though poor in history and law, and destitute of dramatic writings, the collection is fairly rich in the poetic, the heroic, the legendary, and more wonderful still, the medical.　The latter treatises have a quaint interest of their own, and offer a basis of comparison for measuring the progress in the medical department of science.　What would our modern savants, for example, think of the " Notes according to Jacques de Forli " ?　Even the old-fashioned doctor himself might be puzzled to get at their meaning.

Jacques de Forli says that there are two ways of administering an electuary ; according as it is intended for the vitals or the extremities.　For the extremities there is tria sandaili for the side, and diamargariton for the head, and pliris for the brain, and sweet electuary to strengthen the parts of the bladder, and diacostum in the folds of the diaphragm, and each of these is to be given before food, that they may affect the part at a distance from the stomach ; for the food prevents the moving of the electuary towards the parts which it is necessary to invigorate.

Dr. Kuno Meyer has described MS. XL. as one of the most important.　Its principal claim on our attention lies in the fact that it contains a considerable number of old texts, of which no other versions or no other equally old and good versions are known to exist.　The handwriting of the oldest part is of the fourteenth century.   Initial letters are coloured, and the contents are seven Aideda or Death-tales of the heroic cycle of early Irish legend.   It supplements the Book of Leinster by relating the death of Conchobar, who was hit in battle by a ball made of lime mixed with the brains of a slain foeman known as Mesgedra, and though the bullet could not be removed from his head, the wound was stitched with thread of gold to match his auburn hair.   Afterwards when debarred from physical exertion, an awful trembling shook creation, and on inquiring, the king learned from his Druids that Christ was pitilessly crucified that day.   Whereupon a great rage seized Conchobar for the iniquity thereof, and drawing his sword he rushed against a wood, attacking the trees till the wood was level.   And with the fury the brains of Mesgedra started out of his head, his own brains following after, so that he fell dead.

From the versions in LIII. and LVI., much valued by scholars, Dr. Whitley Stokes has published the Tale of the Sons of Uisneach (*Irische Texte :* Stokes and Windisch, Leipzig, 1887).

Specially interesting, from the purely Scottish point of view, are the three well-known literary monuments hailing from the Western Highlands, and they deserve more than a passing reference.

The first figures in the Advocates' Library as a MS. collection of Gaelic poetry taken down from oral recitation as early as 1512 to 1526.   It is known as "The Book of the Dean of Lismore," the accepted belief being that Sir James Macgregor, at that time Dean of Lismore in Argyllshire, and his brother Duncan were the compilers.

Originally it was brought into notice by John Mackenzie, Esq., of the Temple, London, literary executor of Macpherson, who gave it among the other documents to the Highland Society.   How it came into his hands or where it lay for the 300 years that elapsed between the Dean's time and the beginning of last century is not known.

The book, as it stands, consists of 311 quarto pages.

Several are amissing at the beginning and at the end. Many of the leaves are stained and almost illegible from the effects of damp. Others are worn by use and exposure. But apart from these defects, which are common to other codexes, the MS. differs from all the MSS. in the Scottish collection in two essential features. It is written in the current Roman hand of the period, and the spelling is phonetic.

There are two distinct handwritings, and thus apparently two compilers. On the lower margin of the 27th page stands the inscription :—

> Liber Domini Jacobi Macgregor Decani Lismoren,

the handwriting of which has a striking resemblance to that of the major part of the volume. And this is really all there is to show that the Dean was compiler.

The other Macgregor, whose name occurs on page 144, is for good reasons identified as his brother :—

> Duncha deyr aclyth Mac Dhowl vic Eone Reawych
> "Duncan (the 'deyr aclyth' is untranslatable), son of Dugald, son of John the Grizzled."

The book is of great interest on account of its age, orthography, and contents. It has a double value, as Dr. Skene has pointed out—linguistic and literary. Linguistic, because its peculiar orthography presents the language at the time in its aspect and character as a spoken language, and enables us to ascertain whether many of the peculiarities which now distinguish the Gaelic were in existence 400 years ago. Literary, because it contains poems attributed to Ossian, and to other poets prior to the sixteenth century which are not to be found elsewhere ; and thus presents to us specimens of the traditionary poetry current in the Highlands prior to that period, which are above suspicion, having been collected nearly 400 years ago, before any controversy on the subject had arisen.

In other words, we have here the oldest written Scottish Gaelic, except that in the Book of Deer, with numerous productions of the time antecedent to the Reformation, and some even of the fourteenth century, for comparison with our modern Gaelic. And we have the complete refutation of Dr. Johnson's bold assertion that the language had nothing written. "The Erse never was a written language," said that vigorous critic; "there is not in the world an Erse (that is, a Gaelic) MS. a hundred years old." Into what strange neglect had our literature fallen when such an emphatic dictum could be made on the housetops.

This one was at that time over 200 years old, and could it have been resurrected from its nameless obscurity would surely have satisfied the unconvinced and sceptical Doctor.

Voluminous and various are its contents, culled from about sixty-six different authors, the whole extending to 11,000 lines of Gaelic poetry, with 800 in the genuine Ossianic style. The pieces vary from half-a-dozen to a hundred lines. And a peculiarity of the Ossianic fragments in this MS. is the frequent introduction of St. Patrick, who is represented as holding dialogues with the bard. Seeing that in the poems of Macpherson the saint never emerges, it is surmised that he regarded all references to him as un-authentic, interpolations of later times, when the Church ideas and dogmas crept into vogue. The Dean's collection is divided naturally into two parts, one more ancient and untouched by Christian sentiment, the other more modern, and not free from ecclesiastical leaven. To the former category belong those poems superscribed "The author of this is Ossian," and of these the finest is the bard's eulogy of his father Finn. "The ideal here set forth is perfectly Homeric," wrote Professor Blackie; "Achilles in his best moments and most favourable aspect might have stood for it."

In its English rendering, which is poetically inferior to the original, it runs thus :—

> 'Twas yesterday week,
> I last saw Finn ;
> Ne'er did I see

A braver man ;
Teige's daughter's son,
A powerful King ;
My fortune, my light,
My mind's whole might.
Both poet and chief,
Braver than kings,
Firm chief of the Feinn
Lord of all lands,
Leviathan at sea,
As great on land,
Hawk of the air,
Foremost always,
Generous, just.
Despised a lie,
Of vigorous deeds,
First in song,
A righteous judge,
Firm his rule,
Polished his mien,
Who knew but victory,
Who is like him,
In fight or song ?
Resists the foe
In house or field.
Marble his skin,
The rose his cheeks,
Blue was his eye,
His hair like gold.
All men's trust,
Of noble mind,
Of ready deeds,
To women mild,
A giant he,
The field's delight.

Ne'er could I tell,
Though always I lived,
Ne'er could I tell,
The third of his praise,
But sad am I now
After Finn of the Feinn !

and so on.

As it is quite impossible to produce in English the euphonious effect of the peculiar rhythm of the original Gaelic, with its alliteration and vocalic concords, here is an example from the above description:—

Dean Text	Modern Version
Fa Filla fa flaa	Fa filidh, fa flath,
Fa ree er gire	Fa righ air gach righ,
Finn flah re no vane	Fionn flath righ nam Fiann,
Fa treat er gyt teir	Fa triath air gach tir,
Fa meille mor marre	Fa miol mor mará
Fa lowor er lerg	Fa luthmhor air leirg,
Fa schawok glan gei	Fa seabhag glan gaoithe,
Fa seit er gi carde	Fa saoi air gach ceird.
Fa hillanit carda	Fa h' oileamhnach ceirde
Fa m'kyt nor verve	Fa marcach nar mheirbh,
Fa hollow er zneit	Fa ullamh air gniomh,
Fa steit er gi scherm	Fa steidh air gach seirm,
Fa fer chart a wrai	Fa fior cheart a bhreith,
Fa tawicht toye	Fa tabhach tuaith,
Fa Ly'seich naige	Fa ionnsaigheach 'n aigh
Fa brata er boye.	Fa breadha air buaidh.

At page 87 there is a curious fragment on Tabblisk, supposed by some to be chess, by others backgammon :—

Ruinous is Tabblisk, few men but know it,
Of what I know myself, I have a little tale to tell,
On a certain day I was travelling through Foytle. The land,
Variegated, beautiful, pleasing. I came there at noon,
When a maiden of red lips met me in the town,
And asked me to join in one of these games ;
She produced a chess-board, etc.

Here follows the description of this game.

They made much of blood in those days, even as we do of heredity now :—

The blood of forty and three kings in the blood of the Great King,
The blood of many races is thy pure blood which we cannot name,
The blood of Arthur in thy gentle veins . . .
The blood of Conn of the two Conns beneath thy soft skin ;
The blood of Grant, as also of the race of Neil, etc.

It is quite interesting to note the names of some of the contributors to the Dean's book. They are so various in rank and character.

Of these Duncan Mor O'Daly was Abbot of Boyle in 1244. Some of his pieces have reference to persons and events in Irish history. One of them, beginning, " Mayst thou enjoy thy belt, O Cathal," gives a very full description of that ornamented article of attire and its adjuncts. There is another whose name has been preserved by tradition, namely, Muireach Albanach, and he has been claimed by Scottish Gaels as the first of the celebrated Macvurichs.

Four of the poems in the MS. are by Campbell, the Knight of Glenorchy, who fell in the battle of Flodden ; three by the Earl of Argyll, and other three by the Countess Isabella.

The compositions generally are very difficult to read, yet the book is not lacking in colour. Here are aphorisms from Phelim Macdougall, reflecting, no doubt, the fashionable virtues and vices and partialities of the age :—

> 'Tis not good to travel on Sunday,
> Not good to be of ill-famed race ;
> Not good to write without learning,
> Not good is an Earl without English.
> Not good is a sailor if old,
> Not good a priest with but one eye,
> Not good a parson if a beggar.
> Not good is a lord without a dwelling,
> Not good is a woman without shame,
> Not good is fighting without courage,
> Not good is entering a port without a pilot ;
> Not good is a maiden who backbites,
> Not good is neglecting the household dogs,
> Not good is disrespect to a father,
> Not good is the talk of the drunken,
> Not good is a knife without an edge,
> Not good is the friendship of devils ;
> And thy Son, oh Virgin most honoured,
> Though he has saved the seed of Adam,
> Not good for himself was the cross.

The Fernaig MS. is another Highland production that was not known in Johnson's day. In 1807 it was in the west of Ross-shire, at the place whose name it bears, and afterwards came into the possession of Dr. Skene. This collection was made between the years 1688 and 1693, in the country of the Macraes, in far Kintail, and breathes the spirit of the times, politically and religiously, as then reflected in Highland Jacobite circles.

The MS. consists of two paper volumes in brown pasteboard cover, containing 4200 lines of poetry. There are several leaves loose, and others blank, a few half pages written upon, and one folded in. The second part was never finished. In one place six leaves closely written on both sides have been neatly removed.

Like the Dean of Lismore's, the handwriting is in the current Roman character, and the spelling phonetic. The collection includes compositions by different authors within the area extending from South Argyll to the north of Sutherland, Bishop Carsewell being among the number. Some of the pieces date back to the beginning of the sixteenth century. Strange to say for a Highland gleaning, there is no love or drinking song. Wine and women have scant notice here. The Gaelic in great part is practically the dialect still spoken in Kintail and district.

Little is indicated of the history of the book or of the author in the text itself. But on the first page of volume I. occurs the significant and suggestive superscription :—

> Doirligh Loijn Di
> Skrijvig Lea Donochig
> Mack rah 1688.

Professor Mackinnon, adopting this clue, made careful search, and is satisfied that the writer was Duncan Macrae of Inverinate, chief of that name. In the course of his investigation, the professor alighted upon some curious and interesting facts, full apparently of local colour.

It appears there were two Duncan Macraes of some

note living on the shores of Loch Duich at that time. Big Duncan of Glenshiel, a warrior who fell at Sheriffmuir, and whose mighty claymore, said[1] to be preserved in the Tower of London as " the great Highlander's sword," with one terrible stroke cut through trooper and steed, ere he succumbed himself in the onslaught. The other, Donnachadh nam Piòs, or Duncan of the silver plate, so called from the magnificence of his table service, was our author. Born about 1640, in early life he studied in the University of Edinburgh, and was known as a man of unique ingenuity and mechanical skill. As evidence thereof it is said he had something to do with bringing the water into Edinburgh, and it is related how, on one occasion, a foreign vessel having got dismasted in passing through Kyle Rhea, he made a new mast for the craft by splicing pieces of wood together. For this the captain, deeply grateful, gave him the famous silver herring, which remained in the family for generations, and was reputed to attract the herring from far and near into Loch Duich.

The oak trees now at Inverinate he reared from French acorns.

Like his brother John, who graduated at the University, King's College, Aberdeen, on July 12th, 1660, Duncan possessed the bardic gift. Poems attributed in the MS. to "an certain harper" and " Tinkler" are, by good authorities, set down to his own Muse, these being simply *noms de plume.*

Cultured, liberal, and deeply religious, he was ecclesiastically an ardent Episcopalian, politically a vehement Jacobite. His wife, the heiress of Raasay, it appears, diddled him out of her property by conveying the title-deeds to a relative to keep the lands for her own clan. Blood was thicker than the marriage bond.

But in spite of this the Kintail chief prospered, and bought lands in Glen Affaric from the Chisholm. Like the passing of Arthur, his death was rather dramatic. He had gone to Strathglass, attended by a single follower, to settle

[1] Professor Mackinnon, in *Transactions of the Gaelic Society of Inverness*, vol. xi.

about this new property, and was returning with the papers in his possession. On coming to Dorisduan he found the Connag River in high flood, but ventured to cross, only to be carried away in the attempt. Unfortunately for him, his companion possessed the fatal gift of *or na h'Aoine*, by which, according to local belief, he could cause the death, if he wished, of any one seen by him crossing the stream on a Friday. And at this juncture the unhappy man, seeing his master battling with the flood, and unable to keep from looking at him, much less to render assistance, in his distress exercised his sinister gift, thereby drowning the poetic Duncan, his own chief.

The Fernaig MS., apart from other considerations, is of great value as representing the literary output of the seventeenth-century period in the Highlands, and so helping to fill the gap between the Dean of Lismore's time and the pregnant Forty-five.

One other very interesting relic of Highland MS. literature remains to be noticed. It is the Book of Clanranald, found in two MSS. known as the Red and the Black. The latter, a thick little paper codex strongly bound in black leather boards, is of the size of a New Testament and of the nature of a commonplace book, containing accounts of the families of the Macdonalds, and the exploits of the great Montrose, together with some of the poems of Ossian.

The history of the book is obscure. Many years ago Dr. Skene picked it up among some old Irish MSS. at a bookstall in Dublin, and, buying it, sent the fugitive back to the family of Clanranald, in whose possession it now is.

But of the two MSS. the Red is far and away the more famous, as it figured largely in the Ossianic controversy, and gives the Macdonald and Montrose histories fuller. On Macpherson's visit to the West he received this MS., by consent of Clanranald, from Nial Macvurich, and it was only after Macpherson's death that the present Red Book was restored. Authorities are not certain that this is the real original, but Clanranald believes that it is, and the editors of *Reliquiæ Celticæ* are of the same opinion.

Since its return it has been much consulted by Ossianic inquirers, as well as by the historians of the country. A transcript and translation, not very accurate, were made of the historical parts early in last century. Sir Walter Scott made use of these in his notes, *Lord of the Isles*, and Mark Napier in his *Montrose*, to throw light upon the obscurer points of Highland conduct in that great chief's campaign. In later times a better rendering has been given by the great Irish scholar, O'Curry, who translated the history for Dr. Skene's *Celtic Scotland*.

Both MSS., the Red and the Black, are closely allied and supplement each other. The only English in the former is a satire on Bishop Burnet, whereas nearly the whole of the last half of the latter is in that language. The writers were the Macvurichs, hereditary bards of the Clanranald chiefs, who traced their descent from Muireach Albanach. The early history of the Macdonalds, down to about 1600, was probably composed by successive members of this line, but the record of the Montrose wars and following events is evidently the work of Nial Macvurich, whose life extended from the reign of Charles the First beyond Sheriffmuir. It may have been written prior to 1700. Its chief purpose is to vindicate the Gael in his marvellous exploits under Montrose. Here Alasdair Macdonald and not the brilliant Lowland leader is hero.

Needless to say, besides Ossianic fragments, old as the *Ages of the Feinn* and *Cnoc an Air*, the MSS. contain genealogies, chronologies, history, poetry, geography, grammar, and various disconnected jottings.

A most curious production is the genealogy of Clanranald as far back as Adam, often with name and date, and some of the names are portentously long.

The Macdonald history begins with the superscription, "The age of the World at the time the sons of Milé came into Ireland 3500" (that is, 1700 B.C.), and in the opening sentence announces that Amergin Whiteknee was poet and historian and judge to them, and the first Gaelic author.

There is a wonderful prose poem on page 210 of the Red Book, on the " Army and Arming of the Last Lord of the Isles," part of which is worth quoting for the way in which it hits off the characteristics of the clans, and the graphic description it gives of the armour of this supreme King of the Gael.

And they were in well arranged battalions, namely, the proud, luminous countenanced, finely-hued, bold, right-judging, goodly, gifting Clan Donald ; the ready, prosperous, routing, very bold, right judging Clanranald ; the attacking, gold shielded Clan Alister ; the protecting, firm, hardy, well-enduring Macphees ; the fierce, strong men, the Maclachlans ; the lively, vigorous, liberally-bestowing, courageous, austere, brown-shielded Macdougalls ; the cheerful, chief-renowned, battle-harnessed Camerons ; the inimical, passionate, hardy Macneils ; the manly, sanguinary, truly noble Mackinnons; the fierce, undaunted, great-feated Macquarries ; the brave, defending, foraging, valiant, heroic, ale-abounding Mackenzies ; the active, spirited, courteous, great-bestowing Clan Morgan (or Mackay) and the men of Sutherland came as a guard to the Royal Prince ; and the powerful, lively, active, great-numbered, arrogant Mackintoshes in a very large powerful force around the Chief of Clan Chattan in active, hardy battalions with their champions. There came along with these warriors earls, princely high chiefs, knights, chiefs, lords, barons and yeomen, at one particular place, to the noble son of Alexander, and these numerous, rejoicing, heroes, and powerful, active, fierce, sounding hosts gathered together.

This is the manner in which they appointed the powerful, fierce, active, mighty-deeded, white-armoured, supreme King of the Gael, viz., the terror-striking, leopard-like, awful, sanguinary, opposing, sharp-armed, fierce, attacking, ready, dexterous, powerful, steady, illustrious, full-subduing, furious, well-prepared, right-judging Earl, as he received on him the armour of conflict and strife against every tumult, that is, his fine tunic, beautifully embroidered, of fine textured satin, ingeniously woven by ladies and their daughters ; and that good tunic was put upon him.

A silk jerkin which was handsome, well-fitting, rich, highly-embroidered, beautiful, many-coloured, artfully-done, gusseted, corded, ornamented with the figures of foreign birds, with branches of burnished gold, with a multiplicity of all kinds of embroidery on the sides of the costly jerkin. That jerkin was put upon him to guard him against dangers.

A coat of mail which was wide, well-meshed, light, of substantial steel, beautifully-wrought, gold-ornamented, with brilliant Danish gems. Such a mail coat as that was possessed by the lithe Luga of Long Arms.

We may conclude this brief account of the Book of Clanranald by a specimen of its poetry—an elegy for Sir Norman Macleod, which Nial Macvurich made. It illustrates how to the Gael, when in grief, all nature seems to suffer and reciprocate his feelings; and the mighty portents associated in the olden days with the birth or demise of a chief.

> A death of the deepest anguish it is
> To his friends and his followers;
> Over his grave as they perform a *neachd*
> They have their turn at the tomb which we cannot get.
>
> The women of every country are in sadness,
> Also their heroes and ecclesiastics;
> Their faithful freemen are in grief,
> The extremity of severe affliction is among them.
>
> The hospitality, the pure generosity,
> The joyous exclamation, the ready welcome,
> They have all gone with him into the earth,
> For an age after him there will be but lamentation.
>
> We are in want of gold and cattle,
> Since the Chief of Rushgarry died;
> The learned men since the hour of his death,
> Have forsaken their havens of watching.
>
> Flaming troubles pervaded the stars of heaven,
> They poured forth the showers of lightning;
> The hills are not illumined by day,
> Their grief for him mastered them.
>
> The rivers are rising over the woods,
> There is a scarcity of fish in the bays;
> The fruitage is not found in the land,
> The roaring of the sea is very coarse.

At the last hours of his death,
Dreadful tokens appeared to us ;
Foreboding clouds which denoted grief,
Were of gold colour in the Northern region.

Such is our heritage of Celtic MSS. in this country, and, in view of the paucity of these existing relics, may we not reiterate the lines of Horace ?—

Full many a chief and warrior lived
Ere Agamemnon saw the day,
Of whom no record hath survived
The glories that have passed away.
Unwept, unsung, unknown they lie,
For want of hallowed Poesy.

CHAPTER VIII

THE MYTHOLOGICAL CYCLE

A rich and abundant saga literature—Three leading periods or cycles—The myths and folk-tales—Problems to men of science—The philologists and anthropologists take opposite sides—Their theories—Attitude of the annalists and romancists of Ireland—Their craze for genealogy—Early settlers in Erin—Advent of the Milesians or Gaels—The Three Sorrows of Gaelic Storydom : (1) " The Tragedy of the Children of Tuireann " ; (2) The fascinating " Aided of the Children of Lir " ; (3) Story of " Deirdre and the Sons of Uisneach "—Extraordinary interest evinced in this saga—Marvellous output of texts and translations.

WITH the arrival of Christianity and its literary promulgators, St. Patrick and St. Columba, authentic history may be said to have begun, first in Ireland, and then in Scotland. Before the fifth century there existed a rich and abundant saga literature transmitted by oral tradition. But even the very oldest of the tales we now have, could hardly have been written down in MS. form before the seventh or eighth century. Such is the general belief of scholars who have sifted and examined the earliest records.

The mass of saga carried over from pagan times, goes back over ages untold and immemorial. And yet it is found to sort out under great leading periods or cycles, three of which seem to stand out distinct and pre-eminent. These are known as the Mythological, the Heroic, and the Ossianic.

Roughly speaking, the Mythological cycle, beginning away back in the vague and dim past, stretches to near the beginning of the Christian era. The other cycles follow, filling up the 400 odd years that elapse before the dawn of written history.

The mythological stories are fewer than the rest, and of course more absurd and unintelligible. Most of them are found in O'Clery's *Leabhar Gabhala, or Book of Invasions,* 1630, of which the more important MSS. are the Books of Leinster and Ballymote. Their chief interest lies in the light they throw upon the early religious ideas of the Celt.

In a practical age like our own, most people are impatient of ancient myth and fairy tales. They seem so utterly unreal, absurd, and impossible, that it is hard to conceive how any sane mortal could have given them credence for one moment. And yet so universal are such stories among every race of mankind, and so credible and far-reaching in their influence in early times, that they have survived when multitudes of recorded facts have perished. They show that men, and especially primitive men, have the same kind of thoughts, desires, fancies, habits, and institutions all the world over.

The myths and folk-tales have a wonderful similarity, reappearing in different guise but in substance the same, among the most varied races and peoples, so that savages to-day in different continents and islands have beliefs and customs corresponding to those which stagger us in the sagas of our own Celtic ancestors, and quite as fantastic.

It is this which lends the fascination to students of comparative mythology and to the folk-lorist. What seems arrant nonsense and the height of absurdity to ordinary intelligence, lures them on to seek in these wild stories for the origins of belief, for the early conceptions which influenced men in their religion and in their life. Removed from primitive man by centuries of progress, and ruled as we are by a scientific view of the world, it is hard for us to put ourselves at the centre of vision and standpoint of our early ancestors, to whom the facts of life were more confused than they appear to us, and in a manner more uncanny and mysterious. Like the savage of to-day, judging from their myths, they conceived all things as animated and personal, capable of endless interchange of form. Men might become beasts, beasts might change into men. Even the gods appeared in human or bestial forms. Animals, plants, stones, earth, winds and waters, spoke and acted like human beings, changing their shapes accordingly.

This is the very essence of myth and fairy tale. Or as Professor Max Müller has expressed it, "What makes mythology mythological in the true sense of the word is what is utterly unintelligible, absurd, strange, or miraculous."

What appears most incredible and repugnant, the ugly blots and scars of these narratives are just the problems to men of science. How to account for them? How to explain their origin? Over this, contending schools are constantly engaged in a kind of guerilla warfare. Leaving the archæologists to pursue their own studies among the material "survivals," the philologists and anthropologists take opposite sides each in defence of his own particular theory.

Briefly stated, the difference between them is this : the philologists maintain that language—language as it were in a state of disease—is the great source of the mythology of the world. Professor Max Müller held this view and gave it a widely accepted vogue. The ugly scars he explained as due to the old words and popular sayings lingering on in a language after their original harmless and symbolic meanings had been lost. Thus what might have been originally a poetical remark about nature, might in process of time be interpreted colloquially and become an obscene, brutal, or vulgar myth. To go no further afield than the Hebrew sacred writings, when we think of an impassioned apostrophe to the sun, and the subsequent popular legend that the sun and the moon stood still, we see that the philologist argument is not without force and cogency.

Yet the anthropologists are more in the line of evolution, for they maintain that mythology on the whole represents an old stage of thought, from which civilised men have slowly emancipated themselves. This is also the view of Mr. Andrew Lang, who recently contributed a work on the subject. The scars so-called are the remains of that kind of taste, fancy, customary law, and incoherent speculation that prevail in human nature in its primitive barbarian state. And indeed when we contemplate the credulity, superstition, and readiness to accept the grotesque and fabulous, that dominate such inhabitants even of a civilised country as are kept ignorant and isolated, this theory seems to point to the main source of myth and fairy tale.

As in the early literature of Greece the gods and heroes are mixed up, so in the records of the Gael. But the annalists and romancists of Ireland, who had a passion for writing history, evidently had no inkling of this. The thought of mythology was far enough removed from their way of thinking, and such floating tales and personages and events as they found wafted towards them on the stream of tradition they took for actual fact. At any rate, they wove them into the story of the past of their nation in such a way as to lead us to believe that the mythical beings were as real to them as the kings and warriors of their own age. And these historians had quite a craze for genealogy ; never satisfied unless they could trace their chiefs or heroes and ancestors up to Adam, which they invariably succeed in doing, bridging the gaps with very fertile ingenuity.

Thus the last great chasm to be spanned in the line of pedigree is the Deluge—to surmount which was a work more intricate and needing more skill in a manner than the Forth Bridge ; for if they could once connect with Noah, the Bible record does the rest.

The feat is accomplished, set down by the annalists of the Middle Ages with all the plausibility of sober fact. Forty days before the Flood, the Lady Cæsair, niece or granddaughter of Noah—it is immaterial which—with fifty girls and three men came to Ireland. This, we are to understand, was the first invasion or conquest of that country. All these were drowned in the Deluge, except Finntan, the husband of the lady, who escaped by being cast into a deep sleep, in which he continued for a year, and when he awoke he found himself in his own house at Dun Tulcha. It is charming to note with what precision and *sangfroid* names are quoted in this legended history. At Dun Tulcha he lived throughout many dynasties down to the sixth century of our era, when he appears for the last time with eighteen companies of his descendants engaged in settling a boundary dispute. Being the oldest man in the world, he was *ipso facto* the best informed regarding ancient landmarks.

After the Flood various peoples in succession stepped on to the platform of Irish history. First the Partholans, then the Nemedians, Firbolgs, Tuatha de Danann, and last of all the Milesians, thus carrying the chronology down to the time of Christ. From the arrival of the earliest of these settlers, the Fomorians or "Sea Rovers" are represented as fighting and harassing the people. Sometimes in conjunction with the plague, at other times with the Firbolgs and Gaileoin and Fir-Domnann, they laid waste the land. The Partholans and Nemedians were early disposed of. And then appeared from the north of Europe, or from heaven, as one author says, the Tuatha de Danann, who at the great battle of Moytura South overcame the Firbolgs, scattering them to the islands of Aran, Islay, Rathlin, and the Hebrides, and afterwards defeating the Fomorians at Moytura North, thus gaining full possession of the land. Much of this fabulous history is taken up with these early struggles between the Fomorians and the Tuatha de Danann, of whom Breas and Lugh of the Longhand, and Dagda are the great heroes.

At length from Spain and the East came the last invaders, known under various names, as the Milesians, the Scots, or Gaels. They are the ancestors of our modern race, called Milesians from an ancestor Milé, and Gaels or Gaidels from an ancestor Gadelus. When they arrived at Tara, a vast army from over the seas, they met the three kings and queens of the Tuatha. The latter complained that they were taken by surprise, and entreated the Milesians to embark again on their ships that they might have a fair chance of opposing them. This they did, retreating for " nine waves " on the sea. But on facing about, lo ! Ireland was not to be seen. The Tuatha de Danann by their enchantment had made the island as small as a pig's back, and therefore invisible from the ships. Besides, they raised a violent storm with clouds and darkness. Many Milesian ships were wrecked, and a crisis was only averted by their leader, Amergin, who was also a Druid, pronouncing a Druidic prayer or oration, addressed it would seem to the Tuatha, when the storm immediately ceased and they landed in peace. After some skirmishes, the Tuatha eventually retire to the Land of Promise, the country of the *Sìdh*— fairy mounds, where in the popular lore they were till lately, taking considerable interest in the affairs of their quondam conquerors.

Druidism, it will be seen, enters largely into all these ancient contests, the opposing parties using spells as well as blows.

The Milesians we are supposed to have some knowledge of — with more or less of their blood in our veins. They are regarded as the main body of the Gaelic people. But who were the Tuatha de Danann and the Fomorians ? Personifications of the forces of nature, or the Gaelic gods of the upper and lower worlds, argue writers on mythology. As Zeus, Poseidon, Pluto, and the rest of the Greek deities rule over the heavens, the earth, the sea, and the shades, so do the Tuatha, the pagan gods of the Gaelic people ; while the Fomorians, vicious and troublesome as they were, may in their origin be none other than the sea powers—the rough chaotic tumult of the Atlantic Ocean, against which in the west of Ireland the various settlers had to contend.

But the early introduction of Christianity, throwing the pagan gods and traditions, as it did, into the limbo of perdition, renders it very difficult for us now to arrive at any definite and certain conclusions on these matters.

The literary interest of the mythological cycle centres largely in the " Three Sorrows of Story-telling," two of which belong exclusively to it, the third to the Cuchulinn cycle. Though connected with the period of the Tuatha de Danann, it is well to remember that these two as well as the third were actually written later than the earliest of the heroic tales.

First comes the " Aided or Tragedy of the Children of Tuireann." It is mentioned by Cormac in his Glossary (ninth or tenth century), and by Flann of Monasterboice (ob. 1056). The story is partially told in the Book of Lecain (cir. 1416), and is found in several MSS., including No. LVI. of the Scottish collection. O'Curry, O'Duffy, and Joyce have each at various times edited and published it with translation ; the first in the *Atlantis*, vol. iv. ; the second for the Society for the Preservation of the Irish Language in Dublin, 1888 ; and the third in his *Old Celtic Romances*, London, 1879.

The scene opens near the ramparts of Tara, in the reign of Nuada of the silver arm. Two handsome, young, and well-formed men are seen approaching. Accosted by the doorkeeper, who had only one eye, they announced them-selves as physicians, and subsequently offered to put his cat's eye in the place of the one he had lost. This done, the substitute proved convenient and inconvenient, for when he desired to take sleep or repose, then the eye would start at the squeaking of the mice, the flying of the birds, and the motion of the reeds ; whereas, when he wished to watch a host or an assembly the same organ continued in deep sleep. Similarly, but to better effect, the king was fitted with a new arm, namely, that of the swineherd, of equal length and thickness with his own. The bones only were removed from its original owner and set by the one leech, while the other sought herbs to put flesh and muscle upon it.

This introduction apparently has no bearing upon the story proper, which now begins.

The Fomorians who dwelt in Lochlann laid Ireland

under heavy tribute. Whoever paid not the tax had his nose cut off. One day, when the King of Sire held a fair upon the hill of Balar, the Tuatha de Danann, who were there assembled, saw a goodly host coming towards them. This was Lugh Lamhfhada and the fairy cavalcade from the Land of Promise. Lugh was mounted on a steed which was as swift as the bleak, cold wind of spring, and sea and land were equal to her, and her rider was not killed off her back. When the troop came where the king was they presently saw a grim and ill-looking band advancing towards them— eighty-one Fomorian ambassadors come to lift the tax. Lugh arose and slaughtered them, leaving only nine to bring back the news. Incensed, the Fomorians, under Breas, the son of Balor of the mighty blows, resolved to invade Ireland and take revenge on Lugh. "And after ye have overcome him and his people," said Balor to the departing warriors, "put your cables round this island of Erin which gives us so much trouble, and tie it to the stems of your ships; then sail home, bringing the island with you, and place it on the north side of Lochlann, whither none of the Tuatha will ever follow it." Thus the Irish difficulty is not of yesterday, and Balor proposed to settle it in a very drastic way.

Lugh heard of their arrival and sent to assemble the fairy cavalcade from every place where they were. Cian, his father, traversing the plain of Muirtheimhne on this quest suddenly encountered three warriors—the sons of Tuireann, with whom, though relatives, he was at deadly feud. The only ruse he could think of for defence in this awkward plight was to strike himself with a Druidical wand into the shape of a pig, and join the herd of swine he saw feeding near him. But the brothers detected the trick, and Brian the eldest, with one swift stroke of a magic wand transformed the others into two slender fleet hounds, who gave tongue ravenously upon the trail of the Druidical pig. While the latter made for a wooded grove Brian's spear transfixed her in the chest, and the pig screamed in human speech, imploring quarter. The only concession

granted the unhappy beast was that she might return into
her original shape and therein get killed. In this Cian had
his revenge, for, instead of the *eric* of a pig, he assured them
they would now be liable for an *eric* altogether oppressive,
because of his rank.

Six times they buried the body and the earth refused
it, but the seventh time they put it under the sod the earth
took to it.

Meanwhile Lugh had joined issue with the Fomorians
and got the victory. And after the slaughter and triumph
of the battle, missing his father, he set out with the fairy
cavalcade to find out what had befallen him. When lo! as
he crossed the scene of his sire's sad fate, the earth spoke to
him and said :—

"Great was the jeopardy in which your father was here,
O Lugh, when he saw the children of Tuireann, for he was
obliged to go into the shape of a pig ; nevertheless they
subsequently killed him in his own shape."

The body was thereupon dug up and examined. Lugh
kissed it three times, uttering words of lamentation, and
ending with a mournful lay.

"Cian was again placed in the grave after that, his
tombstone was erected over his tomb, his dirge was sung,
and his name inscribed in Ogam."

And now it will be ill with the sons of Tuireann.
Having reached Tara, and as he sat in honourable position
next the King of Erin, Lugh looked round on the miscreants
and ordered the Chain of Attention of the Court to be shaken,
that all present might listen. Of the entire company the
children of Tuireann were the best in agility and dexterity ;
they were the handsomest as well as the most honoured. So
Lugh approached the subject of the death of his father and
the vengeance due with circumspection and inquiry. Brian
denied : "Nevertheless," he said, speaking for himself and
his brothers, "we shall give *eric* for him to thee, as though
we had done the act."

Thereupon, in presence of all, Lugh announced the

compensation required, "namely, three apples, the skin of a pig, a spear, two steeds, a chariot, seven pigs, a whelp, a cooking spit, and three shouts on a hill." A mere trifle this *eric* may seem, but it turned out afterwards, when the special items demanded were characterised, that there was as much hazard involved in getting any one of them as there was for the youthful David in another Court, and for another king, to get one hundred foreskins of the Philistines. Brian suspected treachery, but he accepted the bill, and with his two brothers went forth to seek the payment. Daring feats of valour have to be faced to get those wonderful apples from the Garden of Hesperides, and the skin of the pig of the King of Greece, and the well-poisoned spear of the King of Persia, and all the rest. But they got a loan of Lugh's curach to ferry them over the wave wherever they wished, and their sister Eithne, going down to the harbour, uttered a lay over them as the warrior band put out from the beautiful and clearly-defined borders of Eire.

Success crowned their extraordinary adventures, much to the chagrin of Lugh, who sent a spell of magic after them to bring them back. They present him with their spoils, taken in strange and distant lands, only to be reminded that the full measure of the *eric* has yet to be discharged. On the morrow they went to their ship, and the maiden, with moist eyes, sees them off once more. Again they are successful. Thereafter, in attempting the last feat of all, namely, to give three shouts on the hill of Midkena in Lochlann, they got severely wounded by the spears of its champion guardians. And on their return they despatched their aged father, Tuireann, to Tara with all haste to seek from Lamhfhada the gifted skin to relieve them, but Lugh refused ; and the life went forth from the brothers three at the same time.

Their father sang their death song, and "after that lay, Tuireann fell upon his children and his soul left him ;" and they were interred, parent and sons, and, it is even alleged, sister too, all in one grave.

The "Tragedy of the Children of Lir" is the second in order of the Three Sorrows. Though set in the earliest cycle, it is not represented in any of the ancient MSS. The oldest as yet known to contain it is No. XXXVIII. of the Scottish collection, written at the latest in the early seventeenth century. There is a copy also in MS. LVI. All the other copies, which are pretty numerous, belong to the eighteenth and nineteenth centuries, and are in the MSS. of Dublin and the British Museum. Monsieur H. d'Arbois de Jubainville in his survey noted no less than seventeen of these. The comparative lateness of the records has led Mr. Alfred Nutt to surmise that this story may simply be the Gaelic version of the "Seven Swans" *märchen*, once common in the country, and worked up by a monk of the sixteenth century — a suggestion Professor Mackinnon thinks not at all unlikely. O'Curry published the tale with a translation in the *Atlantis*, and Dr. P. W. Joyce included it in his *Old Celtic Romances*.

The incidents of this once very popular tale are as follows : In a conflict with the Milesians the Tuatha de Danann were defeated, and found it necessary to deliberate on the policy they must pursue and the king they should elect. Various candidates are eligible, but Bodhbha Dearg is ultimately chosen. In high dudgeon, Lir, who sought the exalted position for himself, left the assembly and returned to his own *Sìdh*. So far from retaliating, the new ruler, when Lir's wife died, sent for him and offered him his choice of three of the most beautiful and best-instructed maidens in all Erin. He took the eldest of these sisters and married her. But she died, leaving four handsome children, a daughter and three sons. A second time Lir had his choice, and Eva, sister number two, came as spouse to his home at *Sìdh* Fionnachaidh. A devoted stepmother she proved to the children, till by and by green-eyed jealousy infected her. She saw that their father would often rise from his bed in the dawn of the morning and go to theirs to fondle them. And fancying herself slighted, " she lay in bed a whole year filled with gall and brooding mischief."

The outcome of this passion was a plot to do away with the children, whom for the purpose she enticed to a lonely spot and bribed her servants to slay. This they refused to do, and although she made the attempt herself she had not the nerve to execute it. " Her woman's weakness prevented her." Yet she had her revenge in a curious way. She got the children to bathe in Lake Dairbhreach, and once there, by Druidical enchantment she transformed them into four beautiful snow-white swans. As such for 300 years they swim back and fore on the smooth lake, then for 300 in the Sruth na Maoile (off Kintyre), and 300 more at Iorus Domnann and Innis Gluaire, in the Western Sea. And in no way could they escape their bird life " until the union of Larguen, a prince from the north, with Becca, a princess from the south," or as the Irish version adds, "until Talchend Adzehead (that is, St. Patrick) shall come to Erin, bringing the light of a pure faith, and until ye hear the voice of the Christian bell."

The vindictive Eva repented her evil deed, but could not undo the mischief. To ameliorate their lot, she granted her enchanted victims the use of their Gaelic speech, of their human reason, and the power of singing sweet, plaintive, fairy music, surpassing all known in the world in its harmony and soothing influence.

Swift retribution ultimately overtook this once beautiful woman ; for when the king heard of her cruel deed, he asked her "what shape of all others on the earth, or above the earth, or under the earth she most abhorred ? To which she replied, " A demon of the air." " A demon of the air you shall then be to the end of time," said the angry Bodhbha Dearg.

Meanwhile the centuries roll over the children of Lir on the peaceful Lake Dairbhreach, not altogether without sunshine, since the people—Milesians and Tuatha de Danann alike—were wont to crowd on its shore to hear their music and watch their graceful movements. But the time came when they found themselves in " the current of Mull," tossed on the stormy seas twixt Erin and Alba, and here they had to dree their weird with much suffering for another cycle ; sometimes separated from each other in the storm and darkness ; at other times almost frozen to death on Carraig-nan-ròn. Hapless birds ! the slow moving ages bring them to the third stage, which is pretty much a repetition of their experiences in the second. For in the Western Ocean round Glora Isle they are still tormented by the restless wave and the cold and vicious winds of winter, till their three hundred years therein are accomplished.

And then at last St. Kemoc comes ; they hear the sound of the Christian bell and their spell is broken. Thereafter the children of Lir, no longer swans, receive Christian baptism and die. For rashly attempting to take the birds prematurely away from his protection one of the MSS. asserts that St. Kemoc cursed King Larguen with righteous energy. And after their death, in the manner of the previous interments, he buried these ill-starred children all in one grave, sang their death-song, performed their funeral rites, raised their tomb, and wrote their names in Ogam. Thus ended their chequered career, which lasted well-nigh a millennium.

The third Sorrow of Gaelic storydom, that of " Deirdre and the Sons of Uisneach," does not belong, strictly speaking, to the mythological cycle ; yet it is prehistoric and mythical in every other respect, though devoid of the absurd and fantastical elements so characteristic of the other two. Indeed it may have sprung, as Mr. J. F. Campbell maintains, from some Indo-European romance, the common heritage in one form or other of the Aryan family from India to Ireland. The tale is at once the oldest and most famous of the three Aideds, and must have had a wide vogue in early times, for it is mentioned in so ancient an authority as the Book of Leinster, that it was one of the *primscela* that the bards were bound to know. Many versions of the saga exist, but chiefly in ballad form.

The oldest and shortest is that in the Book of Leinster,

twelfth century, with which may be classed one in the Yellow Book of Lecain, fourteenth century, and in the Egerton MS., British Museum. The best and fullest version, now published, is generally held to be that obtained from MSS. LIII. and LVI. of the Scottish collection, the former a vellum of the fifteenth century. In addition to various other documents in the Advocates' Library, such as Nos. V. and XLVIII., which contain fragments, Monsieur H. d'Arbois de Jubainville found seventeen copies of the legend in later MSS. in London and Dublin.

The extraordinary interest evinced in this saga is not confined to ancient or medieval times, but continues unabated down to our own day, if we may judge by the attention it has received at the hands of authors, editors, and translators. Nearly every foremost scholar of the nineteenth century has dealt with it in text, or notes, and translation.

Of many and various publications in modern times, the following will suffice to show the place it holds in Celtic literature. The texts, printed sometimes with notes and translation, are usually of different versions.

O'Flanagan, *Transactions of the Gaelic Society of Dublin*, 1808 ; O'Curry, *Atlantis*, vol. iii. 1860, from Yellow Book of Lecain ; Campbell, *Leabhar na Feinne*, 1872 ; Windisch, *Irische Texte*, vol. i. Leipzig, 1880 ; Dr. Whitley Stokes, *Irische Texte*, vol. ii. Leipzig, 1887, the former from Book of Leinster, the latter from MSS. LIII. and LVI., Advocates' Library. Dr. Cameron's *Reliquiæ Celticæ*, also from MS. LVI. Windisch, O'Curry's and O'Flanagan's texts, reprinted *Gaelic Journal*, Dublin, 1882-84. Carmichael, *Transactions of the Gaelic Society of Inverness*, vol. xiii. 1887, an admirable folk-lore version taken down in the Western Isles from oral recitation. Angus Smith, in his *Loch Etive and Sons of Uisneach*, treats it fictionally in dialogue form, 1879.

Keating tells the tale in his *History of Ireland*. It is found in part in the Welsh story of Peredur, taken apparently from a fifteenth century MS. Mr. Joseph Jacobs has given in English dress, in *Celtic Fairy Tales*, an abridged account from Carmichael's version. Of French translators, H. d'Arbois de Jubainville, M. Georges Dottin, and M. Louis Ponsinet may be mentioned. Of poetical English versions there is no lack. Macpherson treated it specially in Darthula, Sir James Ferguson dramatised it, Dr. Joyce published it in America (Deirdre: Boston and Dublin), and Drs. Todhunter and Douglas Hyde have given other renderings. Mr. T. W. Rolleston made it the subject of the Prize Cantata of the Fèis Ceoil in Dublin in 1897.

Truly a marvellous output of texts and translations, rivalling any in the whole range of our Gaelic literature. And the above catalogue does not by any means exhaust the list. The wonder is that the saga should be found in remote and outlying corners of the Highlands floating by oral tradition down to our own time. Fletcher got a version about 1750, Irvine took down part of the verse about 1801 from a fox-hunter on Tayside, Carmichael from an old Macneill in Barra in 1871. The story is of additional interest to us because it is laid partly in Ireland and partly in Scotland, among that beautiful scenery around Loch Etive so well known to native and tourist.

The story opens at Emain Macha, or Emania, where, with the nobles of Ulster, King Conchobar is feasting in the house of Feidhlim the bard. During the entertainment Feidhlim's wife gave birth to a daughter; and Cathbad the Druid forthwith prophesied that the child would grow up "a maiden fair, tall, long-haired, for whom champions would contend." Her lips would be cherry-red over pearly teeth; her lovely form the envy of high queens. Deirdre, the Druid named her, and thrilled the company by announcing that her queenly beauty would yet involve the province in heavy woes.

All the nobles present, instantly wished to circumvent such destiny by having the child put to death. Conchobar intervened: "Let not that be done," said he; "I will take her with me and send her to be reared that she may become my own wife." Deirdre was accordingly removed and kept apart in a fortress, seeing no one but her tutor and nurse and Lebarcham, the king's *banchainte* or conversation woman. Shot up at length into the fair maiden of Cathbad's prediction, she happened one snowy day to be looking out, when she observed her *oide* (tutor) killing a calf, and a raven came to drink the blood. "Dear to me," she exclaimed, "would be the man who would have the three colours yonder on him, his hair like the raven, his cheek like the blood, and his body like the snow." "Such an one is Naois, son of Uisneach," suggested the *banchainte*.

They met, Deirdre and he. A kinsman of the king and one of three gifted brothers, this Naois stood head and neck taller than any man in Erin, and peerless in strength, courage, and manly beauty. When he or his brothers sang, the cows gave two-thirds additional milk and people were enchanted. Their prowess was such that the three together could meet all Ulster in arms.

Deirdre adored Naois, and proposed that they twain should elope. At first he refused, but bewitched by her charms and entreaties he yielded. The brothers went off, taking their followers, 150 men with their wives and greyhounds. For a time they were pursued round Erin to Ballyshannon, Howth, Rathlin, till they sought refuge in Alba and sailed for Loch Etive. From that beautiful centre they made many excursions inland, living in hunting booths, chasing the deer on the mountains, assisting the King of Alba, who needed their help, and living joyous and free ; a most romantic life, full of incident and full of happiness.

After a time Conchobar hatched a plot to lure them back. First he approached Cuchulinn and Conall Cearnach to undertake a mission. But these champions, suspecting treachery, gave blunt refusal. At length Fergus Mac Roich was induced to go, not without misgivings. When he arrived with his two sons and bargeman, Naois and Deirdre were sitting together in their hunting booth playing at chess. Fergus went into the glen and raised his sweet-voiced warning cry, after the manner of a hunter. Naois heard the

sound and said, " I hear the cry of a man of Erin." Deirdre
dissimulated at first, "That was not the cry of a man of
Erin but the cry of a man of Alba." Afterwards she
explained it was because of a dream she had had, which she
felt foreboded evil. The emissaries spend the night with
them and win over Naois.

Next morning they all sail away, returning to Erin, and
as the land fades from her view, Deirdre with mingled regret
and presentiment, sings or recites a beautiful lay, describing
the shores of Loch Etive and the charms of the life she led
in the glens. The following rendering is from Dr. Skene, the
few verses here quoted indicating the feeling and passion of
the old lyric :—

> Glen Etive ! O Glen Etive !
> There I raised my earliest house ;
> Beautiful its woods on rising
> When the sun fell on Glen Etive.
>
> Glen Orchy ! O Glen Orchy !
> The straight glen of smooth ridges ;
> No man of his age was so joyful
> As Naois in Glen Orchy.
>
> Glenlaidhe ! O Glenlaidhe !
> I used to sleep by its soothing murmurs ;
> Fish and flesh of wild boar and badger,
> Was my repast in Glenlaidhe.
>
> Glendaruadh ! O Glendaruadh !
> I love each man of its inheritance,
> Sweet the noise of the cuckoo on bended bough,
> On the hill above Glendaruadh.
>
> Glenmasan ! O Glenmasan !
> High its herbs, fair its boughs ;
> Solitary was the place of our repose,
> On grassy Invermasan.

The upshot of this fateful voyage was that Fergus, their

guardian, was unwittingly decoyed to a feast through the King's strategy, his son Buinne Borb was bribed to act the traitor, and the sons of Uisneach were slain. But not before they had done mighty execution against the hosts of Conchobar, and kept them at bay till his Druid put a sea with high waves across the plain before them, while their foes had the benefit of dry land on which to attack from behind.

Deirdre was distracted at the loss of her lover. Taken to the King's palace, for the space of a whole year even the raising of her head or the giving of a smile she did not concede, till Conchobar, chagrined with such moping, resolved to send her away for a time with Eogan who slew Naois. On the way the evil man flung her a brutal taunt, suggestive of her defencelessness, which when Deirdre heard she gave a start, made a wild leap from the chariot, and her brains were dashed in fragments against a pillar stone that stood opposite. But the manner of her death is otherwise told in the popular version, apparently with more romantic effect and less probability. All through, the narrative is interspersed with touching lays, expressive of the heroine's feelings at various times. Thus after her loss :—

> Long is the day without Uisneach's children,
> It was not mournful to be in their company,
> Sons of a king by whom pilgrims were rewarded ;
> Three lions from the hill of the cave.

> Thou that diggest the tomb,
> And that puttest my darling from me,
> Make not the grave too narrow ;
> I shall be beside the noble ones.

Cathbad, the Druid, in retaliation for Conchobar's dissimulation, curses Emain Macha ; and Fergus Mac Roich, resenting the dastardly treachery that brought the noble sons of Uisneach to an untimely grave, took service under Queen Meve of Connaught and harassed Ulster for years. At length Nemesis overtook the guilty Conchobar. Emania is levelled to the ground, never again to be rebuilt. None of his race inherit the proud walls of that ancient citadel.

Thus, like Helen of Troy, was Deirdre the unhappy cause of strife and calamity to the land and its people, to the lover and friends she held so dear—fateful Deirdre and hapless sons of Uisneach!

CHAPTER IX

THE HEROIC CYCLE

The golden age of Gaelic romance—Number of the tales—Cuchulinn—His early adventures—The Wooing of Eimer—Training in Skye—The Bridge of the Cliffs—Tragedy of Conlaoch—Elopement—The "Táin Bó Chuailgné," and exploits of Cuchulinn—Ferdia at the ford—The two champions of Western Europe—Cuchulinn in the Deaf Valley—Death—The Red Rout of Conall Cearnach—Instruction of Cuchulinn to a prince—His "Phantom Chariot" —Modern translations of these rare sagas.

THE Heroic, or, as it is sometimes called, the Cuchulinn, or Red-Branch cycle, corresponds with the period immediately before and after the opening of the Christian era.

This was really the golden age of Gaelic romance, at once the most complete, productive, and brilliant of the three traditional epochs. And happily of it almost all the larger and more important tales have been preserved. What a world of human interest is conjured up even by the names and titles of these old-world sagas. Among them we find the " Táin Bó Chuailgné " ; Deirdre and the Sons of Uisneach ; Conchobar's Vision ; The Battle of Rosnaree ; Conchobar's Tragedy ; The Conception of Cuchulinn ; His Training ; The Wooing of Eimer ; Death of Conlaoch ; Cuchulinn's Adventure at the Boyne ; Intoxication of the Ultonians ; Bricriu's Banquet ; Eimer's Jealousy ; Cuchulinn's Pining ; Conall's Red Rout and the Lay of the Heads ; The Capture of the Sìdh ; The Phantom Chariot of Cuchulinn ; and that hero's Death ; The Recovery of the Táin through the Resurrection of Fergus. These and many other episodes, quaint and suggestive, give us curious glints into the past.

In her recent book on the Cuchulinn saga, Miss Eleanor Hull has classified the tales of this cycle under eight heads, which may be briefly summarised as follows :—

I.	Tales personal to	Conchobar	. . . .	5
II.	,, ,,	Cuchulinn	. . . .	16
III.	,, ,,	Fergus Mac Roich .	. .	5
IV.	,, ,,	Conall .	. . . .	4
V.	,, ,,	Celtchar	. . . .	2
VI.	,, ,,	Curigh .	. . . .	4
VII.	,, prefatory to	"Táin Bó Chuailgné"	. .	24
VIII.	Miscellaneous .	. . . . .	.	36
			Total . .	96

A goodly aggregate, indeed, to survive the dim forgetfulness of time ! These narratives now constitute the main body of early Celtic tradition. They breathe the spirit of the race in the long distant past, and consequently are of unique value and import.

It is evident they bear marks of pre-Christian origin, but we must remember they have reached us through the transcription of monks, and hence be prepared to find in them many interpolations, suppressions, and alterations. Indeed one very old legend represents the longest—the "Táin," as having been taken down by St. Ciaran at the grave of Fergus Mac Roich, and to the dictation of that hero, who, it appears, was conjured up from the dead for the purpose. St. Columba and the other chief saints of Ireland are reported as witnesses of this proceeding, and on their departure with the coveted writing, after they had offered up thanksgiving, Fergus also retired to his lone tomb.

There are Scotch versions of some of the sagas, but the vast majority are Irish. The earliest written copies are those in the Leabhar Na h'Uidhre and Book of Leinster—the latter the fullest of all the saga documents.

Ulster was the chief theatre of the Heroic drama. In that province, under the patronage of King Conchobar, arose the renowned order of knighthood which included such celebrities as Conall Cearnach, Cuchulinn, and the sons of Uisneach. Yet of all the knights of the Royal Branch, the second, above-named, was *facile princeps*, the most out-standing and representative man ; in fact, a kind of demigod, round whom whole armies and many champions fatefully gyrated.

Fortissimus heros Scotorum, says the Annals of Tighernach, " vii years was his age when he took arms, xvii when he was in pursuit of the ' Táin Bó Chuailgné,' xxvii when he died." The Book of Ballymote, a later MS., gives him a much longer career, asserting that the year of the " Táin " was the fifty-ninth of Cuchulinn's age, from the night of his birth to the night of his death.

To get at once a direct and luminous glimpse into the literature of his cycle, we have only to follow this champion in his varied fortunes and exploits. And so we turn to the story of his extraordinary career, recognising that the Celtic imagination has here full play, untrammelled by the limita-tions of physical science or modern thought, and that in these rich and varied creations of fancy we have fact and fiction so intricately commingled that it is vain to try to differentiate between them.

Some of the sagas tell us that Cuchulinn was super-naturally descended from the god Lugh. But later versions with more restraint affirm that his father's name was Sualtam, his mother's Dechtine, and that she was a sister of King Conchobar. When a boy he was known as Setanta, till he got the name Cuchulinn, which came to him in a manner quite characteristic and worthy of mention.

Culand, a smith and Ulster retainer, it appears, had asked the king and his retinue to spend a night and a day with him. In response to this invitation " all the Ultonian nobles set out : a great train of provincials, sons of kings and chiefs, young lords and men-at-arms, the curled and rosy youth of the kingdom, and the maidens and fair-ringleted ladies of Ulster. Handsome virgins, accomplished damsels, and splendid fully-developed women were there ;

satirists and scholars were there ; and the companies of singers and musicians, poets who composed songs and reproofs, and praising-poems for the men of Ulster. There came also with them from Emania, historians, judges, horse-riders, buffoons, tumblers, fools, and performers on horseback. They all went by the same way behind the king."

Late that evening Culand inquired if any more were expected, and on receiving a reply in the negative, he closed the doors and let loose the house-dog. No sooner was the place thus shut up for the night than the boy Setanta arrived, and was set on by the dog. A fierce struggle followed, but the youth got the better of his canine assailant and laid him lifeless. For this loss Culand demanded *eric*. Unable to pay, Setanta offered to watch the house himself until a pup of its slain guardian grew up. Hence the name Cu-Chulaind, that is, Culand's dog, by which he was subsequently known. So runs the myth.

Afterwards, with the consent of his mother, he paid a visit to his uncle the king. Happening to arrive at Emania when the boys were playing shinty, the mischievous frolics began to throw their balls and *camags* at him. Whereupon Cuchulinn's "war-rage seized him," and "he shut one eye till it was not wider than the eye of a needle ; he opened the other till it was bigger than the mouth of a meal goblet." No wonder that the terrified youngsters fled in every direction.

Presently King Conchobar recognised his nephew when he presented himself at the Court, and he introduced him to his youthful compeers. Suitable arms, a suitable chariot and charioteer were given him, and he soon proved himself a unique warrior.

The women of Ulster admired him " for his splendour at the feat, for the nimbleness of his leap, for the excellence of his wisdom, for the melody of his language, for the beauty of his face, and for the loveliness of his look." " There were seven pupils in his royal eyes, four in the one and three in the other; seven fingers on each of his two hands, and seven toes on each of his two feet." " I should think," says the writer of one text, " it was a shower of pearls that was flung into his head. Blacker than the side of a black cooking-spit, each of his two eyebrows, redder than ruby his lips."

He was too young, too daring, too beautiful, in the opinion of the chiefs, to be a gallant unwed ; for their women and maidens loved him greatly. So they took counsel with the king to have him married.

Emissaries were sent to the courts and princes of all Erin in quest of a partner whom it might please Cuchulinn to woo, but they returned after a year unsuccessful.

Left to fend for himself, the hero got ready his chariot and set out for the house of Forgaill of Lusk, whose daughter Eimer was renowned for the six victories she had upon her : the gift of beauty, the gift of voice, the gift of music, the gift of embroidery and all needlework, and the gifts of wisdom and virtuous chastity. In the pleasure-ground of the mansion, surrounded by the fair daughters of the neighbouring chiefs and men of wealth, the lady descried the famous chariot in the distance, and one of her maidens describes the appearance of the horses, the chariot, charioteer, and hero. The latter she reports thus : —

Within the chariot a dark sad man, comeliest of the men of Erin.
Around him a beautiful crimson five-folded tunic, fastened at its opening on his white breast with a brooch of inlaid gold, against which it heaves beating in full strokes. A shirt with a white hood, interwoven red with flaming gold. Seven red dragon gems on the ground of either of his eyes. Two blue-white, blood-red cheeks, that breathe forth sparks and flashes of fire. A ray of love burns in his look. Methinks a shower of pearls has fallen into his mouth. As black as the side of a black ruin each of his eyebrows. On his two thighs rests a golden hilted sword, and fastened to the copper frame of the chariot is a blood-red spear with a sharp mettlesome blade, on a shaft of wood well-fitted to the hand. Over his shoulders a crimson shield with a rim of silver, ornamented with figures of golden animals. He leaps the hero's salmon-leap into the air and does many like swift feats.

Such was Cuchulinn in the damsel's eyes. Eimer declined his suit at first on the plea that she was a younger daughter, and advised him to approach her father for leave to pay court to her elder sister, whose brilliant accomplishments she fully rehearsed. This suggestion the hero spurned and love sprang up between them.

After he departed Forgaill heard of the visit of the remarkable unknown stranger, and quickly divined who he was. Not wishing to have this professional champion as son-in-law, the wily father disguised himself as a Gaulish or Scandinavian envoy and set out for Emania. There he was well received by the king, and while witnessing the feats of the knights he took occasion to recommend the king to send his nephew to Skye to complete his special training in arms, at the celebrated school of the lady Scathach. His sinister idea was that so many dangers and difficulties would beset Cuchulinn on the way that he would never return. The latter vowed he would go. And on setting out he encountered many perils. Among others he had to traverse "the plain of misfortune," which he did by the aid of a wheel and of an apple given him by a chance acquaintance. He took instruction from the Albannach Donall by the way, and declined the love of his ugly daughter. But departing from their home he arrived in safety at Dun Scathach.

The Grianan or sunny house of his future instructress, "built upon a rock of appalling height," "had seven great doors and seven great windows between every two doors of them, and thrice fifty couches between every two windows of them, and thrice fifty handsome marriageable girls in scarlet cloaks and in beautiful and blue attire, attending and waiting upon Scathach."

Here he met his one match in arms, Ferdia Mac Daman, the Firbolg champion. Naois, Ardan, and Ainnle, the three sons of Uisneach, were also pupils. To pass the " Bridge of the Cliffs" was the first great feat to be learned. " Wonderful was the sight that bridge afforded when any one would leap upon it, for it narrowed until it became as narrow as the hair of one's head, and the second time it shortened until it became as short as an inch, and the third time it grew slippery as an eel of the river, and the fourth time it rose up on high against you until it was as tall as the mast of a ship."

It was while practising the feat of the bridge that Scathach's lovely daughter Uathach fell in love with him as she spied the hero from one of the windows of the Grianan. And then " her face and colour constantly changed, so that now she would be as white as a little white flowret, and again she would become scarlet." Cuchulinn and she were afterwards married. During his sojourn at the Dun, Scathach was carrying on war against other tribes over whom her rival the Princess Aoife (Eva) ruled. When the two hosts met, Aoife challenged Scathach to single combat, and Cuchulinn went out instead to encounter the heroine. This was his chance introduction to the lady who bore him his famous son Conlaoch. Before he went back again to his native land, he left instructions with her that the child to be born if a girl would be hers, if a boy she was to train him in all hero feats, except the gaebolg or belly dart—a mysterious weapon that could only be cast at fords on water. Then she was to send him to Erin, bidding him tell no man who he was.

Conlaoch's amazing exploits in his father's country are related in a special tale, which tells how he killed the Ulster warriors sent against him, and how Cuchulinn himself unwittingly opposed him in arms till, hard pressed by his skilful opponent, he called for his gaebolg and despatched him.

It was then the unhappy father discovered that he had killed his own son.

This is apparently the Gaelic version of the well-known Persian tale of Sohrab and Rustum—a story of Aryan origin. Just as Cuchulinn recognised when too late his kinship with Conlaoch, and mourned over him, so did the father of the young Tartar, for the brief moments the latter survived his mortal wound.

On his return from Skye, prior to the birth of his ill-fated son, Cuchulinn had been joyously welcomed

home by King Conchobar and his knights. Losing no
time he proceeded to Lusk to claim Eimer. The young
lady had in his absence become deeply enamoured of him,
though her father and brothers remained obdurate. Forti-
fying themselves against the intrusion of the champion for a
whole year, they denied him entrance, or even a sight of his
faithful lover, until Cuchulinn, getting desperate, scaled the
walls, overcame his opponents and carried off Eimer, her
maid, and much treasure in his chariot. All the way north
to Emania he had frequent combats with the men who
followed to frustrate this heroic elopement.

Commenting on the story, O'Curry makes the interesting
remark that "there is scarcely a hill, valley, river, rock,
mound, or cave in the line of country from Emania in the
present county of Armagh to Lusk in that of Dublin of
which the ancient and often varying names and history are
not to be found in this singularly curious tract," namely,
the Wooing of Eimer. "So that, if we look upon it even
as a highly-coloured historic romance, it will be found one of
the most valuable of our large collection of ancient compositions on account of the light which it throws not merely on
ancient social manners, and on the military feats and terms
of those days, but on the meaning of so vast a number of
topographical names. And it records, too, I may add, very
many curious customs and superstitions, many of which to
this day characterise the native Irish people."

Other exploits of the wonderful Cuchulinn are related in
the " Táin Bó Chuailgné " or " Cattle Raid of Cooley "—the
greatest and longest of the heroic sagas. Here we encounter
that remarkable Amazon, Queen Meve of Connaught, and
her third husband, Ailill. When at Rath-Cruachan it seems
they had spread their royal couch, and between them there
ensued a pillow conversation, ending in a controversy as to
which of the two was the richer. In this debate comparison
was made between their mugs and vats and iron vessels,
their urns and brewers' troughs, and kieves. Their jewels
also were brought out, such as finger-rings, clasps, bracelets,

thumb-rings, diadems, and gorgets of gold ; their apparel of crimson, blue, black and green, yellow and chequered and buff, wan-coloured, pied and striped. Comparison was made between their flocks of sheep and steeds and studs, and herds of swine and droves of cows. But all were found to be exactly equal.

Then Ailill recollected that he had a young bull named " Finn-bheannach " or "White-horned," which had been calved by one of the Queen's cows, but which had left her herd and joined his own because the high-minded animal did not " deem it honourable to be under a woman's control." Meve's disappointment was keen that no bull of hers was found to match this one ; so, when Fergus Mac Roth the herald assured her that Daré, in Cuailgne, Ulster, possessed a brown one, the best in all Erin, she immediately sent him with nine subordinates to fetch it, offering its owner liberal terms for a year's loan. Daré treated the messengers with kindly hospitality, and agreed to the royal request. But, unhappily, while the men were imbibing too freely that night, his steward overheard one of them boasting that if the bull had not been willingly sent they would have taken it by compulsion.

On this coming to Daré's ears, he swore by the gods that now they would not have his Donn Chuailgne either by force or consent.

Meve was not a woman to be thus lightly denied or insulted. *Nolens volens* she would have the bull, and summoned her native forces for action. She also invited the men of Leinster and Munster to join her in avenging past indignities received at the hands of the men of Ulster. Fifteen hundred men from the latter province, who happened to be at feud with King Conchobar for his treachery to the sons of Uisneach, were prevailed upon to answer her summons, and a great army set out. At a place near modern Louth, where they halted on the march, a feast was held, at which the Queen contrived to promise to each of the leaders, without the knowledge of the rest, the hand of her beautiful daughter Finnamhair in marriage as a stimulus to valour and fidelity. "On one of the nights the snow that fell reached to men's legs and to the wheels of the chariots, so that it made one plain of the five provinces of Erin, and the men never suffered so much before in camp. None knew throughout the whole night whether it was his friend or his foe who was next him until the clear shining sun rose early on the morrow."

Though the Ulster men had sufficient warning of the approach of this host, they were not in readiness. A childish helplessness, to which they were subject for an unmanly crime, had overtaken them and left them at the mercy of their foes.

It was Cuchulinn's country the enemy had invaded, and he kept them at bay. Hovering around them unseen all day, he killed as many as a hundred each night with his sling. In vain Meve tried to buy this boyish hero off, first by a mutual conference, with the glen between them, and second by sending an embassage with Mac Roth as messenger-in-chief. On this occasion Cuchulinn discarded the twenty-seven cunningly prepared undershirts which with cords and ropes were secured about him. And this he did to escape the difficulty that would arise in throwing them off, should his paroxysm come to boiling point and he in them still. Anon for thirty feet all round the hero's body the snow melted with the intense heat generated in his system. His charioteer, we are told, durst not come nigh him. From a safe distance he informed his master of Mac Roth's approach and described him.

Cuchulinn demands single combat, enjoining his opponents by the laws of Irish chivalry not to pass the ford till he was overcome. Queen Meve reluctantly consents, deeming it better to lose one warrior a day than a hundred each night. With her messenger came a youth anxious to see the renowned hero, and he, deceived by the boyish appearance of Cuchulinn, determined to fight him. To warn the rash stripling of his danger, the latter plays upon him two sword-feats. By the first, "the under-cut," he slices away the sod from under this Etarchomal's soles and lays him supine, with the sod upon his upturned chest. By the second, "the vigorous edge-stroke," he takes off all his hair from poll to forehead and from ear to ear, as clean as though he had been shaven with a razor, but without drawing blood. Finally, he despatches him with the "oblique transverse stroke," whereby in three simultaneously fallen segments the youth reaches the ground.

Champion after champion falls in single combat, until Meve, getting desperate, had at length to call in the aid of magic. So we read that one warrior was helped by demons of the air in bird shape, but in vain ; and the great magician Cailatin and his twenty-seven sons, despite their spells, also met their doom. Cuchulinn was further persecuted by the war-goddess, the Morrigan, who appears in all shapes to plague him and to frighten the life of valour out of his soul. He himself is not behind in demoniac influence, for with the help of the Tuatha de Danann—Manannan especially — he does great havoc among Meve's troops, circling round them in his chariot and dealing death with his sling.

It was during one of these exploits that he gave his chariot the heavy turn, so that its iron wheels sank into the earth and their track was in itself a sufficient fortification, for the stones and pillars and flags and sand rose back high on every side round the wheels.

His foes are baffled. Impatient Meve cannot forget that the Ulster men will soon be rid of their childish feebleness, and then the game is up. So she approaches Ferdia, the only warrior fit to match Cuchulinn, with the view of arranging a combat whereby the latter may be laid low. Ferdia at first refuses to fight his former comrade, with whom he had made a compact of undying friendship while attending the lady Scathach's school in Skye. The Queen then promises him Finnamhair for wife, with land and riches. It is probable that even this bait would not have fetched the unwilling warrior had she not further threatened that her druids and ollamhs would " criticise, satirise, and blemish him," enough to " raise three blisters on his face," if he refused. Thereafter he consented, thinking it better to fall by valour and championship than by druids and reproach.

Fergus was accordingly sent forward to tell Cuchulinn that his friend Ferdia was coming to fight him. " I am here," retorted the champion, "detaining and delaying the four great provinces of Erin from Samhain till Feill Brighde, and I have not yielded one foot in retreat before any one during that time, nor will I, I trust, before him." The charioteer gets ready the chariot, and into it sprang " the battle-fighting, dexterous, battle-winning, red-sworded hero, Cuchulinn, son of Sualtam, and there shouted around him Bocanachs and Bananachs and Genîtî Glindi, and demons of the air. For the Tuatha de Danann were used to set up shouts around him, so that the hatred and the fear and the abhorrence and the great terror of him should be greater in every battle, in every battle-field, in every combat, and in every fight into which he went."

The heroes met at the ford. After the first day's fight, " each of them approached the other forthwith and each put' his hand round the other's neck and gave him three kisses. Their horses were in the same paddock that night, and their charioteers at the same fire; and their charioteers spread beds of green rushes for them with wounded men's pillows to them. The professors of healing and curing came to heal and cure them, and they applied herbs and plants to the stabs and cuts and gashes and to all their wounds. Of every herb and of every healing and curing plant that was put to the stabs and cuts and gashes and to all the wounds of Cuchulinn, he would send an equal portion from him westward over the ford to Ferdia, so that the men of Erin might not be able to say, should Ferdia fall by him, that it was by better means of cure that he was enabled to kill him."

As the days pass the fighting becomes more serious.

Early on the fourth Ferdia arose and went forward alone to the ford. He knew that that day would decide the contest, and that either or both of them would fall. Having put on his wonderful suit of battle, he displayed many extraordinary feats which he never learned from any other, —not from Scathach, or Uathach, or Aoife, but which were invented by himself.

On seeing these, Cuchulinn said to his charioteer, " I perceive there, my friend Laeg, the noble, varied, wonderful, numerous feats which Ferdia displays on high, and all these will be tried on me in succession. Therefore if it be I who shall begin to yield this day thou must excite, reproach, and speak evil to me, that the paroxysm of my rage and anger shall grow the more. If it be I who shall prevail then thou shalt laud and praise and speak good words to me, that my courage may be the greater."

" It shall be so done indeed, O Cuchulinn," replied the faithful Laeg.

The champions then arranged to try the ford feat. And the saga remarks : " Great was the deed, now, that was performed on that day at the ford—the two heroes, the two warriors, the two champions of Western Europe, the two gifted and stipend-bestowing hands of the north-west of the world, the two beloved pillars of the valour of the Gael, and the two keys of the bravery of the Gael, to be brought to fight from afar through the instigation and intermeddling of Ailill and Meve."

First, they began to shoot with missive weapons, till, getting more furious, Cuchulinn sprang at his opponent twice for the purpose of striking his head over the rim of his shield, but each time Ferdia gave the shield a stroke of his left knee or elbow, and cast Cuchulinn from him like a little child on the brink of the ford.

Laeg perceived that act, and, true to the instructions of his master, began taunting him. " Alas ! indeed," said he, " the warrior who is against thee casts thee away as a lewd woman would cast her child. He throws thee as a mill would grind fresh malt. He pierces thee as the felling axe would pierce the oak. He binds thee as the woodbine binds the tree. He darts on thee as the hawk darts on small birds, so that henceforth thou hast not call, or right, or claim to valour or bravery to the end of time and life, thou little fairy phantom."

At that word up sprang the fallen hero with the rapidity of the wind, and with the readiness of the swallow, and with the fierceness of the dragon, and the strength of the lion, into the troubled clouds of the air the third time, and he alighted on the boss of the shield of Ferdia, but with the same humiliating result.

"It was then that Cuchulinn's first distortion came on, and he was filled with swelling and great fulness, like breath in a bladder, until he became a terrible, fearful, many-coloured Tuaig, and he became as big as a Fomor, or man of the sea, the great and valiant champion in perfect height over Ferdia."

So close was the fight they made now that the Bocanachs and Bananachs, and wild people of the glens, and demons of the air screamed from the rims of their shields, and from the hilts of their swords, and from the hafts of their spears.

At length Ferdia found an unguarded moment upon his opponent and wounded him sorely. Cuchulinn, unable to endure this, or Ferdia's stout quick strokes and tremendous great blows at him, called for the gaebolg. It was a weapon that used to be let down the stream and cast from between the toes. It made the wound of one spear in entering the body, but it had thirty barbs to open, and could not be drawn out of a person's body until it was cut out. So Laeg set the gaebolg down the stream, and Cuchulinn caught it between the toes of his foot and threw an unerring cast of it at Ferdia.

"That is enough now indeed," said the wounded man. "I fall of that."

Thereafter a trance, a faint, and a weakness fell on Cuchulinn as he saw the body of Ferdia. But Laeg roused him, and then he began to lament and mourn, and to utter a panegyric over his slain rival as David did over Jonathan :—

> O Ferdia (he said) treachery hath defeated thee.
> Unhappy was thy fate—
> Thou to die, I to remain,—
> Grievous for ever is our lasting separation.
>
> When we were far away, yonder
> With Scathath, the gifted Buanand,
> We then resolved that till the end of time
> We should not be hostile one to the other.
>
> Dear to me was thy beautiful ruddiness,
> Dear to me thy perfect form,
> Dear to me thy clear grey-blue eye,
> Dear to me thy wisdom and thine eloquence.
>
> There hath not come to the body-cutting combat,
> There hath not been angered by manly exertion,
> There hath not borne shield on the field of spears
> Thine equal, O ruddy son of Daman.
>
> Never until now have I met,
> Since I slew Aoife's only son,
> Thy like in deeds of battle,
> Never have I found, O Ferdia.
>
> Finnamhair, daughter of Meve,
> Notwithstanding her excellent beauty,
> It is putting a *gad* on the sand or sunbeam
> For thee to expect her, O Ferdia.

He continued to gaze on his fallen friend, and when at length, tempted by his charioteer to come away and get healed of his grievous wounds, he said, " We will leave now, O my friend Laeg, but every other combat and fight that ever I have made was to me but as a game and a sport compared to the combat and the fight of Ferdia."

There is a most beautiful rendering of his further eulogy in Dr. Sigerson's *Bards of the Gael and Gall.* Here it is.

The repetition and rhythm have been adapted from the original :—

> Play was each, pleasure each,
> Till Ferdia faced the beach ;
> One had been our student-life,
> One in strife of school our place,
> One our gentle teacher's grace,
> 　Loved o'er all and each.
>
> Play was each, pleasure each,
> Till Ferdia faced the beach ,
> One had been our wonted ways,
> One the praise for feat of fields,
> Scathach gave two victor shields—
> 　Equal prize to each.
>
> Play was each, pleasure each,
> Till Ferdia faced the beach ;
> Dear that pillar of pure gold,
> Who fell cold beside the ford.
> Hosts of heroes felt his sword
> 　First in battle's breach.
>
> Play was each, pleasure each,
> Till Ferdia faced the beach ;
> Lion, fiery, fierce, and bright,
> Wave whose might nothing withstands,
> Sweeping, with the shrinking sands,
> 　Horror o'er the beach.
>
> Play was each, pleasure each,
> Till Ferdia faced the beach ;
> Loved Ferdia, dear to me ;
> I shall dree his death for aye,
> Yesterday a mountain he,—
> 　But a shade to-day.

Queen Meve with her army ravaged the province of Ulster and secured the Donn Chuailgne. Ultimately, through the recovery of the Ultonians from their temporary debility, she was thoroughly defeated. Yet, notwithstanding the loss of so many warriors, the masterful woman congratulates herself on having accomplished the two great objects of her expedition—the securing of the brown bull and the chastisement of her former husband, King Conchobar.

The story of the Táin ends in an anti-climax, relating in the most ludicrous and fantastic manner the tragic fate of the bulls,[1] the unwitting cause of all this frenzy.

But Queen Meve was determined to avenge herself on Cuchulinn, and in the course of time collected another large army. Among all his foes none was more venomous than were the descendants of the wizard Cailatin, who, with his twenty-seven sons, had been killed at the ford combat. The malignant efforts of these sorcerers to get the warrior into their power are vividly described. For a time he was kept and entertained in the royal palace by his wife Eimer and the ladies of Emania, and poets, and musicians, and wise men. The wizards made noise as of battle, and when Cuchulinn looked out he imagined he saw battalions drawn up upon the plains smiting each other unsparingly. It was with difficulty he was withheld from going out.

So, by Conchobar's command he was taken at length by the druids and ladies of the Court to a far away lonely glen, called the Deaf Valley. Even here the wizards found him, and in consequence the very dogs were terrified with the goblins, prodigies, and eldritch things with which the place was haunted. A full account is given of the manner in which they ultimately decoyed him from his retreat, and it is related how all the omens were against him. For example, his brooch fell and pierced his foot. His noble steed, the Liath Macha, refused to be yoked, and when finally persuaded, let fall down his cheeks two large tears of dusky blood.

But Cuchulinn met his foes in battle array. And as many as there were of grains of sand in the sea, of stars in heaven, of dewdrops in May, of snowflakes in winter, of hailstones in a storm, of leaves in a forest, of ears of corn in Magh Breagh, of stalks of grass beneath the feet of the

---

[1] See p. 110.

herds on a summer's day, so many halves of heads and of shields, so many halves of hands and of feet, so many red bones, were scattered by him throughout the plain of Muirtheimhne. Grey was that field with the brains of his enemies, so fierce and furious the hero's onslaught.

When he fell, he fell pierced with his own spear, which Lewy, the son of Curigh, had hurled back upon him, but rising again, he went against a pillar of stone that he might die standing up. And the Liath Macha defended him with teeth and hoofs to the last, killing as many as thirty in the struggle. So died the mighty Cuchulinn.

In the Red Rout of Conall Cearnach we read how that famous knight, who had been previously sent for, came back from Pictland to avenge the death of his friend, and how he brought the heads of the chief offenders to Eimer.

Satisfied with this retribution, Eimer desired Conall to dig a grave for Cuchulinn wide and deep ; and she laid herself down in it with her mate, saying, " Love of my soul, O friend, O gentle sweetheart, many were the women who envied me thee until now, and I shall not live after thee." After she expired Conall performed the customary funeral obsequies, wrote their names in Ogam, and raised the stone over their tomb.

In the Leabhar Na h'Uidhre there is a detached episode entitled, " The Instruction of Cuchulinn to a Prince." It occurs in the romance known as " The Sickbed of Cuchulinn," and on the authority of the Brehon Law we know that many of the precepts therein enjoined were rules legally incumbent on the chieftains in aftertimes.

The occasion was the election of a king to rule over Erin in Tara.

Lugaid, destined for this exalted office, was at the time the pupil of Cuchulinn, sitting over his pillow as he lay ill. When news came, suddenly the prostrate hero arose and began to instruct the young prince. Among other precepts he gave voice to these, which show not only the traditional estimate of the hero's character, but also the high moral qualities expected in the chief ruler of Erin and his satellites.

"Speak not haughtily. Discourse not noisily. Mock not, insult not, deride not the old. Think not ill of any. Make no demands that cannot be met. Receive submissively the instructions of the wise. Be mindful of the admonitions of the old. Follow the decrees of your fathers. Be not cold-hearted to friends; but against your foes be vigorous. Avoid dishonourable disputes in your many contests. Be not a tattler and abuser. Waste not, hoard not, alienate not. Submit to reproof for unbecoming deeds. Do not sacrifice justice to the passions of men. Be not lazy lest you become weakened, be not importunate lest you become contemptible."

"Do you consent to follow these counsels?" the distinguished tutor asked.

To which the prince made answer, "These precepts without exception are worthy to be observed. All men will see that none of them shall be neglected. They shall be executed, if it be possible."

Little wonder that in later Christian times the old pagan hero was held in high esteem, and even exalted into a medium for the conversion of King Laoghaire, whom the preaching of St. Patrick himself failed to convince. In the "Phantom Chariot of Cuchulinn" it is related that Patrick went to Tara to enjoin belief upon the King of Erin, that is, upon Laoghaire, son of Nial, for he was King of Erin at the time, and would not believe in the Lord, though he had preached unto him. "By no means will I believe in thee, nor yet in God," said the heathen monarch to the saint, "until thou shalt call up Cuchulinn in all his dignity, as he is recorded in the old stories, that I may see him, and that I may address him in my presence here; after that I will believe in thee."

Upon this St. Patrick conjured up the hero, so that he appeared to the King in his chariot as of old. Laoghaire's description of Cuchulinn as thus seen in his phantom chariot is even more graphic than that of the maid in the Wooing of Eimer.

The spectre proved a most earnest preacher, endeavouring to persuade his royal hearer to believe in God and Patrick, and so escape the pains of hell, of which it appears he had had some experience.

> My little body was scarred—
> With Lugaid the victory :
> Demons carried off my soul
> Into the red charcoal.
>
> I played the swordlet on them,
> I plied on them the gae-bolga ;
> I was in my concert victory
> With the demon in pain.
>
> Great as was my heroism,
> Hard as was my sword,
> The devil crushed me with one finger
> Into the red charcoal.

It is somewhat ludicrous to read that he practised the gae-bolg even on the spiteful units of the under world, though apparently with less success than on Ferdia and the rest.

The tale consistently enough concludes that " great was the power of Patrick in awakening Cuchulinn, after being nine fifty years in the grave."

To appreciate the vigour and spirit of these remarkable sagas as they figure in the original, one requires to read them through. No quotations, however well chosen, can do full justice to their wealth of imagination and descriptive power, especially when depicting stirring incidents, curious customs, men, horses, chariots, arms, ornaments, vesture, and colours. Then they are profuse, fantastic, minute, and boldly original, tedious, sometimes through the very prodigality of their adjectival resources. In perusing them the reader feels that he is in a fresh field of literature and breathing an atmosphere entirely different to anything modern.

Though Homeric in form, there is always the Celtic tinge in the literary style as well as in the facts seized on and made prominent. Within the last half century these early tales have been frequently translated into various languages, and excellent versions are now available from the pens of such distinguished scholars as Eugene O'Curry, Dr. Whitley Stokes and O'Flanagan, M. d'Arbois de Jubainville and M. Louis Duvan, Dr. Ernst Windisch, Dr. Kuno Meyer, Standish Hayes O'Grady and O'Beirne Crowe.

CHAPTER X

THE OSSIANIC CYCLE

The old order changes—Who were the Feinn ?—Ossian, his name and relation
to the bardic literature—The Ossianic tales and poems very numerous—
Earliest references—First remarkable development—Original home of the
Ossianic romance—The leading heroes—A famous tract—Legends regarding
Fionn, and curious details of his warrior-band—The literature divided into
four classes—Most ancient poems of Ossian, and the Feinn—Quotations—
"The Dialogue of the Ancients"—Ossian and Patrick—Story of Crede—
Miscellaneous poems—Prose tales—"Pursuit of Diarmad and Grainne"—
"Lay of Diarmad"—Norse Ballads—Dream figures, a remarkable Gaelic
tradition.

THE Ossianic cycle brings us down to the middle of the third
century A.D.   It is clearly much later than the Heroic.   For
in the interval the old order peculiar to the days of Cuchulinn
has passed away, and new manners and customs are in
vogue.   No longer is our attention engrossed with descriptions of chariots and war-horses and cow-spoils.   The heroes
are an organised body of men, who engage in the peaceful
pastimes of hunting and feasting when not occupied with the
more serious business of warfare.   They appear less mythical
than the demi-gods and champions of earlier times; yet
they move in that dim background of history where figures
are always seen in chiaroscuro, and we cannot even be
remotely confident of their historical reality.

Indeed, it has long been a moot question who the Feinn[1]
were, and we still have the most conflicting opinions on the
subject.   For example, the native Irish have always regarded

---

[1] Fiann, gen. Feinne, means the band, troop; the plural Fianna, the troops
or the soldiers.—Dr. Ludwig Stern.

them as an actual martial caste, maintained during several reigns by the kings of Erin for national defence. And there is documentary evidence to show that as early as the seventh century Fionn [1] was generally looked upon as a quondam popular hero. Eugene O'Curry shared the belief of his countrymen, for he says : " I may take occasion to assure you that it is quite a mistake to suppose Finn Mac Cumhaill to have been a merely imaginary or mythical character. Much that has been narrated of his exploits is, no doubt, apocryphal enough, but Finn himself is an undoubtedly historical personage ; and that he existed about the time at which his appearance is recorded in the Annals is as certain as that Julius Cæsar lived and ruled at the time stated on the authority of the Roman historians." And O'Curry supports this opinion with the statement that the hero's pedigree is fully detailed in the Book of Leinster, and his death is chronicled in the *Annals of the Four Masters*, as having taken place in 283 A.D.

Yet more recent scholarship inclines to other and very different views. Dr. Hyde fancies the school of Mr. Nutt and Professor Rhys would recognise in the Feinn tribal deities euhemerised or regarded as men. Dr. Skene and Mr. Macritchie believed they were a race distinct from the Gaels, probably allied to, or even identical with, the Picts, the latter venturing the opinion that they might be the *sìdh* or fairy folk of the mounds so frequently in evidence in Gaelic literature ; while Dr. Alexander Macbain speaks of Fionn as probably the incarnation of the chief deity of the Gaels, and his band of heroes as a kind of terrestrial Olympus.

From these latter the popular Ossian, son of Fionn, has been singled out as the representative bard of early times. The most ancient forms of the name were Ossin, Oisin, or Oisein, meaning " the little fawn." It is variously spelt in the Book of the Dean of Lismore. And only in

[1] Said to be so named from his white head.—Dr. Macbain. Finn, ancient form.

Macpherson's time and through his usage did the word acquire its modern familiar orthography.

In the same manner as the name of David is traditionally associated with the Hebrew Psalter, or the name of Homer with the Homeric poetry, so is that of Ossian the warrior bard with the classic poems of the Gael. His will always be identified with the bardic literature that celebrates the deeds of the Feinn, even though scholars cannot affirm with historic certainty that he actually lived or was the real author of one of the ballads attributed to him.[1]

The Ossianic tales and poems are very numerous. Indeed O'Curry says that if printed at length in the same form as the text of O'Donovan's edition of the *Four Masters* they would occupy as many as 3000 pages of such volumes. And that statement was made before the publication of Campbell's Scottish collection, known as *Leabhar na Feinne*. Apart from the tales, it is believed that the poetry alone extends to upwards of 80,000 lines.

Yet, compared with the wealth of ancient texts that represent the Heroic saga, we have very few old vellum MSS. representing the Ossianic. Of many of the pieces there are two redactions, one on vellum, the other on modern paper— the latter usually the longer and more profuse. It would seem as if the Ossianic tales took hold of the imagination of the Gael much more powerfully than did those of the Heroic cycle, with the result that they have been in process of evolution down almost to the present day—certainly to the end of the eighteenth century, which witnessed that wonderful recrudescence of production, associated in Scotland with the names of Macpherson, Smith, Clark, Maccallum, and others.

The earliest references to Fionn occur in two Irish poets, one of the tenth and the other of the eleventh century ; in the Annals of Tighernach, who died in 1088 ; and in the

---

[1] The age of the oldest existing Ossianic poems, according to Dr. Ludwig Stern, is the eleventh and twelfth centuries, though a few of them may be more venerable.

venerable Leabhar Na h'Uidhre and Book of Leinster.
So that as early as the origin of these latter two MSS. we
have written Ossianic or Fionn tales ; and, seeing these
literary monuments were compiled from older documents it
is at least possible, as scholars affirm that some of the tales
may have been written down in MS. before the end of the
seventh century.

The first remarkable development in the evolution of
the saga took place between the thirteenth and fifteenth
centuries, the most characteristic feature of the change being
the prominence given to foreign invasion, especially the
invasion of Lochlanners. Fionn is no longer a tribal chief
in one locality, but the acknowledged leader of all Gaeldom
against the intruding aliens.

The stories of his own exploits and of those of his
warrior band are Gaelic variants of tales common to all
Celtic, indeed to all Aryan races. In his essay on the
" Development of the Ossianic or Fenian Saga," printed in
vol. ii. of *Waifs and Strays of Celtic Tradition*, Mr. Alfred
Nutt says that " in the redactions which substantially reach
back to the twelfth century, these tales are profoundly
modified in two ways : firstly, the euhemerising process
begun in the ninth to tenth centuries has fully developed,
and the saga has been fitted into a framework of tribal and
personal conditions, which necessarily determine the growth
along certain lines ; secondly, mythic features and incidents
have been translated, as it were, into historic terms, borrowed
from the comparatively recent history of the race, and the
saga has in consequence been enriched by a new series of
personages, and by a wider geographic horizon. At this
stage it is taken up by the literary class of the day, the professional story-tellers, and metrically fixed. It is literary
in so far as the form is artificial, that is, due to a given man
who did not hesitate to embellish and amplify out of his
acquired stock of knowledge ; popular in so far as it is kept
in close touch with tradition. This semi-literary form continued to develop until the eighteenth century in both

divisions of Gael-land, but the guiding impulse ever came from Ireland. During the last hundred years and more, large fragments of it have been preserved in Scotland orally, and offer the most instructive object lesson with which I am acquainted to the student of traditional diffusion and transmission. Side by side with the semi-literary development, the purely popular forms continued to exist and grow. With regard to Scotland, the chief Ossianic problem is, how far these may be looked upon as independent of the semiliterary twelfth century forms, that is, as derived substantially from the earlier traditions brought by the Gael to Scotland in the early centuries of the Christian era. There is much to be said for and against this view. There is practically nothing to be said in favour of the Fenian saga being older on Scotch ground than the Dalriadic colonisation. Both Scotland and Ireland have an equal claim to the saga in this sense—that both countries were inhabited by Gaels, who told and localised it wherever they went ; but Ireland's claim is so far superior that these tales were told in Ireland earlier than in Scotland ; that whatever admixture of fact there is in them is Irish fact, and that the chief shapers of the cycle have been Irish, and not Scotch Gaels. On the other hand, the Gaels seem both to have preserved the popular form in a more genuine state, and the semi-literary form orally with greater tenacity."

Ireland we may therefore regard as the original home of the Ossianic romance, which in time diffused itself to the west of Scotland, to the Hebrides, and even to the Isle of Man. And it is significant that while the theatre of the Cuchulinn drama was mainly the north of that country—Ulster and Connaught, that of the Feinn was the south—Leinster and Munster.

The leading heroes of this cycle were :—

1. Fionn, son of Cumhail, son of Trenmor, who is represented as having been a druid.

2. Gaul Mac Morna, leader of the clan Morna in Connaught. The first name of Gaul was Aedh Mac Morna,

but in the battle of Cnucha he lost an eye and was henceforth known as Gaul, that is, the *Blind* Mac Morna.   In this
battle he slew Cumhail, Fionn's father, the leader of the
Leinster band, and though he afterwards served under Fionn,
they had no great love for each other.

3. Ossian, son of Fionn, who in later times became
famous as the great poet of the Celtic people.

4. Oscar, son of Ossian, and grandson of Fionn, who is
represented as handsome and kind-hearted, and generally one
of the bravest of the Feinn.

5. Diarmad O'Duibhne, with the beauty spot — " ball
seirc "—which compelled any woman who saw it to fall in
love with him.

6. Caoilte Mac Ronan, a nephew (or cousin) of Fionn, the
swiftest of all the Fenian heroes.

7. Fergus Finne-bheoil, " the eloquent," who figures as
a wise counsellor as well as a great warrior.

8. Conan Maol, the fool and coward of the party.

The greater number of the incidents of this cycle are
represented as having taken place during the reign of Cormac
Mac Art Mac Conn of the hundred battles, and that of his
son, Cairbre of the Liffey.   The former reigned from 227
to 268 A.D., but it was during the reign of the latter that the
battle of Gabhra was fought, in the year 283 A.D., which for
ever put an end to the Fenian power.

In O'Flaherty's " Ogygia " it is said, " *Cormac* exceeded
all his predecessors in magnificence, wisdom, and learning,
as also in military achievements.   His palace was most
superbly adorned and richly furnished, and his numerous
family proclaim his majesty and munificence ; the books he
published and the schools he endowed at Temor bear
unquestionable testimony of his learning ; there were three
schools instituted, in the first the most eminent professors of
the art of war were engaged, in the second history was taught,
and in the third jurisprudence was professed."

There is a famous tract entitled, " The Instruction of
a Prince," ascribed to this king, which has evidently been

redacted in Christian times. It is preserved in the Book of Ballymote, and takes the form of question and answer between the son Cairbre and his royal father.

"O Grandson of Conn, O Cormac," said Cairbre, "what is good for a king?"

"That is plain," said Cormac, "it is good for him to have patience and not to dispute, self-government without anger, affability without haughtiness, diligent attention to history, strict observance of covenants and agreements, strictness mitigated by mercy in the execution of laws . . . let him enforce fear, let him perfect peace."

"O Grandson of Conn, O Cormac," said Cairbre, "what is good for the welfare of a country?"

"That is plain," said Cormac, "frequent convocations of sapient and good men to investigate the affairs, to abolish each evil and retain each wholesome Institution, to attend to the precepts of the elders; let the law be in the hand of the nobles, let the chieftains be upright and unwilling to oppress the poor."

"O Grandson of Conn, O Cormac," said Cairbre, "what are the duties of a prince at a banqueting house?"

"A Prince," said Cormac, "should light his lamps and welcome his guests with clapping of hands, procure comfortable seats, the cup-bearers should be respectable and active in the distribution of meat and drink. Let there be moderation of music, short stories, a welcoming countenance, a welcome for the learned, pleasant conversations, and the like."

"O Grandson of Conn, what is good for me?" to which Cormac answers :—

"If thou attend to my command, thou wilt not mock the old although thou art young, nor the poor although thou art well-clad, nor the lame although thou art strong, nor the ignorant although thou art learned. Be not slothful, nor passionate, nor penurious, nor idle, nor jealous. . . ."

Again Cairbre asks how he is to conduct himself among the wise and among the foolish, among friends and among strangers, among the old and among the young, to which Cormac, his father, replies :—

Be not too knowing nor too simple; be not proud, be not inactive, be not too humble nor yet haughty; be not talkative but be not too silent; be not timid, neither be severe. For if thou shouldst appear too knowing thou wouldst be satirised and abused ; if too simple thou wouldst be imposed upon ; if too proud thou wouldst be shunned ; if too humble thy dignity would suffer ; if talkative thou wouldst not be deemed learned ; if too severe thy character would be defamed ; if too timid thy rights would be encroached upon.

There are various versions of the story of Fionn's birth. In Leabhar Na h'Uidhre it is told shortly as follows : Tadg, chief druid of Conn, had a beautiful daughter called Muirne. Cumhail, son of Trenmor, who was head of the Militia in King Conn's time, asked Muirne in marriage, but her father Tadg refused to give her, because he knew from his druidical knowledge that if Cumhail married her, he himself would lose his ancestral seat at Almhain, now Allen, in Leinster. So Cumhail took Muirne by force and married her. Tadg appealed to King Conn, who sent his forces after the delinquent, resulting in the battle of Cnucha being fought, in which Cumhail was killed by Aedh son of Morna, who in turn lost his eye. Muirne fled to Cumhail's sister, and gave birth to a son, who was at first called Demni. When he grew up he demanded *eric* of his grandfather Tadg for the death of his father, and so, according to druidical anticipation, he got possession of Almhain. He also made peace with Gaul, who afterwards figured as one of his band of warriors.

In the Bodleian Library, Oxford, there is a MS. written about the fifteenth century, in which is preserved a treatise entitled " Boyish exploits of Fionn." It is interesting to note here how he was reputed to have come by the gift of seeing into the future. At that time on the banks of the Boyne there lived a famous poet called Finn Eges, and young Fionn was sent to him to complete his education. There was a prophecy that if one of the name of Fionn ate a salmon caught in Fiacc's pool on the Boyne he should no longer be in ignorance of anything he might wish to know. The poet had industriously fished the pool for seven years and never landed a single fish. However, one was caught shortly after Fionn's arrival, and Finn Eges sent the lad to cook it, with strict injunctions not to taste it. While turning the salmon on the fire Fionn burnt his thumb, and instinctively thrust it into his mouth to cool. On reporting the incident to his master, the poet asked him his name. " Demni," said the lad. " Your name is Fionn," muttered the poet, " and it is you who were destined to eat of the salmon of knowledge, you are the real Fionn ! "

Thus it was that knowledge came to the young hero. Through the chance incident of suddenly inserting his thumb in his mouth, the hidden was revealed to him.

The legend, as given in a vellum MS. in Trinity College, Dublin, is somewhat different. It says that on a certain occasion Fionn was hunting near *Sliabh nam Ban*, and while standing at a spring, presently a strange woman came along, filled a silver tankard at the well, and without saying a word walked away with it. The hero's curiosity was aroused. He followed, unperceived, until she reached the side of the hill, where a concealed door opened to admit her. In by this entrance she walked, and Fionn attempting to do likewise got his thumb trapped between the door and doorpost as the former suddenly swung back. It was with great difficulty he managed to extricate the *ordag*, but having succeeded, he at once thrust it, bruised as it was, into his mouth to ease the pain. And no sooner had he done this than he found himself possessed of the gift of foreseeing future events. Hence the expression, " ordag mhor an eolais " (the great thumb of knowledge).

Irish scholars invariably represent the Feinn as a band of Militia, or kind of standing army, that fought battles, and defended the kingdom from invasion. Before a soldier could be admitted into this select corps, he had to promise, " first, never to receive a portion with a wife, but to choose her for good manners and virtues ; second, never to offer violence to any woman ; third, never to refuse any one in the matter of anything he might possess, that is, he ought to be charitable to the weak and the poor ; and fourth, no single warrior should ever flee before nine champions." It was necessary that "both his father and mother, his tribe, and his relatives should first give guarantees that they would never demand an *eric* or revenge from any person for his death."

In a fifteenth century MS. in the British Museum it is stated that (1) Not a man was taken until he was a prime poet versed in the twelve books of poetry. (2) No man was taken till in the ground a large hole had been made such as to reach the fold of his belt, and he put into it with his shield and a forearm's length of a hazel stick. Then must nine warriors having nine spears, with a ten-furrows' width between them and him, assail him, and in concert let fly at him. If he were then hurt past that guard of his, he was not received into the Fian-ship. (3) Not a man of them was taken until his hair had been interwoven into braids on him, and he started at a run through Ireland's woods, while they seeking to wound him followed in his wake, there having been between him and them but one forest bough by way of interval at first. Should he be overtaken he was wounded, and not received into the Fian-ship after. (4) If his weapon had quivered in his hand he was not taken. (5) Should a branch in the wood have disturbed anything of his hair out of its braiding he was not taken. (6) If he had cracked a dry stick under his foot, as he ran, he was not accepted. (7) Unless that, at full speed, he had both jumped a stick level with his brow, and stooped to pass under one on a level with his knee, he was not taken. (8) Unless also without slackening his pace he could with his nail extract a thorn from his foot, he was not taken into the Fian-ship. But if he performed all this he was of Fionn's people.

Keating, who wrote about 1630, and who had access to documents now no longer extant, gives some curious details :—

The members of the Fenian body (he says) lived in the following manner. They were quartered on the people from November Day till May Day, and their duty was to uphold justice and to put down injustice on the part of the kings and lords of Ireland, and also to guard the harbours of the country from the oppression of foreign invaders.   After that, from May till November, they lived by hunting and the chase, and by performing the duties demanded of them by the kings of Ireland, such as preventing robberies, exacting fines and tributes, putting down public enemies, and every other kind of evil that might afflict the country.   In performing these duties they received a certain fixed pay. . . .   However, from May till November the Fenians had to content themselves with game, the product of their own hunting, as this right to hunt was their maintenance and pay from the kings of Ireland.   That is, the warriors had the flesh of the wild animals for their food, and the skins for wages.   During the whole day, from morning till night, they used to eat but one meal, and of this it was their wont to partake towards evening. About noon they used to send whatever game they had killed in the morning by their attendants to some appointed hill, where there were wood and moorland close by.   There they used to light immense fires, into which they put a large quantity of round sandstones. They next dug two pits in the yellow clay of the moor, and having set part of the venison upon spits to be roasted before the fire, they bound up the remainder with *sugans*—ropes of straw or rushes—in bundles of sedge, and then placed them to be cooked in one of the pits they had previously dug.   There they set the stones which they had before this heated in the fire round about them, and kept heaping them upon the bundles of meat until they had made them seethe freely, and the meat had become throughly cooked.   From the greatness of these fires it has resulted that their sites are still to be recognised in many parts of Ireland by their burnt blackness.   It is they that are commonly called *Fualachta nam Fiann*, or the Fenians cooking spots.

As to the warriors of the Fenians, when they were assembled at the place where their fires had been lighted . . . there every man stripped himself to his skin, tied his tunic round his waist, and then set to dressing his hair and cleansing his limbs, thus ridding himself of the sweat and soil of the day's hunt.   Then they began to supple their thews and muscles by gentle exercise, loosening them by friction, until they had relieved themselves of all sense of stiffness and fatigue.   When they had finished doing this they sat down and ate their meal.   That being over, they set about constructing their hunting-booths, and preparing their beds, and so put themselves in train for sleep.   Of the following three materials did each man construct his bed—of the brushwood of the forest, of moss, and of fresh rushes. The brushwood was laid next the ground, over it was placed the moss, and lastly rushes were spread over all. It is these three materials that are designated in our old romances as the *Tri Cuilcedha nam Fiann* (the three beddings of the Fenians).

The literature of the Ossianic cycle is divided by O'Curry into four classes—

1. The first consists of poems in ancient MSS., ascribed to Fionn Mac Cumhail, to his sons Ossian and Fergus Finnbheoil, and his nephew Caoilte. There are seven in Fionn's name, five in the Book of Leinster, and two in the Book of Lecain. Other two are attributed to Ossian in the Book of Leinster, of which one is a description of the battle of Gabhra, which took place in the year 283, and in which Oscar, the brave son of Ossian, and Cairbre Lifeachair, the monarch of Erin, fell by each other's hands.

The original of this latter has both alliteration and assonance, which we miss in the English version here given :—

> An Ogam on a stone, and a stone on a grave,
> Where once men trod ;
> Erin's prince on a white horse
> Was slain by a slender spear.
>
> Cairbre made a cruel cast,
> High on his horse good in the fray ;
> Shortly before they both were lamed—
> He struck Oscar's right arm off.
>
> Oscar made a mighty cast,
> Raging bold like a lion :
> Killed Cairbre, grandson [1] of Conn,
> Whom warriors bold obeyed.
>
> Youths, mighty and daring,
> They met their death in the strife ;
> Not long before their combat,
> More heroes had fallen than lived.

---

[1] Really great-grandson.

> I myself was in the fight,
> Southward there of Gabor green ;
> Twice fifty men I slew—
> With my own hand I slew them.
>
> The Ogam is here on the stone,
> Round which many ill-fated fell ;
> Were Finn, in prowess great, alive
> Long in mind would be the Ogam.

The facts of Cairbre fighting on horseback and the Ogam on the stone seem to point back to early times, though alternatively the ideas might be used afterwards to give an air of antiquity to the piece.

Ossian's second describes the great fair and festival games of Liffey, and sketches a visit he paid with his father and accompanying warriors to the court of the King of Munster.   These are the only poems of the bard that O'Curry knew, that could positively be traced as far back as the twelfth century.   The earliest written pieces superscribed with his name that we have in Scotland are the nine in the Book of the Dean of Lismore.   Mr. J. F. Campbell was of opinion that the Dean regarded them as actual compositions of the warrior-bard, contemporary with Cormac Mac Art.

Of one of these, well known as a lament of Ossian in his old age, Professor Blackie has given an English rendering from the Dean's text, and Dr. Douglas Hyde another more recently from a similar text in the Belfast Museum.   The latter runs thus :—

> Long was last night in cold Elphin,
> More long is to-night on its weary way.
> Though yesterday seemed to me long and ill,
> Yet longer still was this dreary day.
>
> And long for me is each hour new-born,
> Stricken, forlorn, and smit with grief
> For the hunting lands and the Fenian bands,
> And the long-haired, generous, Fenian chief.

I hear no music, I find no feast,
I slay no beast from a bounding steed,
I bestow no gold, I am poor and old,
I am sick and cold, without wine or mead.

I court no more, and I hunt no more,
These were before my strong delight.
I cannot slay, and I take no prey;
Weary the day and long the night.

No heroes come in their war array,
No game I play, there is nought to win;
I swim no stream with my men of might,
Long is the night in cold Elphin.

Ask, O Patrick, thy God of grace,
To tell me the place he will place me in,
And save my soul from the Ill One's might,
For long is to-night in cold Elphin.

As in the beautiful poem entitled " Finn's Pastimes," so in the following verses from the Dean's Book, the bard shows that he is in intimate touch with nature, revelling in her sights and sounds:—

Binn guth duine an tir an ôir,
Binn a ghlòir a chanaid na h'eoin;
Binn an nuallan a ni a chorr,
Binn an tonn am Bun-da-treor,
Binn am fabhar a ni a ghaoth;
Binn guth cuach os Cas-a'choin,
Aluinn an dealradh a ni grian,
Binn a nithear feadail nan lon, etc.

Sweet is man's voice in the land of gold,
Sweet the sounds the birds produce;
Sweet is the murmur of the crane,
Sweet sound the waves at Bundatreor,
Sweet the soft murmuring of the wind;
Sweet sounds the cuckoo at Cas-a'choin,
How soft and pleasing shines the sun,
Sweet the blackbird sings his song, etc.

There is one genuinely ancient poem ascribed to Fergus, the bard's brother. It was copied from the lost "Dinnsenchus" into the Book of Lecain and Book of Ballymote. It tells of a remarkable adventure Ossian once had. While out hunting with a few followers he was decoyed into a mountain cavern by some of its fairy inhabitants, and detained there with his companions for a whole year. During all that time the bard was in the habit of cutting a small chip from the handle of his spear, and casting it upon the stream that issued from his rocky prison. Fionn, who had searched in vain for his missing men, happened one day to come to this river, and observing a floating chip, picked it up, and knew at once that it was from Ossian's spear, and intended for a sign. He thereupon followed the stream to its source, entered the cavern, and rescued the captive hunters.

A poem by Caoilte Mac Ronan, found in the same two MSS. as the last, and copied from the same source, is not a legend of the Feinn, but a love story, in which Cliodhna, a fair-haired, foreign lady, figures as heroine.

2. The second class of Ossianic literature consists of tracts made up of articles in prose and poetry, attributed to one or other of the bards already mentioned, but related by some other person. The most important in this category, and perhaps the only genuine one now existing, is that known as "Agallamh na Seanórach," or "Dialogue of the Ancients," the latter being Ossian and Caoilte. Full of curious and really valuable historical information, it is the largest Fenian or Ossianic tale, and has recently been edited by Dr. Whitley Stokes. The text preserved in the Book of Lismore, and more or less fully in other collections, asserts that after the battle of Gabhra, the Feinn were so shattered and diminished in numbers that they dispersed themselves over the country.

Ossian and Caoilte survived their brethren in arms, and after wandering for a time among the new and strange generation that had grown up, they agreed to separate.

The former went to his mother in the enchanted mansion

of Cleitech, as some MSS. say, to "Tir nan Og." The latter passed over Magh Breagh southwards, and ultimately joined St. Patrick, who was delighted to add so remarkable a convert to his following.

Nearly 150 years passed since their early warrior days, when Ossian suddenly returned from "Tir nan Og" and the enchanted mansion to seek his old friend and comrade Caoilte. On finding him, henceforth they both became St. Patrick's constant companions in his missionary journeys through Erin. They give him the history and topography of every place they visit and of numberless other places, all of which is noted down by Brogan, the saint's faithful scribe, for the benefit of future generations. So says the wonderful "Colloquy of the Ancients." As an instance of this service, Patrick and his company were one day sitting on the hill Finntulach, now better known as Ard-Patrick, in the county of Limerick, when the saint inquired regarding the origin of the name. Caoilte explained how it used to be called Tulach na Feinne until Fionn altered it ; and went on to relate how that great leader of men and his following were once on this same hill when Cael O'Neamhain came to him, and the conversation of the two heroes turned on Crede, the daughter of Cairbre, King of Kerry.

"Do you know," said Fionn, "that she is the greatest flirt of all the women of Erin ; that there is scarcely a precious gem in the land that . she has not obtained as a token of love ; and that she has not yet accepted the hand of any of her admirers." "I know it," said Cael, "but are you aware of the conditions on which she would accept a husband ?" "Yes," replied Fionn, "whoever is so gifted in the poetic art as to write a poem descriptive of her mansion and its rich furniture will receive her hand." "Good," said Cael, "I have with the aid of my nurse composed such a poem, and if you will accompany me, I will now repair to her court and present it to her."

Fionn consented, and setting out on their journey they in due time reached the lady's mansion, which was situated at the foot of the well-known Paps of Anann in Kerry. On their arrival, the lady asked their business. Fionn answered that Cael came to seek her hand in marriage. " Has he a poem for me ? " queried she. " I have," said Cael. And he then recited his poem, of which the following are a few characteristic verses :—

> Happy the house in which she is,
> Between men and children and women,
> Between Druids and musical performers,
> Between cup-bearers and door-keepers.
>
> Between equerries without fear,
> And distributors who divide (the fare) ;
> And over all these the command belongs
> To fair Crede of the yellow hair.
>
> It would be happy for me to be in her *dùn,*
> Among her soft and downy couches,
> Should Crede deign to hear my suit,
> Happy for me would be my journey.
>
> A bowl she has whence berry-juice flows,
> By which she colours her eyebrows black,
> She has clear vessels of fermenting ale ;
> Cups she has and beautiful goblets.
>
> The colour (of her *dun*) is like the colour of lime
> Within it are couches and green rushes,
> Within it are silks and blue mantles,
> Within it are red, gold, and crystal cups.
>
> Of its grianan the corner stones
> Are all of silver and of yellow gold,
> Its thatch in stripes of faultless order,
> Of wings of brown and crimson red.

Crede seems to have been very well pleased with this song, for she married Cael. But, sad to tell, on being called away soon after to the battle of Finntraigh, he was there killed. His widowed partner gave vent to her grief in an elegy replete with interest, because it exhibits the Celtic characteristic of imputing to all nature—birds, deer, waves, and rocks, one's own mournful feelings ; and because it contains allusions to ancient customs. Her wail sounds like a Highland coronach of other days : " A woeful note, and O a woeful note is that which the thrush in Drumqueen emits, but not more cheerful is the wail which the blackbird makes in Letterlee. A woeful sound, and O a woeful sound is that the deer utters in Drumdaleish. Dead lies the doe of Drumsheelin, the mighty stag bells after her sore suffering, and O suffering sore is the hero's death, his death, who used to lie by me. Sore suffering to me is Cael, and O Cael is a suffering sore, that by my side he is in dead man's form ; that the wave should have swept over his white body, that is what hath distracted me, so great was his delightfulness. A dismal roar, and O a dismal roar is that the shore's surf makes upon the strand. . . . A woeful booming, and O a boom of woe is that which the wave makes upon the northward beach, butting as it does against the polished rock, lamenting for Cael, now that he is gone."

3. The third class of this literature consists of miscellaneous poems attributed chiefly to Ossian, with a few also to his brother poets, and a large number without any ascription of authorship. They are found mostly in paper MSS. of the last 250 years, and are generally transcripts from older books. In whole or in part they often take the form of dialogues between Patrick and Ossian. Apparently following the idea suggested by the " Colloquy of the Ancients," the Gaelic dreamers have instituted talks and debates between these representatives of Paganism and Christianity. Such dialogues are to be found in earlier MSS., like those of the Book of Lismore and the Book of the Dean of Lismore, but more frequently in later ones. Besides dealing with the exploits of the Feinn, they somewhat humorously accentuate the antagonism between the pagan and ecclesiastical ideals. Specimens of the more famous of these may be seen in the chapter dealing with the influence of the Church on Celtic literature. Of the other poems of

this class, the best known is perhaps that entitled "Cath-Chnuic-an-Air, or, more shortly, "Cnoc-an-Air. In addition to giving an account of the battle, it describes the treasures of the Feinn hidden under Loch Lenè (Killarney).

The delightful "Ossian and Evir-Alin" may also be noted here. Pattison thought it possibly one of the oldest of all the Ossianic fragments, but he was well aware that it is not easy to determine its age. These verses from his English rendering suggest its peculiar charm :—

> We came to the dark Lake of Lego ;
> There a noble chief came to meet
> And conduct us with honour to Branno—
> With honour and welcomings sweet.
>
> .   .   .   .   .   .
>
> Branno inquired, "What is your purpose ?
> What would you have of me ? "
> And Cailta said, " We seek thy daughter,
> Her would we have of thee."
>
> .   .   .   .   .   .
>
> "So high the place, O Ossian,
> Do men's tongues to thee assign,
> If I twelve daughters had," said Branno,
> " The best of them should be thine."
>
> Then they opened the choice and spare chamber,
> That was shielded with down from the cold ;
> The posts of the door were of polished bone,
> And the leaves were of good yellow gold.
>
> Soon as generous Evir-Alin
> Saw Ossian Fingal's son,
> The love of her youth, by the hero
> By me, young maid, was won.
>
> Then we left the dark Lake of Lego
> And homeward took our way ;
> But Cormac, fierce Cormac, waylaid us
> Intent on the furious fray.

Ossian and Cormac fight for the lady. The personal combat is described, and the victorious Ossian continues—

I swept the head from his shoulders
And held it up in my hand ;
His troops they fled, and we came with joy
To Fingal's mountain land.

4. The fourth class consists of prose tales, describing in a romantic style the exploits and daring deeds of Fionn and of individuals of his band. The two best known are the " Pursuit of Diarmad and Grainne," and the " Battle [1] of Ventry Harbour." Of the former the leading details are these :—

Fionn in his old age asked the monarch Cormac Mac Art for the hand of his celebrated daughter Grainne in marriage. The king agreed to the hero's proposal, and invited him to Tara to obtain the princess's own consent, necessary in those days as in these to their union. Accepting the invitation, he proceeded thither, attended by a chosen body of his warriors, among whom were his son Ossian, his grandson Oscar, and a chief officer Diarmad O'Duibhne. A grand feast was provided, over which the monarch presided, and the Feinn were entertained with every mark of favour and distinction.

It appears to have been a custom on such occasions in ancient Erin, says O'Curry, for the mistress of the mansion or some other distinguished lady to fill her own rich drinking cup with choice liquor, and send it round by her maid-in-waiting to the leading gentlemen at the banquet, who in turn passed it on to certain others next them, in order that every guest might enjoy the distinction of participating in the special favour. The lady Grainne in this instance did the honours of the occasion, and all, with the exception of Ossian and Diarmad, had drunk from her cup. But while the imbibing company were yet proclaiming their praises of the liquor and their profound acknowledgments to the hostess, they fell one by one into a heavy sleep.

The slim hostess had caused the drink to be drugged,

---

[1] Finntraigh.

and, as soon as she recognised the effect, went and sat beside Ossian and Diarmad, addressing the former, and complaining to him of the folly of his father Fionn in expecting that a maiden of her youth and beauty should ever consent to become the wife of so old and war-worn a veteran. Had it been Ossian himself, gladly would she accept him ; but since that could not be in the circumstances, she saw no chance of escaping the evil her father's rash promise threatened to bring upon her than by flight. Ossian could not dishonour his own sire by being partner to such a course, so she conjured Diarmad, by his manliness and chivalry, to take her away, make her his wife, and thus save her from a fate more tragic in her eyes than death itself.

After much persuasion, for the step was serious in view of his leader's ire, Diarmad consented, and they both eloped, gaining the open country before the somnolent company awoke.

But no sooner had Cormac and Fionn rallied than they perceived how they were duped, and, raging desperately, they vowed vengeance against the absent pair. Organising a party for pursuit, the jilted lover immediately set out to scour the country. In this search he sent forward advance parties of his swiftest and best men in every direction. Apparently to little purpose at first, for Diarmad was a favourite with his brethren-in-arms, and the peculiar circumstances of the elopement invested it with such an element of romance, and of sympathy on the part of the young heroes, that those in pursuit never could discover the retreat of the lovers. Even if Fionn himself did happen to get on their track, he was thwarted by means of some wonderful stratagem on the part of Diarmad.

Such is the outline of " The Pursuit of Diarmad and Grainne," a pursuit which extended all over Erin. In the course of its narration in the original a large amount of curious information on social manners, ancient tales, superstitions, topography, and the natural products of different parts, is introduced. The absconding pair were caught at last, but the Fenian heroes would not permit Fionn to punish Diarmad.

Ultimately, the chief had his own peculiar revenge. When at the hunt of the magic boar Diarmad killed that formidable quarry, and escaped scatheless, with sinister intention Fionn asked him to measure its length against the bristles. In doing so Diarmad's foot, his only vulnerable part, was pierced by one of the poisonous points. And although Fionn could have restored him by a draught from his life-giving shell, he would not. Thus died the hapless Diarmad O'Duibhne, an officer of fine person and most fascinating manners. Famous in family annals too, for from him the Campbells trace their descent. Not only does he figure in their genealogical tree,[1] but the Dukes of Argyll still have the boar's head on their coat-of-arms.

The "Lay of Diarmad" has for generations been very popular. There are various versions of it. Pattison's English rendering is mainly from the text in Maccallum's collection. Fionn afterwards repenting that he did not save his young rival, lamented thus :—

> Alas, that, said Fionn, for a woman
> I've slain my own sister's son—
> For an ill woman slain him! too noble
> To be slain for the loveliest one.
>
> Sad stood the heroes beside thee,
> O youth of the noble race ;
> And dim grew the eyes of each maiden
> When the mould went over thy face.
>
> And now like the tree, I stand lonely—
> Wither'd and wasted and sear ;
> With the rude howling tempest to tear me,
> Where the shade of no green bough is near.

Quite a large collection of ancient Ossianic ballads are

[1] Dr. Skene has shown, *Celtic Scotland*, vol. iii. p. 459, that another O'Duibhne is in question.

concerned with the wars between the Feinn and the Norse
invaders from Lochlann.   They are quite manifestly of
dates posterior to the Viking age, and might constitute a
class by themselves.   In " The Banners of the Feinn," the
heroes are marshalled before us one by one.   And here also
Diarmad O'Duibhne takes the lead.   The ballad, in rollicking
modern verse, has been thus rendered by Dr. Macneill :—

> The Norland king stood on the height
> And scanned the rolling sea ;
> He proudly eyed his gallant ships
> That rode triumphantly.
>
> And then he looked where lay his camp
> Along the rocky coast,
> And where were seen the heroes brave
> Of Lochlann's famous host.
>
> Then to the land he turn'd, and there
> A fierce-like hero came ;
> Above him was a flag of gold,
> That waved and shone like flame.
>
> "Sweet Bard," thus spoke the Norland king,
> "What banner comes in sight ?
> The valiant chief that leads the host,
> Who is that man of might ?"
>
> "That," said the bard, " is young MacDoon,
> His is that banner bright ;
> When forth the Feinn to battle go,
> He's foremost in the fight," etc., etc.

Dream-figures of the dim and distant past, Fionn and
his warriors have not quite lost their sway over the Celtic
imagination.   Indeed, Gaelic popular tradition has it that
they are not dead, but sleeping under great green knolls
somewhere in the Highlands, and that one day they will
awake to restore the Gael to his ancient power, just as the
Cymri look for the return of Arthur.   It is even related
that once a wight obtained entrance to their place of rest,

and was asked to blow three times on the *dudach* or horn. This he did, and, after the first blast, behold ! the sleeping forms of men and dogs moved to life ; after the second, the Feinn warriors got up on their elbows and stared at him. The sight so unnerved the rash intruder that, throwing down the instrument, he fled in terror from the ghostly place ; while after him came the awful imprecation, " Milè mollachd, is miosa dh'fhag na fhuair " (" A thousand curses on you ; you left us worse than you found us "). These were the last words he heard as he made good his escape— the last account of the Feinn borne to the upper world.

CHAPTER XI

THE INFLUENCE OF THE NORSE INVASIONS ON GAELIC LITERATURE

The dreaded Vikings—In English waters—Descents on Iona—Monasteries favourite objects of attack—Destruction of books—Their own eddas and sagas—Modern discovery of the wonderful Icelandic literature—The Northmen in a new light—Literary effects of their invasions—Arrested development—Lamentable dispersion of the literary classes—Pilgrim Scots—The rise of Scottish Gaelic—Present-day differences between it and Irish—Introduction of Norse words—Decay of inflection—Gaelic examples of Viking beliefs and superstitions—The Norseman still with us.

BRITAIN owes her proud pre-eminence among the nations as much to the sea as to any other external factor. Her empire seems to sit stable upon the waves. So far from disconnecting the broadcast parts, it is the ocean that links them well together into one mighty whole which keeps "the fretful realms in awe." Thus as citizens of the British Empire we are wont to regard the sea as our most powerful ally and friend. We connect with it the idea of national defence. It is our bulwark. With it we associate also the spirit of freedom, and pleasure in summer time, when multitudes frequent the coast and drink in new life and energy there. And in reflective moments it wafts our thoughts to larger issues, and we recognise that the sea helps towards the realisation of the brotherhood of man, for it brings the nations into close touch with one another, and through the quiet channels of trade and commerce, tends to exorcise old and distant race antagonisms. And so in this country we are born to view the ocean with kindly eyes, and to rely upon it almost as our national foster-parent.

Yet it was not ever thus. We go back to a time in these western lands when the briny wave was a terror to men, for out there, in storm and shine, lurked their chief danger. Any morning they awoke, or any evening they retired to rest, they might see the dragon-prowed galleys of the wild Norsemen bearing down upon them. And in the night, when the winds howled or there came a moaning from the deep, they could not be sure but the dreaded Vikings were upon them. No part of the coast of these islands or of north or west France was safe from their incursions. The blue waves and the distant horizon of the watery main were then scanned with different feelings from ours. A secret fear haunted the imagination as it saw or fancied it perceived a distant sail on the seascape. The very children inherited the awe inspired by these ruffians of the deep ; for ruffians they were, many of them, who massacred and laid waste, sparing not even the peaceful abodes of piety and learning.

Sometimes they bore down upon a reach of coast when the unsuspecting inhabitants had not the faintest presentiment of peril from the waves. A medieval writer (Monachi Sangale, Gesta Caroli, II. 14) tells how Charlemagne himself and his courtiers were thus surprised. They were seated at a banquet one day in the town of Narbonne, when all of a sudden some swift barks were seen putting into the harbour. The company started up, wondering who the strangers might be. Were they Jews, or Africans, or simply British traders ? None could tell. The keen eye of the king alone hastily divined the situation. " No bales of merchandise," said he, " are borne hither by yonder galleys. They are manned by terrible foes." And then advancing to the window, he stood for a long time reflecting, his eyes moist with tears and bent on vacancy. No one durst ask him the cause of his foreboding, till at length he broached it himself. " It is not for myself," muttered he, " that I am weeping, nor for any

harm that yonder barks can do to me ; but it grieves me
sore to think that during my lifetime they have made bold
to approach these shores, and greater still is my dejection
when I reflect on the evils they will yet inflict on those who
come after me." And he was right. The crews that he saw
in the offing were plundering Northmen, who were soon to
be followed by kindred sea-rovers bent on conquest. Of
little avail in his own time were his strong forts and garri-
son towns built to withstand the foe, and after his death his
less imperious successors hardly dared lift a dagger to stem
the tide of invasion that laid waste their fairest lands
and cities. "Take the map," wrote Sir Francis Palgrave in
his history of *Normandy and England*, "and colour with
vermilion the provinces, districts, and shores which the
Northmen visited, as the record of each invasion. The
colouring will have to be repeated more than ninety times
successively before you can arrive at the conclusion of the
Carlovingian dynasty. Furthermore, mark by the usual
symbol of war—the two crossed swords—the localities
where the battles were fought by or against pirates,—where
they were defeated or triumphant, or where they pillaged,
burned, or destroyed; and the valleys and banks of the Elbe,
Rhine and Moselle, Scheldt, Meuse, Somme and Seine,
Loire, Garonne and Adour, the inland Allier, and all the
coasts and coastlands between estuary and estuary, and the
countries between the river streams will appear bristling as
with *chevaux de frise*.

"The strongly-fenced Roman cities, the venerated abbeys
and their dependent bourgades, often more flourishing and
extensive than the ancient seats of government, the opulent
seaports and trading towns were all equally exposed to the
Danish attacks, stunned by the Northmen's approach, sub-
jugated by their fury."

According to Paul B. du Chaillu, one of the more recent
and exhaustive writers on the subject, the Viking age
extended from the second to the middle of the twelfth century A.D. For a long time—centuries no doubt—individuals

were wont to come as traders, and in that capacity may have been welcomed. But towards the end of the eighth century an alarming development took place. Issuing from the viks or bays of Norway and Denmark, the notorious Vikings appeared as depredators and conquerors. 787 is given as the date when first their hostile vessels were seen in English waters. And henceforward concerted attempts were made to land on our shores and annex our territory. In 793 the work of plunder was effectively inaugurated by an attack on Lindisfarne and other points in Northumbria. The monastery on that island was laid waste, and the Northumbrian kingdom itself so crippled that it lost the commanding influence it wielded in the days of Adamnan and Bede and their friend King Aldfrid.

Next year the marauding Norsemen emerged in the Western Isles, which from this time till the middle of the thirteenth century were destined to be favourite haunts and special theatres of their operations.

They quickly found and sacked defenceless Iona, and for years took spoils of the sea between that Island and Erin. The Hebrides and the Isle of Man were at their mercy in 798, and still insatiate with former booty, in 802 they revisited Iona and burned its sacred buildings to the ground. Returning four years later, they put the whole community to the sword, numbering no fewer than sixty-eight persons.

Iona truly had cause to dread the unceasing attentions of these terrible strangers, for each visit seemed more appalling than the other. Baulked in their efforts to get the silver shrines and relics of the departed Columba, the freebooters made another swift and dire descent upon the island in 825. Trained by sad experience, the monks on this occasion had taken the precaution to bury their treasure-trove in a hole in the earth, covering the surface with sods. And when their fierce assailants burst upon the unprotected sanctuary, they found the holy St. Blathmac, who was probably acting-abbot at the time, standing before the altar. Of him they impetuously demanded the way to the hidden objects of their pursuit—the precious silver shrines—and when he calmly refused, insisting that he did not know the place of concealment which his brethren had selected, they savagely murdered him on the spot. The Annals of Ulster record the martyrdom, and Walafridus Strabo, a contemporary on the Continent, gives an interesting metrical account of the event in Latin, gathered no doubt from one or other of the monks who had fled to him from these islands through terror of the Norse.

Once more, on Christmas eve in 986, the famous monastery of Hy, ever rising on its own ashes, was attacked and destroyed by the successors of these old Danes, and this time the abbot and fifteen monks were put to a violent death. From Orkney and Shetland, and the coasts of Caithness and the Hebrides the hardy Norsemen swooped down upon Eastern Scotland as well as upon the English and Irish seaboards, until at length they made themselves for a time masters of a great part of the country.

How they went to work may be gathered from their own records. For example : Harold Fairhair's saga, c. 22, says, " They ravaged in Scotland and took possession of Katanes (Caithness) and Sudrland (Sutherland) as far as Ekkjalsbakki. Sigurd slew the Scotch Jarl, Melbrigdi, and tied his head to his saddle-straps ; the tooth which protruded from the Jarl's head wounded the calf of Sigurd's leg, which swelled and he died therefrom ; he is mounded at Ekkjalsbakki."

From these details it will be seen that they had much of the Vandal and the rough buccaneer in their composition. Monasteries were favourite objects of attack. They contained the richest plunder, and from their nature, as religious centres, offered the least resistance. And not content with merely carrying off the loot, the rovers mingled blood with their depredations. Hence the peculiar fitness of the introduction into the Litany of the significant petition : " From the fury of the Northmen, good Lord, deliver us." And this coarse grain in their character accounts for their reckless conduct in other directions. They seem to have had a special aversion to monks and clerics and learning. They made short work of the books and bells of monasteries. We have contemporary evidence of their vandalism towards literature in a remarkable book of the period entitled, *Wars of the Gael with the Gaill* (Northmen). It is in Gaelic, and appears in the Book of Leinster, copied about 1150. The author may have been an eye-witness of many of the scenes, and particularly of the battle of Clontarf, which he so realistically describes. His accuracy on matters of fact has been fully attested. We can, therefore, credit his statement when he affirms regarding the few men of learning who had survived the Viking ordeal that "their writings and their books in every church and in every sanctuary where they were, were burnt and thrown into water by the plunderers from beginning to end" (of the Norse invasion).

Countless numbers of the illuminated books of the men of Erin and Alba thus perished. It was a mania with these illiterate rovers to destroy all learning. Eloquent testimony to this is borne by the historian Keating also. "It was not allowed," he says, "to give instruction in letters. . . . No scholars, no clerics, no books, no holy relics were left in church or monastery through dread of them. Neither bard nor philosopher nor musician pursued his wonted profession in the land."

And if modern evidence were necessary it might be found in the fact that while Gaelic MSS. of the Viking age are to be found in almost every other country of Europe, there is not one to be gleaned in the lands whence the Norsemen came. From which circumstance it may be inferred that they set so little value upon these literary acquisitions that they took no care to preserve them, or even to carry them away to their own territory. When the tide of invasion had well nigh spent itself, Ireland, once so rich in native literature, was found to be so depleted that King Brian Boru had to send delegates abroad, "to buy books beyond the sea and the great ocean," as the records affirm, so scarce had they ultimately become.

Yet even in their roving days the strenuous Norsemen had rare *eddas* and *sagas* of their own, to which they were passionately devoted. These were not then written down, but recited orally, like the Celtic tales, till they found a literary embodiment in MS. books.

It was only towards the middle of the last century that their wonderful national sagas burst upon Europe, and thrilled and surprised the learned quite as much as if they had felt a whiff of the old Viking breath upon them. Prior to that time historians were largely dependent upon the English, Irish, and Frankish chronicles for their knowledge of this northern race and their deeds of spoliation, but since the discovery in Iceland of the literary remains of their immediate descendants, quite a fresh light has been cast upon their disposition and habits. And we recognise that they were not quite the demons and fiends the monkish scribes believed them to be. It is clear that, having suffered so much from the hardy invader the latter had the tendency to exaggerate his ferocity. For example, the author of the *Wars of the Gael with the Gaill:* "In a word, although there were an hundred sharp, ready, cool, never-resting brazen tongues in each head, and a hundred garrulous, loud, unceasing voices for each tongue, they could not recount nor narrate nor enumerate nor tell what all the Gael suffered in common, both men and women, laity and clergy, old and young, noble and ignoble, of hardship and of injury and of oppression in every house from these valiant, wrathful, foreign, purely pagan people."

In every war and conquest there are dreadful happenings, and the Viking was not troubled with sentiment or too much conscience in his proceedings. He was rough and ready— like his trade, as we should say—as he needed to be in that age if he meant to be master or even to get a living.

Great upheavals, we must remember, were taking place in his mother country and driving him from his home.

To take one example, Harold Fairhair, in bringing the whole of Norway under his sway effected quite a revolution, changing the old ödal tenure by which the land was held into a feudal one. Rather than submit to the new order many nobles and people simultaneously sought freedom elsewhere. They settled in Shetland, Orkney, and the Hebrides, occasionally raiding back to harass the king. But by the year 872 the latter had so far established his rule at home that he was free to tackle these islands with their Norwegian rebels and annex the territory to Norway. Whereupon the more daring and independent spirits who had settled there and in Ireland, and had contracted alliances in marriage with leading native families, once more hived off, this time sailing away for Iceland to join friends and relations who had migrated thither from the mother country. And these were the nucleus of the colony whose descendants produced the wonderful Icelandic literature which is now reckoned among the most valuable assets of medieval Europe. Among the settlers were men who bore Gaelic names and left their impress upon this Norse heritage. From the parchments lately discovered upon which the history of the Vikings is written, and which are begrimed by the smoke of the Icelandic cabin and worn by the centuries that have passed over them, we learn many things that tend to show the Northmen in a new light. These men, who held undisputed sway of the seas for more than nine centuries, were not by any means barbarians. They had a civilisation rivalling that of the Gael, though of a different warp and woof, and they were not even without a script or mode of writing. The characters they used are known as runes, and may have been in use as early as the second or third century.

In the sagas we are often told that drawings on shields and embroidery on cloth were made by them to preserve the memory of heroic deeds and important events. And though the set who invaded our shores, in the stress of war and sailing were not likely to trouble much with learning or letters, their nation had doubtless retired *literati* just like our own.

To trace the effect of these Norse invasions on Celtic literature will now be our main endeavour.

I. The first and immediate influence was doubtless to arrest its progress. After ages of apparent barrenness, the genius of the Gaelic-speaking peoples had at length produced the germ of a literature which in the days of St. Patrick and St. Columba took root and began to grow. For wellnigh four centuries it had gone on developing in a most promising way. The quiet and leisure of the monasteries furnished the atmosphere most suitable for its inception and subsequent growth. These religious retreats were then the centres of learning and nurseries of thought, and many men were arising within their sacred walls who had a genuine love and taste for writing—a love so great that they were not merely content with copying books, composing poems, or writing history, but they embellished them in a way which has excited the admiration of modern times.

Gaelic literature both in Ireland and Scotland was thus bidding fair to yield a rich and abundant harvest when the blight of the Norse invasion fell suddenly upon it, and effectually hindered its farther advance for several centuries. The history of literary work in every age and country shows that it is mostly in times of peace that this delicate plant flourishes. In the stormier periods, when wars are waged, changes frequent, and a spirit of unrest abroad, production of books is rare or even non-existent.

When the Celts themselves were a warrior race, living for the most part by the sword, and migrating from land to land, they had no literature that we know of. The conditions of life were not such that men could quietly cultivate the art and practice of writing. Life was too full of change, too turbulent, and too uncertain.

Similarly the Norsemen during the Viking age, till they gained a peaceful retreat in Iceland, were no litterateurs. Sailing and fighting were more exciting, and with these the habits of the scribe or of the author were not entirely compatible. And so when the tide of invasion burst upon the monasteries of Ireland and Scotland, when rest from strife and security from change could no longer be had, authorship, if it did not entirely cease, became more rare and spasmodic. This is particularly true of Scotland, for with the exception of the Book of Deer, with its Latin contents of the ninth century, and its Gaelic entries written towards the end of the Viking period, we have nothing to show, of known Scottish origin, from the beginning to the end of these incursions. Ireland was more fortunate in that in spite of invasion her literary output was more continuous, especially in the department of poetry.

II. Contemporary with this arrested development, the sinister influence of the Norse depredations may be traced in another result, and one which has left a deep and permanent mark in the history of Celtic literature. It is the lamentable dispersion of the literary classes—monks and missionaries—to the Continent with such books and MSS. as they were able to save from the violence of the invaders. Long before the inroads of these Norsemen became a terror to the Gael, we know that Irish missionaries had spread themselves over England, France, Germany, Switzerland, and Italy. And in addition to their peripatetic preaching, they had established monasteries and colleges for the diffusion of Christianity and learning. From MSS. preserved in St. Gall, Switzerland, we gather that these pilgrim Scots usually travelled in companies, provided with long walking-sticks, leathern wallets, and water-bottles. They wore long flowing hair, and were clad in rough garments. Though thus rude and uncouth in appearance, they were accomplished scholars, many of them, and easily acquired the languages of the countries through which they passed, or in which they settled and preached with all the perfervid eloquence so natural to the Celt. To show the extent of their wanderings, and the distinguished calibre of the missionaries themselves, a few names may be given which still live in books and tradition. St. Columbanus, perhaps the best known of all, died in 615. His name is perpetuated in the town of San Columbano. It was he who founded the monasteries of Luxueil in France, and Bobbio among the Apennines.

Almost equally prominent as an evangelist was St. Gall, his companion, who gave his name not only to the town which subsequently grew up beside his monastery, but also to a whole canton of Switzerland.   Then there were St. Catald, from the school of Lismore in Ireland ; St. Donnatt his brother, Bishop of Lupice in Naples ; St. Kilian the apostle and martyr of Franconia, still annually commemorated at Würzburg.   At a monastery near Strasburg, also founded by an Irish bishop, there is a charter of date 810, which specifies grants made to that house, to the poor, and to the pilgrim Scots—the nine of whom therein mentioned are all bishops except the abbot.   In the ninth century there was a convent of Scots at Mont St. Victor near Feldkirk.   Dungall, of the same Scotic nationality, figures as the author of the famous letter to Charlemagne on the eclipses of 810, and he held the office of preceptor at the cathedral school at Pavia. Besides the numerous other places in which they laboured, from the middle of the seventh to the twelfth century, Scotic monasteries were founded at Ratisbon, Vienna, Eichstadt, Würzburg, Erfurt, Kelheim, and Constance.

These earlier retreats served as so many houses of refuge for the poor monks and scholars flying from the fury of the Norsemen, when life and property became insecure at home, in Iona, and elsewhere.   It is known that a fresh tide of Gaelic pilgrims set out for the Continent from the time that the new peril appeared, seeking safe custody for themselves and their books among their countrymen abroad.

And thus it has come to pass that there are to-day hundreds of Celtic MSS. in Latin and Gaelic widely scattered throughout Europe, in places as far apart as Paris, Brussels, Dresden, Berne, Vienna, Rome, Florence, Milan, Schaffhausen, St. Gall, etc.   And while in the British Isles we have only seven of these with Gaelic writing prior to the eleventh century, on the Continent there are as many as twenty.

It is surmised that it was in this manner in 825, after the attack on Iona and murder of St. Blathmac, that the famous *Vita Columbæ* of Adamnan found its way to Reichenau on the Rhine, where it remained for nearly a millennium, till it was ultimately transferred to Schaffhausen.

These are two far-reaching and long-lasting effects of the Viking troubles—the arrest of the literary development and the dispersion of the documents, but they by no means exhaust the category.

III. We have now to take into account the severance of Ireland from Scotland. Anterior to the Norse invasions the language and literature of both were one. There is no distinction to be made, for they were common to both countries from the time of St. Columba, and there was constant coming and going between Scotland and Ireland. But when the Norsemen came they effectually put a stop to this. For two centuries they kept the kindred realms apart, and never again was the original unity restored.

During the period of disjunction the separated parts began to travel on different lines, and when the Viking sway ceased to sever them, the language and literature of each had already taken on a character of its own sufficiently divergent to keep them for ever asunder. The Book of Deer is the first monument of this departure in Scotland, even as the Leabhar Na h'Uidhre and *Liber Hymnorum* are the earliest in Ireland.

The Norse invasions were thus directly responsible for the rise of the Scottish Gaelic and our native vernacular literature as distinct from the Irish. Had it not been for their interception there is no knowing how long the two dialects might have continued as one.

As it was, notwithstanding the growing divergence, the written, though not the spoken language of both countries might be regarded as still, for the most part, the same in form till the fourteenth century. After that they ceased to be even apparently identical, and to-day the chief differences between the two tongues are these four :—

1. The Irish has a future in the verb, whereas Gaelic uses the present tense to indicate futurity.

2. Inflection is fuller in written Irish than in written Gaelic.

3. In Irish (south especially) the accent remains on the end syllable, whereas in Gaelic it is nearly always on the first.

4. In Gaelic every noun outside the *o* declension forms the plural in *n*, whereas in Irish *n* is shown very rarely.

IV. Instead of the parent Irish, there was from henceforth a Norse linguistic influence upon the language of Scotland. There can be no doubt that the new element thus imported into the Gaelic is very considerable. Yet this is a department of philology which has never been adequately worked. It offers an interesting field for further research and inquiry, and it is gratifying to know that the study of Irish-Norse relations, in its various aspects, claims the attention of such eminent writers as Professor Zimmer, Professor Sophus Bugge, Dr. Alexander Bugge, Dr. Craigie of Oxford, and Miss Faraday.

We have to reckon with the fact that the Norsemen came in large numbers, and freely intermarried with the native races, so that to-day the inhabitants of Orkney, North-east Caithness, North and West Sutherland, and North Lewis, differ very little in physique and general appearance from the people of Norway and Iceland. And in Skye, Islay, and Kintyre there is a large admixture of Viking blood, as well as in the other Hebridean Islands, though not so marked in Mull and Jura.

As we should expect, the Norse element in the Gaelic is most in evidence in maritime terms and place names.

As examples of the former, we have *vata*, a boat; *sgoth*, a skiff; *birlinn*, a yacht; *sgioba*, a crew; *stiuir*, a rudder; *ailm*, a helm; *sgod*, the sheet of the sail; *rac*, the mast-hoop; *stagh*, the stay; *reang*, the rib; *tobhta*, the thwart; *tearr*, tar; *spor*, a flint.

Then we have *eilean* for island; *haf*, the open sea; *ob*, a land-locked bay, as in Oban; *uig*, a creek; *aoi*, an isthmus; *geodha*, a gully; *sgeir*, a reef; *bodha* and *roc*, sunken rocks; *cleit*, a cliff; *grunnd*, the bottom; *bruic*, sea-weed.

Of place names there is no lack. It has been calculated that in Lewis, Norse are still to Gaelic names as three or four to one ; in Skye as three to two ; in Islay as one to two ; in Kintyre as one to four ; in Arran and the Isle of Man as one to eight.

The Minch they called Skottlandsfjord. The smaller isles were nearly all renamed, Eriskay, Eric's isle ; Jura, deer's isle ; Pladda, flat isle ; Staffa, stave isle ; Sanda, sand isle. To the larger islands the invaders left their original names, though these were occasionally sounded in Norse fashion, as, for example, Sgith' (Skye) as Skiō with long vowel.

Personal names were also imported ; Rognvald as Raonall or Rao'all, Ragnhilda as Raonailt, Torcull, Goraidh, etc. The Latin Magnus, which was common as a personal name in Norway, we borrowed in the Gaelic form Manus ; and such surnames as Macleod, Nicolson, Macaulay, and Macaskill with the Celtic Mac prefixed.

Other common words of Norse derivation are *traill*, a slave ; *nabuidh*, a neighbour ; *sgillinn*, a penny ; *mòd*, a court of justice, meeting ; *gadhar*, a greyhound ; *toraisgean*, a peat knife, half Norse, half Gaelic ; *suith*, soot ; *shearradair*, towel ; *mal*, rent ; *gleadhraich*, noise.

The Vikings were called *sumarlidi*, "summer wanderers," because they were most abroad at that season, and from this came the name once famous in the West—"Somerled" of the Isles. To the Norse is also attributed the insertion of *t* in words like *struth* for *sruth*, *stron* for *sron*.

V. But more important even than the introduction of new words was the influence upon the structure of the language. And competent authorities hold that to it we must assign the main share in accelerating the decay of inflection noticeable in the Scottish Gaelic and Manx as compared with the Irish. The latter was not so much exposed to Norse influence as the former. And it is very apparent that the change referred to began to assert itself soon after the Norse had ostracised the Irish, and taken its place as a rival language in the West, destined to influence the local Gaelic.

It is not contended that the Gaelic writers derived any help from the Norsemen. They were themselves the more advanced of the two. On the other hand, the Icelandic scholar Viglisson has traced Gaelic rhymes and measures as well as Gaelic ideas in the old Norse literature, and Professor Zimmer even suggests that the Icelander owes to the Gael his prose style. In the Islendinga Book, c. i., we read that when Iceland was first settled from Norway in the days of Harold Fairhair there were Christian men, whom the Norsemen called Papa, but who afterwards went away because they would not remain with the heathen, and left behind them Irish books and croziers and bells, from which it could be seen that they were Irishmen.[1]

VI. How far the Norse ideas have entered into the warp and woof of Gaelic literature is perhaps the most interesting aspect of the whole subject, and one that offers a wide field for research. It cannot yet be said that we have sufficiently differentiated between the two sets of legends, beliefs, and customs to be able to affirm with certainty that such and such belong to the one race, and such and such belong to the other. The mythologies of peoples have so much in common, so much that seems characteristic of the thinking of the whole human race at certain stages of its development, that many ideas and legends have no exclusive value, and cannot be claimed as the original heritage of one people more than another.

Yet conceptions pass from land to land and folk to folk, like an epidemic, and become assimilated by each new race that breathes or imbibes them, and as the Gaels have contributed to the thought of the Norsemen, so have the Vikings in turn impressed their ideas, especially their legends and beliefs, upon the imaginative race with whom

---

[1] Iceland, first settled by the Irish in 795, perhaps sixty-five years earlier than the Norse. According to M. Letronne, 860 is the date of the arrival of the latter.

they mingled, and by whom they ultimately became absorbed.

When we remember that, in the opinion of the best authorities, even the very oldest of the Gaelic sagas could hardly have been written down before the seventh or eighth century, and that many of them are of much later date, we can well conceive how a Norse element might enter largely into them.

It is well known that the Lochlanners or Norsemen figure largely in the Ossianic poems, and " it is quite evident," says Dr. Hyde, " that most of them, at least in the modern form in which we now have them, are post-Norse productions."

In the Mythological, which is really the latest in point of writing, while the Fomorians who dwelt in Lochlann, vicious and troublesome invaders as they were, may in their origin be conceived as none other than the sea-powers personified — the rough chaotic tumult of the Atlantic Ocean, against which in the west of Ireland the various settlers had to contend, they might more literally represent the Viking rovers which later ages had to encounter, and by whom they were so often harassed and overcome.

In such stories as The Children of Lir, and more particularly The Children of Tuireann, we have Gaelic examples of Norse beliefs and superstitions. Take, for instance, shape-changing, of which there are many illustrations in the Viking sagas. We are reminded at once of the unhappy fate of the children of Lir, when we read in the Hrolf Kraki, cc. 25, 26, that " King Hring of Uppdalir in Norway had a son Björn, and when his wife died, he married a woman from Tuinmôrk. She changed her stepson into a bear in this way. She struck him with a wolf-skin glove, and said that he should become a fierce and cruel lair-bear, and use no other food than the cattle of his father." She went on to say, " Thou shalt kill it for thy food, so much of it that it will be unexampled, and never shalt thou get out of this spell, and this revenge shall harm thee."

Then it is told that the king's cattle were killed in large numbers, as a big and fierce grey bear began to attack them. One evening the Bondi's daughter (Björn's sweetheart) happened to see this fierce bear, which came and fondled her much. She thought she recognised in the animal the eyes of her lover, and followed him to his den, where, strange to relate, she saw, not the bear, but a man. And Björn, for he was no other, told her he was a beast by day and a man by night.

As in this Norse saga we have the marriage, the stepmother, the revenge, the striking with the wolf-skin glove, the spell, all corresponding to the similar details in the Gaelic tale, with the exception that in the latter the objects are usually struck by a magic wand instead of by a wolf-skin glove. And comparing it with the story of the children of Tuireann, Cian went into the shape of a pig, while Björn figured as a bear.

The two Gaelic stories above referred to, though they profess to belong to the Mythological age, centuries before Christ, were actually written down much later than the Heroic tales. The Norse story, on the other hand, is supposed to be laid in the sixth century A.D., and it would be hard to say, we daresay, which originated first or found the earliest expression in writing.

Another Viking idea which has found its way into Gaelic literature is the belief in a Valhalla, or hall of the slain. It was held that to fall gloriously on the field of battle secured undisputed entrance into this heaven. In the "Aged Bard's Wish," an attractive poem of the Macpherson period, we find the bard desirous of obtaining entry at death into the hall where dwell Ossian and Daol. This conception of the future was evidently adopted from Norse traditions, for the Gael, so far as is known, had not originally the idea of a Valhalla. Transmigration was more in his line. And curious was the occupation of the warriors in the hall of the slain.

" Every day after having dressed, they put on their war

clothes, and go out into the enclosure and fight and slay
each other. This is their game ; near day meal they ride
home to Valhalla and sit down to drink." (later edda, c. 40).

The unworthy and fushionless had not this bliss. Their
portion was a region cold, foggy, and cheerless. And it is
thought that the author of Adamnan's vision may have got
his cold and wet imagery of the place of woe from the pagan
invaders. St. Brendan, in his *Navigatio Brendani,* a book
well known in medieval Europe, gives a legend which is
one of the most singular products of Celtic imagination.
He found Judas upon a rock in the midst of the Polar seas.
Once a week he passes a day there to refresh himself from
the fires of Hell. A cloak that he had given to a beggar
is hung before him and tempers his sufferings. As St.
Brendan lived in the middle of the sixth century the subject of the legend is pre-Norse, and it is the heat that is
represented as infernal. Dante, it will be remembered,
reserves the ice and cold for the last degree of torment in
the Inferno. And of Highland bards, Duncan Macrae,
David Mackellar, and others, down to the eighteenth century, have introduced the same idea. Indeed, it has even
been hinted that the tendency of the Highland preacher to
dwell upon the sterner aspects of our faith may well be due
to the lingering influence of the northern paganism. But
this we think rather far-fetched and unlikely, for other less
ancient influences, local and potent, have been at work to
depress the outlook of the Gael.

The Norseman, however, is still with us in hidden and
often unknown corners of our life, our literature, and our
history. Perhaps to him we owe our continuance as a race
to this day. He has carried with him over the wave the
breath of freedom and strenuous endeavour, and infused
them into the life of this great nation, helping Britain to
build up and maintain a world-wide empire and supremacy
upon the seas.

But judging his influence upon Gaelic literature solely,
we cannot say that, so far as it is known, it was of a helpful

or even far-reaching kind. In the first shock of invasion it would rather seem to have been ruinous and deleterious in its effects, arresting development and dispersing the rising literary activity.

But what if it could be proved by further research that while distinctly hostile to the ecclesiastical order in all its manifestations and productions, and therefore its books, the appearance of the Norsemen in these islands revived the interest in the native sagas, so that the scribes were encouraged to write them down and preserve them for future ages. Then verily it might with strictest veracity be said that to the Vikings we owe the cream of our literature, for it is a recognised fact that "the sagas and historic tales, and the poetry that is mingled with them, are of far greater importance from a purely literary point of view" than all the ecclesiastical transcriptions and contributions of the period. But this is a suggestion we offer as not at all improbable, and, like the whole subject of Norse influence, is worthy of a fuller investigation than any it has yet received.

CHAPTER XII

THE FOUR ANCIENT BOOKS OF WALES

The *Myvyrian Archaiology*—Oldest texts—The Black Book of Caermarthen—
The Book of Aneurin—The Book of Taliessin—The Red Book of Hergest
—Gildas and Nennius—The ancient Laws and Institutes—A great dialectic
battle—The princes of song—"I Yscolan"—A Welsh Ossianic poem—
Characteristics of the early poetry—The medieval romances—Their history
—Modern translations of the Mabinogion—Two classes of tales—The legend
of Taliessin—His curious odes—Kilhwch and Olwen—The Lady of the
Fountain—Three striking features of the Arthurian romances—Their influence
on Western Europe.

THE arrival of James Macpherson marks a great moment in
the history of Celtic literature. It was the signal for a
general resurrection. It would seem as if he sounded the
trumpet, and the graves of ancient MSS. were opened, the
books were read, and the dead were judged out of the
things that were written in them.

This is true not only of the Highland and Irish barderie,
but also of the poetry of Wales. The sudden popularity of
the Ossianic publications led to a desire on the part of the
Welsh to show that they also were in possession of a body
of native poems not less interesting, and with far better
claims, as they thought, to authenticity. It is significant to
note that though Edward Lhuyd gave an account of the Welsh
MSS. in the *Archæologica Britannica* as early as 1707, none
of the poems were printed till the era of Macpherson. His
famous *Fragments of Ancient Poetry Collected in the Highlands
of Scotland*, 1760, was soon followed by a succession of
rival publications from the sister country, such as *Speci-*

mens of the Poetry of the Ancient Welsh Bards, 1764; *Musical and Poetical Relics of the Welsh Bards*, 1784; " Poems of Taliessin," in the *Gentleman's Magazine*, 1789-90; *The Heroic Elegies and other Pieces of Llywarch Hên*, 1792, and in the year 1801 the text of the whole of the poems. This latter figures as the now oft-quoted *Myvyrian Archaiology of Wales*, containing all the chief productions of Welsh literature, and was published in 1801-1807 by Owen Jones, a wealthy furrier in Thames Street, London. Interested scholars, among them Aneurin Owen, Thomas Price, William Rees, and John Jones set themselves to finish the work of the Myvyrian peasant.

There was no lack of venerable MSS. from which to draw, for many transcripts had been made from time to time in the past. But the sources to which we must go for the oldest texts are mainly four, known as *The Four Ancient Books of Wales*, namely :—

> The Black Book of Caermarthen.
> The Book of Aneurin.
> The Book of Taliessin.
> The Red Book of Hergest.

The Black Book of Caermarthen is the oldest. It is a MS. of the twelfth century in the Hengwrt collection, and contains only poems. It consists of fifty-four folios of parchment in small quarto, with illuminated capitals. There are four different handwritings, apparently of the same period, with the exception of a few insertions made by a subsequent writer. The MS. belonged originally to the six black Canons of the priory of Caermarthen. Hence the name. After the dissolution of that religious house at the Reformation, it passed into the hands of Sir John Price, a native of Brecnockshire, and before the year 1658 was in the Hengwrt collection. Last century it changed hands again, when the whole of the latter most valuable collection was bequeathed to W. W. E. Wynne, Esq., of Peniarth.

The Book of Aneurin, second in point of antiquity, belongs to the thirteenth century. It also is a small quarto, consisting of nineteen folios of parchment. Here we have, perhaps, the most ancient copy now extant of that truly venerable and illustrious relic of Welsh poetry called the "Gododin," as well as the four Gorchanau, not quite so old. The capitals which mark the beginning of the stanzas are coloured alternately red and green. This literary monument belonged formerly to the Hengwrt collection, but in more recent times was bought from Mrs. Powell of Abergavenny by Sir Thomas Phillipps, Bart., of Middle Hill.

The Book of Taliessin, third in order, is still in the same collection. A small quarto MS. written on vellum, in one hand throughout, of the early fourteenth century, it consists now of thirty-eight leaves, and wants the outer page both at the beginning and at the end. Hence it begins in the middle of one poem and ends in that of another.

The last, but certainly not the least of this wonderful series, is the Red Book of Hergest in Jesus College, Oxford. It is a thick folio containing 360 leaves of vellum, and has been written at different times from the early part of the fourteenth century till the middle of the fifteenth. From this valuable codex Lady Charlotte Guest got eleven of her far-famed stories.

The book takes its name from Hergest Court, a seat of the Vaughans, near Knighton, Radnorshire, and before it was finally gifted to Jesus College in 1701, it passed through several hands.

It is written in double columns, in three different hand-writings. There is reason to infer that it was begun in 1318 at the very latest, a date given in one of the columns, and that it was finished in 1454. The book is an enormous compilation of Welsh compositions in prose and verse, of all the periods from the sixth century till the middle of the fifteenth.

Embellished lately in a magnificent binding of red

morocco with steel clasps, and preciously preserved in a
case, it is now shown as one of the curiosities of Oxford.

If we except this codex and others in Jesus College,
and those in the British Museum, most of the Welsh MSS.
are in private hands.   They used to belong to the religious
institutions, but when these were done away with in the
reign of Henry VIII., the ancient documents were dispersed.   Various leading families of Wales afterwards made
collections, thus helping to preserve the MSS. from destruction, but more than one of these collections have since been
destroyed by fire.

It must be understood that though the four great books
of poetry and romance here considered have been called
The Four Ancient Books of Wales, they are not the only
compositions of a remote origin.   For there are three other
notable works represented in very old MSS.   These are,
first, the history and epistle of Gildas, forming one Latin
treatise on the early history of the country, and written by
him in the year 560.   Of this work there have been three
MSS.   The oldest perished, but not before a printed copy
had been taken of it in 1568.   The other two, one of the
thirteenth and the other of the fourteenth century, are still
extant in the public library of Cambridge.

Next to this very ancient history of Gildas is that of
Nennius—an edition of the *History of the Britons* made
by him in 858.   There are three MSS. extant of this
venerable book dating as early as the tenth century—
one in the Vatican, one in Paris, and one in the British
Museum.

Not less celebrated is the great native compilation
entitled *The Ancient Laws and Institutes of Wales*.   The
oldest of them, namely, The Laws of Howeldda, belong to
the tenth century.

Wales thus possesses a literature which for antiquity
carries us back as far as the age of St. Columba.   In the
sixth century, when the Abbot of Iona was opening the page
of poetic history in Scotland, the little land in the west had

many distinguished bards, such as Aneurin, Taliessin, Llywarch Hên, Myrddin, Kian, Talhaiarn. For the preservation of their pieces we are mainly indebted to *The Four Ancient Books*.

As in the case of the Ossianic compositions, a great dialectic battle was fought over the origin of these Cymric poems, some, such as Malcolm Laing and John Pinkerton, denying, and others affirming their antiquity, but the outcome of the controversy has been to establish their genuine authenticity. While it is freely admitted by the best critics that many of the pieces traditionally attributed to Taliessin are not older than the twelfth century, no one now disputes that Aneurin, Taliessin, Llywarch Hên, and Myrddin were famous bards who lived and composed in the sixth century, and that we have some of their poems preserved in the above - mentioned books with the exception, perhaps, of Myrddin's. The honour of the title " King of the bards " lies between the first two, both of whom have been so designated. Stephens, in his *Literature of the Cymry*, gives the palm to Aneurin. His great poem, the " Gododin," has attracted much attention on account of its peculiar character and recognised historic value. It is practically divided into two parts by stanza forty-five, where the author speaks in his own name. The first part is consistent throughout, and Dr. Skene regards it as the original, as distinguished from the second, which may be a later continuation made up of other incidents. The poem is found in the Book of Aneurin, and various theories have been advanced as to the locality and date of the battle it treats of. One of these assumed that the subject was a struggle between the tribe Ottadeni and the Saxons in the sixth century. Another, that it referred, on the contrary, to the traditional slaughter of the British chiefs at Stonehenge by Hengest in " The Plot of the Long Knives." A third would find in it the battle mentioned by Bede as having been fought between Aidan, King of the Scots of Dalriada, and Ethelfrid, King of Northumbria, in 603. A fourth theory suggests *that* between Oswy and

Penda. But the name of the Scottish Donald Brec emerges in the story, " A phen dyvynwal vrych brein ae cnoyn," which in English means, " And the head of Donald Brec the ravens gnawed it." The scene of the struggle appears to have been Catraeth and Gododin. And it is interesting to note that one of the editors of the *Myvyrian Archaiology* (Mr. Edward Williams) locates it in Roxburghshire, as the battle fought between the Cymry and Saxons in 570. Villemarqué, on the other hand, in his, *Poems des Bardes Bretons*, places the contest on the banks of the Calder in Lanarkshire in 578. While Dr. Skene is equally sure that the requirements of the case are met " in that part of Scotland where Lothian meets Stirlingshire in the two districts of Gododin and Catraeth, both washed by the sea of the Firth of Forth, and where the great Roman wall terminates at Caredin, or the Fort of Eidinn."

The style of the poem may be gleaned from the following rendering :—

A grievous descent was made on his native place,
The price of mead in the hall, and the feast of wine ;
His blades were scattered about between two armies ;
Illustrious was the Knight in front of Gododin,
Eithinyn the renowned, an ardent spirit the bull of conflict.
A grievous descent was made in front of the extended riches,
The army dispersed with trailing shields—
A shivered shield before the herd of the roaring Beli,
A dwarf from the bloody field hastened to the fence ;
On our part there came a hoary-headed man to take counsel
On a prancing steed bearing a message from the golden-torqued leader.
Twrch proposed a compact in front of the destructive course,
Worthy was the shout of refusal.
We cried, Let Heaven be our protection ;
Let his compact be that he should be prostrated by the spear in
    battle.
The warriors of the far-famed Alclud
Would not contend without prostrating his host to the ground.

Like Ossian, Aneurin appears to have been a warrior-bard. Where he speaks of himself he says :—

I am not headstrong and petulant.
I will not avenge myself on him who drives me.
I will not laugh in derision.
Under foot for a while,
My knee is stretched,
My hands are bound
In the earthen house,
With an iron chain
Around my two knees.
Yet of the mead from the horn,
And of the men of Catraeth,
I, Aneurin, will compose,
As Taliessin knows,
An elaborate song
Or a strain to Gododin
Before the dawn of the brightest day.

Taliessin, on the other hand, was no warrior, simply a bard. Several of his pieces possess more real poetry than any part of the "Gododin." As Stephens has remarked, they show more skill in composition, finer ideas, bolder images, and more intense passion than any poet of the same age. There are seventy-seven pieces attributed to him, twelve of which, this critic thinks, may be genuine, and as old as the sixth century; among these the "Battle of Gwenystrad," the "Battle of Argoed Llwyvain," the "Battle of Dyffryn Gwarant," and some of the Gorchanau. In after life Taliessin became the bard of Urien Rheged, to whom and to his son Owain his chief poems are addressed. These contain some passages of exquisite beauty.

Llywarch Hên does not rival the other two as a prince of song, yet his poems are not lacking in poetic excellence. They are undoubtedly old, and valuable from his descriptions of manners, and the incidental allusions he makes that are strikingly illustrative of the age, and all the more interesting because we have so few other authorities to enlighten us as to its manners. His forte lay not so much in heroic poetry as in elegies and pathetic lamentations. Of the poems

attributed to him in the Red Book of Hergest the following
is a specimen :—

> Sitting high upon a hill, battle inclined is
> My mind, and it does not impel me onward.
> Short is my journey, my tenement is laid waste.
>
> Sharp is the gale, it is bare punishment to live,
> When the trees array themselves in gay colours
> Of summer, violently ill I am this day.
>
> I am no hunter, I keep no animal of the chase,
> I cannot move about ;
> As long as it pleases the cuckoo, let her sing.
>
> The loud-voiced cuckoo sings with the dawn,
> Her melodious notes in the dales of Cuawg ;
> Better is the lavisher than the miser.
>
> At Aber Cuawg the cuckoos sing
> On the blossom covered branches ;
> The loud-voiced cuckoo, let her sing awhile.
>
> At Aber Cuawg the cuckoos sing,
> On the blossom covered branches ;
> Woe to the sick that hears their contented notes.
>
> At Aber Cuawg the cuckoos sing,
> The recollection in my mind ;
> There are that hear them that will not hear them again.
>
> Have I not listened to the cuckoo on the ivied tree ?
> Did not my shield hang down ?
> What I loved is but vexation ; what I loved is no more.

In such doleful strains the bard continues his parable.
The sad note of the Gael is not lacking in him.

Myrddin is the fourth great poet of the sixth century.
Various poems are reputed his in the *Myvyrian Archaiology*,
but they are all probably of a much later date, as Stephens
and others think. One of the most interesting to us of
these traditional Myrddin pieces is the " I Yscolan." It

appears in the Black Book of Caermarthen. Yscolan is represented as having held a dialogue with Myrddin. To have done so he must have lived in the sixth century. Welsh writers, like Davies and Stephens, identify the name as St. Colan or Columba. " Instead of being unknown to the Cymry of the Middle Ages, no person was better known than Yscolan," says Stephens. From their view Dr. Skene dissents, and Professor Rhys also holds it utterly impossible that Yscolan was St. Columba, as the two names cannot be connected, *Columba* being in Welsh *Cwlum*. It is not maintained by any of these critics that the poem, as it stands, is anything like so old as the period of Myrddin. But older it evidently is than the time of Edward I., and this shows, as the Welsh writers affirm, the existence among the bards, from an early date, of a tradition that St. Columba had, in his zeal for Christianity, destroyed some druidic books. This tradition got mixed up with a later one about the books of Cambria, which had been sent to the White Tower of London for security, having been destroyed there by some Vandal of an Yscolan, who must have lived after the twelfth century.

But whoever the Yscolan of the dialogue was, Myrddin assails him thus (Stephens' version) :—

> Black is thy horse, and black thy cap,
> Black thy head, and black thyself,
> Black-headed man, art thou Yscolan ?

And Yscolan answers :—

> I am Yscolan the Scholar,
> Light is my Scottish knowledge.
> My grief is incurable for making the ruler take offence[1] at thee.

For having burnt a church,[2] destroyed the cattle of a school,

---

[1] The belief was that Myrddin was persecuted by Rhydderch Hael at the instance of Yscolan.

[2] Stephens has here, " For having hindered school instruction," wrongly translated, we believe.

And caused a book to be drowned,
I feel my penance to be heavy.

Creator of all creations,
And greatest of all supporters,
Forgive me my fault.

A full year I have been
At Bangor on the pole of a weir.
Consider thou my sufferings from sea-worms.

If I had known as well as I now do
How clearly the wind blows upon the sprigs of the waving
wood,
I should not have done what I did.

Had he known of certain proofs of druidic excellence he would have refrained. Though the tradition of St. Columba having destroyed some pagan books may have actually been current among the Welsh bards, it is very unlikely that he ever met Myrddin. As Dr. Skene suggests, the black Yscolan may well have been one of the black Canons of Caermarthen connected with some book-episode in the Tower. For we know from Adamnan that the dress of Columba was white, and the above sketch hardly fits in with his history. It is interesting to note that in the book called Taliessin, there is " The Death-song of Corroi, son of Dayry," curiously enough the only specimen of a Welsh Ossianic poem which has come down to us. It tells the story of Curigh of Munster; and Cuchulinn, the famous hero of Ulster :—

Tales will be known to me from sky to earth
Of the contention of Corroi and Cocholyn,
Numerous their tumults about their borders.

This poem is fully noticed by Dr. Skene in his edition of the *Book of the Dean of Lismore*, p. 141.

Taking the Welsh poems as a whole, the difficulty has always been to differentiate between the historical and the mythological. They are usually so obscure in themselves, especially the so-called mythological ones, that some think there lurks in them a system of mystical and semi-pagan philosophy handed down from the Druids, and which our age cannot fathom.

Others think that they are nothing but the wild and extravagant vapourings of bards of the twelfth and subsequent centuries. Referring to this, Dr. Skene wrote in his edition of the poems, and translations of the poems, in *The Four Ancient Books of Wales*, vol. i. pp. 15, 16 :—

I consider that the true value of these poems is a problem which has still to be solved. Whether they are genuine works of the bards whose names they bear, or whether they are the production of a later age, I do not believe that they contain any such system of Druidism or Neo-Druidism as Davies, Herbert, and others attempt to find in them, nor do I think that their authors wrote, and the compilers of these ancient MSS. took the pains to transcribe, century after century, what was a mere farago of nonsense and of no historical or literary value. I think that these poems have a meaning, and that, both in connection with the history and literature of Wales, that meaning is worth finding out; and I think further, that if they were subjected to a just and candid criticism, we ought to be able to ascertain their true place and value in the literature of Wales.

Renan, on the other hand, held that bardism lasted into the heart of the Middle Ages under the form of a secret doctrine, with a conventional language and symbols almost wholly derived from the solar divinity of Arthur. " This," he says, " may be termed Neo-Druidism, a kind of Druidism subtilised and reformed on the model of Christianity, which may be seen growing more and more obscure and mysterious until the moment of its total disappearance."

One remarkable fact in connection with these early poems is how few of them contain any notice of Arthur. Out of the whole number there are only five which mention him at all, and then it is the historical Arthur, the Guledig, to whom the defence of the wall was entrusted, and who fought the twelve battles in the north, perishing at Camlan.

For accounts of the ideal Arthur we need to turn to the medieval romances, and this is the part of Welsh literature which has most fascinated the world and influenced the literatures of Europe. It is well known how there arose on the Continent in the twelfth and thirteenth centuries a body of Romance, popular in England, France, Germany, Norway, Sweden, and even Iceland, down to the Reformation, and it is equally well known that the origin of these tales may be traced to Wales through the north-west of France—the modern Brittany.

First appeared the *Historia Britonum* of Gruffydd ap Arthur, commonly known as Geoffrey of Monmouth, who was a Welsh priest, born in 1128. In this book he professed to have translated into Latin from an ancient Welsh MS. the history of Britain from the days when the fabulous Brut, the great-grandson of Aeneas, landed on its shores, down through the whole period of King Arthur and his Round Table to Cadwaladr, a Cymric king who died in 689. From the Latin the stories were put into French verse by Gaimar, and getting to France they fell into the hands of Robert Wace, a native of Jersey (and Norman trouvère), who, with the help of other independent sources of information, made them into a poem in 1155, which he called the "Brut."

In this form the Romance found its way back to England, and about 1205 was told for the first time in English verse by Layamon, an English priest who dwelt on the banks of the upper Severn, and who was thus, besides being indebted to Wace, near enough the original source to have access to the great body of Welsh literature then current on the subject.

Through these, and French authors, the Cymric tales soon passed to other Continental lands, and since then have been retouched, paraphrased, and amplified in all the languages of Europe. They belong to the age, and breathe the spirit of chivalry.

In modern times these romances have again attracted attention, and become famous through the publication of Lady

Charlotte Guest's English translations of the Mabinogion, 1st edition, 1837-49, and reprint, 1877; Vicomte de la Villemarqué's French translations of the Welsh poems and Round Table romances in 1841 and subsequently; and later still, Professor Loth of Rennes' translation of the Mabinogion.

As in the case of the Gaelic sagas, traditions had been floating among the Welsh people for hundreds of years, and when the general awakening of the twelfth century took place, a natural desire sprung up to have these collected, arranged, and written down. The Mabinogion were thus originally tales penned to be repeated at the fireside, to while away the time of young chieftains and their following, but ultimately they reacted very powerfully upon the national literature and character. The name Mabinogion was not at first so generally applied to all the tales as it is to-day. Only four were so designated.

In point of antiquity these tales sort out into two distinct classes,—one older, the other less ancient. The latter celebrate heroes of the Arthurian cycle, and are full of ecclesiastical terms and of allusions to Norman customs, manners, arts, arms, and luxuries. The former refer to persons and events of an earlier period, are more mythological, and contain very few of these later allusions. As Professor Rhys [1] thinks, they are essentially Goidelic stories, and their machinery is magic, not the laws of chivalry.

To the older class belong—

> The Tale of Pwyll, Prince of Dyfed.
> The Tale of Branwen, daughter of Llyr.
> The Tale of Manawyddan, the son of Llyr.
> The Tale of Math, son of Mathonwy.

These only are the Mabinogion.

[1] "I don't believe that Goidelic was extinct in Wales till the seventh century; the bulk of the people of the north and the south of Wales are in point of race to this day probably more Goidelic than Brythonic. The Ordovices of Mid Wales were the Brythons of the west, and hardly any others in Wales."—Prof. Rhys.

The Contention of Llud and Llevelys.
The Story of Kilhwch and Olwen.
The Dream of Rhonabwy.

This last Professor Rhys regards as a hash or after-composition, in spite of the respectability of the MS.

To the later class—

The Tale of the Lady of the Fountain.
The Story of Peredur, son of Evrawc.
The Story of Geraint, son of Erbin.
The Dream of Macsen Gudelig.

And to these eleven, in her third volume published in 1849, Lady Charlotte Guest added the Hanes Taliessin, compiled in the fourteenth century, but, according to Ernest Renan, belonging to the more ancient of the two classes above mentioned. The great beauty, originality, and antique flavour of these stories may here be exhibited by means of a few characteristic extracts.

And the first to be given is from the legend of Taliessin.

" In times past (it begins) there lived in Penllyn a man of gentle lineage, named Tegid Voel, and his dwelling was in the midst of the lake Tegid, and his wife was called Caridwen. And there was born to him of his wife a son named Morvran at Tegid, and also a daughter named Creirwy, the fairest maiden in the world was she ; and they had a brother, the most ill-favoured man in the world, Avagddu. Now Caridwen his mother thought that he was not likely to be admitted among men of noble birth by reason of his ugliness, unless he had some exalted merits or knowledge. For it was in the beginning of Arthur's time and of the Round Table.

" So she resolved, according to the arts of the books of Fferyllt, to boil a cauldron of Inspiration and Science for her son, that his reception might be honourable, because of his knowledge of the mysteries of the future state of the world.

"Then she began to boil the cauldron, which, from the beginning of its boiling, might not cease to boil for a year and a day, until three blessed drops were obtained of the Grace of Inspiration.

"And she put Gwion Bach, the son of Gwreang of Llanfair in Caereinion in Powys, to stir the cauldron, and a blind man named Morda to kindle the fire beneath it, and she charged them that they should not suffer it to cease boiling for the space of a year and a day. And she herself, according to the books of the astronomers, and in planetary hours, gathered every day of all charm-bearing herbs. And one day towards the end of the year, as Caridwen was culling plants and making incantations, it chanced that three drops of the charmed liquor flew out of the cauldron and fell upon the finger of Gwion Bach. And by reason of their great heat he put his finger to his mouth, and the instant he put these marvel-working drops into his mouth he foresaw everything that was to come, and perceived that his chief care must be to guard against the wiles of Caridwen, for vast was her skill.

"And in very great fear he fled towards his own land, and the cauldron burst in two, because all the liquor within it, except the three charm-bearing drops, was poisonous, so that the horses of Gwyddno Garanhir were poisoned by the water of the stream into which the liquor of the cauldron ran, and the confluence of that stream was called the Poison of the Horses of Gwyddno from that time forth.

"Thereupon came in Caridwen, and saw all the toil of the whole year lost. And she seized a billet of wood and struck the blind Morda on the head until one of his eyes fell out upon his cheek. And he said, 'Wrongfully hast thou disfigured me, for I am innocent. Thy loss was not because of me.'

"'Thou speakest truth,' said Caridwen; 'it was Gwion Bach who robbed me.'

"And she went forth after him running. And he saw her and changed himself into a hare and fled.

"But she changed herself into a greyhound, and turned him. And he ran towards a river and became a fish. And she in the form of an otter-bitch chased him under the water until he was fain to turn himself into a bird of the air. She as a hawk followed him, and gave him no rest in the sky, and just as she was about to stoop upon him, and he was in fear of death, he espied a heap of winnowed wheat on the floor of a barn, and he dropped among the wheat and turned himself into one of the grains. Then she transferred herself into a high-crested black hen, and went to the wheat and scratched it with her feet, and found him out and swallowed him, and, as the story says, she bore him nine months, and when she was delivered of him she could not find it in her heart to kill him, by reason of his beauty. So she wrapped him in a leathern bag, and cast him into the sea, to the mercy of God, on the 29th day of April."

And, Moses-like, was Taliessin afterwards found in the Weir of Gwyddno by that prince's only son Elphin, who took him to the house of his father. Some of the extraordinary tales which this prodigy of a boy told in verse are given, and it is related how he bewitched the bards of King Mælgron by pouting out his lips after them, and playing "Blerwm, blerwm" with his finger upon his lips as they went to court. His own answers to the king are always in song. Among the curious odes that he sang are those known as—

The Excellence of the Bards.
The Reproof of the Bards.
The Spite of the Bards.
One of the Four Pillars of Song.

This latter begins :—

The Almighty made
Down the Hebron Vale,
With his plastic hands
Adam's fair form.

And five hundred years,
Void of any help,
There he remained and lay
    Without a soul.

He again did form,
In calm paradise,
From a left side rib,
    Bliss-throbbing Eve.

Seven hours they were
The Orchard keeping,
Till Satan brought strife
    With wiles from Hell.

Thence were they driven,
Cold and shivering,
To gain their living
    Into this world, etc.

Of the story of Kilhwch and Olwen, which has a particularly antique character, Renan felicitously says that by its entirely primitive aspect, by the part played in it by the wild boar in conformity to the spirit of Celtic mythology, by the wholly supernatural and magical character of the narration, by innumerable allusions, the sense of which escapes us, it forms a cycle by itself. Passing by the unique adventures of Kilhwch, he quotes as a typical sample the remarkable passage on the finding of Mabon, where his followers said unto Arthur, "Lord, go thou home; thou canst not proceed with thy host in quest of such small adventures as these," and Arthur commissions Gwrhyr, because he knew all languages, and was familiar with those of the birds and the beasts, to accompany others, whom he named, in search of the lost cousin. They went forward first to the ousel of Cilgwi, and got its weird and quaint answer, then to the stag of Redynvre. From him to the owl of Cwm Cawlwyd, to the eagle of Gwern Abwy, and, lastly, to the salmon of Llyn Llyw. Each tells its tale, and passes them on to the next. The speeches of these ancient denizens of the land are very old-fashioned and curious, typical of all the primitive extravagance of the Celtic imagination.

But it is in tales like the " Lady of the Fountain " and " Peredur " that we tap the later, full-blown, and most characteristic Arthurian romance. The former begins: " King Arthur was at Caerlleon upon Usk ; and one day he sat in his chamber, and with him were Owain, the son of Urien, and Kynon, the son of Clydno, and Kai, the son of Kyner, and Gwenhwyvar and her handmaidens at needlework by the window. And if it should be said that there was a porter at Arthur's palace, there was none. Glewlwyd Gavaelvawr was there, acting as porter to welcome guests and strangers, and to receive them with honour, and to inform them of the manners and customs of the court ; and to direct those who came to the hall or to the presence chamber, and those who came to take up their lodgings.

" In the centre of the chamber King Arthur sat upon a seat of green rushes, over which was spread a covering of flame-coloured satin, and a cushion of red satin was under his elbow. Then Arthur spoke, ' If I thought you would not disparage me,' said he, ' I would sleep while I wait for my repast ; and you can entertain one another with relating tales, and can obtain a flagon of mead and some meat from Kai. And the king went to sleep.' "

Kynon tells a tale : " I was the only son of my mother and father, and I was exceedingly aspiring, and my daring was very great. I thought there was no enterprise in the world too mighty for me, and after I had achieved all the adventures in my own country, I equipped myself and set forth to journey through deserts and distant regions. And at length it chanced that I came to the fairest valley in the world, wherein were trees of equal growth, and a river ran through the valley, and a path by the side of the river. And I followed the path until midday, and continued my journey along the remainder of the valley until the evening, and at the extremity of the plain I came to a large and lustrous castle, at the foot of which was a torrent. And I approached the castle, and there I beheld two youths."

He describes the wonderful dress of these, and of a man in the prime of life clad in a robe and a mantle of yellow satin with band of gold lace, shoes of variegated leather fastened by two bosses of gold. This man went with him towards the castle. "And there I saw four-and-twenty damsels," he says, "embroidering satin at a window. And this I tell thee, Kai, that the least fair of them was fairer than the fairest maid thou hast ever beheld in the island of Britain, and the least lovely of them was more lovely than Gwenhwyvar, the wife of Arthur, when she has appeared loveliest at the offering on the day of the Nativity or at the feast of Easter. They rose up at my coming, and six of them took my horse and divested me of my armour; and six others took my arms and washed them in a vessel until they were perfectly bright. And the third six spread cloths upon the table and prepared meat. And the fourth six took off my soiled garments, and placed others upon me, namely, an under vest and a doublet of fine linen, and a robe and a surcoat, and a mantle of yellow satin with a broad gold band upon the mantle, and they placed cushions both beneath and around me, with coverings of red linen, and I sat down. Now, the six maidens who had taken my horse unharnessed him as well as if they had been the best squires in the Island of Britain. Then, behold, they brought bowls of silver wherein was water to wash, and towels of linen, some green and some white; and I washed, and in a little while the man sat down to the table, and I sat down next to him, and below me sat all the maidens except those who waited on me."

After he divulged the object of his journey, the host directed him to a black man of great stature on the top of a mound, ill favoured, with but one foot, one eye in the middle of his forehead, a club of iron, and a thousand wild animals grazing around him.

Next day Kynon set out and found this giant. And

when I told him," he says, "who I was and what I sought, he directed me. 'Take,' said he, 'that path that leads towards the head of the glade, and ascend the wooden steep until thou comest to the summit; and there thou wilt find an open space like to a large valley, and in the midst of it a tall tree, whose branches are greener than the greenest pine-trees. Under this tree is a fountain, and by the side of the fountain a marble slab, and in the marble slab a silver bowl attached by a chain of silver, so that it may not be carried away. Take the bowl and throw a bowlful of water upon the slab, and thou wilt hear a mighty peal of thunder, so that thou wilt think that heaven and earth are trembling with fury. With the thunder there will come a shower so severe that it will be scarce possible for thee to endure it and live. And the shower will be of hailstones. And after the shower the weather will become fair, but every leaf that was upon the tree will have been carried away by the shower. Then a flight of birds will come and alight upon the tree, and in thine own country thou didst never hear a strain so sweet as that which they will sing. And at the moment thou art most delighted with the song of the birds thou wilt hear a murmuring and complaining coming towards thee along the valley. And thou wilt see a knight upon a coal-black horse, clothed in black velvet, and with a pennon of black linen upon his lance; and he will ride unto thee to encounter thee with the utmost speed. If thou fleest from him he will overtake thee, and if thou abidest there, as sure as thou art a mounted knight he will leave thee on foot, and if thou dost not find trouble in that adventure thou needest not seek it during the rest of thy life.'"

In these tales the principal part belongs to the women, and here it is the Lady of the Fountain. In reading the romances we instantly find ourselves on the top wave of chivalry. Three things strike the modern reader.

First, the ideal here presented of King Arthur and his Queen Gwenhwyvar, the pure and homely atmosphere of their Court in that wild and barbarian age, and the sterling qualities and integrity of the Knights of the Round Table. Each fights not for any national cause, but to show his personal excellence and satisfy his taste for adventure. It is an epic creation representing the dream of medieval times.

Second, not less surprising to us is the *sang-froid* with which the warriors carry out their adventures, the supreme indifference to danger, or to the pain and death they inflict when they set to, to try each other's mettle. Knight attacks knight for no other reason than that he is superior in prowess to himself, and he will risk his life any day to get the mastery over a rival in arms. They reck nothing of sword cuts. Enough for them that it is in accordance with the laws of chivalry.

Third, and perhaps most wonderful of all, is the delicacy of the feminine feeling breathed in these romances. There is nothing sensual in the love here portrayed. It is angelic. Never an impropriety or gross word is to be met with in all these pages, never a prurient suggestion for all the roughness of that rude age. Women figure as divine, the most charming creatures in the world, to protect whose honour and win whose love and esteem, danger and even death are freely braved. This was a new element introduced into European literature—the creation of woman's character and the place given her in chivalry. " Nearly all the types of womankind known to the Middle Ages,—Guinevere, Iseult, Enid,"—says Renan, " are derived from Arthur's court."

The influence of these tales upon the literature, the taste, the social life of the whole of Western Europe has been immense, and they are still as fresh and enchanting to the intelligent reader as any Arabian Nights' Entertainment.

Lady Charlotte Guest's literary monument is for English readers the standard classic. There we find a charming translation with luminous notes of these famous Mabinogion, a collection which Renan has called " the pearl of Gaelic literature, the completest expression of the Cymric genius," and for the early Welsh poetry, both in the original and in translation, we have the sumptuous edition of Dr. Skene, culled from *The Four Ancient Books of Wales*, to delight us.   The poetry and romance of the Cymry are really two literatures essentially distinct from each other.   Springing from the same soil, each reflects in its own way the same national character which had so much in common with that of our own ancient Gaelic ancestry, so that we feel to-day with regard to that long past, that " distance only lends enchantment to the view."

CHAPTER XIII

CELTIC LITERARY REVIVALS

Sixth century awakening throughout Celtdom—Illustrious names—Brittany's wonderful cycle of song—Charming examples—Dearth of tenth century—A strange trait of Celtic life—The brilliant medieval renaissance—Output of Ireland, Wales, and Brittany—The Cornish dramas—Last speaker of that dialect—Period of inactivity and decline—Recrudescence—1745-1800 the high-water mark of Highland production—A galaxy of poets—Splendid lyrical outburst—New Ossianic cycle—Seana Dana—Caledonian bards—The Welsh Eisteddfod—Latest Celtic renaissance—Some characteristic features, results, manifestations—Antiquity, thou wondrous charm !

THERE comes a time in the history of races when, passing from simplicity to reflection, their deepest nature finds expression in some form of literature. That time for the Celtic people has been the late fifth, but more especially the sixth century of our era. And the remarkable fact confronts us then of a simultaneous poetic awakening in all the chief groups into which the Celtic remnant had been divided. Ireland, Scotland, Wales, and Brittany were all involved in this primal literary activity.

A most curious phenomenon to contemplate is this racial renaissance. When the great Celtic empire had crumbled, and its defeated fragments were driven to their last resorts on the outmost confines of Europe, vanquished by the alien who kept them at bay, suddenly the sundered remnants burst into song. Plaintive and sad for the most part has been this utterance, but full of the wealth of sentiment, fancy, and old-time peculiarities of conception so characteristic of this ancient people.

St. Patrick, St. Sechnall, Dubthach, Fiacc, Dallan Forgaill, and others, inaugurated the new time in Ireland ; St. Columba and his following accomplished a similar transition for Scotland, opening the pages of literary history with beautiful hymns and lyrics, which have continued to this day. In Wales the pregnant sixth century which gave us Columcille was *the* great age of bardic literature—the age of such princes of poetry as Aneurin, Taliessin, Llywarch Hên, and Myrddin.

These are among the most illustrious names of the Celtic past. And in Brittany the same period is believed to have produced that wonderful cycle of song, some of which has been taken down from oral recitation so late as last century by the learned and enthusiastic M. de Villemarqué,[1] the Macpherson of Brittany, and published in his delightful *Barzaz-Breiz, Chants populaires de la Bretagne,* a number of which Mr. Tom Taylor has rendered into English. Those entitled—

> The Wine of the Gauls,
> The Prediction of Gwenc'hlan,
> The Lord Nann and the Fairy,
> The March of Arthur,
> The Plague of Elliant,
> The Drowning of Kaer-Is—

are held to belong to the period with which we are dealing, and to have been in existence prior at least to the close of the sixth century. They are all distinguished by the presence of alliteration as well as rhyme, by a more or less complete division into triplets, like the ancient Welsh triads, as well as by a distinctly archaic impress in the manners described, and the feelings of the singer.

The names of the authors have not come down to us, as in the other three countries, but, having already quoted specimens of the fifth and sixth century poetry of Ireland,

---

[1] He collected Breton ballads and folklore songs, added to them, revised and altered, and published the collection as authentic.

Scotland, and Wales, it might not be uninteresting now to give characteristic examples of the early compositions of Brittany.

The Wine of the Gauls is undoubtedly ancient, so ancient indeed, that Part II. is regarded as a fragment of the song that accompanied the old Celtic sword-dance in honour of the sun.　It runs thus :—

> Blood wine and glee
> 　Sun to thee—
> Blood wine and glee.
> 　　Fire ! Fire ! steel, oh ! steel !
> 　　Fire ! fire ! steel and fire.
> 　　Oak ! Oak ! earth and waves,
> 　　Waves, oak, earth and oak.
>
> Glee of dance and song
> 　And battle throng.
> Battle, dance and song.
> 　　Fire ! fire, etc.
>
> Let the sword blades swing
> 　In a ring,
> Let the sword blades swing.
> 　　Fire ! fire, etc.
>
> Song of the blue steel
> 　Death to feel,
> Song of the blue steel.
> 　　Fire ! fire, etc.
>
> Fight, whereof the sword
> 　Is the Lord,
> Fight of the fell sword !
> 　　Fire ! fire, etc.
>
> Sword, thou mighty King
> 　Of battle ring,
> Sword, thou mighty King !
> 　　Fire ! fire, etc.
>
> With the rainbow's light
> 　Be thou bright,
> With the rainbow's light.
> 　　Fire ! fire, etc.

Far more charming is the episode of Lord Nann and the Fairy, and genuinely typical of the powerful fancy and natural magic of the Celt.

> The good Lord Nann and his fair bride,
> Were young when wedlock's knot was tied—
> Were young when death did them divide.
>
> But yesterday that lady fair
> Two babes as white as snow did bear :
> A man-child and a girl they were.

For making him a manchild's sire, Lord Nann offered to get his bride any dainty food she liked, "meat of the wood-cock from the lake or of the wild deer from the brake." She chose the latter, while she grudged sending him to the wood.

> The Lord of Nann when this he heard
> Hath gripp'd his oak spear with never a word,
>
> His bonny black horse he hath leap'd upon ;
> And forth to the greenwood he hath gone.
>
> By the skirts of the wood as he did go,
> He was 'ware of a hind as white as snow ;
>
> Oh fast she ran and fast he rode,
> That the earth it shook where his horse-hoofs trode.
>
> Oh fast he rode, and fast she ran,
> That the sweat to drop from his brow began,
>
> That the sweat on his horse's flanks stood white
> So he rode and rode till the fall o' the night.
>
> When he came to a stream that fed a lawn
> Hard by the grot of a Corrigaun.
>
> The grass grew thick by the streamlet brink,
> And he lighted down off his horse to drink.
>
> The Corrigaun sat by the fountain fair,
> A-combing her long and yellow hair ;

A-combing her hair with a comb of gold—
(Not poor, I trow, are those maidens cold)—

Now who's the bold wight that dares come here
To trouble my fairy fountain clear?

Either thou straight shalt wed with me
Or pine for four long years and three,
Or dead in three days' space shalt be.

This proposal he spurned, asserting that he was already married, and would die on the spot ere he would take a Corrigaun to wife. Her spell she cast, and instantly he feels sick. On return he bids his mother make his bed, for in three days she would hear his passing-bell, but adjures her never to tell the tale to his bride. The three days expire, and the latter inquires of her mother-in-law why the Church bells toll and the priests chant in the street below, all clad in their white vestments? "A strange poor man had died," was the evasive answer. Then she asks whither her husband had gone, and on being assured he would soon be back, the unsuspecting lady concerns herself with the kind of gown she would wear for her churching. Said her mother-in-law :—

"The fashion of late, my child, hath grown,
That women for churching black should don."

And then :—

As through the churchyard porch she stept
She saw the grave where her husband slept.

And the dialogue proceeds :—

"Who of our blood is lately dead
That our ground is new raked and spread?"

"The truth I may no more forbear,
My son—your own poor lord—lies there."

She threw herself on her knees amain,
And from her knees ne'er rose again.

> That night they laid her, dead and cold
> Beside her lord beneath the mould ;
> When lo !—a marvel to behold !—
>
> Next morn from the grave two oak trees fair
> Shot lusty boughs into the air ;
>
> And in their boughs—oh wondrous sight—
> Two happy doves all snowy white—
>
> That sang as ever the morn did rise
> And then flew up—into the skies.

In addition to the songs, Villemarqué published *The Breton Bards of the Sixth Century*, but Renan preferred the songs as by far the better.

The impulse given by the first literary awakening continued in Ireland, Scotland, and Wales for two or three centuries, until the confusion and disintegration of the Norse invasions put an end to it. During this early and brilliant period the Celt poured forth the richest treasures of his nature. Before the foe triumphed, many valuable pieces of literature, including the heroic sagas, had been committed to writing, and thus preserved for posterity, though it is known that much was destroyed by the reckless invader. It was a bright morning—this dawn of letters—too suddenly clouded and overcast.

For a century or two after, the Celtic field in its various parts remained singularly barren and unproductive. Ireland was not altogether without poets and scholars, though greatly fallen from her pristine glory, but in Wales, from the middle of the seventh century till the year 1080, hardly any poetry of merit was produced, and the same might be said of Scotland, and, it would appear, of Brittany also.

No illustrious bards or outstanding writers redeemed the general dearth of the tenth century. That was the darkest hour before another brilliant dawn.

Ossian, St. Patrick, and Columcille ; Dubthach and King Laoghaire ; Prince Arthur and his knights ; Taliessin and the Royal Urien, Aneurin, Llywarch Hên ; what were

these but memories? vanished heroes and bards of the past.
Already the walls of Balclutha were desolate, the harp hung
mute in Tara's hall; nay, Tara itself was now a simulacrum,
—a ruin, deserted for ever. And even from Caerleon and
Dun-Reged had not the glory departed? Too soon the sun,
late-risen, had sunk upon the unhappy Celts, defeated in
war and now dumb and helplessly inarticulate in literature.
It seemed as if, swan-like, the pathetic remnants of this old
race had at length sung their dying song, and sunk into
silent and finished oblivion.

To such a pass to all appearance, through Carlyle's
" star-fire and immortal tears," had Destiny led these hapless
peoples by the advent of the tenth century, that he would
be a visionary indeed who should prophesy any renaissance,
and a true seer, for the time being, who should say—

> . . . Look
> Upon that poor and broken bankrupt there.

Yet, phœnix-like, is it not ever the fate of the hidden
and precarious Celtic genius to rearise from its ashes and
reassert its vitality? And so in the eleventh and twelfth
centuries there was such a wonderful literary awakening
throughout Celtdom, that it was as when :—

> . . . A sable cloud
> Turns forth her silver lining on the night.

And this new activity, be it noted, was not confined to the
Gaels of Ireland and Scotland, but, as in the sixth century,
comprehended the Cymri of Wales and Brittany also.

Herein lies a strange trait of Celtic life, that the great
literary revivals should be thus simultaneous, and common
to all the sundered groups, though these latter are isolated
so much linguistically and locally. Not once or twice in
their history has this curious affinity of genius and sentiment
been evinced.

In the case of the Gael, no sooner was the grip of the
Vikings relaxed than the bards and schools began to

flourish again. The new Irish king, the semi-usurper Brian Boru, helped much towards this happy consummation, as he was a real patron of letters and worked hard to restore the fallen fortunes of Gaelic literature. Early in the eleventh century he was on the throne, and that and the following century witnessed the new and copious revival of art and learning. To this period belong the great monuments, such as the Leabhar Na h'Uidhre, the Book of Hymns, the Book of Leinster, as well as the Scottish Book of Deer.

During these two centuries a host of poets and some annalists lived, the chief of whom were Flann of Monasterboice and Tighernach. Quite a number of the names of prominent bards who wrote then are given by Dr. Hyde in his *Literary History of Ireland*. And we know that from this time the interest taken in the past gave rise to that rich and abundant medieval succession of books of saga common to Ireland and Scotland. But though these latter were compiled, some of them after the twelfth century, the actual revival did not last beyond the Norman Conquest of Ireland, which culminated at the close of that same twelfth century, arresting Irish development and disintegrating Irish life. So that for 300 years after, Erin produced nothing comparable to her former achievements.

Turning to the Cymri, on the other hand, we find the remarkable intellectual awakening of the eleventh and twelfth centuries ushered in in a similar way as in Ireland, by the advent of new rulers. Rhys ap Tewdwr, who had taken refuge in Brittany, returned in 1077 and ascended the throne of South Wales, to which he laid claim as true heir. And Gruffyd ap Kynan, similarly exiled in Ireland, came back to reign in North Wales in 1080. Uniting their forces in one first great attempt, these two hereditary princes overthrew the reigning monarch, and were confirmed on the thrones of their ancestors.

Like Brian in Ireland, they also in their own fatherland were instrumental in introducing a new era of literature. In North Wales it showed itself in a revival of poetry, while in South Wales it took the form of prose. Thomas Stephens mentions no less than seventy-nine bards who lived between 1080 and 1400, many of whose pieces are still extant in MSS.

To this period belong the greatest monuments of Welsh genius — *The Four Ancient Books of Wales*, and the wonderful cycle of romance treasured for us in the Mabinogion, besides those numerous compositions traditionally attributed to Taliessin, Myrddinn, and others. Chronicles, romances, poems, mabinogion, and a large collection of moral and historical triads—these constitute the result of that extraordinary outburst of creative energy which dates from the days of Gruffyd ap Kynan.

Nor was Brittany asleep during this literary activity, for she too had her share in common with Wales in the origin and dissemination of the Arthurian romance.

It is one of the problems of criticism to-day, rightly to apportion the credit between the two countries.

Robert Wace undoubtedly drew from independent Breton sources as well as from Geoffrey of Monmouth. And from the eleventh century onwards date the historic and narrative ballads so characteristic of Brittany. A selection of these have been translated into English by Mr. Taylor, and all of those he gives came into existence, he assures us, before the end of the fourteenth century. So we have such medieval titles as, "The Evil Tribute of Nomenöe," "Bran," "The Return from Saxon-land," "The Crusader's Wife," "The Clerk of Rohan," "Baron Jaüoz," "The Battle of the Thirty," Jean of the Flame," "Du Guesclin's Vassal," and "The Wedding Girdle"—titles not unlike Chaucer's own.

Bran, the hero of the second ballad, is believed to have been taken prisoner in the great battle recorded in history as having been fought in the tenth century near Kerloän, between the Norsemen and the Bretons, under Ewen the Great.

> Sore wounded lies the good knight Bran
> On the foughten field of Kerloän.

On Kerloän's field, hard by the shore,
Lieth the grandson of Bran-Vor.

Maugre our Bretons won the day,
He's bound and o'er sea borne away.

Borne over sea, shut up, alone,
In Donjon tower he made his moan.

Bran dies in activity.

On the battlefield of Kerloän
There grows a tree looks o'er the lan';

There grows an oak in the place of stour,   (*i.e.* battle)
Where the Saxon fled from Ewen-Vor.

Upon this oak, when the moon shines bright,
The birds they gather from the night.

Sea-mews, pied-black and white are there
On every forehead a bloodspeck clear.

With them a corbie, ashgrey for eld
And a young crow [1] aye at her side beheld.

Wayworn seem the twain, with wings that dreep,
As birds that flight o'er sea must keep.

So sweetly sing these birds, and clear,
The great sea stills its waves to hear.

And aye their songs one burden hold
All save the young crow's and the corbie's old.

And this is ever the crow's sore cry,
"Sing, little birds, sing merrily."

"Sing, birds o' the land, in merry strain,
You died not far from your own Bretayne."

Besides these narrative ballads, Brittany produced at various periods idyllic songs and religious canticles.

As for Cornwall, whose dialect is now extinct, she never produced much of a Celtic literature. What there is still extant is preserved in MSS. of the fifteenth century, representing

---

[1] Bran means crow in Breton dialect.

possibly all the ancient literature she ever had, and dates from that or the preceding fourteenth century. These pieces consist of one poem, entitled " Mount Calvary," and three dramas, or miracle plays, with nothing distinctly Celtic about them save the language. With the exception of these and another drama of the seventeenth century (1611), and the Lord's Prayer translated, the obsolete and defunct Cornish dialect has no literature to show, and therefore is not concerned in the special Celtic revivals characteristic of the literature in the other dialects. A translation of the ancient dramas from the original Cornish has been made and published thirty years ago by Edwin Norris. Their value now is almost solely linguistic. " The last survivor of those who spoke in their youth pure Cornish is said to have been Dolly Pentreath of Mousehole near Penzance, who died in 1778, aged 102. And even she would not have talked Cornish in her youth if she had not lived in one of the few parishes along the coasts of Mount's Bay and St. Ive's Bay, and a few districts to the west of those bays, where alone at the beginning of the last century (eighteenth) the ancient dialect existed." (Morley's *English Writers*, vol. i. p. 750.)

After the brilliant medieval renaissance came another period of inactivity and decline. From the sixteenth century it is true that a new series of poets and prose writers began to arrive in the different Celtic nationalities. In Ireland, during the first half of the seventeenth century, there was quite a distinguished recrudescence of national scholarship, associated with the names of Geoffrey Keating, the Four Masters, and Duald Mac Firbis, all of whom were prose writers of eminence ; and in the Highlands of Scotland flourished Mary Macleod and her contemporaries.

But we must come down to the period immediately following the Forty-five to encounter a more general and splendid resuscitation.

And this time the Highlands especially were prominently to the front. Hitherto, though possessing bards of mark, not

since the days of Columcille did the Scottish Gael burst so
richly and abundantly and tunefully into song.   It seemed as
if the accumulated and pent-up sentiments of generations, at
last overflowing, had found outlet and expression.   The great
Jacobite risings furnished the incentive.   Involving, as they
did, the profoundest issues for the individual, the family life,
and the whole structure of society in the Highlands, these
far-reaching events stirred the deepest emotions in the Gaelic
breast, which found utterance on tongues which otherwise
might for ever have remained silent.

Surpassing the story even of Arthur and the Knights of
the Round Table, because more near, more real and historical,
the romance of Prince Charlie and the Highland chiefs has
taken a lasting hold of the popular imagination.   It has
woven itself into deathless song and story.   The poetry and
music it has elicited in the Highlands alone are among the
sweetest creations of Celtic genius.   They convey a pathos
of sound, richness of rhythm, and perfection of harmony that
is captivating even to foreign ears.

The period between 1745 and 1800 may be regarded as
the high water-mark of Highland poetry.   For quality and
quantity combined, it has never been reached in the past,
and is not likely now ever to be rivalled in the future.
Never before in Gaelic Scotland had there been such a quick
and splendid succession of bards.   In fact, within those fifty
years after Culloden we have nearly all the great names of
Highland poetry—certainly those best known and which
rank highest in the national esteem.   A mere list of the
more important is sufficient to attest this.

There were living then Alexander Macdonald, better
known as Alasdair Macmhaighstir Alasdair ; John Mac-
codrum, the North Uist bard ; Hector Macleod of South
Uist ; Dugald Buchanan ; David Mackellar ; Rob Donn ;
Duncan Macintyre, popularly called Donnachadh Bàn ;
Lauchlan Macpherson, John Roy Stuart, Kenneth Mackenzie,
James Macpherson, Dr. John Smith, John Clark, Mrs. Grant
of Laggan, William Ross, Allan Macdougall, James Shaw,

James Macgregor, Ewan Maclachlan, Alexander Mackinnon, Donald Macdonald, and Donald Macleod—a goodly
number and highly representative to appear in that single
half century.

It is somewhat remarkable that Ireland, too, shared in
the Jacobite poetic reawakening, though she had so partial
and distant a hand in the actual warfare. Without doubt,
her people thoroughly sympathised with the gallant attempt
of Prince Charlie. And this is abundantly evidenced by the
popularity and amount of the national poetry. Not only might
a list of names be given, similar to the above, though fewer
in number, but Dr. Hyde assures us that the Jacobite poems
of Ireland would, if collected, fill a large-sized volume.
Hardiman printed about fifteen in the second volume of his
Irish Minstrelsy, and O'Daly about twenty-five more in his
Irish Jacobite Poetry, second edition.

Comparing this splendid lyrical outburst of that period
in the two countries, Dr. Hyde expresses his own opinion in
the following interesting criticism : "There seems to me," he
says, "to be perhaps, more substance and more simplicity
and straightforward diction in the poems of the Scottish
Gaels, and more melody and word-play, purchased at the
expense of a good deal of nebulousness and unmeaning
sound in those of the Irish Gaels ; both, though they utterly
fail in the ballad, have brought the lyric to a very high
pitch of perfection."

But the literary revival of the eighteenth century was
not by any means confined to the work of the lyrical poets
either in Scotland, Wales, or Ireland. It was this period,
the latter half of the century, that witnessed the new Ossianic
cycle, associated with the name of Macpherson. Though
popularly supposed to be, the latter was not the earliest
pioneer of this movement. In 1756, four years before
Macpherson's *Fragments* appeared, Jerome Stone, who was in
youth a packman, and afterwards a teacher at Dunkeld, gave
to the public the first translation of old Gaelic poems ever
published. On his death, that same year at the age of thirty,

he left a collection, gleaned by himself, of ancient Ossianic ballads, which has recently passed into the possession of Edinburgh University.

Stone undoubtedly had the bardic gift ; his rendering of the original is quite as free as Macpherson's own. The following may be quoted as an example of his style. It is taken from " Fraoch's Death," published in the *Scots Magazine*, 1756, shortly before he died :—

> But now he's gone and nought remains but woe
>   For wretched me ; with him my joys are fled ;
> Around his tomb my tears shall ever flow,
>   The rock my dwelling, and the clay my bed ;
> Ye maids and matrons from your hills descend,
>   To join my moan and answer tear for tear ;
> With me the hero to the grave attend,
>   And sing the songs of mourning round his bier,
> Through his own grove his praise we will proclaim,
> And bid the place for ever bear his name.

Stone did not catch on, like his more brilliant successor.

Before then, except for the fragments that survived, mainly on the lips of oral tradition throughout the Highlands, the old-time volume of saga and heroic poetry had well nigh sunk into oblivion. The MSS. lay neglected in odd and distant corners of the land, hidden and inaccessible, so that the new generations of Gaels as they appeared were wholly ignorant of their existence. The stirring events of the times themselves were not conducive towards the more peaceful study and pursuit of literature. Hence, with the better known publication of Macpherson's contributions there came to the view of modern times, with startling suddenness, an old deposit of literary wealth, which quite astonished the age. It was as if by some convulsion, ancient strata of underlying rock had suddenly upheaved and found access to the surface, much to the wonder and curiosity of all.

The heather was immediately ablaze. A new enthusiasm was awakened in the past. Gaelic scholarship was taxed to the uttermost to substantiate the credit of this new fame.

Libraries were scrutinised, ancient houses searched, memories ransacked, and every remote township and glen scoured to find material. And when material was not forthcoming in sufficient amount, the Muses were invoked to supply the deficiency.

It is now well understood that the period was one of abnormal activity in the production of Ossianic poetry. This might be inferred from the existing British collections of Gaelic MSS., most of which are posterior to the age of Macpherson. Many imitators sought to emulate the ancient bards, and even to palm their modern productions upon the public as part of the original deposit. So late as the day of Mackenzie of " The Beauties" such pieces as " Mordubh," " Collath," and " The Aged Bard's Wish " were regarded as ancient and authentic, though there are few people now, and certainly no recognised authority on the subject, prepared to maintain that.

Certain of these eighteenth century creations are of great merit. Though they lack the antiquity they profess, they are worthy to rank alongside the poetry of the period. Dr. Smith's *Seana Dana* or *Old Lays*, for example, are reckoned fully as interesting and poetical in the original Gaelic as Macpherson's *Ossian ;* yet, unlike the latter, his English translation is a poor substitute for the really fresh and idiomatic vernacular which he published. One of his finest poems, "Dan an Deirg," has been rendered into English, edited, and annotated by an accomplished Englishman, Mr. C. S. Jerram, a scholar and graduate of Cambridge.

In Mr. Pattison's *Gaelic Bards* we have a translation in dainty verses of another of his poems, entitled "Finan and Lorma." Here the young people around the ancient Ossian are represented as addressing the bard in these lines :—

> While on the plains shines the moon, O Bard !
> And the shadow of Cona holds ;
> Like a ghost breathes the wind from the mountain,
> With its spirit voice in its folds.

There are two cloudy forms before us,
Where its host the dim night shows ;
The sigh of the moon curls their tresses,
As they tread over Alva of roes.

Dusky his dogs came with one,
And he bends his dark bow of yew ;
There's a stream from the side of the sad-faced maid,
Dyes her robe with a blood-red hue.

Hold thou back, O thou wind ! from the mountain,
Let their image a moment stay ;
Nor sweep with thy skirts from our eyesight,
Nor scatter their beauty away.

O'er the glen of the rushes, the hill of the hinds,
With the vague wandering vapours they go ;
O ! Bard of the times that have left us,
Aught of their life can'st thou show ?

To which Ossian replies :—

The years that have been they come back as ye speak,
To my soul in their music they glide ;
Like the murmur of waves in the far inland calm,
Is their soft and smooth step by my side.

Smith's translation appeared in 1780, and the originals,
nominally from the Gaelic of Ossian, Ullin, and Orran, etc.,
in 1787. The poems were fourteen in number, with titles as
follow : " The Lay of the Red," " The Death of Gaul,"
" The Lay of Duhona," " Diarmad," " Clan Morni," or " Finan
and Lorma," " The War of Linne," " Cathula," " The War of
Manus," including " The Lay of the Great Fool," " Trahul,"
" Dargo," " Conn," " The Burning of Taura," " Calava," and
" The Death of Art."

In the lay of Taura there occurs the much admired
word-portrait entitled, " Aisling air dhreach Mna," or " The
Vision of a Fair Woman." This is how she looked in the
eye of her Gaelic admirer, and one can judge if her charms
match those of Aspasia or of Cleopatra :—

Innseam pàirt do dreach nan reul;
Bu gheal a deud gu h-ùr dlù;
Mar channach an t-sléibh
Bha cneas fa h-eideadh ùr.

Bha a bràighe cearclach bàn
Mar shneachda tlà nam beann;
Bha a dà chich ag eiridh làn;
B'e'n dreach sud miann nan sonn.

Bu shoitheamh binn a gloir;
S' bu deirge na'n ròs a beul;
Mar chobhar a sios n'a taobh
Sinte gu caol bha gach meur.

Bha a dà chaol mhala mhine
Dûdhonn air liomh an loin.
A da ghruaidh dhreachd nan caoran;
'Si gu iomlan saor o chron.

Bha a gnuis mar bharra-gheuga
Anns a cheud-fhás ùr;
A falt buidhe mar óradh shleibhtean;
'S mar dhearsadh gréine bha sûil.

The Gaelic is not easily translated into felicitous English, but it has been given by Dr. Macneill, somewhat literally thus :—

Tell us some of the charms of the stars;
Close and well-set were her ivory teeth;
White as the cannach upon the moor
Was her bosom the tartan bright beneath.

Her well-rounded forehead shone
Soft and fair as the mountain snow;
Her two breasts were heaving full;
To them did the hearts of the heroes flow.

Her lips were ruddier than the rose,
Tender and tunefully sweet her tongue;
White as the foam adown her side
Her delicate fingers extended hung.

> Smooth as the dusky down of the elk
> Appeared her two narrow brows to me ;
> Lovely her cheeks were like berries red ;
> From every guile she was wholly free.
>
> Her countenance looked like the gentle buds
> Unfolding their beauties in early spring ;
> Her yellow locks like the gold-browed hills,
> And her eyes like the radiance the sunbeams bring.

In the same year, 1780, in which Dr. Smith issued his renderings, another small volume of translations of so-called ancient Gaelic poetry appeared under the title *Caledonian Bards*. It was by John Clark, apparently a very much poorer imitator of Macpherson, and hailing from the latter's own native district, Badenoch. Among the poems submitted, appears the " Mordubh," already referred to, and which in its vernacular garb has misled more than one Celtic enthusiast. Of the latter, besides Mackenzie, Mrs. Grant of Laggan, 1755-1838, was so far deceived that, taking Clark's eighteenth century contribution for genuine ancient poetic material, she set herself to render some of it into more beautiful verse of her own. A contemporary and friend of Sir Walter Scott, this lady takes a high place in the Highland English literature of the period. A third who lived in her time, and who had no mean poetic gift, was the Rev. Duncan Maccallum of Arisaig, the author of " Collath," that other composition which passed for a time as a specimen of ancient poetry. But enough has been said to show the range of this derived and imitative activity.

It will be seen that while on the one hand the Jacobite romance gave rise to a new poetic revival, the Ossianic compositions, on the other hand, proved also a source of general Celtic inspiration during the latter half of the eighteenth century, and for two decades, at least, of the nineteenth. Though the impulse of the Prince Charlie episode did not carry to Wales as it did to Ireland, that of the Ossianic cycle did, and issued in a similar enthusiasm in the production and publication of books of Welsh poetry. This interest became so widespread that in 1819 the national Eisteddfod was revived once more at Caermarthen, and regained its old place in the hearts of the people. Without discussing the tradition that ascribes its origin to the sixth century, it is now fairly well ascertained that it is, at least, as old as the twelfth or thirteenth century. History shows that Prince Griffith of South Wales held a great Eisteddfod at Caermarthen in 1451, at which the twenty-four metres of Welsh poetry were settled for all time. Since then it has had a chequered career ; officially patronised by the Tudors, it seems to have declined under the Stuarts, and nearly perished under the first three Hanoverians. But now, since its revival in 1819, nearly every hamlet in Wales holds its annual Eisteddfod, and the national one has grown to such a magnitude that it tends not only to keep alive the Celtic spirit, but also to foster the love of music and poetry in the Principality.

Like much of our own Highland barderie, the Welsh poetry is the product of workmen who have never been taught to read or write their own language in the schools. Yet such is their natural taste and sense of style that some of their best modern lyrics need not fear comparison with those of Tannahill or even of Burns. Undoubtedly such poetry has serious limitations, but it has a charm and beauty of its own, and is as fresh and limpid as the mountain streams. The fragrance of the heather is upon it quite as much as it is upon the lyrics of our own bards in the Highlands. And as these latter felt the charm of the towering mountain, the gloomy glen, the forest solitude, the lonely mysterious sea, the bubbling stream, the wildflower, and the changing seasons, and gave felicitous and sympathetic expression to the emotions these awakened in their breasts, so did the peasant poets of Wild Wales. All through last century, both in the Highlands and in that country, there have been a succession of minor bards who have maintained the native tongue sweet and warm and tuneful by their lyrics, though in Ireland the same cannot be said, as the language there until quite recently had not been fostered so much as in the sister countries.

But to-day we constantly read of ourselves as passing through another Celtic renaissance, and this is the last which falls to be noticed. It took its rise half a century ago in the work of the scholars, and doubtless was the natural sequence of the wide-spread interest aroused at home and abroad by the Ossianic compositions. It was recognised that there was material to work upon, which could be dealt with from a scientific as well as a literary point of view. And so the renaissance in the first instance was a revival of interest in the language itself, and the ancient MS. monuments that contained its oldest forms.

Two sets of scholars interested themselves in this new line of research. On the one hand, distinguished Irishmen like John O'Donovan and Eugene O'Curry devoted themselves to the task of bringing to light the neglected and hidden MS. remains, which had hitherto for centuries lain in the obscurity of religious or public libraries unread and uncatalogued. And through these treasures they sought to interpret the Gaelic past. On the other hand, Continental savants such as Bopp, Zeuss, and Ebel, deeply absorbed in philological studies, were already at work on the linguistic problem, which has rescued the Celtic dialects from an unnatural isolation and equally unmerited contempt.

Zeuss's book in particular, published in 1853—the Gaelic part of it founded on the study of Gaelic Continental MSS., illuminated the whole field, just as much as if the searchlight had been turned on a dark and hidden landscape. From that day a Celtic renaissance was assured. His philological results, and the fact that the ancient dialects had now been proved beyond question to belong to the great Aryan group, and closely akin to the classic languages of Europe, gave the Celtic a new importance and fired the enthusiasm of that subsequent galaxy of scholars, who have made Celtic studies famous.

Surprised and charmed with the prestige their own language and literature had thus suddenly acquired in the eyes of Europe, and especially of learned philologists, many of the Celts themselves now began to look with kindlier interest upon their own literary legacy and to recognise its value. The attention thus drawn to the past gradually aroused enthusiasm for every surviving relic of tradition, of literature, of history, of social custom, and of music. It has led to the foundation of Celtic chairs for the study of the language and literature, notably at Oxford, Edinburgh, and Berlin. It has given rise to the Gaelic Mòd, Irish Text Society, and numerous other Highland, Irish, and Welsh Associations, and kindred periodicals, British, American, and Continental. Never before has such a mass of Celtic tradition and lore been brought to view, and published in book or magazine, as there has been within the last few decades.

It cannot indeed be said that this renaissance has added any new masterpieces to the native literatures, either in prose or poetry. A wonderful outburst of literary activity there has been, and distinguished authors have arrived ; but the remarkable thing is, and it is worthy of note, that the so-called Celtic renaissance, if we regard it solely from its literary side and apart from the work of scholars, has found its fullest expression in English, and addresses itself not so much to the native Gaels or Cymri as to the English-speaking world in general. Highland, Welsh, and Irish litterateurs have taken to placing their wealth of dream, of poetic sentiment and imagination, as well as their marvellous gift of story-telling, at the service of English literature, which is accordingly enriched, while the old river dries up in proportion as the number of readers and writers of the original tongue declines.

There are some things that we cannot hope to resuscitate. They pass in the nature of things. Some that we would not wish to recall even if we might. They have served their day. And if the current Celtic renaissance has not contributed as much to the vernacular literature as might be desired, it has certainly immensely enhanced the glories of the past, and it has otherwise exhibited a revival of Celtic *esprit de corps* which shows that—

> The ancient spirit is not dead—
> Old times, methinks, are breathing there.

That this race-feeling survives, this kinship of blood, and is ever and anon reasserting itself, may be inferred from the recent Pan-Celtic Congress in Dublin, where representatives of Wales, of Brittany, of the Highlands, of Ireland, and even of Celtdom beyond the seas, assembled in all their ancient *tailoring* to do homage to the past, to reckon with the present, and formulate afresh their aspirations—to ask, in fact, what does this latest renaissance mean? and whither tends it?

A truly heterogeneous gathering, and eminently characteristic of the race, who still look wistfully for the return of Arthur or of the Feinn, and some new age of magic and romance, and whose forte it is unceasingly to pursue the unknown, the undefinable, the ideal.

We can picture the bewildered surprise and irrepressible mirth of the average, unimaginative, unbelieving Sassenach, as he suddenly encounters the extraordinary Pan-Celtic pageant on the living streets of Dublin. Whence this resurrection of phantoms—these apparitions of long dead ancestors? " Nay, good citizen, 'tis no phantasy," sober reason replies, " but one of various manifestations, perhaps the most evanescent of the present Celtic renaissance, which finds little in our modern, materialistic civilisation answering to its deepest aspirations." And, falling into reverie over the unwonted spectacle, we ourselves in our wonderment musingly repeat the words of Charles Lamb :—

Antiquity! thou wondrous charm, what art thou? that being nothing, art everything! When thou wert, thou wert not antiquity —then thou wert nothing, but hadst a remoter *antiquity*, as thou calledst it, to look back to with blind veneration ; thou thyself being to thyself, flat, jejune, *modern !* What mystery lurks in this retroversion? or what half Januses are we, that we cannot look forward with the same idolatry with which we for ever revert? The mighty future is as nothing, being everything ; the past is everything, being nothing.

CHAPTER XIV

HIGHLAND BARDS BEFORE THE FORTY-FIVE

"The Owlet"—Three Macgregor songs—The old bardic system superseded—Era of modern Gaelic poetry—Mary Macleod—Details of her life—Famous songs—Iain Lom—Ardent poet and politician—His "Vow"—Eventful career —Poems—Created Gaelic Poet-Laureate—Influence on Highland history— Other minor bards and bardesses—Imitations by Sir Walter Scott—The blind harper, and the blind piper —A comic poet —Two major bards— Maccodrum's Muse—Characteristics of the group before the Forty-five.

THE Book of the Dean of Lismore may be regarded as having gathered up the best of the available, medieval, Gaelic poetry, and as having closed the old bardic period. After it there came a break of nearly a hundred years. It is true that there are some pieces which hail from this interval, but they are isolated and few, with no certain dates.

Of these, the most remarkable is that styled "The Owlet," and it is worthy of notice here as being the only composition of the kind in the language. The poem is attributed to Donald Macdonald, a native of Lochaber, and perhaps the most expert archer of his day. Withal a famous wolf-hunter, he appears to have lived in the days before firearms, and to have composed the verses when old. Their occasion is briefly summarised by Mackenzie of " The Beauties," in a foot-note. In his declining years the poet had married a young woman who proved a very unmeet helpmate. For when he and his dog were worn down with the toils of the chase, and infirmities rendered them stiff and decrepit, this " crooked rib " took a pleasure in teasing them. Finding an old feeble owl one day, she installed it in the house as a more fitting companion than herself for the aged bard and his dog. The poem is an ingenious performance in the form of a dialogue between the outraged husband and the bird.

Three Macgregor songs of that period have likewise a wonderful charm and pathos. They are entitled "Macgregor's Lullaby," "Macgregor's O'Ruara," and "The Braes of the Ceathach." The authoress of the first laments the death of her husband, who, with his father and brother, were beheaded at the instigation of Colin Campbell of Glenorchy; her own sire, Campbell of Glenlyon; and Menzies of Rannoch. The following verses are from Pattison's rendering :—

> Early on a Lammas morning,
> With my husband was I gay;
> But my heart got sorely wounded
> Ere the middle of the day.

> (chorus) Ochan, Ochan, Ochan uiri,
> Though I cry, my child, with thee—
> Ochan, Ochan, Ochan uiri,
> Now he hears not thee nor me.

> Malison on judge and kindred—
> They have wrought me mickle woe;
> With deceit they came about us,
> Through deceit they laid him low.

> Had they met but twelve Macgregors,
> With my Gregor at their head;
> Now my child had not been orphaned,
> Nor these bitter tears been shed.

> On an oaken block they laid him,
> And they spilt his blood around;
> I'd have drunk it in a goblet
> Largely, ere it reached the ground.

When the rest have all got lovers
Now a lover have I none ;
My fair blossom, fresh and fragrant,
Withers on the ground alone.

While all other wives the night-time
Pass in slumber's balmy bands ;
I, beside my bedside weary,
Never cease to wring my hands.

Far, far better be with Gregor
Where the heather's in its prime,
Than with mean and Lowland barons
In a house of stone and lime.

.   .   .   .   .

Bahu, bahu, little nursling—
Oh ! so tender now and weak ;
I fear the day will never brighten
When revenge for him you'll seek.

Ochan, Ochan, Ochan uiri,
Though I cry, my child, with thee—
Ochan, Ochan, Ochan uiri
Yet he hears not thee nor me.

We pass by the few existing lines of Bishop Carsewell
and Sir John Stewart of Appin, who both lived in the
sixteenth century, and forthwith emerge upon the new time,
the era of modern Gaelic poetry. Almost simultaneously
in Scotland and Ireland, a great change took place in the
form and complexion of this vernacular poetic literature.
From the early part of the seventeenth century, the intricate
metres and technicalities of the old bardic system, which had
been in vogue for a thousand years, began to be discarded
and superseded, and more freedom in versifying introduced.
Dr. Douglas Hyde sums up the principles of this new
departure in two sentences : first, the adoption of vowel
rhyme in place of consonantal rhyme ; second, the adoption
of a certain number of accents in each line in place of a
certain number of syllables. And in consequence of these

changes, he holds that the Gaelic poetry of the last two centuries is probably the most sensuous attempt to convey music in words ever made by man. He who has once heard it and remains deaf to its charm can have little heart for song or soul for music. It is absolutely impossible, he says, to convey the lusciousness of sound, richness of rhythm, and perfection of harmony in another language. The sweetest creation of all Gaelic literature, this new outburst of lyric melody was a wonderful arrangement of vowel sounds, so placed that in every accented syllable, first one vowel and then another fell upon the ear in all possible kinds of harmonious modifications. Some verses are made wholly on the à sound, others on the ò, ù, è, or ì sounds, but the majority on a unique and fascinating intermixture of two, three, or more ; as, for example, in Mary Macleod's vowel-rhyming over the drowning of Mac-Ille Chalum in the angry Minch between Stornoway and Raasay :—

> Mo bhèud, 's mo bhròn,
> Mar dh'eirich dhò
> Muir beucach, mòr,
> Ag leum mu d'bhòrd,
> Thu féin, 's do shèoid
> 'Nuair reub 'ur seòil,
> Nach d'fhaod sibh treòir
> A chaitheadh orr.

> 'S e an sgeul' craiteach
> Do'n mhnaoi a d'fhag thu,
> 'S do t-aon bhrathair,
> A shuidh na t'aite,
> Diluain Càisge,
> Chaidh tonn bàit ort,
> Craobh a b'aird' de'n ubhal thu.

To give the effect in English the original has been some-what freely, though not quite accurately, rendered thus :—

> My grief, my pain,
> Relief was vain
> The seething wave
> Did leap and rave

> And reeve in twain,
> Both sheet and sail,
> And leave us bare
> And foundering.
>
> Alas ! indeed,
> For her you leave.
> Your brother's grief
> To them will cleave.
> It was on Easter
> Monday's feast
> The branch of peace
> Went down with you.

It has been acknowledged even by Dr. Hyde, one of our greatest Irish authorities of the present, that the Scottish Gaels led the way in this great change that transformed the Celtic poetry of both Islands, and to Mary Macleod, popularly known as " Mairi nighean Alasdair Ruaidh," has been assigned the honour of being the first of the modern Highland bards to inaugurate the new system.

Before her day most of the Gaelic poetry was Ossianic, or of uncertain authorship ; fugitive, and generally in the ancient style. The poets were bound by the rules of their order, and to excel within the very narrow limits of the old-world prosody, hedged about as it was with so many technicalities, required years of severe bardic study and preparation. Mary, apparently without any tuition, without even the power to read or write, suddenly burst these unnatural bonds asunder, and gave to the spirit of her poetry the freedom of the elements, unhampered and unfettered by the intricate metres of the Schools. She invented rhythms of her own, often making the music of sound an echo of the sense. And from her time scores of new and brilliant metres have made their appearance.

Only a few biographical details of this remarkable woman are known, but they are characteristic, and extremely interesting, revealing a personality outside the common order of Highland intellect. Born in Roudal, Harris, in the year

1569, she was the daughter of Alexander Macleod, son of Alasdair Ruadh, a descendant of the chief of that distinguished clan ; and at an early age, apparently, she became a nurse in the family of the Macleods at Dunvegan Castle.   Though otherwise illiterate, the poetic Mary must have derived some culture, independently of book learning, from her association with the chiefs and their following in the ancestral home where, nearly 200 years afterwards, Dr. Johnson and his friend were so hospitably entertained.   In the course of her long career, for she lived to be 105 years old, she nursed no less than five lairds of the Macleods,[1] and two of the lairds of Applecross.

There is no evidence that she was much addicted to the making of poetry until somewhat advanced in life.   It was then at least that she composed those pieces that have survived and made her name illustrious in Highland literature. Most of them have reference to events that happened in the Macleod family.

Thus the song, "An Talla 'm bu ghna le Mac Leoid," was produced extempore during the last illness of one of the lairds.   Happening to ask Mary facetiously what kind of a lament she would make for him after he was gone, she declared in response that it would be a very mournful one. "Come nearer me," said the aged chief, "and let me hear part of it," whereupon the clever bardess sang this pathetic dirge.   The power of extemporising poetical compositions still lingers in the Highlands.

Again, " Hithill, uthill agus hò," owes its existence to the gift of a snuff-mull bestowed on Mary by a son of Sir Norman.

All her barderie, however, did not suit the proud chief of Dunvegan, who objected to the scope of the publicity he and his menage received at the hands of the family nurse, exercising, as she freely did, the privileges of the poet.   And therefore he banished her to the island of Mull, under the care of a relative.

---

[1] The late Mr. Alexander Mackenzie has offered other suggestions.   See *Transactions of the Gaelic Society of Inverness*, Vol. XXII. pp. 43-49.

But if one song sent her away, another brought her back. It was hard to be exiled from Eilean-a-Cheo, and the castled seat of the clan, and so seizing the opportunity which the advent of the young laird's birthday offered, she composed the now well-known " Luinneag Mhic Leoid," or " Ode to Macleod," in which she presented a portrait so flattering that the stubborn chief relented and sent a boat to bring her back, on condition that henceforth she should no more exercise her gift of song. The delighted poetess readily assented.

Yet even on the way from Mull to Skye she could not restrain the poetic afflatus, and though for a time after her return she kept her word, as Blackie says, " a bird is a bird and will sing"; and Mary Macleod, this irrepressible daughter of the red-haired clansman, once more incurred the displeasure of her chief by composing a new poem on the recovery of his son from some illness; and in extenuation of the charge laid against her, she naively maintained, " It is not a song; it is only a crònan," that is, a crooning.

The ode she produced in Mull in the days of dreary exile is one of the finest of her poems; wild and beautiful, with a very peculiar charm. It generally appears in all the best collections of Gaelic songs, and has been translated into English verse both by Pattison and Blackie. The rendering of the latter is, perhaps, the more euphonious, and brings out better the repetition at the beginning of each stanza, as :—

> I sit on a knoll,
> All sorrowful and sad,
> And I look on the grey sea
> In mistiness clad,
> And I brood on strange chances
> That drifted me here,
> Where Scarba and Jura
> And Islay are near.
>
> Where Scarba and Jura
> And Islay are near;
> Grand land of rough mountains,
> I wish thee good cheer,

I wish young Sir Norman
On mainland and islands
To be named with proud honour,
First chief of the Highlands !

To be praised with proud honour
First chief of the Highlands,
For wisdom and valour,
In far and nigh lands ;
For mettle and manhood
There's none may compare
With the handsome Macleod
Of the princeliest air.

And the blood through his veins,
That so proudly doth fare,
From the old Kings of Lochlann
Flows richly and rare.
Each proud earl in Alba
Is knit with his line,
And Erin shakes hands with him
Over the brine.

And Erin shakes hands with him
Over the brine ;
Brave son of brave father,
The pride of his line,
In camp and in council
Whose virtue was seen,
And his purse was as free
As his claymore was keen.

.   .   .   .

With my heart I thee worship
Thou shapeliest Knight,
Wellgirt in the grace
Of the red and the white ;
With an eye like the blaeberry
Blue on the brae,
And cheeks like the haws
On the hedge by the way.

With a cheek like the haws
On the hedge by the way,
'Neath the rarest of locks
In rich curly display ;

> And the guest in thy hall
> With glad cheer shall behold
> Rich choice of rare armour
> In brass and in gold, etc.

It needs some of Mary's own imagination to picture her going about in after days wearing a tartan *tonnag*, fastened in front with a large silver brooch, and carrying a silver-headed cane. Hardy to a degree in mind and constitution, the venerable nurse and poetess, when long past the natural span of years, was much given, we are told, to gossip, snuff, and whisky. After her death, which took place at Dunvegan in 1674, she was buried in her native isle of Harris.

Mackenzie of "The Beauties" appraised this quaint personage as the most original of all our poets, who borrowed nothing. Her thoughts, her verse, and rhymes were all equally her own; her language simple and elegant; her diction easy, natural, and unaffected. There is no straining to produce effect; no search after unintelligible words to conceal the poverty of ideas. Her thoughts flow freely, and her versification runs like a mountain stream over a smooth bed of polished granite. She often repeats her rhymes, as in the above instance, yet we never feel them tiresome or disagreeable, for, more than most of her Gaelic compeers, Mary was mistress of the poetic lyre.

After her came another striking figure in the history of Highland bardic literature. This was John Macdonald, the Lochaber poet, popularly known as Iain Lom, probably from lack of hair either on his head or face, and sometimes styled Iain Manntach, from an impediment in his speech. Singular in these physical respects, he was no less remarkable for his mental characteristics. A man of great force of character, he combined in his personality the ardent poet and the keen politician, the intuitive dreamer and the restless man of action.

Macdonald belonged to the Keppoch family, lived through the stirring times of Charles I., Charles II., James II., the Revolution, and subsequent reign of William and Mary, dying at an advanced age in 1710, when Anne was on the throne.

This is the wonderful schemer whom some regard as the real genius of the Montrose Campaign during the Civil War. Were it not for him, it is certain, events could not have developed so favourably and so brilliantly for the victorious Marquis as they did. Keen Jacobite as he always was, he accompanied the latter on most of his marches, and it is marvellous that the great Border minstrel, Sir Walter Scott, especially in his account of the battle of Inverlochy in the *Legend of Montrose*, makes no reference to him.

The Keppoch bard first came into prominence as a man to be reckoned with, in connection with the murder of his chief, which, it is said he foresaw, but was unable to avert. Sent abroad as a minor to be educated, the heir of Keppoch was supplanted in his absence by his own faithless and intriguing cousins, who murdered both him and his brother on their return home. The dastardly crime rankled in the bosom of the fiery bard. Among the faithless clansmen he alone remained fearlessly true to the stricken family, and he determined to have revenge. "The Vow of Iain Lom," published in Mrs. D. Ogilvy's *Highland Minstrelsy*, graphically depicts his state of mind at the time. He went from house to house, and castle to castle, calling for vengeance on the assassins, and having at last obtained a commission from Government to take them dead or alive, he first addressed himself to Glengarry, who declined the dangerous task, and then to Sir Alexander Macdonald, who put a company of chosen men at his disposal, the "Ciaran Mabach," poet and soldier, at their head.

Under the Keppoch bard's directions the murderers were summarily attacked and beheaded in their own barricaded house. A gruesome monument of seven heads, representing those of the father and six sons, now marks the well on Loch Oich side, known as *Tobar-nan-ceann*, where these bleeding trophies are said to have been washed on their way to Glengarry Castle, whence they were carried to Skye as a tribute to the Knight of Sleat.

The bard has a poem on " Mort na Ceapach," the murder of Keppoch ; and another entitled " A Bhean Leasaich," in which he begins by praising Sir Alexander Macdonald of Sleat and his son Sir James, evidently with the intention of provoking Glengarry for his remissness in the matter of retribution upon the usurpers.   His own persecution by the traitors furnished the poet with another theme.   From this time he became a man of mark in the Highlands, feared and respected.   Though not a soldier himself, when the Civil War broke out he identified himself with the cause of the Stuarts, and was the means of bringing the armies of Argyll and Montrose into deadly conflict at Inverlochy on February 2nd, 1645.   The wily John, a willing spectator, evaded taking a personal hand in the encounter by the following ruse.   When asked to make ready to march to the fight, by the Macdonald commanding the Irish contingent, he slyly replied, " If I go along with thee to-day, and fall in battle, who will sing thy praises to-morrow ?   Go thou, Alasdair, and exert thyself as usual, and I shall sing thy feats, and celebrate thy prowess in martial strains."

The result was that the bard feasted his eyes from a safe distance on the disaster of the Campbells, with whom he was ever at feud, and moved by all the passion and prejudice of the event composed the heroic stanzas entitled, " The Battle of Inverlochy."   So realistic and graphic is the description given in the original Gaelic that it seems to photograph many of the details just as they happened.   " The spirit of poetry, the language, and boldness of expression," says Mackenzie, with perhaps the Celtic leaning to hyperbole, " have never been equalled."   Yet to-day we read these vindictive strains with different feelings from those that animated the bard.

A few verses may be quoted from the rendering of Professor Blackie, which, though they lack the fire and intensity of the original, give a good idea of the gist of the poem :—[1]

[1] There is a spirited translation also by Mark Napier, Esq., in his *Life of Montrose.*

Did you hear from Cille Cummin
How the tide of war came pouring?
Far and wide the summons travelled,
How they drave the Whigs before them!

From the Castle tower I viewed it
High on Sunday morning early,
Looked and saw the ordered battle
Where Clan Donald triumphed rarely.

Up the green slope of Cuil Eachaidh
Came Clan Donald marching stoutly;
Churls who laid my home in ashes,
Now shall pay the fine devoutly!

.   .   .   .

Many a bravely mounted rider,
With his back turned to the slaughter,
Where his boots won't keep him dry now,
Learns to swim in Nevis water.

On the wings of eager rumour
Far and wide the tale is flying,
How the slippery knaves, the Campbells,
With their cloven skulls are lying!

O'er the frosted moor they travelled,
Stoutly with no thought of dying;
Where now many a whey-faced lubber,
To manure the fields is lying!

From the height of Tom-na-harry
See them crudely heaped together,
In their eyes no hint of seeing,
Stretched to rot upon the heather!

Warm your welcome was at Lochy,
With blows and buffets thickening round you,
And Clan Donald's groovèd claymore,
Flashing terror to confound you!

Hot and hotter grew the struggle
Where the trenchant blade assailed them;
Sprawled with nails on ground Clan Duiné,
When the parted sinew failed them.

Many a corpse upon the heather,
Naked lay, once big with daring,
From the battle's hurly-burly,
Drifting blindly to Blarchaorainn.

.   .   .   .   .

If I could, I would be weeping
For your shame and for your sorrow,
Orphans' cry and widows' wailing,
Through the long Argyll to-morrow.

All this to the weird and exulting chorus :—

H-i rim h-ŏ-rò, h-ò-rò leatha,
H-i rim h-ŏ-rò, h-ò-rò leatha,
H-i rim h-ŏ-rò, h-ò-rò leatha,
Chaidh an la le Clann-Dòmhnuill.

His dangerous strategy and stinging sarcasm at length
roused the Marquis of Argyll to offer a reward for his head,
and it is characteristic of the impetuous John that he
appeared in person in the audience-hall of this mighty chief
to claim it, relying for safety, no doubt, on the sacred regard
in which Highlanders always held the professional bard.
The Marquis received him courteously, and as they passed
through a room hung round with heads of moor-fowl, he
asked him, " Have you ever seen, John, so many black-
cocks together ? "   " Yes," he replied.   " Where ? "   " At
Inverlochy."   " Ah ! John," muttered Argyll, " will you never
cease gnawing at the Campbells ? "   " I am only sorry,"
added the implacable bard, " that I cannot swallow them."

For his services in the Stuart cause he was created
Gaelic poet-laureate, and received from Charles II. a yearly
pension. Iain Lom thus holds the unique distinction of having
been the first and only Gaelic poet-laureate. Altogether
his poems would occupy a considerable volume, though they
have never been so issued.[1] Pattison has not translated
any, but Iain Lom has nevertheless obtained a well-merited

[1] D. Campbell, in his *Language, Poetry, and Music of the Highland Clans*,
says that Mr. James Munro was preparing his poems for publication with a
memoir. This projected book has never appeared.

niche in Messrs. Blackie, the publishers, *Poets and Poetry of Scotland*, 1876, compiled by James G. Wilson ; and the romantic side of his character is charmingly represented incidentally in Neil Munro's novel, entitled *John Splendid.*

Long after his death his Jacobite effusions still exercised a powerful influence over his countrymen, counteracting in no small degree the efforts of the Government to suppress the Stuart factions. "Children were taught to lisp them," says the *New Statistical Account of Scotland.* "They were sung in the family circle on winter nights, and at weddings, lyke-wakes, fairs, and in every company. They attributed to the Stuarts and their adherents the most exalted virtues, and represented their opponents as incarnate fiends. In 1745, Moidart and Kilmonivaig were called 'The Cradle of the Rebellion,' and they were the very districts where the songs of Iain Lom leavened the whole mass of society with Jacobite sentiments."

> Mightier was the verse of Iain
> Hearts to nerve, to kindle eyes,
> Than the claymore of the valiant,
> Than the counsel of the wise.

Contemporary with Iain Lom, and his confederate in bringing retribution upon the Keppoch traitors, was a minor bard, known as Archibald Macdonald, or "An Ciaran Mabach," an illegitimate son of Sir Alexander Macdonald, sixteenth baron of Sleat. In after life he lived in easy circumstances, well adapted for the cultivation of his poetic tastes, on an estate granted him in North Uist by his influential father, in return for numerous services rendered as a sagacious and practical man of affairs. Otherwise his life was uneventful and his poetry limited in amount.

But the field held various other less prominent bards, for to this period belonged several of those whose productions appear in the Fernaig MS. of Duncan Macrae. Nor was the Highlands then lacking in poetesses. Two at least figure in the record of the remembered.

Dorothy Brown, a native of Luing Island, Argyllshire, composed many poems, of which perhaps that to Alasdair Maccolla is the only one now extant, yet as a poetess she alone of women in that age approached the standard of Mary Macleod.

Cicely Macdonald, her contemporary, was daughter of Ronald of Keppoch, in youth a frolicsome maiden and clever at epigrams. Marrying a gentleman of the Lovat family, she lived with him farther north, and came to be known for her bardic gifts. Songs and laments were her chief productions, but after her husband died at Inverness in a fit of inebriety, she took to hymn-making. The names of her earlier pieces are suggestive, such as : " Moràghach Mhic Shimidh," " Slan gu bràth le ceòl na clarsaich," and " Alasdair a Glinne-Garaidh." The latter beautiful one, Mackenzie assures us, has served as a model for many Gaelic songs.

The next name in the succession is that of Nial Macvurich, family bard and historian of Clanranald, distinguished also as a descendant, through a long line of bardic ancestors, from the ancient and historic Muireach Albannach, whose poetry figures in the Book of the Dean of Lismore. To Nial we are indebted for the history of his illustrious clan, written in Gaelic and preserved in the Red Book of Clanranald. But it is to be regretted that of his own poems none is now extant, except two pieces treasured in " The Beauties." Solicitous to perpetuate the history and ancient poetry of others, it appears that Nial took no thought for his own to have them written down, and so they have mostly disappeared. He lived to a great age, like the majority of these early Highland bards, and was an old man living on his farm in South Uist at the time of the first Jacobite rising in 1715.

Still another poet of Clanranald fame, John Macdonald, or Iain Dubh Mac Iain 'Ic-Ailein, born about 1665, and resident in Eigg ; and then we reach the Aosdan Matheson, who was bard to the Earl of Seaforth in the seventeenth century. Appurtenant to this post he held free lands in

Lochalsh, Ross-shire, and composed as many poems as would fill a large volume, but most of these, like Nial Macvurich's, and for the same reason, have long been forgotten. One of those preserved has been very freely rendered or imitated in English by Sir Walter Scott, under the title "Farewell to Mackenzie, High Chief of Kintail," 1815.

The original verses are arranged to a beautiful Gaelic air, of which the chorus is adapted to the double pull upon the oars of a galley, and which is therefore distinct from the ordinary boat-songs. They were composed on the occasion of the embarking at Dornie, Kintail, of the Earl of Seaforth, who was obliged to take refuge in Spain, after an unsuccessful effort in favour of the old Chevalier in 1718. Sir Walter's version runs thus :—

> Farewell to Mackenneth, great Earl of the North,
> The Lord of Lochcarron, Glenshiel, and Seaforth;
> To the Chieftain this morning his course who began,
> Launching forth on the billow his bark like a swan.
> For a foreign land he has hoisted his sail,
> Farewell to Mackenzie, High Chief of Kintail!
>
> O swift be the galley, and hardy her crew,
> May her captain be skilful, her mariners true,
> In danger undaunted, unwearied by toil,
> Though the whirlwind should rise, and the ocean should boil;
> On the brave vessel's gunnel, I drank his bonail,
> And farewell to Mackenzie, High Chief of Kintail!
>
> Awake in thy chamber, thou sweet southland gale!
> Like the sighs of his people, breathe soft on his sail;
> Be prolong'd as regret, that his vassals must know,
> Be fair as their faith, and sincere as their woe;
> Be so soft, and so fair, and so faithful, sweet gale,
> Wafting onward Mackenzie, High Chief of Kintail!
>
> Be his pilot experienced, and trusty, and wise,
> To measure the seas and to study the skies;
> May he hoist all his canvas from streamer to deck,
> But oh! crowd it higher when wafting him back—
> Till the cliffs of Skooroora, and Conan's glad vale,
> Shall welcome Mackenzie, High Chief of Kintail!

Hector Maclean, of the same period, was bard to Sir Lachlan Maclean of Duart, from whom he had a small annuity. Two poems of his, the " Chief's Elegy " and " Song," are reckoned among the beauties of Gaelic poetry, and have also attracted the attention of Sir Walter Scott, who translated or imitated in the abrupt style of the original a fragment of the latter, entitled " War-Song of Lachlan, High-Chief of Maclean." This song, like many of the early Gaelic productions, makes a rapid transition from one subject to another. From the situation of a forlorn maiden of the clan, who opens with an address to her absent lover, it passes finally to an eulogium over the martial glories of the chieftain. Thus :—

> A weary month has wandered o'er
> Since last we parted on the shore ;
> Heaven ! that I saw thee, Love, once more,
> Safe on that shore again !
> 'Twas valiant Lachlan gave the word ;
> Lachlan, of many a galley lord ;
> He call'd his kindred bands on board,
> And launched them on the main.

> Clan Gillian is to ocean gone,
> Clan Gillian, fierce in foray known ;
> Rejoicing in the glory won
> In many a bloody broil ;
> For wide is heard the thundering fray,
> The rout,-the ruin, the dismay,
> When from the twilight glens away
> Clan Gillian drives the spoil.

> Woe to the hills that shall rebound
> Our banner'd bagpipes' maddening sound ;
> Clan Gillian's onset echoing round,
> Shall shake their inmost cell.
> Woe to the bark whose crew shall gaze
> Where Lachlan's silken streamer plays !
> The fools might face the lightning's blaze
> As wisely and as well !

Lachlan Mackinnon of Strath, Isle of Skye, is the next to figure in this succession. Unlike so many of the others, he was not unlettered, nor ignorant of such knowledge of the language as may be gleaned from a critical study of its structure. Hence his Gaelic is wonderfully pure and correct. In early life he filled the rôle of a strolling musician, carrying his violin about with him from place to place, till certain personal considerations obliged him to desist.

After him came a blind harper and a blind piper, both famous in Highland minstrelsy. The harper was Roderick Morrison, son of an Episcopal clergyman in the island of Lewis. He was born in the year 1646, and in his boyhood had been sent along with his two brothers to be educated at Inverness, all three having been destined by their father for the ministry of the Church. But, unhappily, while there the youthful islanders were seized with smallpox, which was then epidemic in the town. His two brothers recovered from the effects of the dread scourge, and afterwards became ministers, one at Contin, the other at Poolewe in Ross-shire. Roderick himself was the chief sufferer, for not only was his face disfigured and contracted, but he also lost the use of his eyes. Incapacitated thus for a profession, he turned his attention to music, and in addition to the skill he acquired in playing other instruments, became an adept at the harp. Hence the name " An Clarsair Dall," by which he was generally known throughout the Highlands.

Visiting Ireland, it is thought he profited by tuition from his fellow-harpers there, who had achieved fame in that form of minstrelsy; and on his return to Scotland he took occasion to call at every baronial residence on the way to exhibit his art. It so happened at the time that many of the Scotch nobility and gentry were at the Court of King James in Holyrood, Edinburgh, and thither the blind musician wended his way, where he found an excellent friend in the person of the Highland chieftain, John Breac Macleod of Harris, who readily engaged him as his family harper.

While holding this office Morrison composed several

beautiful tunes and songs, living the life of a farmer at Totamòr in Glenelg, on a piece of land which his patron granted him rent-free. On the death of the latter he returned to his native island, and died there in a good old age, and was buried in a country churchyard near Stornoway.

Morrison was a poet of power and culture. His elegy, " Creach nan Ciadan," on the chieftain who befriended him, is reckoned one of the most pathetic, plaintive, and heart-touching of Highland laments.

The blind piper, John Mackay of Gairloch, was a contemporary, though twenty years his junior. Like his father before him, who hailed from the Reay country, this Mackay was born blind. Taught music first of all under the paternal roof, he was sent later on to the Isle of Skye to perfect his studies under the direction of the celebrated Mac Crimmon. There he excelled all other pupils, and soon learned to compose pipe-music himself. In fact, it is recorded that one of the Mac Crimmons, jealous of his powers as a pipe-music composer, bribed some of the youths to. throw him over a precipice, which they did one day, the blind stripling falling a distance of twenty-four feet, but without physical hurt. The rock is still known as " Leum an Doill," or " The Blind Man's Leap," since he had the good fortune to land on his soles.

After seven years' tuition in Skye he returned to his native parish, succeeding his father as family piper to the Laird of Gairloch, and subsequently marrying. Numerous pibrochs, strathspeys, reels, and jigs are placed to his credit. When at length he was superannuated on a small but competent annuity, the old man used to pass his time visiting gentlemen's houses in the Reay country and the island of Skye. On one of these peregrinations in Sutherlandshire he composed the beautiful pastoral " Coire an Easain," lamenting Lord Reay. Of this poem Mackenzie says, " It is not surpassed by anything of the kind in the Celtic language—bold, majestic, and intrepid, it commands admiration at first glance, and seems on a nearer survey

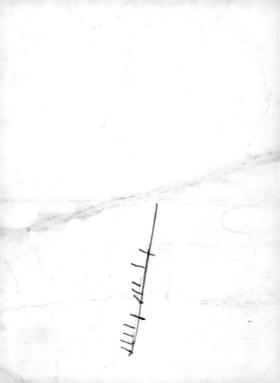

of the entire magnificent fabric as the work of some supernatural agent." Could Highland admiration go farther?

The "Piobaire Dall" lived till he was about ninety-eight
years of age, and sleeps with his father Ruairidh Dall within
the clachan of his native parish in the west.

Other minor bards of the period were, John Whyte,
William Mackenzie, John Maclean, Malcolm Maclean, the
poet Macdonald of Muck, who composed the "Massacre of
Glencoe," Angus Macdonald, Hector Macleod, Archibald
Macdonald, and Zachary Macaulay.

Archibald Macdonald excelled as a comic bard—one of
the few that Highland Gaeldom has produced. His "Elegy"
on Roy while living—a piper and favourite companion of
his own—and his "Resurrection" of the same individual, are
counted very clever. He it was who composed the famous
satire, "Tha biodag air Mac Thomàis," which, when played
at a wedding memorable in Highland history, ended so tragi-
cally for the player, and, indeed, for Mac Thomàis himself,
the alleged heir to the Lovat estates, who had to fly from
the country, and whose descendants have on more than one
occasion in recent times contested the right of the present
Lovat family to the ancient inheritance.

Tradition still pathetically relates how on that occasion,
enraged at the playing of the piece which so cleverly
satirised himself, this young Master of Lovat stabbed the
bag of the piper, to silence it, with his biodag, but the
weapon entered the player's heart also, and bag and piper
both collapsed with a mournful groan.

Zachary Macaulay is worthy of note on another account.
From his family was descended the brilliant Lord Macaulay,
so famous in letters, and it may very well have been from
this source that the gifted essayist and historian derived
his vivid pictorial style. Zachary was born in the island of
Lewis early in the eighteenth century, and was the son of an
accomplished Episcopalian clergyman there. His productions as a poet exhibit true bardic power, though he is
believed in his youth to have been given to writing wanton

songs. The air of one of his popular pieces was in after days a great favourite with Burns.

Two major bards remain to be noticed, who lived partly before and partly after the Forty-five—John Maccodrum and Alexander Macdonald. The latter, the more distinguished of the two, claims fuller mention hereafter. Meanwhile, no more fitting subject might be found wherewith to conclude this chapter than an account of the original and witty Maccodrum, with examples of his poems.

Born in North Uist, he became in manhood bard to Sir James Macdonald of Sleat, who died at Rome in 1766. It was a curious circumstance that first commended him to the notice of this nobleman. The poet happened to make a satire on the tailors of the Long Island, who were so exasperated that they refused one and all to make him any clothing. Consequently he went about for a time in tatters, and meeting Sir James one day, the latter naturally inquired the reason why his trousers were so ragged. Maccodrum explained, and was asked to repeat the offending verses. On complying he was there and then promoted to be bard to the family, and obtained, as was usual in such circumstances, free lands on the estate for his maintenance.

A lively wit and biting sarcasm seem to have been characteristics of Maccodrum's Muse. Yet he could be very tender, as on the occasion when he laments the untimely death of his patron, at the early age of twenty-five. Then was the bard unusually serious and even pious :—

> As I awake it is not sleep
> That strives with me in troubles deep ;
> My bed beneath the tears I weep
> Is in disquiet ;
> My bed beneath, etc.

> Of him, my patron bright, bereft,
> I have no fair possession left ;
> While pain of loss my soul has cleft
> In sight and hearing ;
> While pain of loss, etc.

Sore tears are ours ; joy is no more,
No hope of smiles ; no cheer in store ;
We seem like the brave Fianns of yore
 And Finn forsaken ;
  We seem like the brave Fianns, etc.

Ah ! true it seems the tale to tell ;
Our cup is filled with doings fell ;
Provoking in a rage of hell
 Bless'd God the Highest ;
  Provoking in a rage, etc.

Blest One, from Thee let us not swerve ;
Above with Thee he goes to serve ;
O Christ ! do Thou for us preserve
 Our loving brothers ;
  O Christ ! do thou for us preserve, etc.

Maccodrum was deemed a witness of no mean weight in the Ossianic controversy, on the strength of the following statement by Sir James Macdonald, in a letter dated from Skye, October 10th, 1763. Addressing Dr. Blair, on that occasion he writes : " The few bards that are left among us repeat only detached pieces of the Ossianic poems. I have often heard them and understood them, particularly from one man, called John Maccodrum, who lives on my estate in North Uist. I have heard him repeat for hours together poems which seemed to me to be the same with Macpherson's translations."

The bard once met the hero of Ossianic fame when the latter had gone to the Outer Hebrides to collect fragments of ancient poetry. From Lochmaddy, Macpherson happened to be travelling across the moor towards the seat of the younger Clanranald of Benbencula, and falling in with a native, he took occasion to ask him if he had anything on the Feinn. This man, who was none other than the quick-witted and sarcastic Maccodrum, taking advantage of Macpherson's badly expressed and ambiguous Gaelic, re-torted literally to the effect that the Feinn did not owe him anything, and even if they did, it were vain to ask for payment now. Unaware of the personality of the bard, and direly offended at the character of the reply, which reflected on his own knowledge of the language, the proud collector passed on his way without more ado. Both men thus met and parted as ignorant of each other as ships that pass in the night.

Maccodrum's poems have never been published separately. A few appeared in Alexander Macdonald's collection. Many of the rest, entrusted to memory, are now merged in oblivion. He had not the versatility either of Mary Macleod or of Alexander Macdonald, for he sometimes imitates the poems of bards more original than himself, yet in purity and elegance of language he frequently approaches Macdonald. His satire on "Donald Bain's Bagpipe," and his poems on "Old Age" and "Whisky," are considered excellent, witty, ingenious, and original. And "Smeorach Chlann-Domhnuill," or "The Mavis of Clan Donald," which has been rendered into English verse by Professor Blackie, is a delightful pæan in praise of his own native Uist.

> The Mavis of Pabal am I ; in my nest
> I lay long time with my head on my breast,
> Dozing away the dreary hour,
> In the day that was dark, and the time that was sour.
>
> But now I soar to the mountain's crest,
> For the chief is returned whom I love best ;
> In the face of the sun, on the fringe of the wood,
> Feeding myself with wealth of good.
>
> On the tip of the twigs I sit and sing,
> And greet the morn on dewy wing,
> And fling to the breeze my dewy note,
> With no ban to my breath, and no dust in my throat.
>
> Every bird will praise its own nest,
> And why shall not I think mine the best ?
> Land of strong men and healthy food,
> And kindly cheer, and manners good.

A land that faces the ocean wild,
But with summer sweetness, mellow and mild,
Calves, lambs, and kids, full many a score,
Bread, milk, and honey piled in the store.

A dappled land full sunny and warm,
Secure and sheltered from the storm,
With ducks and geese and ponds not scanted,
And food for all that live to want it, etc.

The poet, apparently, made the most of his own rugged island, and now lies buried in an old churchyard not far from the village of Houghary, where a rough boulder of gneiss, of uneven, battered surface, spotted with nodules, but without any inscription, marks his grave. He himself, while living, had picked it out from the beach and destined it for this purpose.

The Highland bards before the Forty-five were thus a goodly company, and they had this in common, that they were independent for the most part of writing, in some cases even of education ; yet they had a wonderful command of their native Gaelic, and an extraordinary ear for the beauties of sound that may be expressed through the medium of language. They were all more or less attached to chiefs, whose praises they sang, and almost without exception these early bards lived into an extreme old age, and died in the land they had never left, and among the friends they had never forsaken.

CHAPTER XV

THE INFLUENCE OF THE CHURCH ON GAELIC LITERATURE

The origins of Celtic literature—Two streams—The Pagan—The Christian—Influence of the early Celtic Church as patron of letters—Originates a written literature—Attitude towards the ancient sagas—Medieval obscurantism—The Dialogues between Ossian and Patrick quoted and discussed—Their significance—Bishop Carswell and the Reformation—The rival influences of Naturalism and the Church—Decline of Gaelic oral literature—The Nineteenth, a century of gleaning rather than of great creative work—Reasons—Present-day return to nature—Splendid services of individual Churchmen.

AS we work our way back through history towards the origins of Celtic literature, we recognise two streams issuing from two very different sources. One has its rise in pre-Christian times, welling up from the pagan heart of the race from a remote antiquity. It is represented by the sagas and the poetry that is mingled with them. These sagas breathe the spirit of the Celtic people in the long past, and are the most characteristic of all their literary products. So old are they, that very few of them deal with events posterior to the eighth century, and those that do are the less meritorious.

In this respect it may be said that the Celts produced their best literature first. This literature was long in coming to the birth. It took centuries to evolve. But when it did appear it proved a new creation. The mind of a people lived in it, spoke through its tales. Generations of ancestors, lost and speechless in the slumber of the ages, found in it life and utterance.

So far as this stream has gained in volume through its

course down the centuries, it has done so by expansion.
Each succeeding age harks back to the past and draws from
the original, imitating and transcribing, until now in the
great books of sagas and modern literature thereon, we have
a mighty river of Gaelic lore.

Yet nothing so original, nothing so characteristic in this
line has ever been added to the early contribution. The
Celtic genius seems to have found its fullest and most distinctive expression then, in the days before writing, and
before Christianity was introduced, and ever since it has
been drawing inspiration from its oldest creations.

Take away this stream, and the peculiar interest of Celtic
literature is gone. How many centuries the sagas were in
the making before they took final shape as we read them,
can never be known. They passed from generation to
generation by oral delivery, and it was only in the seventh
or eighth century of our era that they ultimately found
embodiment in writing. This much can be inferred, though
we have no copies earlier than the end of the eleventh
century and middle of the twelfth, those from which these
latter drew their texts having perished long ago.

But as this stream flowed on from a past as remote and
mysterious as the sources of the Nile were in the days of
Herodotus, suddenly a new and independent one takes its
rise. And this latter stream can be traced to its source in
the fifth century of our era. It emanated not, as in the
other case, from the pagan heart of the race in its more
primitive phase, but in that heart overtaken and surprised
by the new doctrines of Christianity.

This was really a new departure—a new beginning.
The two streams had little in common. In essence and
colour they seemed as if they belonged to two different
worlds, which indeed was the case, in point of outlook and
underlying thought.

As literature the old was better. It represented the
real quintessence of the Celtic genius before it was diverted
into new channels. And this is what makes critics like

M. Darmesteter, while fully admitting the glorious significance of the new stream as a literary renaissance, yet consider it a decadence in contrast with the earlier.

For all this, the far-reaching significance of the new creation must not be lost sight of. It is probable that even then the ancient stream had reached its full flood, and but for the advent of the latter, which came with the new thought, it may have gradually subsided with the old order and never have found a way to posterity.

Historically, then, it is with the introduction of Christianity that Celtic literature first finds its embodiment, and when we consider the condition of continental Europe at the time, this early beginning in the writing of books is quite marvellous. It is to the Church, therefore, in the person of its missionary pioneers, that we owe the initial force that resulted in a written Gaelic literature.

In bringing Christianity to bear on the old pagan life and thought of the race, the missionaries effected a reanimation, which brought latent powers into action in a new direction. They furnished the people with fresh ideas, new material for thought, and an entirely changed outlook. The movement, indeed, might be described as the passage from Celtic naturalism to Christian spiritualism. And when we consider what the old paganism really was in many of its features, this emancipation cannot be regarded in any other light than that in which history uniformly regards it, as a salvation of the country, preparing the way for the realisation of all those grand possibilities that lay in the future.

With the coming of St. Patrick Ireland entered upon a new epoch, and with the advent of St. Columba the political and literary history of Scotland may be said to have begun. Every credit is due to the Church, therefore, as the importer and originator of a written literature, as well as of a true religion. To it we owe the remarkable arrival of letters which not only tapped a new fountain head, causing a new stream of literary composition to flow, but which also secured for us the preservation and continuance of the old to this day.

" Few forms of Christianity," wrote Renan, " have offered an ideal of Christian perfection so pure as the Celtic Church of the sixth, seventh, and eighth centuries. Nowhere, perhaps, has God been better worshipped in spirit than in those great monastic communities of Hy or Iona, of Bangor, of Clonard, or of Lindisfarne."

And it is this purity of motive and sincerity of purpose that led the early missionaries, in contrast to the obscurantists of later ages, to recognise the high value of literature and use it in the service of religion. In the primitive Celtic Church we find no conflict between the two, such as the sickly piety of some more modern periods has instituted and maintained. Learning and culture were then never regarded as enemies to religion. On the contrary, they were deemed not only helpful, but even indispensable to the progress of Christianity in the land. And they were encouraged as such. They were the most powerful agents for the removal of racial ignorance, superstition, and prejudice.

All honour, therefore, to the Church that first kindled the lamp of literature and the love of knowledge in these once dark islands.

The attitude of this early Celtic Church towards the original oral traditions and compositions of the people was perfectly consistent, and can be easily understood. It simply ignored them as far as that was possible, offering in their stead a substitute infinitely better fitted, as it thought, to elevate the life and character of these pagan peoples.

With a zeal that is entirely praiseworthy, it set itself to the multiplication of copies of the Psalter, of the Gospels, and other parts of Scripture. It is really marvellous, when we consider that these had to be patiently and laboriously and beautifully handwritten, how much was accomplished in this way by the early missionaries. St. Columba alone was credited with having written " three hundred gifted, lasting, illuminated, noble books," all of them transcriptions of some portions of the Bible, no doubt.

It is this which accounts for the fact that almost all the

existing literary monuments of the early Celtic Church are copies of the Gospels or of the Psalter, with or without Gaelic or Latin glosses.

Thus the " Domhnach Airgid," the " Cathrach," the Books of Durrow, Dimna, Kells, Molling, Armagh, Deer, the " Gospel of Maeielbrid Macdurnain," the " Psalter of Southampton," with correlative books like the " Irish Canons " and " Missal of Stowe," in the British Islands, besides those on the Continent.

It is significant that the missionaries used the Latin versions of the Scriptures rather than Greek or Hebrew ones, with the reading and writing of which latter they seemed to have been less familiar.   They did not attempt, so far as we know, to make a Gaelic translation of the original, but contented themselves, no doubt, with rendering from Latin into the Gaelic in course of their preachings and expositions.

One thing is evident, that these scholarly men had no aversion to textual criticism or any fear of it, like so many of their Highland and Irish successors to-day, for they freely indulged in it for their own and the popular benefit.   Thus the Celtic Church of Scotland and Ireland had Jerome's recension of the Vulgate almost as soon as it was issued, and, to judge from the youthful Columba and his master St. Finnian's avidity for it, welcomed it with great enthusiasm. And more than that, the Celtic Church appears to have collated Jerome's text with older native texts of their own, to make if possible even a better version, such as they might use in all their monasteries, and such as we find to this day in most of their great books of Gospel, as quoted above.

But in the same way that Knox unfortunately found it expedient to destroy many beautiful buildings, books, and customs of the Roman Catholic Church at the time of the Reformation, so the early Celtic Church in conflict with an ancient and debasing paganism felt it necessary, while tolerating many ancient customs and superstitions, to resist the leaven of heathenism in every shade and form, and thus even to ignore the compositions which breathed so freely its spirit and atmosphere.

There is a high probability that the best minds felt the hardship of having to turn their backs upon the most beautiful of these literary products of their race. For example, in the "Dialogue of the Sages," found in the Book of Lismore, it is recorded that St. Patrick himself felt rather uneasy at the delight with which he listened to the stories of the ancient Feinn, and feared it might be wrong in him to enjoy or show his appreciation of those pagan narratives, yet when he consulted his guardian angels, they not only assured him that there was no harm in listening to the tales, but even counselled him to have them written down in the words of ollamhs, " for," said they, " it will be a rejoicing to numbers and to the good people to the end of time to listen to these stories."

The missionaries appear to have been too earnest and consistent in their struggle with the gnarled roots of paganism to indulge their taste in writing what they could not help admiring as tales of great literary beauty, and very fascinating. And so for two or three centuries, though the cultivation of writing and bardic compositions went steadily on, none of the ancient pagan products found patrons sufficiently literary to commit them to MSS.

The new school followed a style and trend of its own, and in addition to endless transcribing, produced Latin prose works of its own, prominent among which may be mentioned St. Patrick's *Confession*, and "Epistle to Coroticus," Cummene's and Adamnan's *Lives of St. Columba*, Brendan's *Navigatio* or *Voyaging*, each of which have had a wide vogue throughout the Middle Ages, and since.

Among its Gaelic contributions are many beautiful poems, some of ancient renown, on account of their theme or author, such as Dallan Forgaill's *Amra Choluimcille*, St. Columba's own numerous lyrics—that on Derry, on Cormac's visit, his " Farewell to Ara," all breathing love of nature and affection for home.

Then we have the verses of Cennfaelad, who died in 678;

Aengus the Culdee's "Feilire," or Calendar, about 800 ; the poems in the Monastery of St. Paul, Carinthia; and the verses in the Codex Boernerianus; the "Saltair na Rann," about the year 1000, a collection of 162 poems in early middle Irish.

Of hymns and prayers, both in Gaelic and Latin—compositions of the early Celtic Church—there is no lack. The most famous of the Latin ones are those of Sechnall (on St. Patrick) and of Columcille ("The Altus," "In te Christo," and "Noli Pater") ; and of the Gaelic ones, St. Patrick's "Deer's Cry," Colman's and Fiacc's hymns, "Ninine's Prayer," Ultan's and Broccan's hymns, both in praise of Brigit, "Adamnan's Prayer," and the hymns of Sanctain and Mael-isu.

When to these we add specimens of homiletic literature and "Cormac's Glossary" (Cormac, King-Bishop of Cashel, 837-903), which is reckoned by far the oldest attempt at a comparative vernacular dictionary made in any language of modern Europe, and the same author's "Saltair of Cashel," we have a very fair representation of what the new literature initiated by the monks and missionaries contained.

It is mainly a religious literature, as contrasted with the purely pagan war-stories and romances of the heroes. This ethical movement for a time tended to supplant the natural spontaneous poetical output of the race, yet it could not crush out these older creations, which were independent of books and MSS., and as intense in feeling and true to nature as anything which the classical literatures contain.

And so in course of time there came a reaction. The votaries of naturalism so far triumphed in their zeal for the ancient sagas and romances, that they began to have them written down. Zimmer thinks that the earliest redaction of the "Táin Bó Chuailgné" dates from the seventh century. But it is difficult to ascertain when the sagas first found embodiment in ink. The interest in them appears to have been revived immediately before or at the time when the Norsemen arrived and were devastating the country. The devotion of the latter to the characteristic sagas of their own race and nation may have quickened the enthusiasm of the Gael for his own.   And the new atmosphere which this rough pagan element introduced to the land, breaking for a time the influence and sway of the Church and of the men of learning in the monasteries, may have conduced further to bring into popular favour the old heroic war-poetry, nerving the heart of the people to withstand the onslaught of the invader in the spirit of the dead heroes.

Christianity suffered eclipse for a while, and with it the interests of learning and the religious literature, cultivated so assiduously in the monasteries.

By the time that the sagas had come to be written down, the old feeling which had prompted the early missionaries to ignore them was apparently giving way, since there were scribes within the Church eager to commit them to MS. This was a natural and inevitable reaction.

But monastic Christianity, ever on its guard against nature, was constantly seeking after the strange and paradoxical.   For it, abstinence was worth more than enjoyment, happiness must be sought in its opposite.   And so there sprung up afresh, this time a more blind and uncompromising orthodox antagonism to the early paganism and all its creations.

The Dialogues between Ossian and Patrick are our witness. These, while professing to bring the spirit of paganism and of early Christianity together in the person of the last great representative of the one and the first of the other, were evidently the work of monkish scribes in the twelfth century or earlier, and they throw a significant sidelight on the situation.   In reality they reflect the posture of affairs, not as it was in the early days when Christianity was first introduced, but as it existed later, when ecclesiastical doctrines had taken on their more lurid, medieval colour.

In form and setting the Dialogues are the nearest approach to a drama that the Gael has ever produced.   And Miss Hull thinks that they were designed simply to popularise the ancient tales.   But such a view seems to us to miss the whole aim and point of these compositions, which are clearly the undisguised result of a reaction,—nay, even revolt in the minds of thoughtful and patriotic men, monks or clerics or laymen, against the narrow and captious spirit that can see no good in any form of natural life and religion other than the contracted faith in which it was itself reared.

Evidently the Church had descended from the high level of faith and policy it had maintained in the days of St. Patrick and St. Columba, and measures which the latter had found necessary as temporary expedients till the need for them had vanished, smaller minds had elevated into principles; and even the simple tenets of Christianity they had distorted by casting them into an ecclesiastical mould, and opposing them to the most natural instincts and enthusiasms of the human heart.

The writers of the Dialogues, we can see, are thoroughly in earnest, and not sparing in their irony and banter of the grim theology which found no place for the natural virtues of the Celts, or for the story of the dreams and ideals of a thousand years. A mocking, derisive humour runs through these pieces, but the humour is all on one side. There can be no mistaking the sympathies of the writers, who themselves are intellectually emancipated from the narrow tenets and intolerant spirit that would consign the heroes without reflection and without scruple to endless pain.

In these Dialogues paganism at its best is brought face to face with ecclesiastical Christianity, and is made to appear more just, more humane, and desirable in every way.

To the spirit of these conversations, or to the form in which they are cast, no exception can reasonably be taken. In one respect only might students of history dissent, and that is, to the selection of St. Patrick as spokesman for the bigotry that is here pilloried.

Those who are familiar with the authentic records of his life and the spirit of his teaching will feel that an injustice is done the apostle of Ireland, by associating his name with such counterfeit sentiment. Had a typical medieval monk or cleric been selected as advocate of the repulsive theology represented here, the rôle would have been more true to life and historical fact. As it is, one feels that a noble character is traduced and put in a false setting. These Dialogues are profoundly interesting, not only because of the struggle between nature and dogma, between the cosmic process and the ethical, here brought into irreconcilable antagonism, but also because the two original and independent streams of Gaelic literature seem here to meet, and, like the rushing together of contrary tides or of two confluent currents, to mingle their waters together in a wild tumult of angry waves, which only subsides as each again gradually finds its own channel.

One of the most interesting of the Dialogues is that which is known as "Ossian's Prayer," and is about 150 lines in length. The bard begins by asking the saint if the Feinn of Erin are in heaven. When he is informed that his father, Gaul, and Oscar cannot be there, he not unnaturally retorts, "If Erin's Feinn are not in heaven, why should I Christian be?" Thereupon the saint taunts him with irreverent fierceness of language, adding "What are all the Feinn of Erin to one hour with God alone?" But Ossian declares he would prefer to see one battle waged by the valiant Feinn than to see the Lord of Heaven and his cleric (Patrick) chanting sin.

The saint tries to impress him with God's omniscience by telling him in effect that it would be impossible for the smallest midge to enter heaven without God's knowledge. "How different from Finn," exclaims the bard, "thousands might enter, partake of his cheer, and depart without notice."

The argument throughout shows complete divergence in their thought.

"Finn is in hell in bonds," says Patrick. "He is now in the house of pain and sorrow, because of the amusement he had with the hounds and for attending the (bardic) schools each day, and because he took no heed of God." And to an interpolation of Ossian, "Misery attend thee, old man," he continues, "who speakest words of madness; God is better for one hour than all the Fenians of Erin."

To which the bard retorts, " O Patrick, who makest me that impertinent answer, thy crozier would be in atoms were Oscar present. Were my son Oscar and God hand in hand on Knock-na-veen, if I saw my son down, it is then I would say that God was a strong man.

" How could it be that God and his clerics could be better men than Finn, the chief king of the Fenians, the generous one, who was without blemish ? All the qualities that you and your clerics say are according to the rule of the King of the Stars, Finn's Fenians had them all, and they must be now stoutly seated in God's heaven. Were there a place above or below better than heaven, 'tis there Finn would go and all the Fenians he had."

Baffled in his attempt to initiate the pagan into his new doctrines, and curious to hear, Patrick relents and calls for a tale. The following is an example of the usual metre of the original mellifluous Gaelic :—

> Ossian, sweet to me thy voice,
> Now blessings choice on the soul of Finn,
> But tell to me how many deer
> Were slain at Slieve-na-man-finn.

And warming to the task, the bard recites the glorious character and deeds of the vanished heroes. " The Fenians never used to tell untruth. There never sat cleric in church, though melodiously ye may think they chant psalms, more true to his word than the Fenians, the men who shrank never from fierce conflicts." And then when he adds, " I never heard that any feat was performed by the King of the saints, or that *He* reddened his hand," the exasperated and dogmatic Patrick stops him short with the assertion, " Let us cease disputing on both sides, thou withered old man, who art devoid of sense ; understand that God dwells in heaven of the orders, and Finn and his hosts are all in pain." Ossian, pathetically, " Great then would be the shame for God not to release Finn from the shackles of pain ; for if God himself were in bonds, my chief would fight on his behalf. Finn never suffered in his day any one to be in pain or difficulty without redeeming him by silver or gold, or by battle and fight, until he was victorious.

"It is a good claim I have against your God, I to be among these clerics as I am, without food, without clothing or music, without bestowing gold on bards, without battling, without hunting, etc." The idea of his well-meaning instructors was to starve the bard into submission, in the intolerant spirit of the Inquisition of later times, or of boycotting in more modern days.

Elsewhere the bewildered Ossian laments as follows :—

"Alas, O Patrick, I did think that God would not be angered thereat ; I think long, and it is a great woe to me, not to speak of the way of Finn of the Deeds." To which Patrick : "Speak not of Finn nor of the Fenians, for the Son of God will be angry with thee for it. He would never let thee into his court, and He would not send thee the bread of each day."

"I will, O Patrick, do his will. Of Finn or of the Fenians I will not talk, for fear of bringing anger upon them, O cleric, if it is God's wont to be angry."

Mingled with these arguments are passages which quiver with the Gaelic enthusiastic love of nature. In *Finn's Pastimes*, for example, we have a lyric of extraordinary beauty. After a couple of verses addressed to his opponent, ending, "Can his doom be in hell, in *the house of cold?*" Ossian goes on to tell of his father's delight in nature. The passage is held to be in the very best style, rhyme, rhythm, and assonance, all combined with a most rich vocabulary of words expressive of sounds, nearly impossible to translate into English. But we quote from Dr. Sigerson's beautiful rendering of the original :—

> The tuneful tumult of that bird,
> The belling deer on ferny steep ;
> This welcome in the dawn he heard,
> These soothed at eve his sleep.

Dear to him the wind-loved heath,
The whirr of wings, the rustling brake ;
Dear the murmuring glens beneath,
And sob of Droma's lake.

The cry of hounds at early morn,
The pattering deer, the pebbly creek,
The cuckoo's call, the sounding horn,
The swooping eagle's shriek.

These Dialogues are quoted at some length, because they bring into clear outline permanent tendencies—the rival influences of naturalism and the Church—Celtic literature struggling to be free, and the Church seeking to saturate it with its own sentiment, and use it solely for its own propaganda. That is the history down to this day. Nature, love, and war on the one side, and religious themes on the other. The one timid of the other, and each on its guard against the undue ascendency of its rival.

Thus it is assumed that James Macpherson ignored these ancient compositions, namely, the Dialogues, as modern and counterfeit, because of the intrusion of the ecclesiastical element into the purely pagan domain. Into none of his own so-called translations did he admit any flavour of Christianity, regarding that only as the genuine and original Ossianic residuum which breathed the spirit of pre-Christian times.

But he lived in the days before textual criticism. We cannot credit the Church as a whole with disinterested love of literature and its encouragement. But in every age there have been men within its fold who were passionately devoting themselves to authorship on their own account, and to the preservation of books and MSS., and literary lore of the past. Every monastery in the Middle Ages was thus more or less a place in which reading and writing were cultivated, and some were active centres of literary work. So that indirectly, and especially in troublous times, we owe to the

Church the splendid heritage of a Gaelic literature continuous from the days of St. Patrick and St. Columba to our own. Down to very recent times, in fact, the men connected with religious institutions have been the real custodiers, if not always themselves the authors, of Gaelic productions. Thus it was Maelmuiri in Clonmacnois that enriched posterity with the wonderful Leabhar Na h'Uidhre, while his contemporary did for the hymns in the *Liber Hymnorum* what he so bravely and intelligently did for the sagas. From their time the fatuous hostility to the sagas had evidently broken down. Perhaps the Dialogues between Ossian and Patrick had been as effective in their own way in pouring ridicule and contempt upon the opposing faction as the poems of Burns in withering the hyper-orthodox tyranny of later times. At any rate, from the monasteries of Ireland in these Middle Ages came the great books of sagas and romance, such as the Books of Leinster, Ballymote, Lecain, Lismore, etc. ; and in Scotland in the corresponding period we have the Glenmasan MS. of the thirteenth century ; MS. XL. of the fourteenth ; and, besides others, the great Book of the Dean of Lismore, which covers the period down almost to the Reformation in Scotland.

But with the Reformation the old spirit of mistaken evangelical zeal against the ancient heroic literature seems to have revived in an aggressive form, for we find no less a man than Bishop Carswell, the most representative Churchman in the Highlands of that age, inveighing against the popularity of the sagas. In the epistle to the reader, which he prefixed to Knox's Liturgy, the first book printed in Gaelic, he says :—

And great is the blindness and sinful darkness and ignorance and perverseness of those who teach and write and compose in Gaelic, that with the view of obtaining for themselves the vain rewards of this world, they are more desirous, and more accustomed to preserve the vain, extravagant, false, and worldly histories concern ing the Tuath de Dananns and Milesians, Fionn, the son of Cumhail, and his heroes the Feinn, and many others, which I shall not here mention, nor attempt to examine, than they are to write, and to teach, and to compose the sincere words of God and the perfect way of truth. For the world loves falsehood more than the truth, and as a proof of it, worldly sinful men will pay for falsehood, and will not listen to the truth though they have it for nothing.

A great portion of the darkness and ignorance of such persons arises, too, from the aforesaid truths not being taught in good books, understood by all who speak the general language or habitual Gaelic tongue.

This was a volte-face from the sympathetic attitude of the Dean of Lismore, and no doubt included him in its sweeping indictment. Yet we may take it as representing the attitude of the leaders of the Reformation towards the literature as well as the beliefs and cults tolerated by the Latin Church. For a time the great evangelical movement, which had spread from Germany over England and Scotland, had little effect in the Highlands. The people remained widely indifferent to religious influences of every kind, except such lingering influence as the Roman Catholic Church continued to exert upon them ; but when at length they came once more under the influence of evangelical preachers, like Robert Bruce and others, the precedent set by Carsewell and the reformers seems to have been less or more uniformly followed; and with every revival of clerical authority there appeared an unmistakable tendency towards a revival of clerical intolerance, painfully detrimental to wholesome literature, as well as to music, athletic sports, and amusements of every kind.

Consequently since the Reformation Gaelic oral literature has been gradually disappearing, until, in the words of Mr. Alexander Carmichael, " it is now becoming meagre in quantity, inferior in quality, and greatly isolated."

In his own collection, which represents the latest gleaning in this field of Gaelic lore, we see the influence of the Church and the old pagan traditions strangely intermingled. The very title, " Hymns and Incantations," suggests the double influence, the two streams which have been running parallel, approaching each other, mingling and separating all through Celtic literature.

However much the Church may have gained the ascendency over rival influences, it has never been able to stifle the heroic poetry of the race. At periods when the latter seemed most to have gone under, and disappeared beneath the ban of religion, it came to life again with amazing vitality, as, for example, in the days of Maelmuiri and after, when the ecclesiastical seemed to have conquered the pagan ; and again in the days of Macpherson, when the Reformation appeared to have made a clean sweep of the heroic saga in the land, leaving neither name nor memorial. And the MSS. had so completely disappeared that they were not known to exist.

But forth they came to testify once more to the hidden and precarious genius of the Celtic people, which produced such diverse characters as Fergus and Ossian, Patrick and Columcille.

While the nineteenth century has been exceptionally brilliant in the department of English literature, the same cannot be said of Gaelic literature. In the former great works of creative genius have appeared, which have added immense lustre to the language in which they were conceived. In the latter the output by comparison has been very poor and meagre, no lengthy sustained production of any originality having · seen the light either in prose or poetry. It would seem as if the genius of the Gaelic language had found more congenial expression in English, for not a few of those who have enriched the younger literature, from Sir Walter Scott onwards to William Black and Robert Buchanan, have derived their inspiration, and sometimes their themes, from Celtic sources. Of native compositions we have nothing to show beyond elegies, songs, and lyrics, some of them of great beauty, and as spontaneous and true to nature as the beating of men's hearts. But no epic, no heroic poetry, no drama, no great prose work worthy to be classed with the masterpieces of English literature, or even with the minor works, has appeared within the last century. Instead of being a century of creative work, as in English, it has rather been a century of gleaning. All the best works in Gaelic are collections—gleanings from the past.

It would be difficult to assign the real reason for the barrenness of production in recent times. Many causes seem to combine. The derelict condition of the Highland and Irish populations in the beginning of last century may have had something to do with it ; the decline and limited use of the language ; the invasion of English and English literature, of Lowland people and Lowland ways.

Gleaners and native lovers of Celtic literature generally ascribe a large share of the decadence to the influence and attitude of the Church in its local testimony. During the greater part of last century, especially in the Highlands, that influence has been such that, had the Dialogues been produced any time within that period, they would have hit the mark quite as surely as in the age in which they were written, if we conceived St. Patrick as orthodox cleric and Ossian as the native genius of the Celtic people.

But times have changed. The lights and shadows on the canvas have again shifted. Our modern habits of thought are different. Like Ossian, men look askance on morbid teaching, and have no great enthusiasm for unnatural asceticism. The prevailing theory of life, impatient of ethical dualism, objects to the identification of nature with evil quite as much as the bard did. If nature is not evil, it asks, where, then, is the necessity or the benefit of a renunciation which is incompatible with the conditions under which men have to exist ? And so, concurrent with the decadence of ecclesiastical ideas and ecclesiastical authority, there is a return to nature ; and in many quarters a fresh interest is being taken in the language, literature, and lore of the Gael. And new writers have arisen who breathe the spirit of the race, and voice its longings, yearnings, strivings, free from theological bias.

Their medium is no longer the Gaelic, but the English,

into which they have carried many quaint idioms, sentiments, and expressions. Indeed it is doubtful if ever the Gaelic will again adapt itself to any great literary work, since the gifted have adopted English as the more comprehensive vehicle.

Yet now, looking dispassionately over the vicissitudes of Gaelic literature from the time it was first cradled in the rough bosom of the race, and nurtured by Christianity, we cannot forget the splendid services rendered by monks and Churchmen in the early days and during the Middle Ages down to the Reformation. Adverse periods of obscurantism there have been, blighting enough and painfully retrograde. But for ages the Church figured as the patron of letters, and even in later times there have been enthusiastic literary workers within its pale. In Scotland men like Sage, Macnicol, Smith, Maccallum, Drs. Norman Macleod, Macdonald, Clerk, Maclauchlan, Cameron, Dowden, Henderson, and Macneill ; in Ireland Drs. Reeves, Todd, Wright, Stokes, and many others.

And taking the influence of the Church at its best, we may surely apply to it, in its relation to literature, the remark of Dean Church in a wider connection : " History teaches us this, that in tracing back the course of human improvement, we come in one case after another upon Christianity as the source from which improvement derived its principle and its motive. We find no other source adequate to account for the new spring of amendment, and without it no other source of good could have been relied on."

So here Christianity, through its medium, the Church, besides saving the soul of a departing oral literature, has been the fruitful spring and inspiration of much that is beautiful, pure, and enduring in our Gaelic heritage.

CHAPTER XVI

THE INFLUENCE OF CELTIC, ON ENGLISH LITERATURE

Earliest contact—Loan-words—Three periods of marked literary influence—
Layamon's "Brut"—A fascinating study for critics—The development of
the Arthurian Romance—Sir Thomas Malory—Question as to origin of
rhyme—A Celtic claim—Elements in Scottish poetry—in English literature
—Gray's "Bard"—Macpherson's "Ossian"—Influence on Wordsworth
and his contemporaries—Moore's "Irish Melodies"—Sir Walter Scott—
Tennyson—Interesting comparison—Arnold, Shairp, Blackie—Novelists
after Scott—Living writers.

ANGLO-SAXON or Old English came into contact with Celtic
from the year 449 onwards. By the end of that century
the latter had the beginnings of a literature, the former had
not. Cædmon's poem dates from nearly 200 years later.

English literature could not, therefore, have been influenced by Celtic for centuries after the first Saxon invasion,
as it had not then come into existence. But the English
language was so influenced. From the earliest contact it
doubtless bore traces of the Celtic in the form of loan-words.

Yet, strange to say, very few such native vernacular
words passed over into Old English till the Norman invasion.
The reason may have been, as suggested by Sweet, that the
Britons were themselves to a large extent Romanised,
especially those of the cities, who were for the most part
descendants of Roman soldiers.

After the Conquest many more Celtic words found their
way into English through the Norman-French, and, as might
be expected, it is very difficult to discriminate between the

contributions of the earlier and the later period.   Names of persons and places, on the other hand, are easily distinguished, because they were generally taken over without change.

Not till the fateful Forty-five had finally broken down the ancient barriers of racial seclusion was there any further great accession of this Celtic element.   But owing to the interest awakened then in the Highlands, the freer intercourse established with England and the Lowlands of Scotland, and especially through the writings of historians and travellers, and of great authors like James Macpherson and Sir Walter Scott, a number of new words passed from this time direct from the Highland Gaelic as well as from the Irish into the English language.   From the former came the well-known clan, claymore, ghillie, plaid, pibroch, sporran, slogan, whisky, reel ; and from the latter, brogue, kern, Tory, shamrock, shillelagh, usquebaugh, bother, and a few others. Words had been dribbling from the Welsh also, as we might expect, from time to time.

The influence on the literature began later, but it has been very marked and continuous down to the present day. Three periods stand out as particularly potent.   The first begins from the end of the twelfth century and extends to the Reformation.   The second, taking its impetus from the Forty-five and the Ossianic revival, carries us forward to the time of Tennyson.   And the third, coeval with the modern Celtic renaissance, reaches from Tennyson to the present time.

Though the different branches of the Celtic people had been producing a literature from the sixth century, that literature does not seem to have affected English authorship, until in the Middle Ages it created the captivating Arthurian romances.   Then, like the other Continental literatures, the English for the first time fell under the sway of the Celtic imagination.

The earliest great poem written in the English language after the Norman Conquest owes its inspiration and theme entirely to that source. In the opening passage the author introduces himself thus: "There was a priest in the land, whose name was Layamon; he was son of Lovenath; may the Lord be gracious unto him! He dwelt at Ernley at a noble church on Severn's bank, good it seemed to him, near Radstone, where he read books. It came in mind to him and in his chiefest thought that he would of England tell the noble deeds, what the men were named, and whence they came, who first had English land."

This Layamon, travelling widely over the land in search of information, found three valuable books on which he based his tale—an English translation of Bede, a Latin book made by St. Albin and the fair Austin, and the French one by Wace.

His own poem he called the "Brut," after the fabulous Brutus, the great-grandson of Aeneas, who, according to Welsh writers, became the ancestor of the Kings of Briton. It deals chiefly with the materials of Wace, but it gives the story of Uther Pendragon and his famous son Arthur in much fuller detail. For example, while Wace's "Brut" contains 15,300 lines, Layamon's has 32,250, more than double, and the composition is characterised by a somewhat rude attempt at alliteration and rhyme.

There are two MSS. still extant of this interesting work, both of them in the British Museum. The oldest is held to have been written not later than 1205, and the language is so purely English, notwithstanding its source, that less than fifty words of French origin have been found in it by Sir Frederick Madden, who in 1847 first edited these texts.

Almost a hundred years pass after Layamon wrote before another English book of the kind appears. And this time it is the rhyming chronicle of Robert of Gloucester, who goes over some of the ground of Geoffrey of Monmouth, and brings the history down to 1272.

A fascinating study for critics is the wonderful way in which the Arthurian romance seems to have developed from a small beginning. This gradual evolution can in the main be traced.

So far as our modern knowledge goes, the Arthur of real life was a Cornish chief with a following in Wales, who met Cedric of Wessex in the stricken field, but who himself at length fell fighting the Picts, most probably in our own native Scotland. Gildas chronicles a great victory won over the Saxons, but omits to record who was the victorious chief. It is Nennius who first mentions Arthur by name, in the ninth century. His story is vastly amplified by Geoffrey of Monmouth, who wrote about 1154, and by the time it comes from the pen of Robert Wace, some ten years later, there is the splendid addition of the Round Table. Layamon is able to go into details, not hitherto mentioned, of the construction of this famous Board, which obviated quarrels over uppermost seats, since no one could have precedence owing to its shape. Up to this point the legend bore no Christian character. It is saturated with the magic, and slaughter, and revenge of the old Pagan North, rich in stories of giants, dwarfs, serpents, and heathen enchantments, far enough removed from the spirit of medieval Christianity. But by the beginning of the thirteenth century it suddenly underwent a great development, and new incidents were added with which the earlier writers could not have been acquainted.

Thomas Arnold thinks that this transformation is due to the genius of Walter Map (*circa* 1210), who introduced the religious element with the view of converting the Arthurian legends, and employing them in the service of Christianity.

From this time we have in French the Story of the Holy Grail, the History of Merlin, Sir Launcelot of the Lake, the Quest of the Holy Grail, and the Death of Arthur. The first two have been attributed to Robert Borron, the latter three to Walter Map himself. But the whole subject appears to be wrapped in singular obscurity, and offers a field for considerable divergence of opinion. The latest dissertation on the question is that by Jessie L. Weston in her recent publications. (Nutt: London, 1901.) After the above, five more stories followed, such as Tristram and the history of

King Pellinore by other writers. These later series of romances seem to have caught on better in France than in England. For only a few metrical compositions of this class are found in English MSS. prior to the days of Sir Thomas Malory, and these in documents of the fifteenth century. One alliterative tale, indeed, that of *Sir Gawayne and the Green Knight*, first printed by Sir F. Madden in 1839, and re-edited by Dr. Morris, is held by the latter to have been written about 1320. Sir Gawayne was Arthur's nephew, and figures in the early stories as one of the purest models of knighthood, though very differently represented by the author of Tristram and subsequent writers, including even Malory, who drew from French sources. About the middle of the fifteenth century Henry Lonelich translated into English verse the prose narrative of the sacred Grail, and possibly this may have led Malory, the author of the more famous *Morte d'Arthur*, to produce, as he did about the year 1470, the remainder of the romances connected with the Holy Grail in English prose. It was one of the earliest books printed by William Caxton (1485), and certainly one of the finest examples of the prose of the pre-Elizabethan period.

Sir Thomas Malory compiled it out of the French versions of " Merlin," " Launcelot," " Tristram," the " Queste du Saint Graal," and the " Mort Artur." His own postscript at the end of the book . fitly describes its scope in very quaint terms. It runs as follows :—

Heere is the end of the whole booke of King Arthur and of his noble Knights of the round table, that when they were whole together there was ever an hundred and fortie. Also heere is the end of the death of King Arthur. I pray you all, gentlemen and gentlewomen, that read this book of King Arthur and his Knights from the beginning to the ending, pray for me while I am alive, that God send mee good deliverance.

And when I am dead, I pray you all pray for my soule. For this booke was finished the ninth yeare of the raigne of King Edward the Fourth, by Sir Thomas Maleor, Knight, as Jesu help me for his great might, as hee is the servant of Jesu both day and night.

Thus endeth this noble and joyous booke entitled *La Mort Darthur*, notwithstanding it treateth of the birth, life, and acts of the said King Arthur and of his noble Knights of the round table, and their mervailous enquests and adventures, the achieving of the holy sancgreall, and in the end the dolorous death and departing out of this world of them all.

As literature, this work of Malory is very interesting, and has been frequently edited within the last hundred years.

Beyond the powerful influences exerted by the Celtic romances, there falls to be noticed another way in which the Gaelic genius is believed to have affected and even moulded English poetry in the later Middle Ages. It is well known that down to Chaucer's time English poetry was characterised chiefly by alliteration. Scarcely any authors attempted rhyme. And those, like Layamon, who tried to combine both, often seem to achieve neither the one nor the other. They failed to produce the real effect of metre. But after Chaucer, rhyme gradually supplanted alliteration. And it is held by various learned authorities that this is due to Celtic influence. The Celts first invented rhyme, they say, and in proof of this it is shown that they used it centuries before the English or any other western nation. " Outside of Wales and Ireland," says Dr. Hyde, "there probably exists no example in a European vernacular language of rhymed poetry older than the ninth century."

And Matthew Arnold, in a footnote to his *Study of Celtic Literature*, asserts that " rhyme,—the most striking characteristic of our modern poetry as distinguished from that of the ancients, and a main source, to our poetry, of its magic and charm, of what we call its *romantic element*,— rhyme itself, all the weight of evidence tends to show, comes into our poetry from the Celts." And in this opinion these litterateurs are supported by the earlier testimony of great philologists like Zeuss and Count Nigra.

From the time of John Barbour, too, it is recognised

that the bards of Scotland who wrote English poetry have been influenced in various ways not peculiar to their own contemporaries in England, by their connection with and descent from the Celt. Stopford Brooke mentions three elements of Scottish poetry that he regards as distinctly Celtic contributions. These are, first, the love of wild nature for its own sake—the passionate, close, and poetical observation and description of natural scenery, which is not found in the poetry of England till near the end of the eighteenth century ; second, the love of colour so characteristic of Gaelic and Cymric authorship ; and, third, the wittier, more rollicking humour, which contrasts with the Teutonic humour, which has its root in sadness. The humour of Dunbar is thus as widely different from that of Chaucer as the humour of Burns is from that of Cowper, or of a modern Irishman is from that of a modern Englishman.

But if there is really humour in the ancient Celtic literature it is entirely unconscious. Many passages tickle our risible faculties now, and we smile as we read some of the narratives, such as the fight between Queen Meve's bull and his opponent in the old saga, but this is because of the very wealth of the Gaelic imagination and the mendacity of its exaggerations. It is questionable if the original Gael, the slave of such a powerful fancy, saw anything in his own extravagant descriptions to laugh at. More likely he perpetrated these fictions quite as unconsciously as his Irish descendant of to-day perpetrates his bulls.

All the same it is quite conceivable that from this early tendency to be carried off the ground by flights of fancy, the Scottish sense of humour, conspicuous in the poets from pre-Reformation times, may have developed.

That Celtic literature revelled from a remote antiquity in nature and love of colour is very manifest from the earliest Gaelic, Welsh, and Breton tales. Take, for instance, the following description of Olwen from the Welsh :—

The maiden was clothed in a robe of flame-coloured silk, and about her neck was a collar of ruddy gold, on which were precious emeralds and rubies.   More yellow was her head than the flower of the broom, and her skin was whiter than the foam of the wave, and fairer were her hands and her fingers than the blossoms of the wood anemone amidst the spray of the meadow fountain.   The eye of the trained hawk, the glance of the three-mewed falcon, was not brighter than hers.   Her bosom was more snowy than the breast of the white swan, her cheek was redder than the reddest roses.   Whoso beheld her was filled with her love.   Four white trefoils sprang up wherever she trod.

The old sagas and romances are full of this sort of vision.   It was impossible that such Celtic compositions could exist without imparting some of their charm, their brilliant colouring, their observation, and delight in nature and the unknown, to English literature.   Naturally, Scottish poetry first felt this influence.   But the wonder is that English literature as a whole was so late in being permeated therewith.   When it did enter, it effected a mighty change both in the style and subject matter.

Beyond rhyme, love of nature, love of colour, and a certain type of humour, which we have just glanced at, Matthew Arnold recognised three elements which are in a manner distinct from these.   " If I were asked," he says, " where English poetry got these three things—its turn for style, its turn for melancholy, and its turn for natural magic, for catching and rendering the charm of nature in a wonderfully near and vivid way—I should answer, with some doubt, that it got much of its turn for style from a Celtic source ; with less doubt, that it got much of its melancholy from a Celtic source ; with no doubt at all, that from a Celtic source it got nearly all its natural magic." . . . .

" The Celt's quick feeling for what is noble and distinguished gave his poetry style ; his indomitable personality gave it pride and passion ; his sensibility and nervous exaltation gave it a better gift still, the gift of rendering with wonderful felicity the magical charm of nature.   The forest solitude, the bubbling spring, the wildflowers are everywhere in romance.   They have a mysterious life and grace there ; they are nature's own children, and utter her secret in a way which makes them something quite different from the woods, waters, and plants of Greek and Latin poetry. Now, of this delicate magic Celtic romance is so pre-eminent a mistress, that it seems impossible to believe the power did not come into romance from the Celts. Magic is just the word for it—the magic of nature ; not merely the beauty of nature,—*that* the Greeks and Latins had ; not merely an honest smack of the soil, a faithful realism,—*that* the Germans had ; but the intimate life of nature—her weird power and her fairy charm." What better example of this distinction between the magic and beauty of nature might be wished for than the following beautiful conception ? " Well," says Math to Gwydion, " we will seek, I and thou, to form a wife for him out of flowers. So they took the blossoms of the oak, and the blossoms of the broom, and the blossoms of the meadow-sweet, and produced from them a maiden, the fairest and most graceful that man ever saw. And they baptized her, and gave her the name of Flower-Aspect."

Shakespeare, in handling nature, while he had the Greek touch, is also credited with sometimes striking the more exquisite and inimitable Celtic note.   Thus :—

> The moon shines bright.   In such a night as this,
> When the sweet wind did gently kiss the trees,
> And they did make no noise, in such a night
> Troilus, methinks, mounted the Trojan walls—
> . . . In such a night
> Did Thisbe fearfully o'er-trip the dew—
> . . . In such a night
> Stood Dido with a willow in her hand,
> Upon the wild seabanks, and waved her love
> To come again to Carthage.

But we must pass on to the second period, the period after the Forty-five, to see a more abundant entrance of the Celtic elements into English literature as a whole.   It might be detected in isolated instances, but during the latter half of the eighteenth century both prose and poetry were influenced by Celtic in a very marked degree.

Collin's ode on the "Popular Superstitions of the Highlands" was perhaps the first contribution after the memorable Rising to herald the new time. If we except Shakespeare's "Macbeth," it is almost the earliest inroad by an English poet into the wild and romantic regions beyond the Grampians.

After him came Gray, with a similar interest in Celtic lore. His well-known poem "The Bard" appeared in 1755. This ode is founded on a tradition current in Wales that Edward I., when he completed the conquest of that country, decreed the death of all the bards who should fall into his power. The original argument of this fine production is set down in the author's commonplace book as follows:—

The army of Edward I., as they march through a deep valley, are suddenly stopped by the appearance of a venerable figure seated on the summit of an inaccessible rock, who, with a voice more than human, reproaches the king with all the misery and desolation which he had brought on his country; foretells the misfortunes of the Norman race, and, with prophetic spirit, declares that all his cruelty shall never extinguish the noble ardour of poetic genius in this island; and that men shall never be wanting to celebrate true virtue and valour in immortal strains, to expose vice and infamous pleasure, and boldly censure tyranny and oppression. His song ended, he precipitates himself from the mountain, and is swallowed up by the river that rolls at its foot.

Gray deviated a little from this original sketch, but the above is, in the main, the gist of the poem.

> "Ruin seize thee, ruthless King!
> Confusion on thy banners wait!
> Though fanned by conquest's crimson wing,
> They mock the air with idle state.
> Helm nor hauberk's twisted mail,
> Nor e'en thy virtues, Tyrant, shall avail
> To save thy secret soul from nightly fears,
> From Cambria's curse, from Cambria's tears!"

Such were the sounds that o'er the crested pride
Of the first Edward scatter'd wild dismay,
As down the steep of Snowdon's shaggy side
He wound with toilsome march his long array.
Stout Glo'ster stood aghast in speechless trance :
" To arms!" cried Mortimer, and couched his quivering lance.

On a rock, whose haughty brow
Frowns o'er old Conway's foaming flood,
Robed in the sable garb of woe,
With haggard eyes the poet stood ;
(Loose his beard, and hoary hair
Stream'd like a meteor, to the troubled air ;)
And, with a master's hand and prophet's fire,
Struck the deep sorrows of his lyre.
" Hark ! how each giant oak, and desert cave,
Sighs to the torrent's awful voice beneath :
O'er thee, oh King ! their hundred arms they wave,
Revenge on thee in hoarser murmurs breathe ;
Vocal no more, since Cambria's fatal day,
To high-born Hoël's harp, or soft Llewellyn's lay," etc.

In addition to " The Bard," Gray translated into English
verse fragments of the " Gododin " and " The Triumphs of
Owen " from Mr. Evans's *Specimens of the Welsh Poetry*,
published in London in 1764.

After Gray came the renowned Macpherson, representing
the very soul of the Celtic genius, and Europe listened
surprised as it felt the thrill of the new notes which he
struck from the old instrument—the passionate, penetrating
regret, the deep melancholy, the sensitiveness to the powers
of nature. In his *Ossian* we are made to feel " the desolation
of dusky moors, the solemn brooding of the mists on the
mountains, the occasional looking through them of sun by
day, of moon and stars by night, the gloom of dark cloudy
Bens or cairns, with flashing cataracts, the ocean with its
storms." And when the wind shrieks and the elements do
frightful battle, there is the eerie sensation of ghostly presences
hovering around the warriors on the hillside or out on the
ocean.

And through all the sadness of sorrow and the clang of conflict there break gleams of tender light and soothing reflection, as, for example :——

Come, thou beam that art lonely, from watching in the night! The squally winds are around thee, from all their echoing hills. Red, over my hundred streams, are the light-covered paths of the dead. They rejoice on the eddying winds, in the season of the night. Dwells there no joy in song, white hand of the harps of Lutha? Awake the voice of the string; roll my soul to me. It is a stream that has failed. Malvina, pour the song.

I hear thee from thy darkness in Selma, thou that watchest lonely by night! Why didst thou withhold the song from Ossian's failing soul? As the falling brook to the ear of the hunter, descending from his storm-covered hill, in a sunbeam rolls the echoing stream, he hears and shakes his dewy locks : such is the voice of Lutha to the friend of the spirits of heroes. My swelling bosom beats high. I look back on the days that are past. Come, thou beam that art lonely, from watching in the night!

No wonder these plaintive notes struck the heart of modern times with overpowering emotion, awakening a sympathy with the past, and opening a new avenue of vision into the life of nature. Englishmen especially, who had hitherto beheld the bleak mountains, the moors, and the naked rocks with feeling almost akin to aversion, began to see a hidden beauty and majesty in these sublime and lonely objects. And a passion for nature gradually crept into English poetry. Thomson had made a beginning in this direction with his *Seasons* as early as 1726-30, but it cannot be said that he quite struck the notes which afterwards so moved and enchanted the readers of Macpherson, Wordsworth, Shelley, Keats, and Tennyson.

The new Ossian had a wonderful mastery of style, rhythmical flow, pathos, and sometimes even sublimity of language, though it can scarcely be said that he represented the realistic force and vivid exactness of the Gaelic he sought to imitate in his English style. Of his *Fragments*, when they appeared, the poet Gray wrote : " I was so struck, so extasié with their infinite beauty, that I writ into Scotland to make a thousand enquiries." And he adds, " In short, this man is the very demon of poetry, or he has lighted on a treasure hid for ages."

English poets and litterateurs from this time found a new well-spring of inspiration in the ancient Celtic fountain thus wondrously and unexpectedly tapped. And so we find men like Pennant, Dr. Johnson, Boswell, and numerous other interested travellers and historians, making pilgrimages through the Highlands, with the view of observing for themselves the old life surviving there, and of gathering up materials for literary work. Each of the above-named, well known in the pages of English literature, have contributed books which are now classic authorities on the social customs and conditions of the Highlands at the time of their visit, and thus helped to carry a stream of Celtic thought and feeling into the prose of the period, which was afterwards more fully developed by the great magician, Sir Walter Scott.

Meanwhile the new elements had entered into the warp and woof of English poetry, and may be traced in all the great masters of the period—Cowper, Burns, Wordsworth, Crabbe, Byron, and their numerous contemporaries. Blake was so enthusiastic that he is generally regarded as an imitator of Macpherson, and Southey, going even farther back, edited, with introduction, in 1817, the *Morte d'Arthur* of Sir Thomas Malory before mentioned.

Yet more characteristically Celtic as a poet than all these, because himself an Irishman, was Thomas Moore, author of *Lalla Rookh*, an Indian tale ; and *Irish Melodies*. It is with these latter lyrics that we are here most concerned, because they exhibit so much the quality of the Gaelic muse in English verse. Take, for example, the following delightful pieces—euphonious, melancholy, and touching—so full of the Ossianic sadness and Celtic sentiment for the past, and for the dead heroes :—

The harp that once through Tara's halls
    The soul of music shed,
Now hangs as mute on Tara's walls
    As if that soul were fled.
So sleeps the pride of former days,
    So glory's thrill is o'er ;
And hearts that once beat high for praise
    Now feel that pulse no more !

No more to chiefs and ladies bright
    The harp of Tara swells ;
The chord alone, that breaks at night,
    Its tale of ruin tells.
Thus freedom now so seldom wakes,
    The only throb she gives,
Is when some heart indignant breaks
    To show that still she lives.

This one, too, sounds a similar note. It is entitled " After the Battle " :—

Night closed around the conqueror's way,
    And lightnings show'd the distant hill,
Where those who lost that dreadful day
    Stood few and faint, but fearless still !
The soldier's hope, the patriot's zeal,
    For ever dimm'd, for ever crost—
Oh ! who shall say what heroes feel
    When all but life and honour's lost ?

The last sad hour of freedom's dream
    And valour's task mov'd slowly by,
While mute they watch'd, till morning's beam
    Should rise and give them light to die.
There's yet a world where souls are free,
    Where tyrants taint not nature's bliss ;
If death that world's bright opening be,
    Oh ! who would live a slave in this ?

From Moore it is but a step to the great master-hand of Celtic romance, the heroic Sir Walter Scott, who has done more than any modern writer to popularise the literature of the Gael, and to make the Gael and his country interesting to Englishmen. With his magic power he threw a halo over the land and the people, and made their past live again in his enchanting pages. What a world of forgotten romance he brought to light alike in his prose and his poetry! In the *Lady of the Lake, Tales of a Grandfather, Waverley*, and *Rob Roy*, we have Celtic life and tradition depicted in a way which has vastly influenced and enriched our English literature, besides showing the gate to subsequent authors into a field near at hand, into which English imagination, much less English sympathy and literary art, had hardly as yet found its way. What Wordsworth in England did for the Lake District, Scott in Scotland did for the Highlands, fostering the love for scenery which the English poets had already begun to awaken.

Yet, more than any of his predecessors who cultivated the poetry of natural description, Scott carried into English literature the Celtic imagination and sentiment, the Celtic magic and wistful veneration for the past, which made him the wizard of modern literary romance.

The enthusiasm aroused by Macpherson, and even more by himself, had not died down before another great period of Celtic influence arrived—the last, and, in certain respects, the most potent and extensive of all. As early as 1842, the *Morte d'Arthur* and some other pieces of Tennyson appeared, but it was in 1859, contemporary with the Celtic renaissance at home and abroad, that he published *The Idylls of the King*. Founding on the old Arthurian romances, as told in English by Sir Thomas Malory, Tennyson depicts anew the more picturesque characters and incidents, idealising them in his own inimitable poetic style. So we have, in twelve books,—

> The Coming of Arthur,
> Gareth and Lynette,
> The Marriage of Geraint,
> Geraint and Enid,
> Balin and Balan,

Merlin and Vivien,
Lancelot and Elaine
The Holy Grail,
Pelleas and Ettarre,
The Last Tournament,
Guinevere, and
The Passing of Arthur.

The charm of these Idylls, which rank among the Poet-Laureate's best work, may be gathered from the opening passage, describing the coming of Arthur :—

Leodogran, the King of Cameliard,
Had one fair daughter, and none other child ;
And she was fairest of all flesh on earth,
Guinevere, and in her his one delight.

For many a petty king ere Arthur came
Ruled in this isle, and ever waging war
Each upon other, wasted all the land ;
And still from time to time the heathen host
Swarm'd overseas, and harried what was left.
And so there grew great tracts of wilderness,
Wherein the beast was ever more and more,
But man was less and less, till Arthur came.
For first Aurelius lived and fought and died,
And after him King Uther fought and died,
But either fail'd to make the kingdom one.
And after these King Arthur for a space,
And thro' the puissance of his Table Round,
Drew all their petty princedoms under him,
Their King and head, and made a realm and reign'd.

And thus the land of Cameliard was waste,
Thick with wet woods, and many a beast therein,
And none or few to scare or chase the beast ;
So that wild dog, and wolf and boar and bear
Came night and day, and rooted in the fields,
And wallow'd in the gardens of the King.
And ever and anon the wolf would steal
The children and devour, but now and then,
Her own brood lost or dead, lent her fierce teat
To human sucklings ; and the children, housed

> In her foul den, there at their meat would growl,
> And mock their foster-mother on four feet,
> Till, straighten'd, they grew up to wolf-like men,
> Worse than the wolves.

This, surely, puts us back into the old days. But "Arthur heard the call and came; and Guinevere stood by the castle walls to watch him pass." The Celtic ideal of woman and the Celtic pursuit of the unknown and mysterious, and the delicacy and passion that characterise the early romances, pervade these nineteenth century Idylls throughout.

It is interesting to compare the Passing of Arthur, for example, as recorded by Layamon, with Tennyson's more elaborate and developed idealisation. According to the former, these were the words of the king's dying speech to Constantine :—

I will fare to Avalun to the fairest of all maidens, to Arganté the Queen, an elf most fair, and she shall make my wounds all sound ; make me all whole with healing draughts. And afterwards I will come again to my kingdom and dwell with the Britons with mickle joy ! Even with the words there approached from the sea a little short boat floating with the waves ; and two women therein wondrously formed ; and they took Arthur anon and bare him quickly and laid him softly down, and forth they gan depart. Then was it accomplished that Merlin whilom said, that mickle care should come of Arthur's departure. The Britons believe yet that he is alive, and dwelleth in Avalun with the fairest of all elves, and the Britons even yet expect when Arthur shall return.

Compare with this the appearance from the wave of Tennyson's wondrous barge with its fair occupants, and the famous farewell speech Arthur made before setting out. After the well-known passage beginning, "The old order changeth, yielding place to new," he goes on :—

> But now farewell.   I am going a long way
> With these thou seést—if indeed I go
> (For all my mind is clouded with a doubt)—
> To the island-valley of Avilion ;
> Where falls not hail, or rain, or any snow,

Nor ever wind blows loudly; but it lies
Deep-meadow'd, happy, fair with orchard lawns
And bowery hollows crown'd with summer sea,
Where I will heal me of my grievous wound.

So said he, and the barge with oar and sail
Moved from the brink, like some full-breasted swan
That, fluting a wild carol ere her death,
Ruffles her pure cold plume, and takes the flood
With swarthy webs.   Long stood Sir Bedivere
Revolving many memories, till the hull
Look'd one black dot against the verge of dawn,
And on the mere the wailing died away.

But when that moan had past for evermore,
The stillness of the dead world's winter dawn
Amazed him, and he groan'd, "The King is gone."
And therewithal came on him the weird rhyme,
"From the great deep to the great deep he goes."

Sir Bedivere was thus the sole survivor of the Knights
of the Round Table.   In the final battle all that remained
of them perished except the king himself and two knights,
who escaped wounded.   But first one and then the other
passed, dying from his hurt.   With what a halo of colour
and real Celtic enchantment poets and romancers have
covered up the last grim tragedy of the wounded knight
watching his master, the royal Arthur die, after all the rest
were fallen and gone, and the Round Table was from henceforth to be but a memory.

Macaulay must have inherited the Celtic power of
pictorial detail and vivid colouring, though he might not
willingly acknowledge it.   Where did he get that brilliant
turn for style and those suggestive tricks of lively fancy if
not from his Celtic ancestry?

After him came three Celtic enthusiasts of great literary
standing, who put Macaulay's apathy towards the Gaelic and
Cymric tradition to the blush.   These were Matthew Arnold;
John Campbell Shairp, Professor of Poetry at Oxford, and

Principal of the United College, St. Andrews; and Professor Blackie of Edinburgh.

Over the first, the apostle of culture, and otherwise dispassionate critic, the Celtic past undoubtedly cast a spell. The finding of its literature seemed to have influenced him in a similar manner as the hoving of a new planet into his ken thrills the eager astronomer. And we have his personal contribution in his well-known *Study of Celtic Literature* (1867), a book which, like Renan's French essay, has done much to enhance the reputation and influence of our ancient heritage in modern times. It was through his strenuous advocacy that the Celtic chair which Professor Rhys now occupies in Oxford was established.

Principal Shairp published *Kilmahoe : a Highland Pastoral, with other Poems*, in 1864; his *Poetic Interpretation of Nature* in 1877 ; and *Aspects of Poetry* in 1881. These books revel in the Celtic sentiment, its melancholy, and love of nature. Their author exhibited the same spirit of admiration for the Gaelic muse that Matthew Arnold did for the Cymric.

In one of his Highland lyrics, entitled, " A Dream of Glen Sallach," Shairp showed that he could be overpowered by the gloom pervading the land of the heather as much as any Gael :—

> In deep of noon, mysterious dread
> Fell on me in that glimmering glen,
> Till as from haunted ground I fled
> Back to the kindly homes of men.
>
> Thanks to that glen ! its scenery blends
> With childhood's most ideal hour,
> When Highland hills I made my friends,
> First owned their beauty, felt their power.

And in " The Forest of Sli'-Gaoil " he muses thus of other days :—

> And doth not this bleak forest ground
> Live in old epic song renowned ?
> Of him the chief who came of yore
> To hunting of the mighty boar,

And left the deed, to float along
The dateless stream of Highland song,
A maid's lorn love, a chief's death toil.
Still speaking in thy name Sli'-Gaoil !
Well now may harp of Ossian moan
Through long bent grass and worn grey stone :
But how could song so long ago,
Come loaded with some elder wo ?
Were then, as now, these hills o'er-cast
With shadows of some long-gone past !
Did winds, that wandered o'er them, chime
Melodies of a lorn foretime ?
As now, the very mountain burns
For something sigh that not returns !

Professor Blackie in later life had a similar passionate regard for Celtic literature, and not only did much by poetic renderings into English from the Gaelic, and in other ways, to introduce English readers to the best treasures of the Gaelic past, but also, like Matthew Arnold, was instrumental in founding a Celtic chair, namely, that in Edinburgh University.

Of novelists who, like Sir Walter Scott, have drawn their themes and inspiration from Celtic sources, there has been a splendid succession from the days of Tennyson till now. Among others, besides the veteran Dr. George Macdonald, we may mention William Black, Robert Buchanan, and Robert Louis Stevenson, all three now dead, but recognised in their time as men of considerable literary genius. Black's descriptions, his scenes and incidents and characters in those graphic stories laid in the West Highlands, are well known, and are as full of nature as Stevenson's thrilling tales of *Kidnapped* and *Catriona* are of Celtic passion and adventure. Buchanan's *Child of Nature* is now perhaps not so well known as these others, but the plot is laid in the extreme north-west corner of Sutherlandshire, and interprets Gaelic life and character with wonderful verve and insight. All the three writers seem to have caught the magic glamour of the North, and to have been influenced in their style by the Celtic elements.

Of living novelists to carry on the succession we have still a distinguished contingent. Besides names, less familiar, the following have achieved a wide reputation, namely, Dr. John Watson (Ian Maclaren), Neil Munro, Fiona Macleod, Katherine Tynan, and W. B. Yeats. These writers are distinctly Celtic in style, idiom, and sentiment. They have all the passion, yearning, imagination, and emotion of the Gael, combined with his wonderful gift of story-telling and of local colour.

There are other writers of distinction, such as Andrew Lang, Dr. Douglas Hyde, Sir Charles Gavan Duffy, Dr. Sigerson, Dr. Todhunter, Stopford A. Brooke, Edmund Jones, T. W. Rolleston, Miss Eleanor Hull, Miss Jessie L. Weston, Miss Goodrich Frere, and Miss Emily Lawless, who have done much of later years to popularise the Celtic lore and literature, and to extend its sway over English letters.

Through books of history and philology which have been issuing from the press in a steady flow for decades past, the tide of Celtic influence still continues to rise and permeate every department of English literature. So that from that little spring we saw welling up in the fifth century, and which at first yielded but a few words of Celtic import to incipient English, we have been able to trace a continuous stream, gaining in volume and momentum through the centuries, until now it is like a mighty Missouri which mingles its waters with the broader and more potent Mississippi, to be carried to the great ocean of human intercourse, and lose itself in the common good.

CHAPTER XVII

THE PRINTED LITERATURE OF THE SCOTTISH GAEL

Two interesting bibliographies—Surprising revelations—First Gaelic printed book—Meagre output prior to the Forty-five—Earliest original works issued —No complete Bible in type before 1801—Nineteenth century activity— The Highlander's favourite books—A revelation of character—His printed literature mainly religious—Translations—The two books in greatest demand —Dearth of the masterpieces of other languages—The most popular of English religious writers—of native bards—Gaelic poetry—The printed succession—Notable books—Account of the Gaelic grammars—Dictionaries —Periodicals—Value of the literature.

A CLOSE study of the printed literature of the Scottish Gael leads to some surprising and even wholly unexpected revelations. Happily, we have the materials for such a scrutiny within moderate compass, a fact which cannot be predicated of the more comprehensive and ubiquitous English.

It is an amazing circumstance—indeed the *Spectator*, some seventy years ago, dubbed it " a piece of Highland dilettanteism"—that one should be found enthusiastic enough to attempt to make an exhaustive bibliography of the printed Gaelic output of Scotland. Yet such a devotee has emerged not once, but twice within the last century.

First, in the person of John Reid, a Glasgow bookseller of Lowland birth, who published in 1832 his *Bibliotheca Scoto-Celtica*, or " an account of all the books which have been printed in the Gaelic language," down to that date.

Second, in the person of the Rev. Donald Maclean, minister of Duirinish, Skye, who brought the catalogue forward to 1900, arranging the authors' names alphabetically, and giving the various editions, with their dates and places of publication. This MS., which has not yet been printed, contains in addition a complete transcript of the title of each work, an account of the author or translator so far as known, the number of copies printed, size of paper, and published price, and in the case of the very rare books, an account of the copies known to exist, and the price they fetched on transfer.

Had it not been for the earlier researches of Reid, it is not likely so elaborate an effort would have ever been attempted. Even Reid seems to have been lured on gradually, all unconscious at first of the magnitude of the task, for he says that his book was not written with the view of being published. On the contrary, its *raison d'être* is thus explained by him in the preface :—

While studying the Gaelic language in 1825 a friend wished me to make up a catalogue of his Gaelic books. It appeared, after the list was made up, scarcely probable that many more should exist, and under the idea of having almost already completed the list, the present work was undertaken. All the Gaelic books in the neighbourhood were examined, but I found the work increase so rapidly on my hands that it became necessary to class them and re-write the whole; and the longer I searched the more I was convinced that the literature of the Gael was richer than even its friends imagined. The number of translations, song-books, etc., which I now met with, many of them works which I had never previously heard of, obliged me four times to extend the plan originally adopted, and to re-write the MS.

Reid ransacked the principal libraries in this country and on the Continent in search of Gaelic books, yet he admits the list must necessarily be imperfect. When finished, the work was awarded a premium by the Highland Society of London in 1831, and printed the following year. It has been the aim of his bibliographic successor to supplement and complete the list by a new classification up to date.

Both men deserve credit for having patiently and persistently pursued what was undoubtedly an interesting but eminently thankless task, so far at least as financial remuneration was concerned.

When we hark back to the period when MS. writing first began to pass into modern type, we discover that no book of any kind was printed in this country before 1477. In that year Caxton issued in London the earliest publication from an English printing press. Other books quickly followed, but nearly a century elapsed before any Gaelic writing passed through the inky mill.

The first printed work in that language is the translation of John Knox's *Liturgy* by Bishop Carsewell, published in Edinburgh in 1567. Carsewell, or Carsuel, as the name is sometimes spelt, a native of Kilmartin, was superintendent of the diocese of Argyll, and well versed in the Highland vernacular. It was he who, in the preface to his work, denounced the ancient *ursgeuls* or Gaelic prose tales as lying fables, and inaugurated a clerical campaign against the popular ballads. Yet he merits our approbation for getting into print so early a book which modern philologists regard as uncommonly valuable.

Only three copies exist of the original issue,—one, complete, in the possession of the Duke of Argyll, and two others imperfect. Of the twain, one is now in Edinburgh University Library, the other in the British Museum.

The Duke's was lost for a time, but recovered in 1842, and doubtless restored to its ancient place in Inverary Castle.

This rare book is five inches long and three and a half broad, containing 247 pages, on the 246th of which occurs the couplet :—

> Gras Dé is na thós atáimid
> Ni ránuic sé fós finid.

And on the last page the following :—

> Do Bvaile
> adh so agclo an
> Dvn Edin Le Ro
> ibeart Lekprevik
> 24 Aprilis 1567.

In 1872 the Rev. Dr. Maclauchlan transcribed it entire for a new edition which was published the following year, 1873.

Nearly another century glides slowly by after the printing press disgorged Carsewell's translation before any further Gaelic printing—that we know of—took place, if we except the translation of Calvin's Catechism issued at Edinburgh in 1631. In fact, three psalm-books complete the list for the whole of that seventeenth century, namely, the first fifty Psalms of David with the Shorter Catechism, published by the Synod of Argyll in 1659, exactly ninety-two years after the Liturgy; another Psalter by John Kirke in 1684, and the Synod of Argyll's finished in 1694. Thus in the sixteenth century we have just one Gaelic printed book; in the seventeenth, three and a catechism; and all these merely translations from other languages.

Not till 1741 do we encounter any original work, and even then it is simply a Gaelic Vocabulary by Alexander Macdonald, the gifted bard of Ardnamurchan. So that till after the Forty-five, Gaelic Scotland had no printed literature of its own—neither poetry nor prose of any kind.

Indeed, with the exception of a few reprints between 1702 and 1725 of the Synod of Argyll's Psalter and Catechism, and Kirke's Irish version of the Bible and Vocabulary in 1690, Lhuyd's Vocabulary in Nicholson's *Historical Library*, 1702, and Macdonald's, 1741, there were no additions to the printed list of the Highlands till Baxter's *Call to the Unconverted* was issued in Gaelic in 1750, Macdonald's *Songs* in 1751, and David Mackellar's *Hymns* in 1752. These two latter volumes were the early precursors in type of that considerable output of song and hymn and story with which we have been familiar in later years.

After them came, in 1752, a small book entitled *Hymn of Praise* (English and Gaelic), Willison's *Mother's Catechism*, and next year Macfarlane's *Translation of the Psalms, with forty-five of the Paraphrases*.

Between 1753 and 1767, Reid could not find that any

Gaelic work was printed, with the exception of reprints of the Mother's and Shorter Catechisms and Macdonald's songs.

Like some slow-moving stream, the output was at first very feeble and irregular, and drawn for the most part from imported sources.

In 1767, however, an event occurred in the Gaelic printing world worthy of special notice. This was the issue of the New Testament for the first time in the language of the Highland people. It was translated by Stewart of Killin, with the assistance of Dugald Buchanan and other eminent Gaelic scholars, and was published by the Society for Propagating Christian Knowledge. Strange to say, the language of this translation was looked upon at that period as perfectly free from Irish idiom, and yet in Reid's day, half a century later, it was regarded as savouring more of Irish than of Gaelic.

The same year in which the New Testament saw the light in the ancient dialect there appeared also the celebrated hymns of Dugald Buchanan, and the year after the no less famous songs of Duncan Ban Macintyre.

As yet no Bible existed in the language of the Highlands, and attention having been drawn to this fact, the Society for Propagating Christian Knowledge set themselves to supply the defect. It was arranged to have the Old Testament translated and issued in four parts, which were ultimately published in Edinburgh as follows :—

> Part I. in 1783.
> Part IV. in 1786.
> Part II. in 1787.
> Part III. in 1801.

The first part contained the Pentateuch, to which was prefixed a vocabulary of five pages and general rules for reading the Gaelic language. The second comprised from Joshua to the end of 1 Chronicles. The third, published last, contained 2 Chronicles and on to the end of the Song of

Solomon. The fourth was made up of the Prophets, and to it was prefixed an advertisement, stating the use that had been made of various English translations.

The Rev. Dr. John Stuart of Luss was responsible for the rendering from Hebrew into Gaelic of the first three parts, and the Rev. Dr. John Smith of Campbeltown for the fourth, which appeared second in point of publication.

Their MS. translations were, before being sent to press, submitted for revision to a Committee of Highland clergymen specially selected ; and by order of the General Assembly of 1782 a collection was made in all the parishes to defray the expense. This appointment was renewed in 1783 and 1784, as the funds of the S.P.C.K. were reduced, and the outlay on publication amounted to £2300 for some 5000 copies, with an additional number of Part I. containing the Pentateuch. The whole work was printed on fine and common paper ; and until the early decades of last century was looked upon as the standard of Gaelic orthography.

Considering that the Bible has since come to be regarded as a kind of fetich in the Highlands, it is somewhat surprising to learn that there was no complete rendering of it in the language earlier than 1801, just a century ago. And apparently not till 1807 were the Gaelic Old and New Testaments finally printed together in one volume. In that year they were thus issued in England for the first time on behalf of the British and Foreign Bible Society, who chose two different colours of paper for the purpose—the one blue for the Old Testament, and the other yellow for the New, which gave the book rather a polychrome appearance. The impression amounted to 20,000 copies, each of which cost the Society 6s. 6d., though they issued them to subscribers at half that price.

Of the Gaelic Scriptures there have been fourteen different recensions.

From the time of the publication of Dugald Buchanan's and Duncan Ban Macintyre's compositions in 1767-68, may be reckoned the real beginning of the new era of printing, so

far as the production of original Gaelic literature was concerned, and that mainly poetry, for of prose the land was
singularly barren, except in translations.   And it will hardly
be credited that from the introduction of printing down to
the end of the eighteenth century, just about a hundred years
ago, if we exclude the translations from other languages, and
extra editions of books already published, there were not in
all three dozen printed original Scottish-Gaelic works to be
found.   The day of copious issue had not yet arrived for the
sweet and tuneful Gaelic.

Even the collected MSS. of Macpherson did not appear
in type till 1807, almost half a century after his so-called
translations electrified the literary world.

Thus it will be seen that the nineteenth century was
really the golden age of Gaelic printing, for, with the
exception of the straggling volumes indicated above, the
literature we now have passed into printed book form within
the last hundred years.   From the beginning of the century
there was a marked increase in the rate of publication—an
activity which has been growing in volume and momentum
to the present day.

And now it will be found highly informing and even
entertaining to review the printed literature of the Gael, to
consider its character, its general features, and specially to
note what the Highlander deemed worthy of putting into
type—his favourite books.   Such a survey, in fact, amounts
to a revelation of character, and throws a wonderful light on
his recent past, his outlook on life, and peculiar habits of
thought.   Indeed, the glimpse we get here of the mental
composition and literary limitations of the purely Gaelic-
speaking or Gaelic-reading section of our countrymen is really
amazing, and if we did not know that they now rely so
much for their knowledge and information on the English
language, would simply be incredible.

It surprised Reid beyond measure that there were so
many Gaelic printed books to catalogue seventy years ago,
and probably he thought the work was well-nigh complete for

all time, but had he lived to-day to scan the amended and supplemented list, it would almost take his breath away, for he expected the Gaelic long before now to be as extinct as the Waldensian or the Cornish.   He just gave it fifty years in which to "die down and drone and cease."   People in general, even Highlanders, are scarcely aware of the very considerable number of printed books that exist in the native tongue.

But a cursory glance at the catalogue shows the derived nature of the material.   A large proportion of the volumes consists of translations, and these translations, if we except the Scriptures, are almost, if not entirely from the English. And here we are face to face with a most striking fact. The literature represented, both in the original and in translations, is mainly religious.

You will search in vain for the masterpieces of other languages and other nations.   The Hebrew Bible and Greek New Testament, *The Arabian Nights' Entertainments*, parts of Homer's *Iliad*, and Thomas à Kempis' *Imitatio Christi*, are perhaps the solitary exceptions.   All the best literature of the world has been given a silent go-by.

And this is true even of the greatest English and Scottish works of genius.   You will not find Chaucer, or Shakespeare,   or   Bacon,   or   Gibbon,   Scott   or   Dickens, Thackeray, Carlyle, or Tennyson here.   Two poems alone of Burns are translated, "Tam o' Shanter" and "Auld Langsyne," but the great masters are to Gaelic print as if they had never existed.   Science is unknown, and art and philosophy ; history, too, we may say, and the drama.   Whole departments of human thought remain practically unrepresented, as if they were alien to the Gaelic mind.

On the other hand, works of religion, pious devotion, theology, and ecclesiastical polemics abound, showing the peculiar cast of the modern Celtic temperament.

And of all the books, that which has been most in demand, if we may judge by the extraordinary frequency with which it has been printed, has been the Shorter

Catechism. We are confronted with the curious fact that between the year 1651 and the Disruption in 1843 no less than seventy editions or reprints of this document were issued, and this notwithstanding the circumstance that it was also usually published with the oft-printed Psalter. The version far and away the most in evidence seems to have been the Synod of Argyll's, though other versions, such as Dr. Ross's, Dr. Macdonald's, Dr. Smith's, and Morrison's were in circulation, besides various other Catechisms, of which Willison's and Watt's were prominent examples. The Gael seems to have had a perfect mania for Catechisms. And next to these in his estimation comes the Psalter, with nearly eighty editions or reprints between the year 1659 and the Disruption.

These editions represent six important versions, without taking into account other four unauthorised ones. The select six may be given in chronological order, as follows :—

1. The Synod of Argyll's translation of the first fifty Psalms, entitled, " An Ceud Chaogad do Shalmaibh," 1659; and the whole, 1694.

2. Kirke's Psalter—a translation by the Rev. Robert Kirke, Balquidder, 1684. This was the first complete version issued, ante-dating the former when finished by ten years.

3. Macfarlane's translation, which is just the Synod of Argyll's amended and altered by the Rev. Alex. Macfarlane, M.A., of Kilninver and Kilmelford, who excluded many of the Irishisms and added forty-five of the paraphrases, 1753.

4. Smith's revised version, including all the Paraphrases, by the Rev. Dr. Smith, Campbeltown, 1787.

5. Ross's Psalter, also an amendment, by the Rev. Thomas Ross, LL.D., Lochbroom, 1807.

6. The General Assembly's authorised translation, 1826.

Of these the most extensively used seems to have been Dr. Smith's, which ran through no less than thirty or thirty-five editions in half a century. Next to his, in popular esteem, came Macfarlane's, represented by twenty. Ross's and the General Assembly's have also had a wide vogue, especially in more recent times.

Besides the Shorter Catechism and Psalter, the *Confession of Faith* has been printed in Gaelic eleven times, and *The Book of Common Prayer* eight times, and Prayers from it once.

Of English religious writers who have captivated the Highland emotions, Bunyan takes first place with his *Pilgrim's Progress*, eleven editions ; *Death of Mr. Badman*, one edition; *The Barren Fig-tree*, one; *The World to Come*, seven; *Visions of Heaven and Hell*, four ; *Heavenly Footman*, three ; *Water of Life*, five ; *Holy War*, two ; *Come and Welcome*, four ; *Grace Abounding*, three.

Then Baxter's *Call to the Unconverted* went through nine editions, and his *Saints' Rest*, seven. Alleine, Boston, Doddridge, Dyer, Jonathan Edwards were also prime favourites, whose works were represented by many editions, especially *The Sinner's Alarm*, *The Fourfold State*, *The Rise and Progress of Religion in the Soul*, *Christ's Famous Titles*, and *Doomed Sinners*.

Though the Gaelic-reading Highlanders had apparently little appetite for general English literature in their own tongue outside works of religion, they had a surprising avidity for hymns, elegies, and sermons, for books on the Church, Christian doctrine, Baptism and the Sacraments. And we meet with such varied titles as *Voluntaryism Indefensible*, *Christ is All*, *Apples of Gold*, *Village Sermons*, *Letters to Sinners*, *The Unspeakable Gift*, *Fame of the Branch*, *The Rose of Sharon*, *Call to Awaken*, *Salvation by Grace*, *Sacramental Exercises*, *The Believer's Hope*, *A Parting Exhortation*, *Blair's Sermons*, *Token for Mourners*, *On the Guidance of the Holy Spirit*, *Short History of the Baptists*, *Lessons on the Sabbath*, *The Declaratory Act*, *A Word of Warning to the People*, *Assurance of Salvation*.

Topics of this kind abound. They formed the favourite pabulum of the more pious of our countrymen, and to this day some of these or similar theological productions may be found in almost every Gaelic household of the North and West Highlands.

While English printing concerned itself first with such works as *The Game and Playe of the Chesse, The Dictes and Sayings of Philosophers, The Æneid of Virgil, The Poems of Chaucer, Lydgate and Gower, The Golden Legend,* and the *Morte d'Arthur,* Gaelic printing took to do with religion. Knox's Liturgy, Catechisms, Psalters, and Vocabularies were its main concern ; and only after the lapse of nearly two hundred years did it give any attention to poetry or native literature of any kind. The original bards, like all other English and foreign writers, had to wait in the outer court of the Gentiles. But after Baxter's *Call to the Unconverted* was issued in 1750 they began to come straggling in, Mackellar with his hymns and Macdonald with his songs. And in addition to Dugald Buchanan's and Macintyre's we have, during the following half century, these books :—

A volume of Hymns published in 1770 by Macfadyen, a Glasgow University student ; and about the same time an Elegy and one or two other Gaelic poems by another Glasgow student. Ronald Macdonald, son of Alexander, published the first issue of old Gaelic poems, including some of his own and his father's, in 1776. Then followed in 1777 an anonymous collection of Mirthful Songs, and in 1780 another of Curious ones ; and a volume entitled *Loudin's Songs.*

John Brown's, Margaret Cameron's, and A. Campbell's appeared in 1785 ; and next year the better known collections of John Gillies, bookseller, Perth, and Duncan Kennedy, schoolmaster, Kilmelford.

In 1787 Dr. Smith published his alleged poems of Ossian, Orran, Ullin, etc., and those entitled *Dargo and Gaul.* And before the century closed Kenneth Mackenzie's, Alexander Macpherson's, Duncan Campbell's, and Allan Macdougall's compositions were all in type, issued separately.

The subsequent years, from 1800 to 1831, were most

prolific in the output of poetical publications. It seemed as if the Highland bards had made a rival rush for the printing presses, and kept the busy machines clicking. Among the names of those whose poems were then issued occur the following: Dr. Dewar, Rob. Donn, William Gordon, George Ross Gordon, Peter Grant, Angus Kennedy, A. and J. Maccallum, J. Macdonald, John Macgregor, Dr. James Macgregor, P. Macfarlane, D. Macintosh, A. Mackay, J. Maclachlan, J. Maclean, D. Macleod, D. Matheson, J. Morrison, James Munro, A. and D. Stewart, R. Stewart, P. Stuart, P. Turner. And in addition to theirs, and some other ten volumes of anonymous poetry, partly original and partly collected, there were published within that period the Highland Society's edition of Ossian's poems, and its reprint, the one in London, 3 volumes, 1807, the other in Edinburgh, 1818.

If the Gaelic muse was at first slow in committing its productions to modern printing, it appears to have cast off all reserve after 1800, and every type of bardic effusion went to the press.

But of all the bards whose poems were appearing then, undoubtedly the most popular was Dugald Buchanan. No other book in Gaelic, if we except the Shorter Catechism and Psalter, has gone through so many editions as his Hymns. In the comparatively short period of 110 years from their first appearance they have been issued from the press forty times—so great has been the demand for these vivid and impressive products of Gaelic genius.

Next in general vogue to Buchanan's comes Peter Grant's *Spiritual Hymns*, a book which has been printed at least nineteen times.

These three instances alone—the Psalter, Dugald Buchanan's and Peter Grant's Hymns—would indicate that this is the type of literature that has gone highest with the Gael, even if we did not observe how frequently volumes of spiritual hymns occur in the list of printed books.

By comparison such a classic as Alexander Macdonald's

Gaelic Songs has only reached eight editions, Duncan Ban Macintyre's ten, and Rob Donn's three.

And this bias, so unmistakably exhibited by the Gaelic printed literature, is not confined to poetry, but may be traced even in the few original prose works that the language possesses.

Only ten such books appeared during the early decades of the nineteenth century, and they are all religious ones of quite indifferent merit. While of forty-five prose translations which were printed, either through the munificence of private individuals, or as booksellers' ventures, forty-two were of a religious and three of a moral kind.

There can be no doubt that this extraordinary preponderance of the religious over every other type of printed literature in the Gaelic list, has exercised its own baneful influence on the Highland character of last century, leaving it lop-sided in some obvious directions and rendering the Gael blind to the wider issues of life, and therefore more or less impervious to new ideas. We can well understand his limitations, if, ignorant of English or other modern languages, he were confined to the books of his native tongue, as many Highlanders of the past generations were. These books absolutely give him no knowledge of science, philosophy, art, or even of the great literatures of the world. And his own poets occupied, as we have seen, a somewhat subordinate place in his list. Taught to look through one particular medium, and deprived of most other means of vision, the unsuspecting Gael grew up almost entirely oblivious of the march of mind, and for the most part ignorant of the thoughts that shake mankind.

It is through the introduction of English, therefore, that he has been getting emancipated of late years from the narrow outlook which his own ill-chosen and limited printed literature affords. And it is the sudden intrusion of this higher knowledge, rendering many of his theories obsolete, which has so painfully convulsed the older generation of Gaelic-speaking Highlanders in recent times, and left them so ill at ease.

Though printing made its first inroad on the Gaelic

language as early as 1567, it is characteristic of the race that the cream of the literature only found type within the nineteenth century. After the early editions of Ossian, Peter Grant, and Rob Donn, the following may be quoted as the most noteworthy literary books that have appeared in the last hundred years from the Highlands, namely: Dr. Norman Macleod's *Caraid nan Gaidheal;* Mackenzie's *Beauties of Gaelic Poetry*, 1841; Campbell's *West Highland Tales*, 1860-62; Dr. Clerk's *Ossian*, 1870; Campbell's *Leabhar na Feinne*, 1872; Sinclair's *Oranaiche*, 1876-79; Nicolson's *Gaelic Proverbs*, 1882; Henry Whyte's *Celtic Garland*, 1880-81; *Celtic Lyre*, 1883-95; Mary Mackellar's *Poems and Songs*, 1881; Neil Macleod's *Clarsach an Doire*, 1883; Dr. Cameron's *Reliquiæ Celticæ*, 1892-94 · Dr. Nigel Macneill's *The Literature of the Highlanders*, 1892; and Alexander Carmichael's *Carmina Gadelica*, 1900.

In addition to the purely literary works, there are three other classes of Gaelic books, intimately associated with the history of the language, which have received considerable attention from the printer, and which are worthy of our notice here. These are School-books, Grammars, and Dictionaries.

Of school-books there were three series that ran through many editions during the first half of last century, namely, the Gaelic Society's School series, the Society for Propagating Christian Knowledge series, and the General Assembly's series. Besides ordinary class books, portions of Scripture, especially from Proverbs, Psalms, Job, and the Gospels were printed for use as reading books in schools. The first of the above series dates from 1811, the second from 1815, and the third from 1826.

John Reid apparently never heard of Fenius Farsaid or the " Uraicept na n-Éigeas," [1] or of the other MS. fragments, for he has the following interesting modern account of Gaelic Grammars.

"The first attempt that we have on record of a Celtic

---

[1] Preserved in the Books of Ballymote and Lecain and MS. I. of the Scottish collection.

Grammar was one written by Florence Gray, a monk who was born in Humond about the end of the sixteenth or the beginning of the seventeenth century ; but we have never been able to find a copy of it, or ascertain if it was printed. It is probable that if it was printed it appeared about 1620, as we know that he was living in Dublin in 1630.

"In 1639 Tobias Stapleton, an Irish priest, published at Louvain a small quarto Catechism for the use of the Irish students on the Continent, in parallel columns, Latin and English. To the end of the Catechism is added a small tract in Latin and Irish, entitled, 'Modus perutilis legendi linguam Hibernicam.'

"After this there appeared various little imperfect compends of Irish Grammar, but nothing of any real value until 1677, when there appeared at Rome Molloy's *Grammatica Latino-Hibernica Compendiata*, which, although deficient in syntax and other important requisites, was decidedly the most important work on the subject until 1728, when Hugh M'Cuirtin published his *Elements of the Irish Language*,[1] which again appeared enlarged in his Dictionary, published in 1732.

"In 1742, Donlevy published at Paris a Catechism in Irish and English, to which he appended 'The Elements of the Irish Language.' This has been followed by the Irish Grammars of General Vallancy, Dr. William Neilson, Dr. Paul O'Bryan, William Halliday, and one or two anonymous authors.[2] It is said by Lhuyd, in the year 1707, that a Scottish gentleman had then some thoughts of publishing a Scottish Gaelic Grammar ; but the earliest attempt known to us is by Malcolm, who, about the year 1736, published

---

[1] "This was no work to commend him to the powers that were, and he appears to have been cast into prison, for, in a touching note at page 64 of the last edition of his Grammar, he asks his readers' pardon for confounding an example of the imperative with the potential mood, which he was caused to do 'by the great bother of the brawling company that is round about me in this prison.' What became of him ultimately I do not know."—Dr. Douglas Hyde, *Literary History of Ireland*, pp. 599, 600.

[2] O'Donovan's, 1847, published since Reid wrote, is the best Irish Grammar.

*Some Elements of the Ancient Scottish, or Caledonian Celtick,
with some Observations.* In the year 1778 Shaw's work
appeared, with the following title : *An Analysis of the Gaelic
Language, by William Shaw, A.M., Forsan et haec olim
meminisse juvabit. Virg., Edin., 1778.*"

A second edition followed the same year, the published
price of the book being 4s. sewed. It is now very rare, but
not of much account.

The next work of the kind to appear was Stewart's,
announced as follows : " Elements of Gaelic Grammar, in four
parts. I. Of Pronunciation and Orthography. II. Of the
Parts of Speech. III. Of Syntax. IV. Of Derivation and
Composition. By Alexander Stewart, Minister of the Gospel
at Dingwall, Honorary Member of The Highland Society of
Scotland, Edinburgh. Printed by C. Stewart & Coy. ; for
Peter Hill, Edinburgh ; and Vernon and Hood, London,
1801."

A second edition, corrected and enlarged, was issued in
1812, a third in 1876, and a fourth in 1879. It is very
much superior to that by Shaw, and is still the best and the
one in common use.

A smaller volume appeared in 1828, entitled, *The
Principles of Gaelic Grammar, designed to facilitate the study
of that language to youth,* by Archibald Currie, formerly
Master of the Grammar School, Rothesay, but at the time of
publication Tutor at Prospect, Duntroon, Argyllshire. It
has never been reprinted. After him Neil Macalpine, of
Dictionary fame, produced one which went through four
editions. The other grammarians have been Munro, 1835-43 ;
Forbes, 1843-48; Dr. Macgillivray, 1858; L. Macbean ; D. C.
Macpherson, 1891 ; Malcolm Macfarlane, for the Highland
Association, 1893 ; Reid, 1895 ; and Gillies, 1896, the latter
based on Stewart's.

A good Grammar of the Gaelic language is still a desider-
atum. Students feel that those already in existence follow
too slavishly the model of grammars of other tongues, from
which the Gaelic diverges, and thus exceptions to the rules

abound. Only a man of the Zeuss type, well versed in philology and the original structure and peculiar idioms of this ancient speech, would be likely to bring order out of the existing chaos, and produce a book which would be a real help to the study of the language. Meanwhile the student has to fall back upon Stewart, whose outlines were put together when philological research was yet in its infancy. Though Zeuss and Windisch have Gaelic Grammars, they are in Latin and German.

The history of the Dictionaries is even more interesting. Michael O'Clery is credited with the first attempts to produce a Gaelic one.[1] His *Seanasan Nuadh*, or glossary of old words, was published at Louvain in 1643. Other Irish lexicographers followed, as many as six Dictionaries appearing before the year 1817 was ended, among them that of the learned Lhuyd of Wales and Oxford in 1706.

The earliest in the Scottish Gaelic, was Kirke's Vocabulary, printed at the end of the Irish Bible in 1690, and consisting of five and a half pages, on which the words were arranged alphabetically. Later, in 1702, another Vocabulary of thirteen pages by him, including additions by Lhuyd, was published in *Nicholson's Scottish Historical Library*. This one is not arranged alphabetically, but under twelve heads or divisions. Neither of Kirke's was issued by itself, apart from other subject-matter.

Afterwards, about the year 1732, the Rev. Dr. Malcolm or M'Colm of Duddingston made an attempt to compile a lexicon, the material for which was said to have been prepared by Lhuyd. He published a prospectus and a specimen of the work, entitled "Focloir Gaoidheilge-Shagsonach," but although he was encouraged by the General Assembly and received a grant of £20, the work never appeared.

Thus the first Gaelic Dictionary published in separate form was Macdonald's Vocabulary, 1741, written for the use of the Charity Schools founded and endowed in the Highlands

---

[1] Of course Cormac's Glossary is the earliest, but does not count among printed ones, because only in MS.

by the Society for Propagating Christian Knowledge. Like its predecessor, it is not arranged alphabetically but divided into subjects or chapters, like the syllabaries used by the ancient Assyrians.

A more ambitious work was " A Galic and English Dictionary, containing all the words in the Scottish and Irish dialects of the Celtic that could be collated from the voice, and old books, and MSS., by the Rev. William Shaw, A.M., followed by an English and Galic Dictionary, containing the most useful and necessary words in the English language, explained by the correspondent words in the Galic," by the same author, 1780. The published price was two guineas, though it was frequently sold for three and a half. Shaw's knowledge of the language was defective. A most furious Highland storm burst over his head on account of his open championship of the Johnsonian side in the Ossianic controversy. Consequently some of the subscribers returned their copies, but on the plea that there were a good many Irish words in the book. Others, who did not return them within a reasonable time, were found liable to pay. The case had gone to the Court of Session, and the author won, the judges finding that though he did not fulfil the terms of his prospectus he was not guilty of fraud or deceit in the preparation of the book, and when a definition of a Gaelic Dictionary was given they held that his legally answered the description. From Shaw himself the curious fact was elicited that, when picking up words among the Highlanders, he found the task nearly impossible, as he had to pay them all except the most educated, the natives being impressed with the idea that he was going to make a fortune out of the language, and of course they should have a share. In consequence he turned to the Irish peasantry, who received him more graciously ; and he had access to Colonel Vallancy's MSS. But the upshot was that the Dictionary did ultimately contain more Irish words than Gaelic. And this, combined with his own unpopularity, gave his controversial foes the opportunity to thwart him, which he resisted, as we have indicated, by litigation. Ultimately he had to seek refuge in the Church of England, where through the influence, it is supposed, of Dr. Johnson, he got a living worth £200 a year.

" A new Alphabetical Vocabulary, Gaelic and English, with some directions *for writing and reading* the Gaelic," by Robert Macfarlane, Edinburgh, appeared in 1795 ; and in 1815 another, in two parts, by Peter Macfarlane, the Gaelic translator of Bunyan's *Pilgrim's Progress*, Doddridge's *Rise and Progress*, and Blair's *Sermons*. The two parts were also published separately in the same year. This was the only really practical Gaelic Dictionary up to date, but on account of its limited size was still very deficient.

A prospectus for a more comprehensive lexicon was issued in 1803 by Alexander Robertson, schoolmaster, Kirkmichael, and a few parts appeared. Thereafter the Highland Society bought his MS., as an aid to the Dictionary contemplated by themselves.

Since then there have been issued as many as five good ones, all more or less well known and serviceable at the present time. The first of these was by Rev. A. Armstrong, A.M., " in which the words in their different acceptations are illustrated by quotations from the best Gaelic writers ; and their affinities traced in most of the languages of ancient and modern times, with a short historical appendix of ancient names deduced from the authority of Ossian and other poets ; to which is prefixed a new Gaelic Grammar, 1825." The work was published at three guineas.

On the other hand, the rival, issued by the Highland Society of Scotland, three years later, on somewhat similar lines, cost seven guineas in demy quarto, and ten in royal. To an advertisement from the publisher the following is attached : " This great work has occupied the attention of the Society since 1814, and presents not only a fully illustrated view of the Gaelic of Scotland, but surpasses in extent any lexicon of the Celtic Language ever offered to the public in this or any other country." Armstrong's and this one are by far the largest and the best.

Next in order comes that projected by the Rev. Dr. Norman Macleod, Minister of Campsie, and the Rev. Dr. Daniel Dewar of Glasgow, 1831. It was superintended through the press and indeed mainly compiled by the Peter Macfarlane already mentioned and his son Donald—both accredited Gaelic scholars; and sold for a guinea. It is now known as Macleod and Dewar's.

Contemporary with it we may say, there appeared, in 1832, the first attempt at a Gaelic pronouncing Dictionary, sold in parts by all the teachers in the Highlands. It was originally issued as "A Pocket Pronouncing Gaelic Dictionary for Schools in the Highlands and Islands; containing a far greater number of pure Gaelic words than any other Dictionary, and three times, in some instances ten times, the number of illustrations and examples in the large Gaelic Dictionaries, from the Bible and other sources; also all words that are exclusively Irish pointed out, and reasons given for rejecting them by N. Macalpine, student in Divinity and Parochial Schoolmaster in Islay.

While Armstrong's and the Highland Society's Dictionary have only had one edition, and Macleod and Dewar's five, Macalpine's has reached as many as twelve, and was last printed in 1890. A small volume of recognised merit by the Rev. Ewen Maceachen bears the date 1842. It has now been re-edited by Dr. Macbain and Mr. John Whyte.

Lately Dr. Macbain's own *Etymological Dictionary*, the most scholarly work of the kind, has been published at Inverness in 1896, of which interesting book a new edition may shortly be expected, so that Highland Vernacular Dictionaries have had a goodly record.

One other department of this study remains to be noted, namely the periodicals, a mere list of which suffices to show their character and history. But indirectly this list throws a pathetic side-light on the waning fortunes, or may we not say, the expiring struggles of our ancient tongue, as well as upon the number and variety of efforts that have been put forth to resuscitate it.

PERIODICALS

Name.	Place.	Date.	Nos.
Ros-Roine (The Rose of the Field)	Glasgow	1803	4
An Teachdaire Gaidhealach (Highland Messenger)	,,	1829–31	24
An Teachdaire Ur Gaidhealach (New Messenger)	,,	1835–36	9
Cuairtear nan Gleann	,,	1840–43	40
An Cuairtear Og Gaidhealach	Antigonish	1851	13
Cuairtear nan Coillte	Ontario	1840	
Teachdaire Gaidhealach Thasmania	Antigonish	1837	
An Fhianuis (The Witness)	Glasgow	1845–50	36
Eaglais Shaor na h'Alba (Quarterly)	,,	1875–93	74
An Fhianuis (Continuation of above)	,,	1893 —	
A Bheithir Bheuma (The Satirist, No. 1)	,,	1845	
Teachdaire nan Gaidheal	,,	1844	8
Caraid nan Gael	,,	1844	5
Caraid nan Gaidheal (No. 1)	Inverness	1853	
Fear Tathaich (The Mountain Visitor)	Glasgow	1848–50	25
An T-Aoidh Miosail	Edinburgh	1847–48	17
An Gaidheal (The Gael)	Toronto	1871–77	6 vols.
Issued afresh	{ Glasgow and Edinburgh		
Monthly Visitor	,,	1858 —	
The Celtic Magazine	Inverness	1876–88	13 vols.
The Highland Magazine	Oban	1885	8
The Banner of Truth	Glasgow	1872–74	2 vols.
The Highland Monthly	Inverness	1889	51
Cuairtear na Coille	,,	1881	
MacTalla	Sydney, Cape Breton	1892	
Supplement to *Life and Work*	Glasgow	1879 —	
Scottish Celtic Review	,,	1881–85	4
The Celtic Monthly	,,	1892 —	

Of these it will be seen the most died in their infancy. The only survivors in Scotland to-day are the Church Quarterly *An Fhianuis*, the Monthly Supplement to *Life and Work*, and the *Celtic Monthly*. There have been about twenty monthly periodicals tried since the beginning of last century. Of the *Gaelic Messenger*, to take a single example, Dr. Nigel Macneill says that the late Mr. W. R. Macphun, the publisher, informed him in 1873 that the parcels of *Messengers* sent to the Highlands and Islands came back at the end of the year, *after they had been read*, without any accompanying payment.   Dr. Macleod, the editor, and his enterprising publisher saw then that it was time to give up the business. " Some who have lost time and money in recent times over Gaelic affairs," adds Dr. Macneill sententiously, " may find some cold comfort in this incident in the experience of our greatest of prose writers."

Further comment on that score is surely unnecessary. Yet is it not suggestive of much that the only paper at present wholly written in Scottish Gaelic is one published in Cape Breton, 3000 miles without and beyond the Celtic fringe of the Old World ?

Taken as a whole, we may see from this survey that the printed Gaelic books extant belong to the past.   They represent a type of thought which has been largely superseded. And no modern outside the world of Gaelic dream could live and thrive on them exclusively.   Nevertheless they represent the literature of a people, ancient and venerable, and as such they will have a value and interest for the future historian, litterateur, philologist, and ethnologist far exceeding what they have to-day ; and in translations the best of the bards will be read when the language in which they breathed their poetry is no longer heard on the lips of men.

CHAPTER XVIII

THE MASTER GLEANERS OF GAELIC POETRY

The work of the gleaner—Authors of the three most precious relics of Celtic literature, Leabhar Na h'Uidhre, Book of Hymns, and Book of Leinster—of the three Highland treasures, Book of the Dean of Lismore, Fernaig MS., and Book of Clanranald—Advent of Macpherson—Collections and collectors between 1750 and 1820—First printed gleaning—Four nineteenth-century monuments, Campbell's Leabhar na Feinne, Mackenzie's Beauties of Gaelic Poetry, Sinclair's Songster, and Carmichael's Carmina Gadelica—Other recent gleaners and their books.

To the gleaners of the poetic heritage of the past we are indebted almost as much as to the poets themselves ; for what mattered it to us that some Homer or Ossian had sung, if none of their contributions ever reached us ?   An unappreciative age may allow its masterpieces to be lost, but the gleaners will not suffer that.   They treasure the best, many a time snatching the fugitive poems from the verge of oblivion.

Sometimes they glean for the pure pleasure of possessing, as the miser amasses his gold.   Often they do it to share with others.   In any case, like the middlemen of commerce, they are the true distributers, for sooner or later their wares reach the market.

Unlike that of the poet, the work of the gleaner demands no originality ; only a certain devotion and enthusiasm for the compositions admired, and a certain critical judgment, the latter not always in evidence, and not necessarily indispensable.   Posterity does the winnowing.

347

To the gleaners we owe the original compiling of the three most precious relics of Celtic literature now in the world—the Leabhar Na h'Uidhre, the Book of Hymns, and the Book of Leinster.

It is away back in the latter end of the eleventh century and early part of the twelfth that we encounter the authors of these. When the gloom of the Middle Ages was settling down upon Europe, and weird apparitions hovered round the camp fires and the cloisters ; when the feudal lords were building their strong castles and the men of peace their churches and monastic retreats, to escape from war and disorder and general wickedness, one might enter the precincts of the great monastery of Clonmacnois in Ireland and find Maelmuiri, the son of the son of Conn nam Bocht, busy with his pen compiling the Leabhar Na h'Uidhre. Many times already had the sacred edifice been attacked and pillaged by the marauding Norsemen, and even then it was surrounded by people rendered violent and half savage by the disorders of the time, so that the studious Maelmuiri with his literary tastes was not secure in his quiet retreat, but in the midst of his peaceful avocations was set upon one night in the church and murdered by a band of robbers, to whom literature, most likely, had no meaning.

But Maelmuiri had already reared his monument, more lasting than brass, in the book which happily escaped the hands of the ruffians.

It is the oldest miscellaneous gleaning we have, and contains, among many valuable productions in prose and poetry, such ancient poems as Dallan Forgaill's " Amra " or " Praise of Columcille," and a pretty large transcript of the " Táin Bó Chuailgné." The Gaelic of the former in the Fenian dialect was so ancient even in Maelmuiri's time that it had to be heavily glossed and commented upon.

Of his contemporary, the compiler of the Book of Hymns, nothing seems to be known. His monument too has survived the ravages and vicissitudes of time, but without his name. A wonderful anthology it is, carrying us back, as in the case of the other, to the days of St. Columba, and even further, to the period of St. Patrick. For here, in the *Liber Hymnorum*, we have the Gaelic hymns of Patrick, Colmán, Fiacc, Ultán, Broccán, Sanctáin, Dallan Forgaill, Máel-ísu, the prayers of Nínine and Adamnán ; a Quatrain on the Apostles ; besides a variety of beautiful Latin hymns with Gaelic glosses and prefaces. Among the more famous of the latter may be mentioned the "Te Deum," the "Magnificat," the "Gloria in Excelsis Deo," and the "Benedictus Dominus Deus Israel," so well known to worshippers throughout the ages since then ; and the three Latin hymns of St. Columba—the "Altus," "In te Christo," and "Noli Pater."

Many of these occur only in the Book of Hymns, except when copied from it elsewhere, and may have been lost to posterity, but for the industry of the unknown gleaner now no more remembered.

Maelmuiri and he, in all probability had made their collection before the close of the eleventh century ; and fifty years later appeared the compiler,[1] who produced the Book of Leinster, containing no less than 187 romances in prose and poetry. After the Leabhar Na h'Uidhre this is reckoned the most important monument of Gaelic literature.

The stories recorded relate to events which for the most part happened before the year 650, and their interest and variety may be inferred from the following category of subjects, into which they have been classified, namely : destructions of fortified places, cow-spoils, courtships, battles, cave-stories, voyagings, tragic deaths, feasts, sieges, adventures, elopements, slaughters, water-eruptions, expeditions, progresses, and visions. A book of old-time and abundant human incident is this middle-age document.

In succession to these three master-gleaners there arose numerous other less famous ones in Ireland.

But our special quest carries us over from this time to the land famed in later song and story as the home of the

---

[1] Finn Mac Gormann, Bishop of Kildare, most probably.

Gaelic tongue. And coming to Scotland three other monuments of Celtic industry and literary taste arise to view, covering the period extending from the fourteenth century to the Forty-five. They are the ·Book of the Dean of Lismore, the Fernaig MS., and the Book of Clanranald. These having been described in detail in Chapter VII., demand no more than a passing reference here. Happily, more is known of their authors than of the compilers of their famous precursors.

It was in that wild and turbulent period of clan feuds in the Northern and Western Highlands, and family quarrels between the Douglases and their rivals in the Lowlands, almost half a century before the Scottish Reformation, that the Dean of Lismore in his island home near Oban, set about collecting his fund of Gaelic poetry. In 1512, just the year before Flodden, he began to write down what he gleaned from oral recitation throughout the Highlands and Ireland, and continued with the help of his brother down to the year 1526, thus conserving not only the poetry of his own generation and of two previous centuries, but also most beautiful and characteristic fragments of Ossianic poems, some of which, but for him, would have been irretrievably lost.

A hundred and sixty years pass stormfully by before we meet the next gleaner in this field of poetic literature. And then arose among the wild Macraes of Kintail the chief of that name, Donnachadh nam Piòs, full of piety and song. Amid the tumults of the Revolution of 1688, while Claverhouse was leading the clans on to fateful Killiecrankie, and Cannon and Buchan were ravaging the Northern Highlands, this friend of the Muses, and learned chieftain, found a pastime in making of verse and committing to manuscript, thousands of lines of poetry current in his own district, from Carsewell's day down to his own, and in point of place from Southern Argyllshire north to the borders of Caithness.

This representative gleaning carries the bardic succession over the long interval since the Dean's time, and it is a pity that though the Fernaig manuscript has been transcribed and annotated by Professor Mackinnon, and again transcribed by Dr. Cameron and Dr. Macbain, and partly transliterated by Dr. Henderson, no English rendering has yet been published.

The poems in the Book of Clanranald are not of the same high order as the earlier survivals, with the exception of the two or three Ossianic fragments, which are likewise to be found elsewhere. But they supplement the Fernaig collection, and help to bring down the poetic tradition nearer the Forty-five. It is to the Macvurichs—the descendants of Muireach Albanach, and the hereditary bards of Clanranald—that we owe this contribution to the gleanings of poetising in by-gone days. They collected throughout their successive generations chiefly elegies and eulogies, from the time of Charles the First to George the Second.

A new era of enthusiasm for bardic compositions opened with the advent of Macpherson and his publication in June 1760 of " Fragments of Ancient Poetry collected in the Highlands of Scotland." The rich field of Celtic lore in the past was by this time almost unknown. Few interested themselves in the Celtic literature of their country. The Book of the Dean of Lismore lay in obscurity, nobody now knows where. For centuries it had never been heard of. The Fernaig MS. and the Book of Clanranald were equally buried, perhaps in old clan chests or lumber-rooms. No better evidence of the great dearth in the land of master-gleaners could be adduced than the challenge of Dr. Johnson, that there were not in the whole world Gaelic MSS. one hundred years old, and the feeble way in which it was met.

Interest in these days had reached a very low ebb indeed, when the controversy over Macpherson's *Ossian* set the Celts a-searching.

Macpherson himself, first in the field of these newly awakened enthusiasts, is believed, in the course of his journey through the North-West Highlands, to have gleaned the best of what remained of the treasure. But for him it is highly probable there would be no Scottish collection of Gaelic MSS. in the Advocates' Library to-day. Many of them were already on their way to decay, as their tattered appearance shows.

Besides the work of the Highland Society and the stock in hand of the Kilbride family, it is quite remarkable the number of minor collections that were made between the years 1750 and 1820. This period was, in fact, a resurrected Ossianic cycle. It would be tedious, and quite unnecessary here to catalogue all the names, but we may mention the Turner, the Jerome Stone, the Macnicol, the Fletcher, the Campbell, the Gillies, the Irvine, the Macpherson, the Kennedy, the Sir George Mackenzie, the Sinclair, the Sage, the Macfarlane, the Grant, and the Maccallum collections. And among these gleaners, the baronet, the clergy, the teacher, the farmer, the printer, the soldier, the advocate, the traveller, are all represented.

It is curious now, looking back on the great Macpherson Ossianic controversy, which called forth all this industry, this laborious writing and research, to reflect on its rise and progress. Doubtless it was felt then, as it is recognised now, that the only real way to solve the riddle was to glean in the fields of poetry and history—a task prior to that period too much neglected. They wanted data. Had they the records we now possess, and had they been able to read the ancient scrolls, there would have been no literary wrangle. How quietly and naturally the question, then a problem, has with the advent of scientific scholarship solved itself. As a controversy the Macpherson squabble is now as extinct as the dodo. And the Celtic champions who heralded the dawn of last century, as we did of this, would perhaps be almost as much taken aback with the issue could they know, as with the wonders of steam or electricity and the camera.

It is an interesting fact that the earliest to achieve a printed collection of ancient Gaelic poetry was Ronald Macdonald, son of the Ardnamurchan bard, who published a volume in 1776, presumably from materials treasured by his father.

But if through the past centuries the master gleaners

appeared only at rare intervals, the nineteenth has not been thus barren. For almost simultaneously with the Celtic renaissance abroad, enthusiastic harvesters entered the field at home. Four works especially, all produced within the last sixty years, call for particular attention. Following the modern method, their authors have each taken up a special line, ransacking the past and the present for their own peculiar pearls. And thus for the first time the whole Scottish field of Gaelic poetry has been well-nigh gone over, and representative poems of every age and class have been gleaned and printed.

First in the order of the antiquity of its contents, though not first in the field, comes Campbell's *Leabhar na Feinne.* It appeared in 1872, its title page announcement sufficiently indicating its aim and scope. As a sub-title, the latter runs as follows :—

" Heroic Gaelic Ballads
Collected in Scotland
Chiefly from 1512 to 1871

copied from old manuscripts preserved at Edinburgh and elsewhere, and from rare books ; and orally collected since 1859 ; with lists of collections and of their contents ; and with a short account of the documents quoted.

Arranged by
J. F. Campbell,
Niddry Lodge, Kensington, London, W."

The author, who was a barrister, and of an ancient and illustrious Highland family in Islay, spent twelve years from 1859 collecting folk-lore and poetry as opportunity offered throughout the Highlands, a work in which he was assisted by various contributors and coadjutors. His first book, entitled *Popular Tales of the West Highlands*, orally collected, was published in Edinburgh in 1862. There are four volumes, and they contain mainly prose stories, such as were wont to be repeated round the firesides in the High-

land Ceilidh in days of yore. Yet, commingled with the
Sgeulachdan, are to be found Ossianic fragments which had
filtered down by oral tradition.

This publication, however, was but a stepping-stone to
the author's real *magnum opus*, the *Leabhar na Feinne*.

For it, he collected about 54,000 lines of heroic poetry,
and these it will be observed are independent of the Irish
MSS., and almost of the Scottish MSS. written in the Irish
character before the year 1512. With regard to the latter
he says, "To publish them is more than I am able to do.
Where extracts have been made I have quoted a few passages to show what the language is like, and how these
ancient writings correspond to later writings."

Since in many cases he had two or more versions of the
same ballad, and in some cases five or six, it was his original
intention to collate and make one perfect copy. This idea
he had ultimately to abandon, and wisely followed the plan
of printing the oldest, with selections from later versions.
Of the first Ossianic fragment he attempted to collate from
two versions, namely, Garbh Mac Stairn, he says, "not a line
of Macpherson's Gaelic was in either version, but the story
seemed to be the foundation of the first book of Fingal, and
therefore a literary curiosity." It is significant that when
Campbell issued his first book he favoured the authenticity
of Macpherson's *Ossian*, but by the time *Leabhar na Feinne*
appeared he was strong the other way. His early attitude
he attributed to "unformed opinions affected by old beliefs."

The ballads of *Leabhar na Feinne* are arranged under
nine heads, according to their chronological sequence, as
follows :—

   I. The Story of Cuchulinn.
  II. The Story of Deirdre.
 III. The Story of Fraoch.
 IV. The Story of Fionn and the Feinn, including the Norse
       Ballads.
  V. Parodies.
 VI. Later Heroic Ballads.

VII. Mythical Ballads.

VIII. Poems like Macpherson's *Ossian.*

IX. Pope's collection of ten Ballads.

These heroic tales read like the *Arabian Nights,* often with the exaggerated fancy of *Don Quixote.* The extraordinary variety and human interest of the ballads may be gleaned even from their names. For example : The Story of Cuchulinn and Eimer, his wife ; his sword ; his chariots ; Garbh Mac Stairn ; and Conlaoch ; and Connal's revenge. The Story of Fionn and his Feinn ; his pedigree ; stories about his birth ; Ossian' and Padruig ; Ossian's last hunt ; how he got his sight ; the loss of the Fenian history ; Ossian's controversy with Padruig ; his lament for his comrades ; their names ; their favourite music ; how nine went forth to seek a whelp. Caoilte ; how he slew a magic boar and a giant.

The following would pass as the titles of chapters in the great classic of Cervantes : The adventure with the timbrel player ; With Silhalan ; The adventure of the hag ; The stealing of Fionn's cup ; The adventure with the enchanter's family ; Roc, the King's one-legged runner ; The smithy song, how they got swords ; The one-eyed giantess and her ships ; The battle with Manus ; Fionn's expedition to Lochlan ; His puzzle ; His enchantment in the rowan booth ; The adventure of the nine with a horseman ; The adventure in the house of the king of the fair strangers ; The Black Dog slain by Bran ; The adventure of the six at the golden castle ; The tightest fight of the Feinn ; The expedition of eight or of the six to foreign lands ; The distressed maiden ; The battle of Fair Strand, in which the Feinn defeated the whole world in arms ; The maid of the fair white garment ; Ossian's courting ; How Bran was killed and Gaul's dog ; Fionn's encounter of wits with Ailbhe, Cormac's daughter ; The elopement of Grainne, Fionn's wife, with Diarmad, Fionn's nephew ; Diarmad's lament for his comrades ; The story of Gaul Macmorna ; his adventure with Lamh-fhad ; Gaul's last words to his wife.

The parodies have these headings : The black wrapper ;
A dream ; The tailor and the Feinn ; The truiseal stone ;
Diarmad's speech.

Among later heroical ballads occur subjects like these :
The lay of the great fool ; Oscar and the giant ; Muirchadh
Mac Brian and the heiress of Dublin ; Muirchadh Mac
Brian's riding dress ; Hugh O'Neil's horse.

Such sumptuous narrative, spiced with no lack of imaginative detail, might satisfy even Chaucer's merry group as they
foregathered to listen to the story-telling at the Tabard Inn
centuries ago.

In 1841, some thirty years before *Leabhar na Feinne,*
Mackenzie's *Beauties of Gaelic Poetry* appeared. It is a
work of more general interest than the other, in so far that
it gives gems of every type of poem. Here are to be found
in concise compass the best productions of the best bards
during the last 300 years, with brief biographical sketches,
critical and explanatory notes, and other elucidations.

John Mackenzie, the compiler, was born in 1806 of
humble parentage in Gairloch, Ross-shire. Educated in
the parish school there, and afterwards at Tain Academy,
he developed a taste for reading and music, and became
very proficient in the making of musical instruments.
His father had him started in life as an apprentice joiner
in Dingwall. This occupation he soon left, however, for
more congenial literary work, such as the collecting of
poetical material for publication. On leaving his native
strath to push his way in the great cities of the South, he
acted for a time as book-keeper in the Glasgow University
printing office, and in addition to compiling " The Beauties,"
wrote much in prose. Afterwards the late Gaelic publishers,
Maclachlan and Stewart, Edinburgh, employed him on
various undertakings for several years. Besides " The Beauties" he wrote a " History of Prince Charlie," the English-
Gaelic Dictionary, usually bound with Macalpine's, the "Gaelic
Melodist," and compiled, wrote, translated, or edited under
surprising difficulties, about thirty other works.

A man of talent and industry, Mackenzie has produced a book which not only enhances the prestige of our native literature, but also places himself in the front rank of Gaelic gleaners.

Like the Dean of Lismore, however, he has inserted certain matters which critics feel might, with advantage, be omitted, as they detract from the dignity of the work as a whole.

On the other hand, the author of *Leabhar na Feinne* feels aggrieved that Mackenzie has not included among " The Beauties" some of the ancient heroic ballads of Ossianic origin. As well might objection be taken to Mr. Campbell himself for omitting the heroic poetry in the Irish MSS. and the Scottish MSS. written in the old Gaelic script. As a matter of fact, Mackenzie does give as samples three very beautiful pieces, the " Mordubh," " Collath," and " The Aged Bard's Wish," which he took to be ancient, but which are now held to belong to the Macpherson period.

Both compilers did well to follow each his own plan and work out his own ideal. The field has thus been all the better harvested.

Mackenzie's undertaking seems to have early undermined his health, and though usually resident in the South, he died at Inverewe on the 19th day of August 1848, among his own people, and was buried with his fathers in the old chapel in the churchyard of Gairloch, near which, at the roadside, a monument now stands to his memory.

A few specimen extracts from " The Beauties " may here be quoted to illustrate their quality. Of the three earlier poems " The Aged Bard's Wish " is the best known, and of it our author gives both the text and a literal translation. It was Mrs. Grant of Laggan who first brought it under public notice, and then it was considered ancient because there is no flavour of Christianity in its composition. On the contrary, the bard desires entrance at death into the hall where dwell Ossian and Daol, and expresses the wish that there be laid by his side at the last a harp, a shell full of

liquor, and his ancestor's shield. In other respects both the
language and sentiment are modern.

> O càiraibh mi ri taobh nan allt
> A shiubhlas mall le ceumaibh ciuin
> Fo sgâil a bharraich leag mo cheann
> 'S bi thùs' a ghrian ro-chàirdeil rium.

> O place me by the purling brook,
> That wimples gently down the lea,
> Under the old tree's branchy shade,
> And thou, bright sun, be kind to me !

> Where I may hear the waterfall,
> And the hum of its falling wave,
> And give me the harp and the shell and the shield
> Of my sires in the strife of the brave.

Of Macintyre's " Ben Dorain," which is also included,
Professor Blackie says, " I shall be surprised to learn that
there exists in any language, ancient or modern, a more
original poem of the genus which we may call venatorial.
What Landseer, in a sister art, has done for animals in
general, that Macintyre, in this singular work, has done for
the deer and the roe." And then Blackie himself gives a
characteristic rendering into English of the poem, very free,
but catching the spirit of its Gaelic author. For example :—

> My delight it was to rise
> With the early morning skies
> All aglow,
> And to brush the dewy height
> Where the deer in airy state
> Wont to go ;
> At least a hundred brace
> Of the lofty antlered race,
> When they left their sleeping place
> Light and gay ;
> When they stood in trim array,
> And with low deep-breasted cry,
> Flung their breath into the sky,
> From the brae ;

When the hind, the pretty fool,
Would be rolling in the pool
  At her will;
Or the stag in gallant pride,
Would be strutting at the side
Of his haughty-headed bride
  On the hill.
And sweeter to my ear
Is the concert of the deer
  In their roaring,
Than when Erin from her lyre
Warmest strains of Celtic fire
  May be pouring;
And no organ sends a roll
So delightsome to my soul,
As the branchy-crested race,
When they quicken their proud pace,
And bellow in the face
  Of Ben Dorain.
O what joy to view the stag
When he rises 'neath the crag,
And from depth of hollow chest,
Sends his bell across the waste,
While he tosses high his crest,
  Proudly scorning.
And from milder throat the hind,
Lows an answer to his mind
With the younglings of her kind
  In the morning;
With her vivid swelling eye,
While her antlered lord is nigh,
She sweeps both earth and sky,
  Far away;
And beneath her eye-brow grey,
Lifts her lid to greet the day,
And to guide her turfy way
  O'er the brae.
O how lightsome is her tread,
When she gaily goes ahead,
O'er the green and mossy bed
  Of the rills;
When she leaps with such a grace
You will own her pretty pace

Ne'er was hindmost in the race,
When she wills ;
Or when with sudden start,
She defies the hunter's art.
And is vanished like a dart
O'er the hills.

At the end of the book Mackenzie gives a select number
of "Beauties" by individuals who invoked the muse only on
rare occasions, or whose history is little known to the world.
Among these we find the anonymous yet exquisitely beautiful and pathetic "Mali Bheag Òg." Our author claims to be
the first to give the whole of it correctly in print.[1] There is
much uncertainty as to the history, circumstance, and locality,
but the occasion of the poem was the elopement of two
lovers, who were pursued. The gallant, a young officer, stood
to the defence of his beautiful fiancée, who stole behind him
in the melée. Unhappily his sword accidentally in the
swing struck her so violent a blow that she expired at his
feet. It was in jail awaiting execution that he composed
this heart-melting song :—

Nach truagh leat mi's mi'm priosan,
Mo Mhàli bheag òg
Do chairdean a' cuir binn' orm,
Mo chuid de'n t-saoghal thù.
A bhean na mala mìne,
'S na'm pogan mar na fiòguis,
'S tu nach fagadh shios mi
Le mi-rùin do bheoil.

'S mise bh'air mo bhuaireadh
Mo Mhàli bheag òg,
'Nuair 'thain an 'sluagh mu'n cuairt duinn
Mo ribhinn ghlan ùr ;
'S truagh nach ann san uair ud,
A thuit mo lamh o m' ghualainn,
Mu'n dh'amais mi do bhualadh,
Mo Mhàli bheag òg.

---

[1] Second stanza he printed for first time.

As another independent gleaning, and valuable supplement to Mackenzie's work, there falls to be mentioned Archibald Sinclair's *An T' Oranaiche*, or the *Gaelic Songster*, published in 1879. "If a man were permitted to make all the ballads, he need not care who should make the laws of a nation," said a wise man. And certainly the songs occupy no mean place in Celtic life and poetry. Of these there is no collection in Gaelic like Sinclair's—humorous, patriotic, satiric, and sentimental. He gleaned, as he tells us, in many a field, saving some from oblivion. Others he snatched from fugitive pieces of paper, ere these latter became food for the moth. In all there are 290 songs in the volume, and upwards of fifty names of composers, some of whom are still living. The songs are mainly of last century, and were compiled in Glasgow by their editor, who was a publisher in that city.

By the well-known gleaners above mentioned, the heroic ballads, the lyric poems, and the songs have been securely garnered. But there still remained one large section of the field from which hitherto there had been no great ingathering, necessary to complete the harvest up to our time. And happily, ere the century closed, the crowning work appeared. It is a remarkable book and sumptuous, published in two volumes, in 1900, by Alexander Carmichael, who was for many years a member of Her Majesty's Inland Revenue staff, and an enthusiastic admirer of Gaelic lore. The work is styled "*Carmina Gadelica*,—hymns and incantations, with illustrative notes on words, rites, and customs, dying and obsolete ; orally collected in the Highlands and Islands of Scotland, and translated into English," by the author. Undoubtedly it places the compiler in the very front rank of Celtic gleaners, and will carry its testimony forward to posterity, as a monument of a phase of thought and life now passing away. Even already its weird and old-world "ortha, urnan agus ubagan," sound like the echoes of a far-off time, from which the race has long since emerged.

Yet its cultured author tells us that this work consists of old lore collected during the last forty-four years, forming but a small part of a large mass of oral literature written down from the recital of men and women throughout the land of the Gael, from Arran to Caithness, and from Perth to St. Kilda. The greater portion, however, was made in the Western Isles, the last refuge of the distinctive Celtic life "expiring on the horizon before the growing tumult of uniform civilisation."

For three centuries Gaelic oral literature has been disappearing, and, as our author tells us, it is now becoming meagre in quantity, inferior in quality, and greatly isolated.

" Several causes have contributed towards this decadence," he says, "principally the Reformation, the rebellions, the evictions, the Disruption, the schools, and the spirit of the age. Converts in religion, in politics, or in aught else are apt to be intemperate in speech and rash in action. The Reformation movement condemned the beliefs and cults tolerated and assimilated by the Celtic Church and the Latin Church. Nor did sculpture and architecture escape their intemperate zeal. The rebellions harried and harassed the people, while the evictions impoverished, dispirited, and scattered them over the world. Ignorant school teaching and clerical narrowness have been painfully detrimental to the expressive language, wholesome literature, manly sports, and interesting amusements of the Highland people."

Mr. Carmichael has classified the contents of his extensive gleaning under the following five sub-titles : Invocations, Seasons, Labour, Incantations, Miscellaneous, and in the general introduction explains his mode of gathering the materials.

The glimpses of Highland life he gives in connection with his visits and colloquies with the people are highly interesting.

" Whatever be the value of this work," he says, " it is genuine folk-lore, taken down from the lips of men and women, no part being copied from books. It is the product of far-away thinking, come down on the long stream of time. Who the thinkers and whence the stream, who can tell ? Some of the hymns may have been composed within the cloistered cells of Derry and Iona, and some of the incantations among the cromlechs of Stonehenge and the standing stones of Callarnis. These poems were composed by the learned, but they have not come down through the learned, but through the unlearned—not through the lettered few, but through the unlettered many, through the crofters and cottars, the herdsmen and shepherds of the Highlands and Islands."

" The poems were generally intoned in a low, recitative manner, rising and falling in slow modulated cadences, charming to hear but difficult to follow. The music of the hymns had a distinct individuality, in some respects resembling and in many respects differing from the old Gregorian chants of the Church. I greatly regret that I was not able to record this peculiar and beautiful music, probably the music of the old Celtic Church."

Following the advice and example of his acquaintance, J. F. Campbell of Islay, whom he knew for a quarter of a century, Mr. Carmichael gives the words and names of the reciters. But, unlike Campbell and Mackenzie and Sinclair, he gives an English rendering of the original in every instance. Thus, while to the vast majority of this nation *their* felicitous poems are locked up in the Gaelic, *his* are available to all, in chaste and beautiful language, with charming letterpress, embellished by old Celtic letters, artistically copied by his wife from the ancient MSS. in Edinburgh and elsewhere.

Speaking of the original, he maintains that, although in decay, the poems are in verse of a high order, with metre, rhythm, assonance, alliteration, and every quality to please the ear and to instruct the mind. Simple dignity, charming grace, passionate devotion, characterise most of these pieces. Again and again he laid down his self-imposed task, feeling unable to render the intense power and supreme beauty of the original Gaelic into adequate English ; but he persevered, thus placing a stone as it were upon the cairn of those who composed and of those who transmitted the work.

And now, a few characteristic specimens from the book may fitly close this study. The first is an incantation beginning :—

> The wicked who would do me harm,
> May he take the (throat) disease
> Globularly, spirally, circularly,
> Fluxy, pellety, horny-grim, etc.

But scarcely any English can convey the vengeance of the vernacular. Even the sounds are terrifying :—

> Ulc a dhean mo lochd,
> Gu'n gabh e'n galar gluc gloc,
> Guirneanach, goirneanach, guairneach,
> Gaornanach, garnanach, gruam.

Next, we quote two verses from " The Invocation of the Graces," interesting as containing beautiful names from the ancient sagas :—

> A shade art thou in the heat,
> A shelter art thou in the cold,
> Eyes art thou to the blind,
> A staff art thou to the pilgrim,
> An island art thou at sea,
> A fortress art thou on land,
> A well art thou in the desert,
> Health art thou to the ailing.

> Thine is the skill of the Fairy Woman,
> Thine is the virtue of Bride the calm,
> Thine is the faith of Mary the mild,
> Thine is the tact of the woman of Greece,
> Thine is the beauty of Eimer the lovely,
> Thine is the tenderness of Darthula delightful,
> Thine is the courage of Meve the strong,
> Thine is the charm of Buine-bheul.

Now follows an example of a charm for sprain :—

> Christ went out
> In the morning early,
> He found the legs of the horses
> In fragments soft ;

He put marrow to marrow,
He put pith to pith,
He put bone to bone,
He put membrane to membrane,
He put tendon to tendon,
He put blood to blood,
He put tallow to tallow,
He put flesh to flesh,
He put fat to fat,
He put skin to skin,
He put hair to hair,
He put warm to warm,
He put cool to cool.
As the King of power healed that
It is in his nature to heal this,
If it be in his own will to do it.
    Through the bosom of the Being of life
    And of the Three of the Trinity.

And, finally, we may take this as a good specimen of an invocation :—

Bless, O Chief of generous Chiefs,
Myself and everything anear me,
Bless me in all my actions,
Make Thou me safe for ever.
    Make Thou me safe for ever.

From every brownie and ban-shee,
From every evil wish and sorrow,
From every nymph and water-wraith,
From every fairy mouse and grass-mouse,
    From every fairy mouse and grass-mouse.

From every troll among the hills,
From every siren hard pressing me,
From every ghoul within the glens,
Oh ! save me till the end of my day.
    Oh ! save me till the end of my day.

In recent years, Dr. George Henderson has done useful work in transliterating several poems from the Fernaig MS., which, along with many songs collected in the West Highlands, he has published in his *Leabhar nan Gleann*. And to Henry Whyte and Malcolm Macfarlane the Gael is indebted for an extensive gleaning in the field of vocal music. In addition to numerous Gaelic melodies, they have rescued a variety of excellent songs from impending oblivion and enhanced their value, especially to those who are unacquainted with the original, by giving literal renderings in English, which serve to exhibit their simple beauty.

Nor have the three sister nationalities been behind in work of this kind. The first important Irish gleaning has been Miss Brooke's *Reliques of Irish Poetry*, consisting of heroic poems, odes, elegies, and songs, which she published in the original with English translations and notes, Dublin, 1789. In more recent times we have the interesting collections in English of Sir Charles Gavan Duffy, Dr. Hyde, Dr. Sigerson, Yeats, and others, besides the *Treasury of Irish Poetry* lately edited by Stopford A. Brooke, and T. W. Rolleston. The latter deals simply with the nineteenth century, but Dr. Sigerson's *Bards of the Gael and Gall* is an Anthology of nearly a hundred and fifty poems metrically translated, " covering the ground from the earliest unrhymed chant ascribed to the first invading Milesian down to the peasant days of the eighteenth century."

Wales is well represented by the extensive Myvyrian Archaiology of Owen Jones, 1801-1807, which capable Welshmen, such as Aneurin Owen, Thomas Price, William Rees, John Jones and others, set themselves to finish ; while M. de la Villemarqué has done for Brittany, in his now famous books, perhaps all the ancient gleaning it was possible to do at a period so late as the middle of last century.

CHAPTER XIX

THE MASTER SCHOLARS OF CELTIC LITERATURE

The bards and seanachies—Six men of outstanding literary eminence—The earliest pioneer of the modern philological movement—Representatives of the older scholarship—Those of the new—The brilliant Zeuss—Foreign periodicals dealing with Celtic—Foremost scholars of the various nations—Italian—German—French—Danish—Scandinavian—American—British, including English, Irish, Welsh, Manx, and Scottish—Many literary problems solved—The promise of future harvests. .

IN the company of the scholars we still breathe the atmosphere of the past. It is they who have resurrected the MSS. These monuments of by-gone days are the quarries among which they work. As Burns "eyed with joy the general mirth," so do they scrutinise with eager glance the much-prized vellum.

Only a scholar can know the pleasure it gives to hap upon a long-lost relic of literature, to turn over its leaves, steeping the book in water, if need be, to make its pages come asunder, and even using acid to help the time-worn ancient one to deliver up its secret.

"Why bother with such defunct lore?" asks the man in the crowd, "the past is over and gone. It is long since superseded." Therein lies the difference between him and the scholar. The scholar thinks it worth while. Nay, he will sacrifice much—we shall repeatedly see—to search out the contribution of the past, and determine its meaning. As Plato, Aristotle, and the master-minds of ancient Greece wrote their books and carried on their studies, knowing full well that these would be read and assimilated by very few in their own day, there being no printing-presses as now, and only a limited education ; so many of the Celtic scholars of our own time labour on in solitude, conscious also that even with the printing-press the circle of their readers must be small, yet knowing they are doing a work which in its own way is ever widening the horizons of knowledge and enriching the common heritage of mankind.

In the bards and seanachies, there have not been lacking from remote times men who have interested themselves in the lore and learning of their race ; but we need to come down to more recent times to encounter the class of writers we have specially in view in this study.

Happily, they are not confined to any one age or any one country.   Yet Ireland, as we might expect from its place in the Celtic group, figures early and largely in the domain of Gaelic scholarship.

During the first half of the seventeenth century—to go no farther back—it produced six men of outstanding literary eminence, who represented a national scholarship in that country, the lustre of which has never since been surpassed. These were Geoffrey Keating, Duald Mac Firbis, and the Four Masters.

Keating, though born in Ireland, was of Norman extraction, and educated abroad for the office of priest.   On his return from Spain, a full-fledged Doctor of Divinity, he was appointed to a church and attracted great crowds as a preacher, till an incident, the most trivial and fortuitous in its origin, drove him from the pulpit into literature.   The incident is worth recording as a determining factor in his illustrious career.   It seems that in his audience one day a young lady, who was reputed to have questionable relations with a high dignitary of the Province, happened to appear, curious, like all the rest, to hear the great preacher.   Keating, as fate would have it, was discoursing on this occasion on a theme not likely to commend itself to the dissolute girl ; still less, since all eyes pointed the moral in her direction.

She had her revenge, for forthwith soldiers were dispatched by her lordly patron to arrest the offending priest and make him prisoner. But the latter hearing of this in time, made good his escape to the famous glen of Aberlow, where he lived for years a hidden life. It was while thus cashiered and ostracised that he conceived the idea of writing the history of Ireland, from the earliest times to the Norman conquest, afterwards travelling through the country in disguise, with Aberlow as base, to consult the ancient MSS., which were then in the families of the hereditary brehons and in the proximity of the old monasteries. Many documents which existed in 1630, and which he perused, have since disappeared. And his work is thus of great value, as he rewrote and redacted their contents in his own words, like another Herodotus.

Duald Mac Firbis, his contemporary, was equally indefatigable in ransacking the past for the benefit of the future. His *magnum opus* is *The Book of Genealogies*. O'Curry thinks it perhaps the greatest national genealogical compilation in the world. In addition, he compiled the *Chronicon Scotorum*, various glossaries, and, according to himself, a dictionary of the Brehon laws.

Almost at the same time that Keating was writing his history in the south of Ireland, the Four Masters were busy with theirs in the north. Michael O'Clery, born at Donegal about 1580, was author of the Leabhar Gabhala, or Book of Invasions, and other important works, but in compiling the famous Annals, the greatest of all, he had the assistance of other three eminent scholars, known as Farfasa O'Mulchonry, Peregrine O'Clery, and Peregrine O'Duigenan. Hence the name "Four Masters," given by John Colgan of Louvain, himself worthy to rank after them as the author of the *Trias Thaumaturga,* a book which owes its origin to the vast collection of material amassed by Michael O'Clery throughout his busy life. The latter work consists of two enormous Latin quartos, the first containing the lives of Patrick, Brigit, and Columba ; the second, those of a number of other distinguished Irish saints.

From the middle of the seventeenth century we are carried forward to the beginning of the eighteenth. And the next great name that illuminates the pages of Celtic scholarship is that of a Welshman, Edward Lhuyd. A peculiar interest and distinction attach to the work of this man, inasmuch as he was the earliest pioneer of the modern philological movement, and almost stumbled on the discoveries of Grimm and Rask, which were only reached upwards of a century after his time.

An Oxford don, of Jesus College, he clearly saw the necessity of laying a solid foundation for the scientific study of his own and kindred languages, and, following up his ideal, he set about publishing specimens of the literature and preparing vocabularies of the various dialects. In pursuit of this laudable object he visited Ireland and Scotland, and when his great work, the *Archæologica Britannica*, began to appear about 1703, enthusiastic Celts from far and near sent him congratulatory odes, some of which he afterwards printed. These poems were either in Latin or in the mother tongue of their contributors. Among the specimens sent from the Scottish Highlands, one, composed by the Rev. John Maclean of Kilninian, Mull, has been justly described by Professor Mackinnon as a "really admirable composition."

> Great praise and thanks, O noble Lhuyd, be thine,
> True learned patriot of the Cambrian line !
> Thou hast awaked the Celtic from the tomb,
> That our past life her records might illume.
> Engraved in every heart in lettered gold
> Thy name remains ; thy silent words unfold
> To future ages what our sires had seen,
> While others say, "A Gaelic race hath been."

Such is one verse of the ode, as rendered in English by Dr. Nigel Macneill.

Completed and printed at Oxford in 1707, the *Archæologica Britannica* was, according to the title page, "delivered to the subscribers at 9s. 6d., being the remainder of their payment, and to others at 16s."

As a scientific linguist, the reputation of its brilliant author was at once established.   His calibre may be inferred from the following pregnant note, which he appended to an edition of Kirke's Gaelic Vocabulary in 1702.   The note is in Latin to this effect :—

Of these 360 Gaelic words, 160 agree, in sound and sense, with the British (Welsh) language.   The letter *p* in Welsh equates with the letter *c* in Gaelic, *e.g.*, pren, crann (tree) ; plant, clann ; pen, ceann ; pedwar, ceithir ; pymp, cuig ; pwy, cia ; pasc, casg.   *Gw* of Welsh equates with Gaelic *f, e.g.*, gwyn, fionn ; gwin, fion ; gwr, fear ; gwair, feur ; gwirion, firinneach.   The Welsh *h* corresponds with the Gaelic *s, e.g.*, hen, sean ; helig, seileach ; heboc, seabhag ; hil, siol ; halen, salann ; hyn, sin.

What was to prevent a man of such critical insight travelling towards the interesting discovery of the position of the Celtic in the Aryan group, or even the generalisation formulated in Grimm's Law ?   Already he was on the track, observing sound changes.   He began with the Celtic dialects, but had he lived, in all likelihood he would have carried his equations to other languages of the Aryan group, and anticipated some at least of the modern results.   As it was, his early death occurred before he had time to work out the idea on the wider platform ; and the honour of having laid a sure foundation for the new sciences of philology, ethnology, and literary criticism passed a century and a half later to the great German masters.

After Lhuyd's time, unhappily in this country, his studies were not followed up.   On the contrary, the investigation of Celtic questions was determined more by sentiment than by scholarship.   Wrangling and partisanship took the place of learning and scientific veracity.   And so far were the methods and results of later criticism from being anticipated, that biassed men like Pinkerton and the Ossianic controversialists had a loud voice in the land.

Gradually a better type of scholarship began to emerge both in Scotland and Ireland.   Not at first the representatives of the new order, but representatives of the traditional seanachies, scholars of the long past, who interested themselves afresh in the literature, history, and antiquities of the race ; and who began with unwearied zest to unearth and bring to light the long lost and forgotten monuments of the past. Of these, in Scotland, the brothers Donald and John Smith, Ewen Maclachlan, Dr. Thomas Maclauchlan, and Dr. Archibald Clerk, were perhaps the most prominent. As scholars they were rather uncritical, and do not rank in the same category with the great names of later times ; but they had strong Gaelic sympathies and a large assortment of traditional knowledge.

In Ireland, on the other hand, there were far more who occupied themselves with the earlier periods. Of these it would be hard to rival in patient, conscientious, and solid learning such men as O'Reilly, Petrie, O'Donovan, O'Curry, Todd, Reeves, Hennessy, and Healy.

The first three were associated with the Ordnance Survey of Ireland, and in that sphere found excellent scope for their Celtic studies, in connection with the place-names of the country.

John O'Donovan was born in 1809. His father, though a small farmer, had been descended from the celebrated O'Donovans of County Cork, and when he died in 1817 his son John, then eight years of age and one of a family of nine, was sent to Dublin to be educated. From the age of seventeen he began to devote himself systematically to Celtic study, and three years later was brought under the notice of the Survey Commission as a youth singularly well qualified to conduct the archæological department of their enterprise. Accordingly he entered the service in 1829, and forthwith instituted a careful investigation of the printed books, MSS., and inscriptions bearing on topography ; in due course contributing articles to the *Dublin Penny Journal*, and laying the first instalment of his research before the British Association in 1835. Subsequently, Petrie and he published the full report.

In 1836 he set about preparing an Analytical Catalogue of the Irish MSS. in Trinity College, and from 1841 was editor of the works published by the Irish Archæological Society. Ever since he undertook the work of the Ordnance Survey, he had in view the idea of writing a *Grammar of the Irish Language*, and after seventeen years' study the book appeared in 1847, and was received with enthusiasm both at home and abroad. It is characteristic of the way in which British scholarship followed in the rear of that on the Continent, that so well informed and interested an exponent as O'Donovan did not know when he published his valuable Grammar that aspiration and ellipsis had been explained in Germany eight years before then. Thus he arrived too early to benefit much by the study of comparative philology, though deeply interested in the science.

His masterpiece is really the edition he issued of the *Annals of the Four Masters* (1848-51). Of this vast effort Dr. Hyde affirms that it is the greatest that any modern Irish scholar ever accomplished. "So long as Irish history exists, the *Annals of the Four Masters* will be read in O'Donovan's translation."

In 1847 he was called to the Bar, but sacrificed his prospects in that line for his Celtic studies. Later, he received the degree of LL.D. from Trinity College, Dublin, and a Government pension of £50 a year, and was appointed Professor of the Irish Language in Queen's College, Belfast. But having a large family to support on a small income, he contemplated emigrating to America or Australia, when in 1852, most opportunely, the Government resolved to appoint a Royal Commission to publish the ancient Laws and Institutions of Ireland, and he and O'Curry, the two greatest savants on that subject, were chosen for the office. Eight years' more arduous work undermined his constitution, and he succumbed to an attack of rheumatic fever about the middle of November 1861.

Eugene O'Curry did not long survive him. Neither of them lived to complete the vast undertaking, though they both wrote and translated volumes of text, which have since been published.

The immense labours and success of O'Curry in the difficult fields of Gaelic research are even more astonishing than those of his coadjutor, as he had never received an academical education, and was mainly self-taught, and had to forge his way in new and unexplored directions. In view of this his surprise was great when offered the Professorship in the Catholic University of Ireland, and so diffident was he that it was with difficulty he was persuaded to accept it. His catalogues, editions of texts and translations, and, above all, his famous books, the *Lectures on the Manuscript Materials of Ancient Irish History* (Dublin, 1861), and *On the Manners and Customs of the Ancient Irish* (London, 1873), have rendered him a kind of quarry for subsequent scholars, British and Continental.

To Dr. Todd is mainly due the inception, in 1841, of the Irish Archæological Society for publishing original documents. He figures also as the first editor of the *Liber Hymnorum*, Dublin, 1855, and as the biographer of St. Patrick, while Dr. Reeves has done masterly service as editor and biographer of Adamnan.

Of the line of scholars we have just passed in review, William Maunsell Hennessy is probably the last great representative. The better part of forty years he spent in close familiarity with the great tomes in Dublin, publishing, translating, and annotating, till the list of his works have become too numerous to mention here. Among the chief of these are his edition of the *Chronicon Scotorum*, in the Master of the Rolls' Series, 1858 ; and his translation of the *Tripartite Life of St. Patrick*, printed by Mary Frances Cusack, 1871, and by O'Leary, New York, 1874.

"Hennessy," says Standish O'Grady, "was born at Castle Gregory, some twelve miles west of Tralee, and in early life visited the United States. Upon his return to Ireland he became a journalist, and was appointed to the Public Record Office, Dublin, in 1868. He enjoyed the friendship of the Cavaliere Nigra, himself an accomplished Celticist, and was his guest at the Italian Embassy in Paris.

In 1885 he was visited by a family bereavement, almost tragic in sadness, and this again was before long followed by a second blow, the effect upon his sensitive and affectionate nature being such that he never fairly rallied, but died at the age of sixty."

Having thus glanced briefly at the representatives of the older scholarship and their work, we shall now have occasion to retrace our steps to consider the representatives of the new critical and philological movement. After Edward Lhuyd's demise no further progress seems to have been registered in the elucidation of Celtic philology till the time of Franz Bopp. Even as late as the first quarter of the nineteenth century, Gaelic was regarded by scholars as a peculiar language, unconnected with the other European tongues. It is true that Sir William Jones, from his study of Sanskrit, had thrown out the hint as early as 1786, that Celtic was of the same original stock with the other languages of Europe and South-Western Asia; but when Bopp first published his *Comparative Grammar* Celtic was omitted. It was Dr. Pritchard, an English ethnologist, who, in 1832, really demonstrated on the lines laid down by Grimm and Bopp, that the Celtic language is a member of the Indo-European group.

His book, entitled *The Eastern Origin of the Celtic Nations*, from this time drew the attention of continental scholars to the excluded and hitherto neglected language, with the result that three important works soon after appeared, namely, first, one *On the Affinity of the Celtic Languages with the Sanskrit*, by Adolph Pictet (Paris, 1837); second, the *Die Celtischen Sprachen*, or *Celtic Philology*, by Bopp (Berlin, 1839); and the *Celtica* of Dr. Diefenbach (Stuttgart, 1839-40).

By this time Bopp had studied the Celtic dialects, and published the above work as a supplement to his great *Comparative Grammar of the Sanskrit, Zend, Greek, Latin, Lithuanian, Gothic, German, and Sclavonic Languages*. Some features of Gaelic phonetics, such as initial aspiration and ellipsis, taking the place of declension, seems hitherto to have baffled scholars, but Bopp's sagacity enabled him to perceive that these are nothing else than the relics and results of the after-action of the old case-endings, and that the rational explanation is to be found in the final sound of the previous word, or, as we now say, vocalic and nasal auslaut. This discovery has since been fully confirmed by Zeuss, Ebel, and Windisch.

It was with the publication of the *Grammatica Celtica*, however, that the great moment in the evolution of Celtic scholarship arrived. Its gifted author, J. Caspard Zeuss, stands supreme as the real founder of Celtic philology. He did for it what Grimm did for the Teutonic, and Diez for the Romance. Since the appearance of his monumental work it has been definitely settled that the Celtic languages are pure Indo-European tongues, without any admixture of foreign elements, and thus that they are members of the family in the same sense that Latin or Gothic is. In addition, it has furnished the means of interpreting the most ancient forms of the Gaelic language found in the very old MSS., which before then had defied the efforts of translators.

Zeuss was born in Bavaria in July 1806, and after a brilliant school career, he went to the University of Munich, as his friends intended that he should be a clergyman. But the youth preferred linguistic studies, for which it soon transpired that he had a unique genius ; and, college life over, he taught for seven years (from 1832-39) in the Gymnasium of Munich. Meantime he pursued his own favourite science, publishing in 1837 a work which is still authoritative. It dealt with the German chiefly, but from the first his studies included the oriental languages.

To settle in Berlin and support himself by teaching there had now become the objective of his desire, as the Metropolis would furnish him with exceptional opportunities, but being a Catholic, he found this impossible. In 1839, however, he succeeded in getting a professorship in the

Lyceum in Spires, and went there from Munich. It was then he began to study Celtic. How enormous the difficulties were for a man in his position one can readily imagine, when it is remembered how widely dispersed, unknown, and unintelligible the materials for the most part were at that time. His income was small, but in order to economise his resources, and have the wherewithal to pursue his researches, it is said that he decided to remain a bachelor. It was his custom annually during the vacation to visit the great libraries of London, Oxford, Würzburg, St. Gall, and Milan for the perusal of the Gaelic documents. In the preface to his great work, he even apologises for not having made full use of the Milan glosses. This we know was not altogether his fault, for he went twice there to study the MS. On the first occasion there happened to be a convention of savants in the city, and the library was closed, much to his disappointment. An epidemic of fever prevailed when he returned the second time, and feeling certain sensations, he imagined he had caught the infection, and left the place without accomplishing the object of his visit. No doubt the overwrought student was nervous on that occasion, and his fears may have got the better of him.

In 1847 he was appointed Professor of History in Munich. But his health not being very robust, though he accepted the chair, he was obliged a few months afterwards to resign. Fortunately, however, he received a similar appointment in the Lyceum of Bamberg, which he was able to maintain. This was his last. The *Grammatica Celtica*, which was to take the learned world by surprise and revolutionise Celtic studies, appeared in 1853, after thirteen years' close and laborious work. It is written in Latin, and is so profoundly erudite that it has the reputation, like some other great German books, of being very difficult to grasp. The numerous sources consulted in the production of this masterpiece of scientific scholarship are all carefully given in the preface. Its publication at once established his fame, but the work killed him. In 1855 he was compelled to resign his chair through broken health. That same year Professor Siegfried of Dublin saw him, and afterward wrote the following interesting impression which the appearance of the devoted scholar made upon him. " I paid a visit," he says, " to this remarkable man in the vacation of 1855, when his health was fast sinking. He was a tall, well-made, rather spare man, with black hair and moustache, giving on the whole more the impression of a Sclavonian or a Greek than a German." He did not long survive his retirement, for in November 1856, less than three years after the completion of his Grammar, this illustrious linguist but modest and retiring man died in his native village in Bavaria. To him, mindful of his outstanding influence, Dr Whitley Stokes has not inaptly applied the Greek line—

Ζεὺς ἀρχή, Ζεὺς μέσσα, Διὸς δ᾽ ἐκ πάντα τέτυκται.

After the publication of the *Grammatica Celtica*, Celtic studies received a mighty impetus and took great strides forward. Now that the Celtic dialects were proved to be Aryan, their further study became a necessity in connection with the comparative grammar of the whole family. Already in Germany there was the well-known *Zeitschrift fur vergleichende Sprachkunde* (Journal of Comparative Philology), a journal specially devoted to the Germanic, Greek and Latin languages; but now in 1856, the *Beiträge zur vergleichenden Sprachforschung* (Contribution to Comparative Etymology) was started in Berlin to deal with the Aryan, Celtic, and Sclavonic tongues, and giving particular attention to the Celtic. The periodical went through eight volumes, one appearing in four parts every two years ; and when it came to an end the *Zeitschrift*, edited by Dr. Kuhn, began to receive articles on Celtic subjects, and continues to do so still.

Among the contributors to the *Beiträge* Dr. Hermann Ebel was the most notable. His Celtic studies in the journal were afterwards translated and issued in book form by the late Professor Sullivan of Dublin (1863). Of these the most important are *On Declension*, and *The Position of the Celtic*. Ebel taught for thirteen years in Schniedmuhl, and when the Chair of Comparative Philology, once occupied by Bopp, in Berlin, fell vacant, he was appointed thereto, but he did not live long to fulfil its duties, for he died in 1875, only two years later. He left, it is said, in MS. a dictionary of Old Gaelic. His greatest Celtic work, however, is the second edition of Zeuss's Grammar published in 1871, which embodies the results of Celtic scholarship down to that year.

In 1870 another important periodical, wholly devoted to Celtic studies, began to be published in Paris, namely the *Revue Celtique*. It was the appearance of this quarterly that ultimately led to the appointment of D'Arbois de Jubainville as Commissioner to the British Isles, to report on the Gaelic MSS. found there. This paper, which still flourishes, has for over thirty years done good service in the interests of scholarship, there being among its contributors such eminent writers as Ebel, Windisch, Max Müller, Count Nigra, Pictet, Jubainville, Stokes, Rhys, Macbain, and others.

Occasional articles continue to appear in several German papers, but it may be of moment in passing to note that a few years ago a new periodical, entitled *Zeitschrift fur Celtische Philologie*, was floated, as well as an *Archiv fur Celtische Lexicographie*, which shows the interest that is still taken by the German philologists in this department of study.

As the great succession of Celtic scholars after Zeuss and Ebel are more or less contemporary, it will be most convenient to deal with them in the order of nationality. Among foreigners of the first rank are two Italians, Count Nigra and Ascoli of Milan. Nigra was for a time his country's ambassador in London and Paris. It will be remembered that Hennessy, who enjoyed his friendship, was entertained by him at the Italian Embassy in the latter city. His most important contribution, founded on his own researches in Italy, is the *Reliquie Celtiche*, published in that land in 1872. Ascoli did similar good work in connection with the Gaelic glosses in the ancient MSS. of Milan and St. Gall, supplementing the labours in that field of Zeuss, Ebel, and Nigra.

In Germany, on the other hand, there are four still actively engaged who rank among the masters. First comes the brilliant Professor Windisch of Leipzig. He is best known for his *Irische Texte* (vol. i.), published in Leipzig, 1880; and again a second series of the same, in collaboration with Dr. Stokes, in 1884. It is a learned work with a vocabulary arranged alphabetically, which goes most minutely into the structure of the words. Such pieces as Cuchulinn's Sick-bed, the Vision of Adamnan, the Tale of the Sons of Uisneach, Hymns from the *Liber Hymnorum*, and Irish glosses from the MSS. in the monastery of St. Paul in Carinthia are among its varied contents. Windisch is Professor of Sanskrit in Leipzig, and besides an Irish Grammar has published other books bearing on Celtic philology. In some instances he has corrected Zeuss, and in various directions developed and extended his principles. At present he is engaged on a second edition of the above-mentioned grammar, and on an elaborate edition with translation of the Táin Bó Chuailgné.

Next to him comes Professor Zimmer, formerly of Greifswalde, now Professor of Celtic in Berlin University. Two books stand to his credit in 1881, *Irish Glosses* and *Celtic Studies*. As a writer he expresses fresh and interesting opinions on a great variety of subjects, such as the pagan character of Irish literature, the ancient Celtic Church, the "Táin Bó Chuailgné," Old Middle Irish MSS., the Irish scholars upon the Continent, Fiacc's *Life of St. Patrick*, and the scansion of the classical Irish metres.

Professor Thurneysen of Jena (now of Freiburg) distinguished himself by preparing, along with B. Gütterbock, an elaborate index to the *Grammatica Celtica*, which renders that work more complete and accessible. It was published in 1881.

He, along with Dr. Christian Stern, Librarian of Berlin, complete the quartette of famous German Celticists who have been for some time in the field, though not the list of able scholars engaged in like studies in that country. Other significant names are Drs. Holder, Finck, Zupitza, Foy, and Sommer.

Nor has France in recent years been lacking in eminent men of similar research. M. de la Borderie, Gaidos, De Jubainville, Lotti, Ernault, Dottin, and Professor Loth of Rennes have all greatly advanced the interests of Celtic philology and literature. Of these, D'Arbois de Jubainville is perhaps the best known, on account of his literary mission to the British Isles on behalf of the French Minister of Public Instruction in 1881, and his subsequent catalogue of the MSS. As Professor at the College of France and editor of the *Revue Celtique*, he made numerous interesting contributions in journal and book form to the modern literature of the subject, such as *Grammatical Studies on the Celtic Languages* and *Epopée Celtique en Irlande*.

Ernault occupied himself more with the Breton dialect and folk-lore, Professor Loth with the Mabinogion and Welsh metrics.

Other Continental savants of great promise remain to be mentioned. They belong to the northern nations, which have recently begun to develop a lively enthusiasm for Celtic studies. Denmark is well to the front with Professor Holger Pedersen, a pupil of Zimmer's, and Dr. Sarauw of Copenhagen, while Scandinavia in represented by Dr. Liden of Gothenburg. Much is expected of these men on the lines on which scholarship now travels. Hitherto America, so much engrossed with the problems of the present, has been slow to enter upon a research which burrows so deeply in the past, yet within the last few years two names have emerged which are intimately associated with this subject, namely, those of the Rev. Professor Henebry and Professor Robinson of Harvard. The one is concerned with the translation of O'Donnell's *Life of St. Columcille*, the other with the collection of certain early Irish poems and sagas.

And now, returning to our own shores after contemplating the masters abroad, it is pleasing to find so many who have distinguished themselves in one way or another in this field. England, Ireland, Wales, the Isle of Man, and Scotland have each furnished enthusiastic and capable men.

Foremost of these British scholars, and apparently now of all living Celticists, stands Dr. Whitley Stokes. Next to Zeuss he has done more than any other single man in this particular department of study and research. His publications are a library in themselves, and deal with Cornish, Breton, Old Welsh, as well as Irish and Gaelic. He has made himself master of the field in a very thorough and scientific manner. Perhaps his best known books are the *Irische Texte*, vol. i., 2nd series, 1884 ; vol. ii., published at Leipzig, 1887 ; *The Tripartite Life of St. Patrick*, 1887, and his *Goidelica* (old and early-middle-Irish glosses, prose and verse) which appeared twenty years before the others, and reached a second edition in 1872. In it are given accurate translations of the Gaelic prefaces and hymns of the *Liber Hymnorum*—that ancient anthology which dates from the eleventh century.

Dr. Stokes, who is a son of Professor William Stokes, Dublin, studied Irish with O'Donovan, and Sanskrit and Comparative Philology with Professor Siegfried in Dublin. After a distinguished career in the Indian Civil Service he retired and took up residence in London. It was in Calcutta that the foundation of his great reputation as a Celtic scholar was laid, and it was from that city that he first issued his *Goidelica*. The preface is striking in its brevity and simplicity :—

I have three objects in printing this book—one, to save the contents of my transcripts of the glosses at Turin, Milan, and Berne from the destruction which in this country anything solely entrusted to paper MSS. must sooner or later meet with ; another, to give those excellent German philologists who, like Schleicher and Ebel, have expressed a desire for trustworthy copies of Old Irish compositions, material on which they may look with confidence ; and, thirdly, to lay the first stone of the cairn which I hope to raise to the memory of my beloved friend and teacher, Siegfried.

The cairn has since been raised, and it is indeed a notable one. Besides his books, contributions from Dr. Stokes may be found in Continental journals, such as the *Beiträge zur vergleichenden Sprachforschung* of Berlin, and the *Revue Celtique* of Paris. He is still busy in his island home at Cowes, editing and translating texts, of which the *Annals of Tighernach*, the *Amra Choluimcille*, *Agallamh na Seanorach*, and the *Bruiden Da Derga* have lately been published.

Other great names in this country are those of Professor Rhys of Oxford, a Welshman ; Professor Atkinson of Dublin, a Yorkshireman ; Dr. Kuno Meyer of Liverpool, a German ; Dr. Strachan of Manchester, Professor of Greek and Comparative Philology, a native of Keith, Banffshire ; Dr. Douglas Hyde, whose interesting book on the *Literary History of Ireland* has just recently appeared ; Dr. Norman Moore, the poetical Dr. Sigerson, and the Professors Gwynne, father and son. Of these Principal Rhys has hitherto perhaps been the most prolific in dealing with the early history and problems of Celtic Britain, while the others have interested themselves more in the language and literature.

There are two other outstanding names very familiar to the student of Celtic, the erudite Standish Hayes O'Grady, author of *Silva Gadelica*, and friend of Windisch for many years, and Mr. Alfred Nutt, an authority on folk-lore and literary antiquities. Besides Rhys, Wales has produced such indefatigable workers as Gwenogfryn Evans and Canon Silvan Evans, the veteran of Welsh philology ; Professors Morris Jones and Lewis Jones, of Bangor ; the late Charles Ashton ; Professor Anwyl of Aberystwyth, and Mr. Brynmor Jones ; while the Isle of Man has Mr. A. W. Moore and Mr. Kermode.

In Scotland during the middle of last century Dr. Skene did much to revive interest in the history and monuments of the past, by collecting MS. materials, editing the *Four Ancient Books of Wales*, and publishing his own voluminous *Celtic Scotland*.

The first scholar north of the Tweed to assimilate the results of Zeuss's labours and follow his lead was the late Dr. Cameron of Brodick; very industrious, as may be seen from his contributions to the magazines, and his posthumous work, the *Reliquiæ Celticæ*, but sadly lacking in system and method.   After him come Dr. Macbain of Inverness, a distinguished philologist, whose Gaelic Dictionary is a valuable contribution to Celtic etymology, and the Rev. John Kennedy; the late Sheriff Nicholson; Professor Mackinnon, occupant of the Edinburgh Chair of Celtic Literature, and Dr. Henderson, a former student of his, who has since studied abroad and written various papers and books, and edited poems or tales collected in the Highlands.

These all represent the forces of scholarship in the highways and by-ways of Celtic literature.   They are not all masters, in the technical sense of the word; not a few of them are, as we have already seen, and the marvel is, looking back for fifty years, the number of men of the first rank who have appeared, in great part on the Continent but also in our own land.   It is truly a recrudescence or re-arising of the Celt.   Spent forces seem suddenly to have re-emerged and overflowed the foremost files of time, taking science captive and using it as their instrument.   And yet people wonder and inquire and continue to ask for evidence of a Celtic renaissance.

Many literary problems have within the last half-century been solved, but many more remain to be unravelled—questions too, of history, ethnology, and sociology.   But so much has already been done—so much that a century ago seemed visionary and impossible, and had not even appeared on the horizon of dreamers, that there is the promise of future harvests, and still unlimited scope for the masters.

Thus the progress.   First the available materials had to be ascertained, catalogued, sifted, and examined in every land.   Then followed the work of publishing and interpreting the texts which have already yielded such interesting philological and ethnical results, and now we look for a further synthesis in other directions from the hints and suggestions scattered all over these published records, which will throw light on the fascinating problems which confront the students of history, ethnology, archæology, and of the beliefs and customs of the race in its earlier stages—a study in keeping with the human experience, that to go on we must often go back.

INDEX OF NAMES

Achilles, 123
Adam, 63, 83, 126, 130, 232
Adamnan, 5, 16, 42, 45, 46, 47, 50, 58-77, 83, 88, 92, 201, 209, 215, 226, 291, 292, 349, 374, 380
Aedh, 54, 105
Aedh, 91
Aedh Mac Morna, 178, 181
Aeneas, 68, 228, 306
Aengus, 48, 292
Aidan, 221
Ailbhe, 355
Ailill, 109, 160, 161, 165
Ainnle, 158
Albin, St. 306
Aldfrid, 65, 68, 201
Alexander I., 89, 94
Alexander the Great, 6, 7
Alleine, 334
Amergin, 131, 139
Amphitrionis, 8
Anderson, Dr., 95
Andlis, 8
Andrew, 91
Aneurin, 218-223, 240, 244
Anne, Queen, 270
Antestis, 8
Anwyl, Prof., 383
Aoife, 159, 165, 167
Ardan, 158
Arganté, 320
Argyll, Earl of, 126, 272, 274, 327
Aristotle, 12, 367
Armstrong, Rev. A., 343, 344
Arnold, Matthew, 2, 97, 309, 311, 321-323
Arnold, Thomas, 307
Art, 179, 186, 193, 254
Arthur, 125, 128, 227-240, 244, 250, 260, 306-308, 318-321
Ascoli, 98, 379, 380

Ashburnham, 103
Ashton, Charles, 383
Aspasia, 254
Athol, 8
Atkinson, Prof., 383
Attila, 2
Aurelius, 319
Austin, 306
Avagddu, 230

Bach, Gwion, 231
Bacon, Francis, 332
Baithene, 48, 61, 71, 83
Balan, 318
Balin, 318
Balor, 141
Bannatyne, Lord, 117, 118
Barbour, John, 309
Baxter, Richard, 328, 334, 335
Becca, 145
Bede, 5, 22, 56, 65, 77, 92, 201, 221, 306
Bede, the Pict, 85, 86, 94
Bedivere, 321
Beli, 222
Benen, 34
Benignus, St., 34
Bernard, St., 39
Bethune, Donald, 116
Björn, 213, 214
Black, William, 301, 323
Blackie, Prof., 123, 186, 268, 272, 284, 322, 323, 358
Blair, Dr., 283, 343
Blake, William, 316
Blathmac, St., 62, 201, 208
Bodhbha, Dearg, 144, 145
Bollandist Fathers, 31, 62
Bondi, 214
Bopp, Franz, 258, 375, 376, 379
Borderie, M. de la, 381

387

Borron, Robert, 307
Boston, Thomas, 68, 334
Boswell, 63, 316
Brachet, A., 9
Bradshaw, Henry, 79-81
Bran, 247, 248, 355
Branno, 192
Branwen, 229
Brash, 14
Breas, 138, 141
Brec, Donald, 222
Brendan, St., 75, 215, 291
Brian, 141-143
Brian Boru, 203, 246
Bricriu, 153
Bride, 365
Brigit, 292, 369
Broccân, 292, 349
Brogan, 189
Brooke, Miss, 366
Brooke, Stopford, 310, 324, 366
Brown, Dorothy, 276
Brown, John, 335
Browning, Robert, 107
Bruce, Robert the, 86, 87
Bruce, Robert, 300
Brude, 46, 72
Brutus, 306
Buchan, Earls of, 87
Buchanan, Dugald, 250, 329, 330, 335, 336
Buchanan, Robert, 301, 323
Bugge, Dr. Alex., 210
Bugge, Prof. Sophus, 210
Buinne Borb, 151
Bunyan, 334, 343
Burnet, Bishop, 130
Burns, Robert, 257, 282, 299, 310, 367

Cadwaladr, 228
Cædmon, 15, 41, 57, 79, 304
Cael, 189-191
Cæsair, Lady, 137
Cæsar, 3, 5, 6, 9, 12, 13, 99
Cailatin, 163, 169
Cailta, 192
Cainnech, 51, 91
Cairbre, 179, 180, 185, 189
Calpornius, 25
Calvin, John, 328
Cameron, Dr., 147, 303, 338, 351, 384
Cameron, Margaret, 335
Camin, St., 104
Campbell, A., 335
Campbell, Alex., 352
Campbell, Colin, 263
Campbell, D., 274

Campbell, Duncan, 335
Campbell, J. F., 146, 147, 176, 186, 338, 353, 354, 357, 363
Campbell, Knight of Glenorchy, 126
Campbell of Glenlyon, 335
Canmore, Malcolm, 89, 92
Caoilte, 179, 185, 188, 189, 355
Caredig, 32
Caridwen, 230, 231
Carlyle, Thomas, 245, 332
Carmichael, A., 147, 148, 300, 338, 361, 362, 363
Carsewell, Bishop, 127, 264, 299, 300, 327, 328, 350
Cassius, Dion, 12
Catald, St., 208
Cathal, 91, 126
Cathbad, 148-151
Cathula, 254
Caxton, William, 308, 327
Cedric, 307
Celtchar, 154
Cennfaelad, 107, 291
Ceolfrid, 66
Ceretic, 32
Chaillu, Paul B. du, 200
Charlemagne, 59, 199, 208
Charles I., 130, 270, 351
Charles II., 270, 274
Charlie, Prince, 250, 251, 256
Chaucer, 309, 310, 332, 335
Church, Dean, 303
Cian, 141, 142, 214
Ciaran, St., 108, 154
Cicero, 12
Clanranald, 129, 130, 276, 283
Clark, John, 176, 250, 256
Cleopatra, 254
Clerk, Dr. A., 303, 338, 372
Cliodhna, 188
Clydno, 234
Cocholyn, 226
Colan, St., 225
Colban, 92
Colgan, 23, 50, 62, 112, 369
Collin, 313
Colman, 292, 349
Columba St. (Columcille), 15-17, 28, 39-72, 76, 77, 85-88, 94, 95, 104, 112, 134, 154, 201, 206, 209, 220, 225, 226, 240, 244, 250, 288-294, 299, 301, 349, 369, 381
Columbanus, St., 41, 207
Comgall, 91
Comyns, 86, 87
Conaill, Cinal, 49
Conall, 42

Conall Cearnach, 149, 153-155, 170, 355
Conan Maol, 179
Conchobar, 121, 148-156, 160, 161, 169
Conlaoch, 153, 159, 355
Conn, 108, 125, 179, 180, 254, 348
Cormac, Abbot of Turiff, 91
Cormac, 51, 140, 291, 292, 341
Cormac Mac Art, 179-181, 186, 192-194, 355
Coroticus, 15, 30, 32, 33
Corroi, 226
Cowper, 310, 316
Crabbe, 316
Craigie, Dr., 210
Crede, 189, 190
Creirwy, 230
Cuchulinn, 149, 153-174, 178, 226, 354, 355, 380
Culand, 155, 156
Cumhail, 178, 179, 181, 185
Cummene, 61, 63, 74, 76, 291
Curigh, 154, 170, 226
Currie, Archibald, 340
Cwlum, 225
Cyclops, 12

Dagda, 138
Daire, 28
Dante, 68, 215
Daol, 214, 357
Daré, 161
Dargo, 254
Darmesteter, 53, 288
Darwin, Charles, 2
David I., 84, 89, 94
David, 91, 143, 167, 176, 328
Davies, 225, 227
Dayry, 226
Dechtine, 155
Deirdre, 146, 148-153, 354
Demni, 181, 182
Devonshire, Duke of, 109
Dewar, Dr., 336, 344
Diarmad, King, 44, 45, 50, 105, 106
Diarmad O'Duibhne, 179, 193-196, 254, 355, 356
Dickens, Charles, 332
Dido, 312
Diefenbach, Dr., 375
Diez, 376
Dima, 51
Diodorus, 12, 99
Dionysius, 12
Doddridge, 334, 343
Domangart, 91
Domnall, 91

Donall, Albanach, 158
Donlevy, 339
Donn, Rob., 250, 336-338
Donnatt, St., 208
Dorbene, 60, 61
Dottin, Georges, 148, 381
Dowden, Dr., 34, 52, 303
Drostan, 85, 86, 94
Drust, 86
Dubthach, 37, 240, 244
Duffy, Sir Charles Gavan, 324, 366
Duhona, 254
Dunbar, 310
Dungall, 208
Duvan, Louis, 173
Dyer, 334

Ebel, Dr. Herdmann, 98, 258, 376-382
Edward I., 225, 313
Edward IV., 309
Edwards, J., 334
Eimer, 153, 157, 160, 169-172, 355, 365
Eite, 92
Eithinyn, 222
Eithne, 143
Elaine, 319
Elphin, 232
Emerson, 1
Enda, St., 29
Enid, 237, 318
Eogan, 151
Eoin o Albain, 116
Ephorus, 12
Erbin, 230
Ercoill, 8
Ernault, 381
Etarre, 319
Ete, 92
Ethelfrid, 221
Ethne, 29
Eua, 92
Eva, 144, 145
Evans, 314, 383
Eve, 233
Evir-Alin, 192
Evrawc, 230
Ewen, 247, 248

Fairhair, Harold, 202, 204, 212
Faraday, Miss, 210
Farsaid, Fenius, 107, 112, 114, 338
Fedelm, 29
Feidhlim, 148
Fercertné, 107
Ferdomnach, 23
Fergus Finne-bheoil, 179, 185, 188

Ferguson, Sir James, 148
Ferry, Jules, 99
Festime, 8
Fferyllt, 230
Fiacc, 23, 25, 26, 37-39, 240, 292, 349
Finan, 253, 254
Finck, Dr., 381
Finn Eges, 181, 182
Finnachta, 64, 65, 67
Finnamhair, 162, 163, 167
Finnian, St., 44, 48, 290
Finntan, 137
Fionn (Finn), 123, 124, 174-196, 283,
    295, 296, 299, 354, 355
Flann, 140, 246
Fletcher, 148, 352
Forbes, 340
Forgaill, Dallan, 16, 55, 57, 61, 108,
    240, 291, 348, 349
Forgaill of Lusk, 157, 158
Forli, Jacques de, 120
Foy, Dr., 381
Francis, St., 31, 39
Fraoch, 354

Gadelus, 138
Gaidos, 381
Gaimar, 228
Gairloch, Laird of, 280
Galates, 8, 12
Galgacus, 6
Gall, St., 41, 208
Garbh, 354, 355
Garnat, 86
Gartnait, 91
Gaul, 178, 181, 254, 295, 355
Gavaelvawr, 234
Gawaine, Sir, 308
Geoffrey of Monmouth, 228, 247, 306,
    307
George I., 80
George II., 351
Geraint, 230, 318
Germanus, 24, 27
Geryon, 8
Gibbon, 382
Gildas, 220, 307
Gillemichel, 92
Gillies, H. C., 340
Gillies, John, 335, 352
Glengarry, 271, 272
Glewlwyd, 234
Gloucester, Robert of, 306
Glûngel, 107
Gobhan, 106
Goldsmith, 7
Gomer, 8

Goraidh, 211
Gordon, George Ross, 336
Gordon, Patrick, 87
Gordon, William, 336
Gordonus, 118
Grainne, 193, 355
Grant, 352
Grant, Mrs. 250, 256, 357
Grant, Peter, 336, 338
Graves, Dr., 14
Gray, 313-315
Gray, Florence, 339
Gregais, 8
Griffith, Prince, 257
Grimm, 370, 371, 375, 376
Gruffydd ap Arthur, 228
Gruffydd ap Kynan, 246, 247
Gudelig, 230
Guesclin du, 247
Guest, Lady Charlotte, 219, 229, 230, 237
Guinevere, 237, 319, 320
Guledig, 227
Gurban, 106
Gwenc'hlan, 240
Gwenhwyvar, 234-236
Gwreang, 231
Gwrhyr, 233
Gwyddno Garanhir, 231, 232
Gwydion, 312
Gwynne, Prof., 383

Hael, Rhydderch, 225
Hailes, Lord, 118
Halliday, William, 339
Hamlet, 81
Hardiman, 251
Healy, Dr., 50, 372
Hecatæus, 2, 11
Helen of Troy, 152
Hên Llywarch, 218, 221, 223, 240, 244
Henderson, Dr. George, 303, 351, 366,
    384
Henebry, Prof., 381
Hengest, 221
Hennessy, W. M., 372, 374, 379
Henry VIII., 220
Herbert, 227
Hercules, 8
Herodotus, 2, 11, 19, 287
Hoel, 314
Holder, Dr., 381
Homer, 176, 332, 347
Horace, 133
Horatio, 81
Howeldda, 220
Hring, 213
Hull, Eleanor, 154, 293, 324

Huxley, 2, 6
Hyde, Dr. Douglas, 32, 46, 50, 57, 113, 148, 175, 186, 213, 246, 251, 264, 266, 309, 324, 339, 366, 373, 383

Irvine, 118, 148, 352
Isabella, Countess of Argyll, 126
Iseult, 237

Jacobs, Joseph, 147
Jafed, 8
James II., 49, 270, 279
James, Prof., 71
Jauïoz, 247
Jerome, St., 44, 49, 82, 290
Jerram, C. S., 253
Jocelin, 23
John, St., 68, 80, 83, 84
Johnson, Dr. Samuel, 123, 127, 267, 316, 343, 351
Jonathan, 167
Jones, Brynmor, 383
Jones, Edmund, 324
Jones, John, 218, 366
Jones, Prof. Lewis, 383
Jones, Prof. Morris, 383
Jones, Owen, 218, 366
Jones, Sir William, 18, 375
Joyce, Dr., 140, 144, 148
Jubainville, H. d'Arbois de, 99, 103, 108, 144, 147, 148, 173, 379, 381
Judas, 215

Kaer-Is, 240
Kai, 234, 255
Keating, Geoffrey, 101, 147, 183, 203, 249, 368, 369
Keats, 315
Keith, Sir Robert de, 87
Keller, Dr., 59, 62, 63
Kemoc, St., 146
Kempis, Thomas à, 332
Kennedy, 352
Kennedy, Angus, 336
Kennedy, Duncan, 335
Kennedy, Rev. John, 384
Kermode, 383
Kian, 221
Kilhwch, 230, 233
Kilian, St., 208
Kirke, John, 328, 341, 371
Kirke, Rev. Robert, 333
Knox, John, 56, 290, 299, 327, 335
Kuhn, Dr., 378
Kynan, 246, 247
Kyner, 234, 235
Kynon, 234

Laeg, 165-167
Laing, Malcolm, 221
Lamb, Charles, 260
Lamh-fhad, 355
Landseer, 358
Lang, Andrew, 137, 324
Laoghaire, King, 28, 29, 34, 171, 244
Larguen, 145, 146
Launcelot, Sir, 307, 319
Lawless, Emily, 324
Layamon, 228, 306-308, 320
Lebarchan, 149
Lekprevik, Roibeart, 327
Leodogran, 319
Leot, 91
Lewy, 170
Lhuyd, Edward, 4, 217, 328, 370, 371, 375
Liden, Dr., 381
Lir, 144-146, 213
Lismore, Dean of, 89, 91, 121-123, 127, 129, 175, 186, 187, 191, 262, 299, 300, 357
Livy, 12
Llevelys, 230
Llewellyn, 314
Llud, 230
Llyr, 229
Lonelich, Henry, 308
Longarad, 48
Lorma, 254
Loth, Prof., 229, 381
Lotti, 381
Lovat, 281
Lovenath, 306
Lugaid, 170, 172
Lugh, 138, 141-143, 155
Luke, St., 80, 83, 84
Lynette, 318

Mabon, 233
Macalpine, Neil, 340, 344, 356
Macaulay, Lord, 281, 321
Macaulay, Zachary, 281
Macbain, Dr. Alex., 4, 86, 95, 175, 344, 351, 379, 384
Macbean, L., 340
Macbeth, 313
Macbrian, 356
Maccallum, 352
Maccallum, A., 336
Maccallum, Rev. Duncan, 176, 195, 256, 303
Maccallum, J., 336
Maccarthenn, 36
Maccodrum, John, 250, 282-284
Maccolla, Alasdair, 276
Mac Crimmon, 280

Maccuirtin, Hugh, 339
Mac Cumachteni, 23
Mac Daman, Ferdia, 158, 163-168, 172
Macdonald, Alasdair, 130, 272
Macdonald, Alexander, 250, 282, 284, 328, 329, 335, 336, 341
Macdonald, Sir Alexander, 271, 272, 275
Macdonald, Angus, 281
Macdonald, Archibald, 281
Macdonald, Archibald (An Ciaran Mabach), 271, 275
Macdonald, Cicely, 276
Macdonald, Donald, 251, 262
Macdonald, Dr., 303, 338
Macdonald, Dr. George, 323
Macdonald, Sir James, 272, 282, 283
Macdonald, John (Iain Dubh), 276, 336
Macdonald, John (Iain Lom), 270, 275
Macdonald of Muck, 281
Macdonald, Ronald, 335, 352
Macdougall, Allan, 250, 335
Macdougall, Phelim, 126
Macdurnain, 103, 104, 290
Maceachan, Rev. Ewen, 344
Macfadyen, 335
Macfarlane, Rev. Alex., 328, 333, 334
Macfarlane, Donald, 344
Macfarlane, Malcolm, 340, 366
Macfarlane, P., 336, 343, 344
Macfarlane, Robert, 343
Mac Firbis, Duald, 65, 112, 249, 368, 369
Macgillivray, Dr., 340
Mac Gormann, Finn, 349
Macgregor, Duncan, 121, 122
Macgregor, Gregor, 263, 264
Macgregor, James, 251, 336
Macgregor, Sir James, 121, 122
Macgregor, John, 336
Mac-Ille Chalum, 265
Macintosh, D., 336
Macintyre, Duncan Ban, 250, 329, 330, 335, 337, 358
Mackay, A., 336
Mackay, John, 280, 281
Mackellar, David, 215, 250, 328, 335
Mackellar, Mary, 338
Mackenzie, Alexander, 267
Mackenzie, Sir George, 352
Mackenzie, Henry, 117
Mackenzie, High Chief of Kintail, 277
Mackenzie, John, 121
Mackenzie, John, 250, 282, 284, 328, 329, 335, 336, 338, 356, 357, 360, 361, 363
Mackenzie, Kenneth, 250, 335
Mackenzie, William, 281

Mackinnon, Alexander, 251
Mackinnon, Prof. D., 56, 105, 127, 144, 351, 384
Mackinnon, Lachlan, 279
Maclachlan, Ewen, 251, 372
Maclachlan, I., 336
Maclachlan, Major, 118
Maclaren, Ian, 324
Maclauchlan, Dr. T., 116, 303, 328, 372
Maclean, Rev. Donald, 325
Maclean, Hector, 278
Maclean, John, 281, 336
Maclean, Rev. John, 370
Maclean, Sir Lachlan, 278
Maclean, Malcolm, 281
Macleod, Alexander, 267
Macleod, Donald, 251, 336
Macleod, Fiona, 324
Macleod, Hector, 250, 281
Macleod, John Breac, 279
Macleod, Mary, 249, 265-270, 276, 284
Macleod, Neil, 338
Macleod, Dr. Norman, 303, 338, 344, 346
Macleod, Sir Norman, 132, 267, 269
Macneill, Dr. Nigel, 196, 255, 303, 338, 345, 346, 370
Macnicol, 303, 352
Macpherson, Alex., 335
Macpherson, D. C., 340
Macpherson, James, 103, 117, 121, 123, 129, 148, 176, 214, 217, 240, 250-256, 283, 298, 301, 305, 314-316, 318, 331, 351-355
Macpherson, Lachlan, 250
Macphun, W. R., 345
Macrae, Duncan, 91, 127-129, 215, 275, 350
Macrae, John, 128
Macritchie, 175
Mac Roich, Fergus, 108, 149-154, 301
Mac Roth, Fergus, 109, 161-164
Macsen Gudelig, 230
Macvurich, Nial, 129-132, 276, 277
Macvurichs, 119, 126, 130, 351
Madden, Sir Frederick, 306, 308
Maelbrigte, 104
Maelcolum, 91
Maelgron, 232
Mael-isu, 292, 349
Maelmuiri, 108, 299, 301, 348, 349
Magnus, 211
Malcolm, 339
Malcolm, Dr., 341
Maledoun, 91
Malory, Sir Thomas, 308, 309, 316, 318

Malvina, 315
Manawyddan, 229
Manus, 211, 254, 355
Map, Walter, 307
Mar, Earl of, 87
Marcellinus, 12
Marcellus, 81
Margaret, Queen, 92-94
Mark, St., 80, 84
Mary, Queen, 270
Mason, W. Monck, 65
Matadin, 91
Math, 229, 312
Matheson, Aosdan, 276
Matheson, D., 336
Mathonwy, 229
Matthew, St. 79, 84
Menteith, Earl of, 87
Menzies of Rannoch, 263
Merlin, 307, 319, 320
Mesgedra, 121
Meve, Queen, 110,151,160-169, 310, 365
Meyer, Dr. Kuno, 120, 173, 383
Milé, 130, 138
Mitchell, Anthony, 52
Mitonis, 8
Mocumin Lugne, 73, 74
Molaise, St., 45
Molloy, 339
Mone, 105
Montalembert, 88
Montrose, 129, 130, 271, 272
Moore, A. W., 383
Moore, Bishop, 80
Moore, Dr. Norman, 383
Moore, Thomas, 316
Morda, 231
Morley, 249
Morna, 178-181
Morni, 254
Morrigan, 163
Morris, Dr., 308
Morrison, 333
Morrison, J., 336
Morrison, Roderick, 279, 280
Mortimer, 314
Morvran, 230
Moses, 107, 232
Muireach, Albanach, 119, 126, 130, 276, 351
Muirne, 181
Munro, James, 274, 336, 340
Munro, Neil, 275, 324
Müller, Max, 136, 379
Mura, St., 61
Muridach, 91
Myrddin, 221, 224-226, 240, 247

Naitan, 56
Nann, Lord, 240, 242
Naois, 149, 150, 158
Napier, Mark, 130, 272
Nectan, 91
Neil, Oig, 116
Neilson, Dr. William, 339
Nennius, 220, 307
Nial, 34, 107, 112, 171
Nicholson, 328
Nicolson, 338, 384
Nigra, Count, 56, 57, 98, 309, 374, 379, 380
Ninine, 38, 292, 349
Noah, 8, 137
Noe, 8
Nomenöe, 247
Norris, Edwin, 249
Nuada, 140
Nutt, Alfred, 144, 175, 177, 383

O'Beirne, Crowe, 173
O'Bryan, Dr. Paul, 339
O'Clery, Michael, 50, 112, 135, 341, 369
O'Clery, Peregrine, 369
O'Connor, 111
O'Curry, 97, 98, 102, 108, 110, 130, 140, 144, 147, 160, 173, 175, 176, 185, 186, 193, 258, 369, 372, 373
O'Daly, 126, 251
O'Donnell's, 381
O'Donnells, 49
O'Donovan, 97, 113, 176, 258, 339, 372, 373, 374, 382
O'Duffy, 140
O'Duigenan, 369
O'Flaherty, 179
O'Flanagan, 147, 173
Ogilvy, Mrs. D., 271
O'Grady, S. H., 173, 374, 383
Olwen, 230, 233, 310
O'Mulchonry, 369
O'Reilly, 4, 372
Orran, 254
Oscar, 179, 185, 193, 295, 296, 356
Ossian, 29, 122, 123, 129, 175-194, 214, 222, 244, 253, 254, 293-302, 314, 315, 323, 336, 343, 347, 355, 357
Oswy, 221
Owain, 223, 234
Owen, Aneurin, 218, 366

Palgrave, Sir Francis, 200
Palladius, 22, 24
Patrick, St., 15-17, 22-43, 53, 57, 68, 78, 112, 123, 134, 145, 171, 172, 187,

189, 191, 240, 244, 288, 291-302, 349, 355, 369, 374, 382
Pattison, 195, 253, 263, 268, 274
Paul, St., 8, 31, 76
Pedersen, Prof., 381
Pelleas, 319
Pellinore, King, 308
Penda, 222
Pendragon, Uther, 306
Pennant, 316
Pentreath, Dolly, 249
Peredur, 147, 230, 234
Petrie, 372
Phillips, Sir Thomas, 219
Pictet, Adolph, 375, 379
Pinkerton, 78, 221
Plato, 12, 367
Pliny, 12
Polybius, 12
Ponsinet, Louis, 148
Posidonius, 12
Potitus, 25
Powell, Mrs., 219
Price, Sir John, 218
Price, Thomas, 218, 366
Pritchard, Dr., 375
Prosper, 22
Ptolemy, 7, 12
Pwyll, 229
Pytheas, 12

Quixote, Don, 355

Ragnhilda, 211
Rao'all, 211
Raonailt, 211
Raonall, 211
Rask, 370
Reay, Lord, 280
Rees, William, 218, 366
Reeves, Dr., 50, 60, 63, 67, 76, 77, 105, 303, 372, 374
Reid, D., 340
Reid, John, 325-331, 338
Renan, 97, 227, 230, 233, 237, 244, 289, 322
Rheged, Urien, 223
Rhys, Principal, 4, 175, 225, 229, 230, 322, 379, 383
Rhys ap Tewdwr, 246
Rhonabwy, 230
Ripley, Dr. W. Z., 11
Robertson, Alex., 343
Robinson, Prof., 381
Roc, 355
Rognwald, 211
Rolleston, T. W., 148, 324, 366

Ronald of Keppoch, 276
Ronan, 63
Ronan, 179, 188
Ronnat, 63, 67
Ross, Rev. Thomas, 333, 334
Ross, William, 250
Ruadh, Alasdair, 267
Rustum, 159

Sage, 303, 352
Samson, 91
Sanctain, 292, 349
Sangale, Monachi, 199
Sarauw, Dr., 381
Scathach, Lady, 158, 159, 163, 165, 167
Schaafhausen, 2
Schleicher, 382
Scott, Sir Walter, 130, 256, 271, 277, 278, 301, 305, 316-318, 323, 332
Scylax, 12
Seaforth, Earl of, 276, 277
Sechnall, 36, 37, 240, 292
Secundius, 36
Setanta, 155, 156
Seth, 83
Shairp, Principal, 321, 322
Shakespeare, 312, 313, 332
Shaw, James, 250
Shaw, Rev. William, 340, 342
Shelley, 315
Siegfried, Prof., 378, 382, 383
Sigerson, Dr., 167, 297, 324, 366, 383
Sigurd, 202
Sinclair, Archibald, 338, 361, 363
Sinclair, Sir John, 352
Skene, Dr., 32, 55, 117, 120, 127, 129, 130, 150, 175, 195, 221-227, 238, 383
Smith, Angus, 147
Smith, Dr., 176, 250, 253-256, 303, 330, 333, 335, 372
Smith, Donald, 372
Sohrab, 159
Somerled, 211
Sommer, Dr., 381
Southey, 316
Stairn, 354, 355
Stapleton, Tobias, 339
Stephens, Thomas, 221-225, 247
Stern, Dr. Ludwig Christian, 174, 176, 380
Stevenson, R. L., 323
Stewart, A., 336, 340, 341
Stewart, D., 336
Stewart, Sir John, 264
Stewart, R., 336
Stokes, Prof. G. T., 36, 303

Stokes, Dr. Whitley, 25, 26, 32, 34, 68, 81, 82, 90, 95, 98, 104-106, 121, 147, 173, 188, 378-383
Stokes, Prof. William, 382
Stone, Jerome, 118, 251, 252, 352
Strabo, 7, 12, 99
Strabo, Walafridus, 202
Strabus, 62
Strachan, Dr., 55, 383
Stuart, Dr., 82, 95, 330
Stuart, John Roy, 250
Stuart, P., 336
Sualtam, 155, 156
Sweet, 304

Tacitus, 5, 12
Tadg, 181
Talchend, 145
Talhaiarn, 221
Taliessin, 218-223, 226, 230, 232, 240, 244, 247
Tannahill, 257
Taylor, Tom, 240, 247
Teige, 124
Tennyson, 305, 315, 318, 320, 323, 332
Tewdwr, 246
Thackeray, 332
Thisbe, 312
Thomson, 315
Thurneysen, Prof., 57, 380
Tighernach, 68, 111, 112, 155, 176, 246
Timæus, 12
Tinne, 63
Tirechan, 23, 24, 29
Tischendorf, 83, 97
Todd, Dr., 25, 33, 38, 303, 372, 374
Todhunter, Dr., 148, 324
Torcull, 211
Townshend, Lord, 80
Trahul, 254
Trenmor, 178, 181
Tuireann, 140-143, 213, 214
Turner, P., 336, 352
Tynan, Katherine, 324

Uathach, 159, 165
Uisneach, 146, 149-155, 158, 161, 380
Ullin, 254
Ultan, 292, 349
Urien, 234, 244
Ussher, 62
Uther, 319

Vallancy, 339, 342
Victoricus, 27
Viglisson, 212
Villemarqué, 222, 229, 240, 244, 366
Virgil, 12, 335
Vivien, 319
Voel Tegid, 230

Wace, Robert, 228, 247, 306, 307
Ward, 68
Watson, Dr. John, 324
Watt, 333
Weston, Jessie L., 307, 324
Westwood, Prof., 82
White, Stephen, 62
Whyte, Henry, 338, 366
Whyte, John, 281, 344
William King, 270
Williams, Edward, 222
Willison, 328, 333
Wilson, James G., 275
Windisch, Dr. Ernest, 57, 89, 90, 98, 121, 147, 173, 341, 376, 379, 380
Wordsworth, 19, 315-318
Wright, Dr., 36, 303
Wynne, W. W. E., 218

Xenophon, 12

Yeats, W. B., 324, 366
Yscolan, 224-226

Zeuss, J. Caspard, 56, 82, 98, 99, 120, 258, 309, 341, 376-379, 380, 382, 384
Zimmer, Prof., 22, 98, 106, 120, 210, 211, 292, 380, 381
Zupitza, Dr., 381

INDEX OF SUBJECTS

Adamnan, 58-79 ; his biography, 61-68 ; writings, 67-79 ; his Life of Columba, 16, 58, 69-79 ; Adamnan's Prayer, 68 ; his Vision, 68
Aged Bard's Wish, 253, 357, 358
Alexander the Great and Celts, 7
American scholars, 381
Amra Choluimcille, 55, 108
Ancestors of the Gael, 138, 139
Ancient Laws and Institutes of Wales, 220
Aneurin, the Book of, 218, 219
Annals, Irish, 111-113
Archæologica Brittannica, 217, 370, 371
Armagh, the Book of, 17, 22, 23, 82
Arnold's *Study of Celtic Literature*, 309-312, 321-323
Arthurian Romances, 227-238, 306-309
Aryan group of languages, 19

Ballymote, the Book of, 109
Bards, the Irish, 54
Bards of the Gael and Gall, 167, 168, 297, 298, 366
Barzaz-Breiz, Chants populaires de la Bretagne, 240-244, 366
Beauties of Gaelic Poetry, the, 356-360
Ben Dorain, 358-360
Bible, Gaelic, 328-330
Bibliographies, Gaelic, 325-327
Bopp's discovery, 375, 376
Breton Bards of the Sixth Century, the, 244, 366
British scholars, 382-385
Brittany, early ballads of, 240-244 ; medieval ballads of, 247, 248
Buchanan, Dugald, his hymns, 329, 336

Caermarthen, the Black Book of, 218
Caledonian Bards, 256

Carmina Gadelica, 361-366
Cathrach, the, 16, 48, 49
Celtic elements in English literature, 309-312
Celtic literary revivals, 239-261
Celtic renaissance, latest, 259, 353
Celts, early history of the, 1-9 ; arrival in British Isles, 3 ; Continental empire, 5-9
Christianity, introduction of, 27, 28, 47, 287-290
Chronicon Scotorum, the, 112, 369, 374
Church, the, its influence on Gaelic literature, 286-303
Churchmen, splendid services of, 303
Clanranald, the Book of, 129-133
Classical authors on early Celts, 11-13
Columba, St., 16 ; his biography, 41-78, 226 ; writings, 47-58 ; his poems, 49-53
Confession of St. Patrick, 15, 25, 30
Cornish dialect, last speaker of, 249
Cornish literature, 248, 249
Coroticus, Epistle to, 15, 30
Cuchulinn, 155-173

Danish scholars, 381
Decay of inflection in Scottish Gaelic and Manx, 211
Decline of Gaelic oral literature, 300
Deer, the Book of, 16, 17, 79-95, 209, 246
Deer's Cry, the, 15, 31, 33
Deirdre and the sons of Uisneach, 146-152
Dialogue of the Ancients, 53, 188, 189
Dialogues between Ossian and Patrick, 29, 292-299
Dictionaries, Gaelic, 341-344

Differences between Irish and Gaelic, 209, 210
Domhnach Airgid, the, 36
Durrow, the Book of, 16, 48, 82

Early Celtic Church and oral traditions, 289
Early missionaries and the Scriptures, 289, 290
Edinburgh libraries in which are Celtic MSS. : Advocates', 115-118 ; University, 118 ; Scottish Antiquaries', 118
Eisteddfod, Welsh, history of, 237
English literature, 305-324
English loan-words from Celtic, 304, 305

Fate of MSS., 119, 120
Feinn, the, 174-197
Fernaig MS., the, 127-129, 350, 351
Fiacc's Hymn, 37, 38
Fionn, 175-197
Foundation of Celtic Chairs, 259
Four Ancient Books of Wales, 217-238, 247
Four Masters, the Annals of, 112, 113, 373 ; authors, 369
French scholars, 381

Gadelic and Brittonic, linguistic difference, 3, 371
Gaelic, earliest written, 17 ; earliest distinctly Scottish, 89; first printed book, 327
Gaelic Bards, Pattison's, 253
Galatian colony, 8
Genealogies, the Book of, 369
Genealogy, Irish, 137
German scholars, 379-381
Gildas, works of, 220
Gleaners, Gaelic, 347-366
Gododin, the, 221, 222
Grammars, Gaelic, 107, 338-341, 373
Grammatica Celtica, 98, 376-378
Gray's *Bard*, 313, 314

Hergest, the Red Book of, 218-220, 224
Heroic Cycle, the, 153-173
Highland bards before the Forty-five, 263-285
Highland bards after the Forty-five, 249-251
Highland Society Collection of Gaelic MSS., 117
Historia Britonum, 228

Hymns, the Book of, 17, 36, 209, 246, 348, 349, 374, 382

Icelandic literature, 205
Influence of Celtic on English literature, 305-324
Iona, 46 ; ravages of Norsemen, 201
Irish Annals, 111-113
Irish missionaries on the Continent, 207
Irische Texte, 380, 382
Italian scholars, 379, 380

Jacobite poems of Ireland, 251
Jones, Sir William ; his suggestion, 375
Jubainville, M. d'Arbois de ; his mission to the British Isles, 99-104

Keating's work, 368, 369
Kells, the Book of, 16, 48, 82
Kilbride collection of MSS., 117, 118
Knox's *Liturgy*, 327, 328

Layamon's " Brut," 305, 320
Leabhar Gabhala, 135, 369
Leabhar na Feinne, 353-356
Leabhar nan Gleann, 366
Leabhar Na h'Uidhre, 17, 108, 209, 246, 348
Learning and culture, 289
Leinster, the Book of, 108, 109
Liber Hymnorum, 17, 36, 209, 246, 348, 349, 374, 382
Lir, Tragedy of the Children of, 144-146
Lismore, the Book of, 109
Lismore, the Book of the Dean of, 121-126, 226, 350, 351
Literary History of Ireland, Dr. Hyde's, 246
Literature, Gaelic, printed, 325-346
Literature of the Early Celtic Church, 288-292
Llywarch Hên's poetry, 223-224

Mabinogion, 229-238
Maccodrum's Muse, 282-285
Macdonald, Alexander, his work, 328, 336, 337
Macdonald, John, life and poetry, 270-275
Macgregor songs, 263
Macleod, Mary, life and poetry, 264-270
Macpherson's Ossian and other poems, 117, 217, 252, 314-316, 331, 351, 352
Malory, Sir Thomas, his *Morte d'Arthur*, 308, 309, 316

Manuscripts, Celtic, 17, 40; on the Continent, 96, 100, 101; in England and Ireland, 97, 102; in Scotland, 115-134; antiquity of MSS., 102-104; MSS. of the Middle Ages, 107; MSS., XL., LIII., LVI., 120, 121; Welsh, 217-238
Milesians, 138, 139
Minor collections of Ossianic poetry, 352
Minor Highland bards, 275-282
Mòd, Gaelic, 259
Modern novelists, 323-324
Moore's *Irish Melodies*, 316, 317
Myrddin's poetry, 224-226
Mythological Cycle, the, 135-152
Myth and folk-tale theories, 135-137
Mythical races in Ireland, 137
Myvyrian Archaiology of Wales, 218, 224, 366

Navigatio Brendani, 215
Nennius' *History of the Britons*, 220
Nineteenth century output of Gaelic literature, 301, 302
Ninine's Prayer, 38
Norris, Edwin, translation of Cornish dramas, 249
Norse eddas and sagas, 204, 205
Norse ideas in Gaelic literature, 212-215; Norse words, 210, 211
Norse invasions, 198; influence on Celtic literature, 205-217; and upon the structure of the Gaelic language, 211, 212

O'Curry's research, 97, 373, 374
O'Donovan's life and work, 97, 372, 373
Ogam writing, 14, 15
Origin of shires, burghs, and parishes in Scotland, 84-95
Ossian, 175; poetry, 185-188
Ossianic cycle, 174-197; heroes of, 178; literature, 185-197; poetry, 123, 185-188; tales, 176, 188-197

P, rarely used in Irish or Gaelic, 4; group, 5
Patrick, St., 15; Lives of, 23; biography, 23-39; writings, 15, 30-39
Patrick and Ossian, 29, 293-298
Periodicals, foreign, 378, 379; Gaelic, 345, 346
Picts, the, 45, 56
Poetesses, Gaelic, 275, 276
Poet-laureate, Gaelic, 274
Poetry, Gaelic, in Continental MSS., 104-106

Psalters, Gaelic, 328, 333

Q., the Aryan guttural changed into *p*, 4; group, 5

Reid's *Bibliotheca Scoto-Celtica*, 325-327
Reliquiæ Celticæ, 384
Reliques of Irish Poetry, 366
Renan, Ernest, on Welsh literature, 227, 230
Rhyme, Celtic claim, 56, 57, 309
Rise of the Scottish Gaelic, 89, 209

Scandinavian scholars, 381
Scholars, modern Celtic, 367-385
School-books, Gaelic, 338
Scott, Sir Walter, renderings from Gaelic, 277, 278, 323; influence, 317, 318
Scottish collection of Celtic MSS., 115-133
Seana Dana, 253-256
Severance of Scotland from Ireland, 209
Shairp, Principal, writings, 322, 323
Skene, Dr., Collection of MSS., 117; on Welsh poems, 227, 237
Songster, Gaelic (An T'Oranaiche), 361
Sorrows of Gaelic Storydom, the Three, 140-152
Statistics of Celtic-speaking peoples, 10, 20, 21
Stephens' *Literature of the Cymry*, 221
Stone, Jerome, a pioneer, 251

Táin Bó Chuailgné, 108-111, 160
Tales of Heroic Cycle, 153-173
Taliessin, the Book of, 218, 219; the bard, 223; legend of, 230-232; odes, 232, 233
Taylor's translations of Breton ballads, 240-244, 247, 248
Tennyson's *Idylls of the King*, 318-321
Tighernach, the Annals of, 111
Treasury of Irish Poetry, 366
Trias Thaumaturga, 369
Tuireann, Tragedy of the Children of, 140-143

Uisneach, Tale of the Sons of, 121, 146-152

Valhalla, 214, 215
Vikings, 198-216
Villemarqué, M. de, Breton ballads and folklore songs, 240-248
Vita Columbæ, Adamnan's, 58-79, 92; criteria of age, 59; copyist, 60, 61;

history of MS., 62 ; contents, 69 ; other MSS. of, 76, 77

Wars of the Gael with the Gaill, 203, 204
Welsh bards of the sixth century, 221
Welsh intellectual awakening of the eleventh and twelfth centuries, 246
Welsh MSS., 220

Welsh poetry, 217, 218, 257
Wordsworth and his contemporaries, 316
Whyte, Henry, his gleanings, 366

Yscolan, 225, 226

Zeuss' life and work, 98, 99, 376-378
Zimmer's books, 380

THE END